# MACROHISTORY AND MACROHISTORIANS

# MACROHISTORY AND MACROHISTORIANS

Perspectives on Individual, Social, and Civilizational Change

*Edited by Johan Galtung and Sohail Inayatullah*

PRAEGER

Westport, Connecticut
London

**Library of Congress Cataloging-in-Publication Data**

Macrohistory and macrohistorians : perspectives on individual, social, and civilizational change / edited by Johan Galtung and Sohail Inayatullah.
    p.    cm.
  Based on a seminar given spring 1989 at the Dept. of Sociology, University of Hawaii, Honolulu.
  Includes bibliographical references and index.
  ISBN 0-275-95755-1
  1. History—Philosophy.  2. History—Methodology.  3. Social change.  I. Galtung, Johan.  II. Inayatullah, Sohail, 1958- .
D16.9.M24  1997
901—dc21          97-8811

British Library Cataloguing in Publication Data is available.

Copyright ©1997 by Johan Galtung and Sohail Inayatullah

All rights reserved. No portion of this book may be reproduced, by any process or technique, without the express written consent of the publisher.

Library of Congress Catalog Card Number: 97-8811
ISBN: 0-275-95755-1

First published in 1997

Praeger Publishers, 88 Post Road West, Westport, CT 06881
An imprint of Greenwood Publishing Group, Inc.

Printed in the United States of America

The paper used in this book complies with the Permanent Paper Standard issued by the National Information Standards Organization (Z39.48-1984).

**Copyright Acknowledgments**

The editors and publisher are grateful for permission to reproduce copyright material from Khaldun, Ibn, *The Muqaddimah*, Copyright © 1967 by Princeton University Press. Reprinted by permission.

Every reasonable effort has been made to trace the owners of copyright materials in this book, but in some instances this has proven impossible. The editors and publisher will be glad to receive information leading to more complete acknowledgments in subsequent printings of this book, and in the meantime extend their apologies for any omissions.

P

---

In order to keep this title in print and available to the academic community, this edition was produced using digital reprint technology in a relatively short print run. This would not have been attainable using traditional methods. Although the cover has been changed from its original appearance, the text remains the same and all materials and methods used still conform to the highest book-making standards.

# Contents

|  | Preface | ix |
|---|---|---|
| Chapter 1 | Macrohistory and Macrohistorians: A Theoretical Framework<br>*Johan Galtung* | 1 |
| Chapter 2 | Twenty Macrohistorians: A Presentation<br>*Edited by Sohail Inayatullah* | 11 |
| 2.1 | Ssu-Ma Ch'ien: The Cycles of Virtue   12<br>*Chang Xie with Sohail Inayatullah* | |
| 2.2 | Augustine: The River to Eternity   18<br>*Brian Shetler* | |
| 2.3 | Ibn Khaldun: The Strengthening and Weakening of *Asabiya*   25<br>*Sohail Inayatullah* | |
| 2.4 | Giambattista Vico: Barbarism and Providence   32<br>*Daniela Rocco Minerbi* | |
| 2.5 | Adam Smith: Self-Love and Love of Others   40<br>*Daniel J. Campbell* | |
| 2.6 | George Wilhelm Friedrich Hegel: Dialectics and the World Spirit   47<br>*Brian Shetler* | |
| 2.7 | Auguste Comte: The Law of the Three Stages   54<br>*Claus Otto Scharmer* | |
| 2.8 | Karl Marx: Techno-Economic Stages   61<br>*Johan Galtung* | |

**2.9** Herbert Spencer: Progress and Evolution  68
*Sohail Inayatullah*

**2.10** Vilfredo Pareto: The Unbreakable Cycle  76
*Daniela Rocco Minerbi*

**2.11** Max Weber: History as Interplay and Dichotomy of Rationalization and Charisma  84
*Claus Otto Scharmer*

**2.12** Rudolf Steiner: History as Development toward Emancipation and Freedom  90
*Claus Otto Scharmer*

**2.13** Oswald Spengler: The Maturation and Decay of Cultures  98
*Sohail Inayatullah*

**2.14** Pierre Teilhard de Chardin: Universal Personalization  105
*Daniela Rocco Minerbi*

**2.15** Pitirim Sorokin: The Principle of Limits  113
*Johan Galtung*

**2.16** Arnold Toynbee: Challenge and Response  120
*Johan Galtung*

**2.17** Antonio Gramsci: Hegemony and the Materialist Conception of History  128
*Marsha Hansen*

**2.18** Prabhat Rainjan Sarkar: Agency, Structure, and Transcendence  132
*Sohail Inayatullah*

**2.19** Riane Eisler: Dominator and Partnership Shifts  141
*Riane Eisler*

**2.20** Cosmic Gaia: Homeostasis and Planetary Evolution  151
*Christopher B. Jones*

**Chapter 3** Macrohistorians Compared: Toward a Theory of Macrohistory                159
*Sohail Inayatullah*

**Chapter 4** Macrohistorians Combined: Toward Eclecticism     203
*Johan Galtung*

**Chapter 5** Social Macrohistory as Metaphor for Personal Microhistory                221
*Johan Galtung*

**Chapter 6** Social Macrohistory as Metaphor for World Macrohistory                237
*Johan Galtung*

# *Preface*

This book grew out of a seminar on social theory in general and macrohistory in particular in the spring of 1989, at the Department of Sociology, University of Hawaii, Honolulu, within the peace studies program. Any other department, for instance, Political Science or History, might have been a venue, but it happened to be Sociology. The seminar became a habit for the participants, over some years, and the result is in your hands.

Galtung wrote Chapters 1, 4, 5, and 6, and Inayatullah wrote Chapter 3. Several authors contributed their insights to the presentation (in chronological order) of twenty macrohistorians, in Chapter 2: Daniel J. Campbell, Riane Eisler, Marsha Hansen, Chris Jones, Daniela Rocco Minerbi, Claus Otto Scharmer, and Chang Xie. Inayatullah edited these twenty sections. Daniela Rocco Minerbi, an architect by profession, contributed the visual understandings of the macrohistorians (see Appendix B). Daniel Campbell also played a major role as administrator of this project in its early phases, for which we are most grateful.

Chapter 1 introduces macrohistory, asking why there is so little macrohistory. Chapter 2 presents the macrohistorians selected for this volume. Chapter 3 articulates a theory of macrohistory and macrohistorians along ten factors, such as stages of history, causes of changes, and the episteme in which macrohistorians write. Chapter 4 combines macrohistorians, asking what each can learn from the other. Chapter 5 asks how microhistory or biography can contribute to macrohistory, and different theories of individuals' life stages are analyzed. The final chapter discusses anti-macrohistory as well as world macrohistory.

As usual, there is a pre-history. There is even a "double-S syndrome," each one of us being fascinated with one of the macrohistorians: Galtung with Pitirim Sorokin and Inayatullah with Prabhat Rainjan Sarkar. Here are the stories.

## Johan Galtung

On my somewhat tortuous road from being a student of mathematics and physics to becoming a peace researcher rooted in the social sciences, I was very much in search of someone who did to the human condition what physics does to space and time: transcend both of them. Physics does so by searching for laws invariant of the where and the when. I had no reason to believe that the human condition was a part of physics, hence I was much more interested in what a social scientist could have to say about the social where and about the social when. I accepted Sorokin's view of the social where as "social and cultural" units, and of the social when as "dynamics." So, when the short version of *Social and Cultural Dynamics* became available in 1957 (at the time, I had just started as a young instructor and assistant professor in the Department of Sociology at Columbia University in New York), I was not only ready to receive but I soaked up every word (and they were many). Some years later, I used his basic ideational–sensate distinction in a study in Sicily, and, in 1961, was gratified to have the occasion to meet the great man.

But why not Marx? I was not so much put off by his analysis as by his message, that renewal comes from the working class, but by its practicality—some years as a member of the Norwegian Labor Party Youth League made Marx's message incredible.

But why not Toynbee? He certainly also had the macro span in space and time. But as a recent student of mathematics and physics, I believed more in the figures reported by Sorokin than in the countless facts told by Toynbee. Today, I might have a more eclectic view as to that particular distinction.

I regard Sorokin as one of the greatest thinkers of our century, one who saw deeply and beyond the horizons in all directions; one who saw it all coming before it happened. Of course, his pessimism in the 1930s did not endear him to the controllers of the marketplaces of optimism in the U.S. academe. He might have done better in Europe, and then perhaps not; after all, Harvard offered him a niche and his books did get published. His scope and domain, the number of social institutions, and the space-time breadth and width might have been too vast for contemporary readers in general and social scientists, including historians, in particular. The twenty-first century may react differently.

## Sohail Inayatullah

My interest in Sarkar was not initially based on his social stages of history, but on his comprehensive worldview, particularly his inclusion of the spiritual in social theory. Sarkar's vision of the future impressed me immediately because it had both modern and traditional components, yet transcended both.

It also appealed to my dual nature as a Pakistani South Asian and as a rootless son of a U.N. intellectual. Having lived all over the planet by the age of seventeen and having been raised in the international relations discourse, I was impressed by Sarkar's universal humanism and his articulation of a theory that was historical–structural, not merely concerned with the day-to-day happenings of leaders and nation-states. By this time, national pride and ambassadorial wealth had ceased to impress me. More important than explaining social reality were theories that could change the living conditions of the powerless. Marx was interesting, but had no spiritual dimensions. And American political science, narrowly centered on modernization and development theory, was utterly boring. I found Sarkar's emphasis on social movements committed to economic self-reliance, cultural strength, and a new environmental ethic far more energizing. His theory of social stages also gave an anchor to my interest in futures studies, which often seemed strong on values but weak on history, theory, and structure.

It is not surprising that Sarkar has become so controversial in India. As he was active at theoretical and community levels, both religious (Hindu) and secular (Western liberal) perspectives find Sarkar's rewriting of history uncomfortable, nor are they accustomed to a theory of economic growth within a theory of the spiritual.

For me, it is individuals such as Sarkar and the many others in this volume who fascinate me. They are the greats who have glimpsed past and future and whose categories of thought we continue to live in today. We invite you to share in this fascination.

## Acknowledgments

Galtung would like to express his gratitude to Tony Marsella, then Vice President of Academic Affairs, and Deane Neubauer, then Dean of Social Sciences, for inviting Galtung as Professor of Peace Studies to the University of Hawaii; to Jim Dator for the encouragment of macrohistory as one approach to futures studies; and to Takeshi Ikeda, then Chair of the Department of Sociology, for his helpfulness.

Inayatullah would like to thank Tony Stevenson, the Director of the Communication Centre, Queensland University of Technology, Brisbane for research time and staff assistance in completing this book. Leanne

Holman took time off from the lovely surf of New South Wales to help edit Inayatullah's Chapter 3, Levi Obijiofor took a break from his work on visions of Africa's future to help edit, and Nicholas O'Donnell not only served as an able administrative assistant but, as an accomplished writer himself, helped with the final editing as did Anne Elliott. Thanks as well to Ivana Milojevic for her encouragement and care in the final stretch.

# Chapter 1

# Macrohistory and Macrohistorians: A Theoretical Framework

*Johan Galtung*

## 1.1 MACROHISTORY: VAST SPACE, VAST TIME, VAST THEMES

Macrohistory is the study of the histories of social systems, along separate trajectories, in search of patterns. Macrohistory is ambitious, focused on the stages of history and the causes of change through time (*diachronic*). Macrohistory is not the study of some little region in space at the same point in time (*synchronic*). The region may hang together and be the only one of its kind, like a study of Western Civilization,[1] or be noncontiguous, like a generalized study of the decline and fall of empires.[2] The distinction between singularizing and generalizing is found in Windelband's *ideographic/nomothetic*,[3] close to Dilthey's *verstehen/erklären* (understanding/explaining).[4] The singular case opens for depth in understanding,[5] the study of several cases for comparisons, generalizations, and explanations.[6]

The social sciences—of person, social, and world systems—have been cut through by these deep and basic distinctions between diachronic and synchronic, and between ideographic and nomothetic approaches. In principle, this gives us twelve different sciences, all dealing with the human condition:

|  | *Level I: The level of person systems* | |
|---|---|---|
|  | Diachronic | Synchronic |
| Ideographic | **Biography** | **Interviews** |
| Nomothetic | **Microhistory, genetic psychology** | **Psychology** |

And then

|  | *Level II: The level of social systems* | |
|---|---|---|
| Ideographic | **History** | **Anthropology** |
| Nomothetic | **Macrohistory** | **Sociology, politology, economics** |

And finally

|  | *Level III: The level of world systems* | |
|---|---|---|
| Ideographic | **World system history** | **Yearbooks** |
| Nomothetic | **World macrohistory** | **International relations** |

Level II is best known and best developed, with separate social sciences for the three pillars of modernity: civil society (sociology); the state and coercive power (politology or political science); capital and exchange power (economics). The other two are less elaborate. Psychology has more of a monopoly on Level I than, for instance, sociology on Level II. And international relations rule alone.

So here it is: *macrohistory*. Of course it is diachronic, but it is not ideographic. Macrohistory is not the same as the history of a unit over macro-spans of time, or the history of a macro-unit over short or long spans of time. To expand the time horizon for a history of England (and Wales, Scotland, Ireland) backwards, beyond the onset of the Roman invasion, opens for new understandings of the North Sea islands. But it is not macrohistory. It is long-range history, shaming the historians whose historiography was more shortsighted, even seeing their own country mainly with Roman eyes.[7] The same goes for the conventional way of writing the history of North America, or the Pacific including Hawaii; very perfunctory up to "contact," with studied inability to locate the European invasion inside native historiography, preparing for the discourse of "settlement."

The same goes for a total world history, certainly grandiose in space and maybe even in time if really "from the beginning" up until today, with adequate scenarios for beyond. (Why should history be bounded at the end, like the occidental soul at the beginning?) It remains ideographic, with very thick descriptions; understandable, as we have only this one world.

Let us only note in passing that a world (system) history should not be confused with some thick book with parallel histories for countries or regions, even when those countries and regions are compared. A world system history would be relational, interactive. Wallerstein's ambitious attempt is probably the first to do this, although it may be said to suffer from excessive economism, covering mainly one type of relations.[8] But to be simultaneously relational, diachronic, and ideographic is not easy.

*Macrohistory is nomothetic.* It compares the histories of social systems, along separate trajectories, in search of regularities—"laws." The descriptions of the single unit will invariably have to be relatively thin; after all, the macrohistorian will be looking for occurrences or recurrences of some well-defined theme. He may be accused of selecting only that which fits; a relevant objection, but not necessarily devastating since he may be in search of a theme more than the final word about how history evolves. Macrohistory should be mined for insight. It should not be seen in strict empirical terms, that is, abused by being believed as the total view, including by the macrohistorian himself.

*Macrohistory is diachronic.* It traces a process through time, a *Zeitverlauf*, if not from beginning to end, sufficiently to see the shape of the trajectories and to identify some underlying mechanisms. This calls for long time spans if we study social systems, even longer for world systems, and shorter for person systems with limited life spans. For example, a comparative theory of revolutions, with cases taken from several points in space and time, will be sociology or politology, not macrohistory. The diachrony for each case would be too short. Macrohistory would have to trace several long-range trajectories and follow them long enough to identify mechanisms of revolutions. The raw material for macrohistory is trajectories, as for history in general.

*Macrohistory makes sense both at levels II and III.* We may even distinguish between two types of macrohistory: for social systems, often called societies or even countries; and for world systems, an underdeveloped field. The former is easier because there are more cases. Comparisons can be made. Of course, that can also be done with one case (meaning one trajectory), cutting the trajectory in periods; comparing them for shape, phases, and mechanisms; and the like, but it is good to have more cases to work with.

The macrohistorical approach also makes sense beyond this. Imagine we discovered other worlds with historical processes. We could then move up one level and write an interworld history as raw material for a macrohistory of interplanetary or even intergalactic systems, incorporating biological and physical systems and their rhythms. Astronomers and cosmologists do this at a basic level.

*Macrohistory makes sense at Level I, as microhistory.* The focus is on the individual person, the smallest social unit; the social atom is called "biography." But a life span is not micro for a person living that life, and psychology gains by comparing many human life cycles. In Chapters 5 and 6, Level II macrohistory will be used as a metaphor for Levels I and III—to understand the other levels better, and to test macrohistory.

## 1.2 WHY SO LITTLE MACROHISTORY?

If it is so important, and if this type of approach cuts across levels of inquiry into the human condition, why is there so little macrohistory around? There could be a methodological error here, a focus on great names only. When most people talk about history it is not only in the detailed ideographic sense. People, also historians, enjoy making "sweeping generalizations" in space and time, protestations to the contrary notwithstanding, and do not rest content with isolated "space-time regions." Societies are like people; they are born, blossom, become old, and fade away would be the type of statement many people would subscribe to, not worried about all the problems implicit in the cyclicity hypothesis and the organism analogy. If this is common folklore, there must be many amateur and professional macrohistorians around, only we do not know them.

However, two good reasons can also be put forward to account for the paucity of professional grand-style macrohistory. First, macrohistory is intellectually difficult. Much is required of the macrohistorian. He (almost always a he, as will be explained) should have a command of the basic empirical features of some single cases, contiguous/continuous or not. The mind has to survey vast terrains in space-time. A high capacity for pattern recognition is a precondition. The macrohistorian has to make sense of enormous amounts of data. Whether the focus is on the long-term trajectory of one unit, for instance a country, or the more ambitious comparison of several trajectories, patterns have to emerge and be imposed on the data, the degree of correspondence between theory and data have to be evaluated, the patterns have to be revised, and so on. The macrohistorian is not producing a diachrony of one unit (historians do) or the more interesting but difficult parallel diachronies of several units, whether organized in tables and charts or in historical atlases. He is looking for recurring patterns in the trajectories of the same and/or different units, and for mechanisms underlying them.

The macrohistorian is not engaged in purely descriptive work. His task is at higher levels of the scientific enterprise, working on theory and data at the same time. This is no denigration of the significance of the painstaking work to establish "data"—*wie es eigentlich gewesen ist* (how it really happened) and those who, literally speaking, dig out data covered by the sand of the deserts, the mud of the garbage heaps, and the dust of the archives. The macrohistorian is usually not working with such primary data, but does secondary or tertiary analysis. If successful, the intellectual feat involved is considerable. Singularizing, ideographic historians may turn that feat into defeat by pointing to major discrepancies between the general theory and "his" case. This should be welcomed but not permitted to debunk macrohistory. The macrohistorian is a guide in social space-time. Like all guides he has favorites, emphasizing some points at the expense of others in the landscape. And he has blind spots.

He should not be blamed for being partial; that is the inevitable concomitant of having a perspective at all. He might be blamed, however, if he insists that his perspective is the only valid perspective there is. Many of them certainly write as if they are of that opinion, but followers are also to be blamed if they accept this monoprophetic tradition.

A more healthy attitude would be to see a perspective as only that—one in an unbounded set of perspectives; settling for something between the barefoot empiricism of no perspective at all, the dogmatism of one only, and the facile formula that the world is so complex that anything said about it is true.

Second, macrohistory is politically problematic. A major reason why we have mesohistory has been to produce identity for nations and states, and more particularly for nation-states. This does not mean it all has to be that glorious. Of course, if the general formula of a Golden Past, a fall due to conquest from without or betrayal from within, Dark Ages, Redemption–Resurrection, and from then on Unlimited Progress, equipped with heroes and villains, can be imposed on the data of history, so much the better. But this is a subconscious macrohistory, and usually a bad one, applying a metascript rather than being innovative.

Authorities usually want history as a school subject to provide identity, dedication, enthusiasm, and optimism in addition to a number of role models that can be claimed as "ours." Truth as correspondence with facts is not even recognized as a casualty in the process designed to produce that highly pragmatic truth. Historians have made their skills available as intelligentsia delivering what is ordered rather than as free intellectuals.

Macrohistory may not be totally incompatible with this tall order (that also provides jobs for a number of producers and distributors of "history," the authors and publishers of school textbooks consumed by millions of school children all over the world). But there is no built-in guarantee that the macrohistory product can serve such purposes, for at least two simple reasons.

Being nomothetic, without proper names, macrohistory tends to make the singularity of nations, states, and people, including their leaders, invisible. They are washed out by the tide of forces and mechanisms. Of course, people are still there, but as represented by their status and status-sets, their roles and role-sets; in short, as embedded in structures seen as more or less complex webs of interrelated positions. Even the leader, the hero, and the villain will be cast in such terms. The focus will be on the conditions producing charisma, not on the attribution of charisma to one particular individual. Macrohistory would use proper names only for illustrations.

Being diachronic in addition to nomothetic, the future is always implied, and often with no promise of unlimited progress. The reason would be that the causes and mechanisms postulated do not cease to exist at time present, but will continue operating. In cyclical macrohistory this means more doom and gloom at some future time(s). For linear macrohistory with a downward slope the situation is even worse. But progressive linearity is also problematic; "linearity" meaning more time for the upswing A-phase to be followed by a downswing B-phase than in a cyclical theory.[9] No reflecting macrohistorian will assume resource inputs into linearity to last forever.[10] On the other hand, infinite travel in the same direction is possible in finite space provided that space is curved, as globetrotters can confirm, and it may be argued that social space-time has some of this property. However, to the extent that progress is seen in terms of production and accumulation of material goods with material inputs, that curvature has at least not been encountered so far.

As a consequence, the macrohistorian is unable to promise unlimited progress. Sooner or later the downswing will come, as predicted by a cyclical theory. A theory of unlimited progress may be very dear to incumbent elites, but offers nothing to an opposition who may buy "doom and gloom" macrohistory, to be discarded when they get into power.[11] Of course, the society studied may exit from the obsession with unlimited progress by changing its own program, which, more likely than not, also means a change in the composition of the elites. This is not a project to be entertained with any pleasure by elites in power.

In addition, the macrohistorian delivers an image of society as driven by impersonal forces rather than by forceful persons, not unique in the world but similar to all other societies of the same type (however defined). There is nothing that special, idiosyncratic, or exceptional about the society scrutinized by the macrohistorian. It is a case of this or that type of society in this or that stage, with people, including their leaders, enacting their preassigned roles. Again, macrohistory clearly appears unacceptable from a nation-state building view.

But why can macrohistory not stop short of the future? Because it is nomothetic, with "laws" disrespectful of borders in time, including the line for "now." Whether the prophecies are optimistic or pessimistic, self-fulfilling or self-denying, they enter the political process, enthusing some and enraging others. People are not left untouched by prophecies; after all, everybody has a stake in however small a portion of the future. Historians may say we cannot learn from the past. Macrohistorians insist we can. That is their promise and problem.

## 1.3 WHO ARE THE MACROHISTORIANS?

Given what has been said in the preceding section, what do we know about the people who became macrohistorians, or at least became recognized as macrohistorians? Nothing much in any detail. But we can make some guesses as to where they come from using humankind's major divisions: gender and generation, race and class, nation and country. Given that, maybe something can be said about the social codes they carry.

Of course, they will tend to be male. Macrohistory is based on abstract thought, deriving basic aspects of the human condition from basic principles, with moral implications, a task that seems more attractive to men than to women.[12] In addition, macrohistorians operate at a level several steps removed from concrete human beings, dealing with great social architectonics.

Macrohistorians will tend not to be young. The young mind can make brilliant dashes in fields accessible at early age. New work in macrohistory requires exposure over a long time to the human condition in many of its manifestations. Not just the military and political phenomena, which are overemphasized in mainstream history, but also a diverse range of economic and cultural manifestations. Wisdom, maturing with age like good wine, is needed for this to come together in daring and original ways.

We would not expect race to be of any significance except insofar as it is correlated with class and nation, which it usually is in the present age of imperialism—the Colombian era—five hundred years so far. But class, nation, and country would certainly be important, and particularly the combination of them. Like for other phenomena, we would not expect random distribution.

If the macrohistorian can stand being rejected or at least not accepted by the elites of his own country, then he would probably tend to be either protected by upper-class arrogance or marginal, as an immigrant or a member of a minority. In either case, he derives strength from not having ambitions incompatible with being rejected by the elites. He would have to see through them and beyond them, for some of the reasons that have been mentioned, and if that meets with their displeasure, that is their problem.

Bringing in the Occident/Orient divide, to some extent representative of many divides in human culture, produces no particular reason why macrohistorians should be occidental. Those from the Occident may become better known given the dominant position of occidental culture. Also, they may write in an idiom more readily identified as "scientific" and not as religious as mystical storytelling. But both Occident and Orient come with the basic format for macrohistories already imprinted on their minds, a cyclical–linear combination for the Occident and a more unambiguous cyclical imprint for the Orient. There is enough to build on and to be filled in with details and new mechanisms in both cosmologies, as we shall have occasion to see in Chapter 2.[13]

Would any country be more likely to produce macrohistorians than others? Possibly countries with much history; in other words, old countries like England and Germany, France and Italy, India and China. They have much to look back on, a long trajectory that provides for intertemporal comparisons, not only comparisons across space. To this may be added crisis as a big stimulus, providing motivation to understand the aberrant and the abhorrent, even if only in terms nonpalatable to the elites.

In conclusion, we offer a possible reflection on their personalities. The alternative to macrohistory is not only history limited to the contiguous and continuous. At one level macrohistory is still history, but stretches history in time to get the real long run, *la longue durée*. Macrohistory then adds vast space to vast time for comparative purposes and uses this to arrive at general (i.e., nomothetic) perspectives, principles, and even laws to history. At this point real macrohistory enters, not only history of the large. World history adds to vast time and vast space a relational and interactive, not only a comparative perspective. But as there is only one world, we have no comparative, not to mention interactive, world histories. We get the history of the Very Big. But eras and regions can be compared. There is enough material for world macrohistory. There can be division of labor.

It has to be kept in mind that in earlier ages in the West the working of history was seen as the unfolding of God's plan, reflected in Augustine and Teilhard de Chardin in Chapter 2. The other macrohistorians are secular and Western or religious in the Oriental sense. What this means is that the macrohistorian either has come on top of God, revealing His scheme, or has come in place of God, telling what the scheme is all about. The macrohistorian is to the historian what Einstein or Hawking is for the run-of-the-mill physicist: in search of the totality of space and time, social or physical. It is certainly not a very modest enterprise. So we might perhaps assume strong personalities, to say the least, perhaps somewhat autistic, drawing on inner resources and heedless of responses (or lack thereof) from the outside. Chapter 2 gives some indications in this direction. Divided into twenty sections, each giving a biography of the selected macrohistorian, Chapter 2 articulates the theory of knowledge behind their macrohistory and presents their theories, stages, and mechanisms of historical change.

## NOTES

1. William NcNeill, *The Rise of the West* (Chicago: University of Chicago Press, 1963).

2. Johan Galtung, *The Decline and Fall of Empires: A Theory of De-development* (Geneva: UNRISD, 1996).

3. Wilhelm Windelband, *Geschichte und Naturwissenschaft* (Spiritual science and natural science) (Munich: Beck, 1894).

4. William Dilthey, *Einleitung in die Geisteswissenschaften* (An introduction to spiritual science) (Leipzig: Duncker and Humblot, 1883).

5. In order to understand from the inside, a thick context is needed. As we have only one unit in an ideographic inquiry we have to use many dimensions so

we can empathize, live the situation through, even enact it in our mind and write down what we experience. In other words, we end up with the Collingwood position, history as reenactment. See R. G. Collingwood, *The Idea of History* (Oxford: Oxford University Press, 1946).

6. For an approach to the methodology of social sciences, see Johan Galtung, "The Data Matrix," chapter 1 in *Theory and Methods of Social Research* (New York: Columbia University Press, 1967). For another discussion of the theme of this section, see Johan Galtung, "The Social Sciences: An Essay on Polarization and Integration," chapter 1 in *Papers on Methodology* (Copenhagen: Ejlers, 1979).

7. Hugh Kearney, *The British Isles: A History of Four Nations* (Cambridge: Cambridge University Press, 1989). For a fine review, see Christopher Hill, "The Raj Quartet," *The New York Review of Books*, 1 June 1989.

8. Immanuel Wallerstein, *The Modern World-System* (New York: Academic Press, 1974).

9. François Simiand, a French economist, argued against the three "idols of the tribe" (the tribe of historians): the idols of politics, of the individual, and of chronology. Peter Burke sees Simiand as a spiritual father of the French *Annales* school of historians, with its focus on cycles and the long run rather than events, and on mentalities and global, very multidisciplinary history. See Peter Burke, *Sociology and History* (London: Allen and Unwin, 1980), 95–96.

10. This is where Smith's worries about moral sentiments and Weber's "iron cage" enter as examples.

11. Thus, Marxism was used to undermine the position of governments favoring capitalist formations, and to cement the position of Marxists in power as being forever. That "forever" lasted about forty years.

12. See Carol Gilligan, *In a Different Voice* (Cambridge: Harvard University Press, 1982). There are few women macrohistorians. Even Elise Boulding's classic *The Underside of History* is not a macrohistory—as she admits—but an attempt to include women in history, not to write a grand theory of history from her own perspective. Riane Eisler comes the closest, although there are some missing elements in her work. See Sohail Inayatullah, "Macrohistory and Social Transformation Theory: The Contribution of Riane Eisler," in *World Futures* (forthcoming 1997).

13. For an early presentation of cosmology, see Johan Galtung, Tore Heiestad, and Erik Rudeng, "On the Last 2,500 Years in Western History, and Some Remarks on the Coming 500," in *The New Cambridge Modern History, Companion Volume*, ed. Peter Burke (Cambridge: Cambridge University Press, 1979), 318–361.

Chapter 2

# Twenty Macrohistorians: A Presentation

*Edited by Sohail Inayatullah*

This chapter presents the selected macrohistorians (see Appendix A for a chart summarizing their positions and Appendix B for diagrams illustrating their theories). Essays focus, in general, on the macrohistorian's biography, theory of knowledge, causes and mechanisms of change, stages and patterns of history, and comparisons with other macrohistorians. While the sample is certainly not perfect—one can make a case for other grand thinkers, such as Gaetona Mosca, Chang Hsüeh-Ch'eng, or Eric Voegelin—it does cover the most important macrohistorians in Western, Indic, Islamic, and Sinic civilizations as well as the feminist and Gaian viewpoints. In addition, Chapter 3 brings in the perspectives of other macrohistorians not included in this presentation.

The selected macrohistorians are the following:

2.1 Ssu-Ma Ch'ien (145–90? B.C.)
2.2 Augustine (354–430)
2.3 Ibn Khaldun (1332–1406)
2.4 Giambattista Vico (1668–1744)
2.5 Adam Smith (1723–1790)
2.6 George Wilhelm Friedrich Hegel (1770–1831)
2.7 Auguste Comte (1798–1857)
2.8 Karl Marx (1818–1883)
2.9 Herbert Spencer (1820–1903)
2.10 Vilfredo Pareto (1848–1923)

2.11   Max Weber (1864–1920)
2.12   Rudolf Steiner (1861–1925)
2.13   Oswald Spengler (1880–1936)
2.14   Pierre Teilhard de Chardin (1881–1955)
2.15   Pitirim Sorokin (1889–1968)
2.16   Arnold Toynbee (1889–1975)
2.17   Antonio Gramsci (1891–1937)
2.18   Prabhat Rainjan Sarkar (1921–1990)
2.19   Riane Eisler (b. 1931 )
2.20   Gaia

## 2.1

### Ssu-Ma Ch'ien: The Cycles of Virtue

#### Chang Xie with Sohail Inayatullah

Ssu-Ma Ch'ien is considered one of China's great historians. His book, *Shi Ji* (*The Record of History* or *Records of the Historian*), has been regarded as one of the main sources of historical research for Chinese and foreign scholars. Based on an analysis of Chinese dynasties, Ssu-Ma Ch'ien's theory of macrohistory has had an enormous influence upon Chinese historiography for the last two thousand years.

### BIOGRAPHY

Ssu-Ma Ch'ien (145–90? B.C.) was born in a well-educated family. His father, Si-Ma Tan, the famous historian, was in charge of the official astronomical affairs in the Han dynasty. When he was young, he was taught to read the classical writings as well as how to observe the natural world. At the age of twenty, he traveled city to city, county to county, where he collected literature of ancient scholars and historical figures. He also studied the customs and practices inherited from the Confucians, for whom he had a deep respect. When Ssu-Ma Ch'ien returned from his journey, he had already gained enough experience and knowledge to become a scholar in a government office. By the time his father died, he had became a prominent historian. When he was forty-two years old, he began to compile the *Shi Ji*. This work continued for seven years and was interrupted only by the "Liling" incident, in which the Han dynasty emperor Wu-ti ordered Ssu-Ma Ch'ien to be castrated for writing a letter of support for a friend who had been unjustly punished by the emperor.

Despite this agonizing humiliation, which placed the historian in the same physical category as the venal court eunuchs he so deeply despised,

Ssu-Ma Ch'ien refused to commit suicide; he maintained his dignity by making his history as grand and comprehensive as possible.[1]

However, several years later, he was appointed as *Hang Shu Ling* (secretary of the emperor) and he devoted even more time to the writing of his book. Unfortunately, his grand history was not published until after his death. During the time of Emperor Xian (73–48 B.C.), Ssu-Ma Ch'ien's grandson made the book known to the public and finally it became widely acknowledged.

## PHILOSOPHICAL BACKGROUND

To understand the wonders of Ssu-Ma Ch'ien, we must first have knowledge of his social background and the causation of his theory. Before Han, the main influential schools of thought were Confucianism, Taoist, and Yin–Yang. The former emphasized problems of politics and human relations. Confucianism did not concern itself with metaphysical or cosmological speculation. But the latter two, the Taoist and Yin–Yang schools, had traditionally been interested in these questions and their explanations of the creation and working of the universe exercised a great influence on Han thought. Thus, the cosmological ideas of the Taoist and Yin–Yang schools passed into Han Confucianism and became a part of the philosophy of the educated class. For example, in the work of Tang Zhong-Shu a great body of correspondence was built up relating the two complementary principles of Yin and Yang to all phases of creation. The Yang was always related to male, the sun, fire, heat, heaven, creation, dominance, spring, and summer, while Yin was equated with female, moon, cold, water, earth, nourishing and sustaining, recessiveness, autumn, and winter. As each force reaches its extreme, it produces its opposite and the two continue to succeed each other in a never-ending cycle. This constant reaction of the two forces on the metaphysical and physical planes was used to explain all processes of growth and change in the natural world.

Si-Ma Tan, Ssu-Ma Ch'ien's father, was a great historian of the Han dynasty. He had written numerous articles discussing the essentials of the Six Schools: the Yin–Yang, the Confucianism, the Moist, the Logician, the Legalist, and Taoist. While most of the original materials may be lost, some can be found in *Shi Ji*. In his discussion, Si-Ma Tan favored Taoism and criticized the others. According to Si-Ma Tan, "Taoist teaching is all sufficient and embraces all things. Its method consists in following the seasonal order of the Yin–Yang school. . . . It modifies its position with the time and responds to the changes which come more about in the world. In establishing customs and practices and administering affairs it does nothing that is not appropriate to the time and place."[2]

Here, the "time and place" means only the natural order, the endless process of alternation or the relation of cause and effect. This idea of Taoism and the Yin–Yang school no doubt had a certain impact on Ssu-

**Appendix A** Chart of the Twenty Macrohistorians  247
**Appendix B** Pictorial Representations of the Twenty Theories  249
*Daniela Rocco Minerbi*
   B.1 Ssu-Ma Ch'ien  249
   B.2 Augustine  250
   B.3 Khaldun  250
   B.4 Vico  251
   B.5 Smith  251
   B.6 Hegel  252
   B.7 Comte  252
   B.8 Marx  253
   B.9 Spencer  253
   B.10 Pareto  254
   B.11 Weber  254
   B.12 Steiner  255
   B.13 Spengler  255
   B.14 Teilhard  256
   B.15 Sorokin  256
   B.16 Toynbee  257
   B.17 Gramsci  257
   B.18 Sarkar  258
   B.19 Eisler  258
   B.20 Gaia  259
   Selected Bibliography  261
   Index  267
   About the Editors and Contributors  273

Ma Ch'ien's historical view. Under the influence of his father, he became dramatically different from the great thinker Confucius. Even though Ssu-Ma Ch'ien showed great respect toward Confucius and wanted to become his second—to make *Shi Ji* the second to Confucius's *Spring and Autumn*—the two historians had different approaches toward history.

## THE CONFUCIAN EPISTEME

Inherited from Confucius, Ssu-Ma Ch'ien attributed the driving force of social change to the alternation of social morality. While Ssu-Ma Ch'ien takes the Confucian ethic of virtue, he rejects his linear evolutionary structure. For Confucius, the first stage was *disorderly*, an anarchic stage of continuous warfare. The next stage was *small tranquillity*, characterized by institutions of family/private property, egoism, and social instability. The third stage was that of *great similarity* marked by mutual concern, social harmony, and respect for learning and virtue.

Among Confucianism's classical literature, there are five main books. *Yi Jing* (the Book of Changes), *Shu Jing* (the Book of History), *Shi Jing* (the Book of Odes), The Ritual, and the *Chun-Qiu* or *Spring and Autumn Annals*. The last is commonly considered a historical record of events in or affecting the state of Lu for the years from 722 B.C. to 481 B.C. The difference between the *Spring and Autumn Annals* and *Shi Ji* is that Confucius had compiled the annals not as an impartial record of historical fact but as a vehicle to convey his personal judgments on the men and events of the past and thereby to suggest to men certain moral laws and principles that would guide them in the management of their affairs.

To the Chinese, history is of critical importance in civilization's social development. The rulers usually regarded the history of the former dynasty as a "mirror" which could be seen as a guide for future political conduct. History was to be learned from. From this point of view, *Shi Ji* and *Spring and Autumn* were both written with the same intention. They were written to advise rulers how to establish good government. But the way each of them took to engage in such historiography was different.

For Confucius, social change is a problem of the moral qualification of a man or a family to rule. A ruler may be extremely powerful, but if he is selfish and cruel and oppresses his people, "heaven" will cease to aid and protect him or sanction his rule and he will fail, like the last king of Shang. And yet a state may be weak or insignificant, but if it is wise or benevolent in its administration and care for its people, then all men will flock to its rule and heaven will aid it to rise to the highest position, just as with the leaders of the Zhou.

Borrowing from the Yin-Yang school, Ssu-Ma Ch'ien rearticulated these ideas into a rise-and-fall theory of virtue—arguing that the exact components that lead to the rise would lead to the fall and vice versa.

Ssu-Ma Ch'ien saw his task as that of arranging the accounts of the early dynasties and feudal states in such a way that the pattern of growth and decay could be most easily perceived. He reinterpreted history so as to make it easier to see historical truth and be virtuous. There was a natural order to all things; good history made this order more intelligible.

## INTERPRETATION AND ORDER

Ssu-Ma Ch'ien's *Shi Ji* is not just a record of history. It is the masterpiece of realism in Chinese history. The three thousand years of social change described in this book represent the evolution of human civilization, the cycles of war and peace in social life, and the social and economic life of the Chinese people. To Ssu-Ma Ch'ien, history is an interpretation of the rules and regulations of order. The central regulation pattern is the rise and fall of each dynasty in the two-thousand-year history of China.

Influenced by the theory of Yin–Yang and the theory of the five agents, Ssu-Ma Ch'ien believed that no matter what type of change—heaven change, time change, man change, things change, or world change—there are always rules to change. The underlying order of change is conceived as a cyclical succession of eras proceeding in an order of growth and decay, rise and fall. This recurrence of certain patterns perpetuate everything: the cosmos, and the social and natural worlds. Like the rest of creation, history is a manifestation of the universal process of change coming to realization in the course of human events. Therefore, for Ssu-Ma Ch'ien, the proper study of mankind is man, and man as revealed in the pages of history.

There are thus two dimensions to Ssu-Ma Ch'ien's theory. The first is the pattern of rise and fall, growth and decay, waxing and waning. This is directly related to the moral order creating a rise and fall of virtue pattern. Second, each dynasty could be understood by its moral characteristics: good faith for the Xia, piety for the Shang, and refinement for the Zhou. As each dynasty declined, its virtue was transformed into a fault. Good faith became rusticity, piety became its opposite of superstition, and refinement turned into hollow show. The Qin dynasty failed because it did not transform the hollow show of the declining Zhou. However, "the Han wisely returned to the good faith of the Xia."[3]

Equally central to Ssu-Ma Ch'ien was the view that each dynasty begins with a sage king of superlative wisdom and virtue (Yu of the Xia and Ch'eng T'ang of the Qin) and each dynasty closes with an unspeakably evil and degenerate monarch (Chieh of the Xia and Ch'eng T'ang of the Qin). Between the good and the evil are merely a list of names of rulers.

However, while history was certainly cyclical, it was not preordained. Burton Watson writes, "History to him was a constant process of growth, and it was impossible to think of returning to the same static golden age of the past. What was possible, however, was the creation of a new golden age in the present by a wise appreciation of the moral values appropriate to the times."[4] History then is not just the repeat of the old story.

The cycle of history is renewed when a new sage overthrows the previous tyrant and a new house or dynasty is established. Of course, the pattern does not always fit so exactly. According to Watson, it is "varied in the middle, as in the case of the Qin dynasty, by the appearance of worthy rulers who restore for a time the original virtue of the dynasty in an act of revival or restoration."[5]

Thus, according to Ssu-Ma Ch'ien, history is a process of the endless and the eternal recurrence of social–cultural life. However, the repeat will never be the same as far as time and space have changed. The regulation of the change is obvious when you observe the main stream of dynasties which follow the route of rise–fall–disappear. For Ssu-Ma Ch'ien, small changes took place in thirty years, medium changes in one hundred years, and great changes in three hundred years.

This explanation indicates the extraordinariness of Chinese history, which can be grouped into the cyclical and the linear conception. From the cyclical point of view, the world is characterized by the eternal alternation of the two opposed and complementary forms: the Yin and Yang. This basic metaphysic is the ultimate cause of the rise and fall in history. From the linear point of view, cycles are short phases in a long-term trend during which there are temporary cyclical trends.

The linear theory comes from Confucius and the cyclical from Ssu-Ma Ch'ien. The cyclical and linear theories of history of these two great Chinese historians and philosophers have became the dominant theories of nearly all other historians.

## APPLYING SSU-MA CH'IEN'S THEORY

The intention of Ssu-Ma Ch'ien's cyclical concept was to write history so as to investigate the rules and regulations behind the success and failure of virtue. Hence, the two thousand years covered in *Shi Ji* moves with a ceaseless rhythm of rising and falling political fortunes, a rhythm which to a Chinese historian is a natural and inevitable reflection in the human realm of the larger rhythm of the seasons and the stars. Going back to the history of China, it is not difficult to discern the tracks which reflect the truths of Ssu-Ma Ch'ien's cyclical theory.

Early Chinese history begins with a number of vague, semidivine culture heroes who are said to have first taught the Chinese people the various arts of civilization. These legendary figures are then followed by three rulers of exceptional wisdom and virtue—Yao, Shun, and Yu—who figure so importantly in later Confucian writings.

Yu was the founder of the first dynasty of Chinese history, the Xia. The dominant virtue for this dynasty is good faith. The following dynasties, with no exception, were dominated by the Shang and Zhou virtues of piety and refinement.

Starting from the Xia, Shang, and Zhou dynasties come the Qin, Han, Sui, and Tang. The period between these six dynasties should be considered a transition from the refinement of Han to the good faith of Sui. It is also the repetition the warring period between Zhou and Qin. Sui and Tang exactly reflected the dynasties of Qin and Han. Like the early dynasty of Zhou, the Han and Tang were also regarded as the period of culture flourishing and high-level prosperity. During these periods, China's population jumped to its peak, especially in the Tang dynasty. Just as the cycle ended with the Zhou, Han, Tang, and Ming, respectively, the cycle began with the Xia, Qin, Sui, and Yuan dynasties, respectively. They were similar in that they were reunified after a period of warring and separated states. This led to highly centralized and standardized thoughts and beliefs, which prepared for cultural growth of the next dynasty.

The cyclical theory not only explains the ancient and middle history of China but can also be applied to modern China. Right after the overthrow of the Qing dynasty by the 1911 Xin-hai Revolution, the cycle of republican government began its form. This revolution had a unique place in Chinese history. It emancipated the Chinese nation from the imperial rule of the Manchu minority people and put an end to the feudalist system. Since 1911 to the present is such a short time compared to China's long history, we can barely estimate how long the cycle will last.

We could perhaps divide modern China into three periods. The first is from 1911 to 1949, when China was under the control of the Kuomingtan. The second period is from 1949 to the present, with China under the control of the Communist Party. Like the Qin, Sui, and Yuan dynasties, the Kuomingtan started the New Culture Movement in 1911, diminished all the warlords, and established the first government of the Republic of China in 1928. This significant New Culture Movement led China to a new period in its history and made it possible for the flourishing of democracy in China. The reason for this description of modern China is that from 1911 to now China has not been able to enter the period of refinement suggested by Ssu-Ma Ch'ien. Even though the economic reforms in the beginning of the 1980s were regarded as a historically significant change, they are not significant enough to call the present a period of cultural and economical flourishing which can be considered a refinement in the history. Furthermore, the political system under Deng Xiaoping and his successors is not that different from the system of Mao Zedong. The June 4, 1989 crackdown of the student pro-democracy movement and the further harassment of its leaders sounds familiar to those who have a fresh memory of the Great Cultural Revolution.

If the grand historian Ssu-Ma Ch'ien was able to predict the future of today's China, he would probably say that the current system of dictatorship is coming to its final period. The soon-to-come political system will be more or less the socialist–democratic system which will bring the period of refinement.

## CONCLUSION

Just as Ibn Khaldun provided the paradigm of the search for objective variables of historiography for a "sociology" of history, Ssu-Ma Ch'ien provides history with the paradigmatic theory of cyclical change. The core of his theory is as follows. First, dynasties are the appropriate unit of analysis. Through them we can see the rise and fall of virtue, the waxing and waning of civilization. The fall comes from the rise, it is inherent in the metaphysic of life. The sage-king can improve conditions for his subjects—there is human agency—but his actions are not eternal; while the sage-king may start a dynasty, a time will come when unspeakable evil will rule and a new sage-king and a new dynasty will begin.

There are many similarities between Ssu-Ma Ch'ien and the macrohistorians who followed him. Ibn Khaldun too uses the variable of the dynasty but focuses less on virtue but on the rise and fall of *asabiya*. It is not the sage-king but the Bedouin-king who begins the new dynasty. Sarkar, following Tantra, the antecedent of Taoism, also uses a similar metaphysic to the Yin–Yang, the *avidya/vidya* (introversial/extroversial) deep structure. Sorokin articulates his pendulum theory of history from Ssu-Ma Ch'ien's model. Of course, Ssu-Ma Ch'ien should not be faulted for his lack of sophistication as compared to these moderns, but should be remembered as the first macrohistorian.

## NOTES

1. Jonathan Spence, "Confucius," *Wilson Quarterly* 17, 4(Autumn 1993): 38.
2. Theodore Wm. Debary, *Sources of Chinese Tradition* (New York: Columbia University Press, 1960), 6.
3. Burton Watson, *Ssu-Ma Ch'ien: Grand Historian of China* (New York: Columbia University Press, 1958), 26.
4. Ibid., 143.
5. Ibid., 6.

## 2.2

# *Augustine: The River to Eternity*

### Brian Shetler

Western thought on the macrohistorical processes of time can be largely traced to the interpretations put on classical thought by Augustine. His interpretations shaped medieval thought in the West. Significant among the last medieval cosmologists affected by Augustine was Thomas Aquinas. This subchapter is devoted to Augustine's views from the fourth century with mentions of Aquinas's additional perspectives from the thirteenth century.

## SKETCH OF AUGUSTINE'S LIFE

Saint Augustine was born Augustinus Aurelius on November 13, 354, in Thagaste (now Souk Ahras, Algeria) to middle-class parents, Patricius and Monica.[1] Since Thagaste was too small for a college or university, his family scraped enough money together to send him to school in Madaura and, in 371, to Carthage.[2] In Thagaste and Madaura he had received comprehensive lessons in the writings of a few authors (especially Cicero and Virgil). In Carthage he began to show signs of breaking the mold, but even then in a typical way. He read Cicero's *Hortensius*, a book known to us now only from fragments quoted by Augustine and other ancient writers, which inspired in him a great enthusiasm for the discipline of philosophy. In Augustine's zeal for wisdom, he joined a religious cult from Persia that had recently planted itself in the Roman world: Manicheism.

The world of the Manichees was torn between two contrary powers: the perfectly good creator and the perfectly evil destroyer. The world seen by human eyes was the battleground for their cosmic conflict. The Manichees and their followers were the few who were on the side of the good spirit and who would be rewarded for their allegiance with eternal bliss. In the meantime, all sorts of misfortune might befall the individual, but none of the wicked things he found himself doing were his fault. If the devil compels sin, then guilt of the individual does not ensue.

But Augustine soon became unsettled with theological questions. In *Confessions*, he recounts a meeting with Faustus, the Manichee sage, whom he had been promised would finally answer all the questions that troubled Augustine. He says he discovered the sage to be half-educated and incapable of reciting anything other than a more complex set of slogans than his local disciples.[3] Disillusioned with the cult, he still did not break with it publicly until 384, more than ten years after his first contact with it.

His enthusiasm fading for the niceties of metaphysics, he turned his attention to his career. At age twenty-one, after about four years at Carthage, he returned to his hometown to teach for a year before returning to Carthage, where he taught for seven years, becoming a formidable scholar and orator. Education in Carthage at that time was a free-market enterprise, with each teacher setting up independently around the city center to make a reputation and collect paying students. Augustine prospered but was bothered by the insecurity of his financial condition—students were always scheming on ways to avoid paying their teachers.

In 383, Augustine left for Rome seeking a more secure position. Some Manichee friends there arranged an audition before the prefect of the city of Rome, who had been asked to provide a professor of rhetoric for the imperial court at Milan. Augustine won the job and headed north to take up his position in late 384 at age thirty. At the time it was one of the most visible academic chairs in the Latin world and promised to provide easy access to a political career.

Augustine recognized his opportunity. He called for his mother (his father died shortly after he began school in Carthage), and when she arrived he allowed her to arrange a good society marriage, for which he gave up his mistress. He had to wait two years, however, for his fiancee to come of age and promptly took up with another woman in the meantime.

His life at this time seemed to be centered around a philosophy of prudent ambition. His public ambitions meant he needed connections. Manicheism had failed him, but with his mother there to press claims of Christianity, he publicly declared that he had been enrolled as a prebaptismal candidate in the Christian Church when he was a child. He began attending sermons by bishop Ambrose, who at the time was one of the most influential men in Milan. With the help of technical vocabulary borrowed from Platonic philosophy, Ambrose proposed a solution for Augustine's oldest dilemma: his sense of evil and his responsibility for the wickedness of his life. As a professor of belles-lettres, Augustine had objected to Christianity as barbaric and inelegant. But Ambrose was elegant and far from barbaric, overcoming Augustine's snobbery.

At the age of thirty-five Augustine returned to Thagaste to set up a monastery. Two years later he was conscripted into the priesthood by a local congregration. Eventually, Augustine became a bishop. As bishop, Augustine devoted most of his time to three battles: a battle with the growing Donatist sect that wanted an outwardly pure church (any Christian who sinned would have to go through baptism again in order to be one of the Donatists); a philosophical battle to stamp approval on the Roman culture under Christian rule; and a theological battle over the essentials of faith and salvation. The first battle led indirectly to Augustine writing his most important work on macrohistory, *The City of God*. This book came about as a result of the imperial commissioner Marcellinus visiting Augustine in Africa to look into the Donatist quarrel on behalf of the emperor. Marcellinus requested that Augustine write a response to charges that the Christian god, with his ideas about turning the other cheek and holding wordly empires in low esteem, was not an efficient guardian of the best interests of the ruling class, as evidenced by the barbarians, under the leadership of the Visigoth Alaric, sacking Rome in A.D. 410. The first books in this twenty-two-book masterpiece were published quickly, beginning in A.D. 412, and were meant mainly to console those who were frightened by the Visigoths. But the later books continued to be published over a period of fifteen years and revealed a broad vision of history and Christianity.

## AUGUSTINE'S THEORY OF KNOWLEDGE

Foundational to Augustine's conception of history and macrohistory is his theory of reality and how it is known by humans. Reality for Augustine has three planes of being: body, soul, and God. In space and time there are three categories of things: that which is (i.e., mere bodies in the physical universe); that which both is and lives (i.e., plants and animals); and that which is, lives, and knows, sharing existence with physical bodies, life with plants and animals, and, by virtue of reason, is capable of knowledge. The body is controlled by the soul, which is controlled by God when things are in perfect harmony.

How Augustine knows "reality" is also God centered. Unlike Aristotle and Saint Thomas Aquinas, Augustine's empiricism does not take sensory data and abstract from them. He instead starts within the man's soul with divine illumination and develops interpretations of appearances within the context abstracted from these illuminations. His epistemology is therefore regularly called one of divine illumination.[4]

Thomas Aquinas summarizes their two theories on knowing as follows:

Augustine, going along with Plato as far as the Catholic faith permitted, did not admit the species of things with their own subsistence [the world of forms] but rather admitted ideas of things in the divine mind, declaring that through these we form judgments of all things by an intellect illumined by divine light, not so as to see the ideas themselves, which would require our seeing the essence of God, but through what these supreme ideas impress upon our minds.... Aristotle, however, took another way. First of all he showed in many ways that there is something stable in sensible realities; second that sense judges truly concerning the proper objects of sense but is mistaken about the common objects of sense and more mistaken about things accidentally perceived; third, that there is an intellectual power above the sense, and this judges of truth not through intelligible things existing outside but through the light of the agent intellect by which things become intelligible.[5]

The consequences for the differing concepts of knowing and being in "time" are very different. Under Augustine's approach, man affirms his existence with the statement, "*Si fallor, sum*" (If I fail [or am deceived], I exist). Unlike Descartes's "*Cogito, ergo sum*" (I think, therefore I exist), for Augustine there is no pure thought as long as we exist. Purity and existence are mutually exclusive for him. To be undeceived is to no longer exist. That does not exclude being. It just means that if a being is undeceived, it is eternal—unconfined by past, present, and future distinctions in time. In Thomas Aquinas's approach, on the other hand, man presupposes human existence and argues backwards from his senses indicating that he cannot create himself that God must exist. Eternity becomes a semantic term for the sensible regression of causation until distinctions between moments in the far-off past become insignificant. Being can be actual or potential in time, and is no less being for its potentiality.[6]

## MACROHISTORY

For both Augustine and Thomas Aquinas, time has a beginning and an end, with history in-between. However, the beginning and end are real for Augustine and appear to be semantic constructs for the intellect for Thomas Aquinas. According to Augustine, the existence of humans has a beginning—man's failure. Illuminated divinely by sacred scriptures, Augustine attempts to interpret the human condition before the deception: Undeceived humans were created and were eternally in the garden of Eden. In that garden, they were without change, without past or future. But through deception by the serpent they lost eternity—they were condemned to existence, change, and death.

For Augustine, history as cyclical events is only an appearance created by our confined existence. The "true" history is in the eternity that transcends all existence. In comparison to this "true" history, existential events and cycles are trivial surface waves on a rolling river. These waves may seem to be without beginning or end in their repetitions, but are really only distractions in a much greater scheme.

Augustine's "true" history is distinctly linear. At one end of the history of man stands his creation, deception, and ejection from eternal paradise. At the other end stands the final judgment in which all deception is eliminated, time is declared no more, and all the just will be awarded with a place inside the walls of the city of God, the unjust in the void beyond its walls. Between the beginning and end of history is time mercifully given to man for repentance. The avenue that makes this repentance possible is the one-time occurrence of God submitting himself, as Christ, to the unjust execution of man's rule as a means of taking the punishment, of paying the price, for man's sins—an event that never before occurred and will not recur.

Some, too, in advocating these recurring cycles that restore all things to their original, cite in favor of their supposition what Solomon says in the book of Ecclesiastes: "What is that which hath been? It is that which shall be. And what is that which is done? It is that which shall be done: and there is no new thing under the sun. Who can speak and say, See, this is new? It hath been done already of old time, which was before us." . . . At all events, far be it from any true believer to suppose that by these words of Solomon those cycles are meant, in which, according to those philosophers, the same periods and events of time are repeated. . . . "For once Christ died for our sins; and, rising from the dead, He dieth no more. Death hath no more dominion over Him"; and we ourselves after the resurrection shall be ever with the Lord, to whom we now say, as the sacred Psalmist dictates, "Thou shalt keep us, O Lord, Thou shalt preserve us from this generation." And that too which follows, is, I think, appropriate enough: "The wicked walk in a circle," not because their life is to recur by means of these circles, which these philosophers imagine, but because the path in which their false doctrine now runs is circuitous.[7]

The river may then seem endlessly full of repetitions, but that appearance is deceptive. Soon enough we will round the last bend of what seemed an age of an age and enter, instead of another age, a boundless ocean of eternity. But in the meantime, according to Augustine, every individual's existence in this stream of time, since the expulsion from paradise, is conceived in the cloudy waters of lust—a deception from the true desires God meant to be expressed in procreation. Because of the deceptive form of our conception, according to Augustine, we inherit deception and existence. In this state of inherited sin man has the illusion of free will, but the only alternatives available in his considerations are those involving error.

The history of man is a struggle to be free from this error, to find Truth, which to Augustine was changeless and eternal. But all men's efforts by themselves fall far short of eternity and always will, according to Augustine. Man's efforts must be motivated by a love for God, even to the contempt of man himself, not the love of self, for it to last—something impossible to accomplish without exogenous intervention in the affairs of men by God. Thus, to him Roman virtues were but splendid vices because they were motivated by national pride or a desire for imperial power or glory, which eventually turn vicious because they have not been inspired by the love of God.

The only way for man to find true (universal and eternal) anything, according to Augustine, is through the true religion: Christianity. But no man can even choose to do this on his own, because man can only will error by himself. Man can only realize the true religion by pursuing the leadings of God in man's innermost and highest thoughts. Thus, he presents a peculiar mix of free will and predestination. He says God as the ultimate reality is omnipotent, omniscient, and perfectly good. As omnipotent, nothing can happen without His willing it to happen. As omniscient, nothing can happen without His knowing it. As perfectly good, nothing can happen that is not good. The catch here is that evil is seen as a lack, a no-thing, an ungood, not a thing itself.

The foreknowledge God has of who will respond to His leadings does not negate free will because the interaction is not coercive. It is like observing how a person approaches a street and knowing by this that the person will cross the street. But in this interplay even the unconscious intentions of people cannot be hidden from the omniscient God, who knows their consequences but does not force them. He empowers people to will things and empowers them to accomplish things. If people do not follow God's leadings and submit to his instructions in order to will good things and accomplish good things with what they are given, they can only blame themselves.

According to Augustine, by following and accepting God's leadings, man becomes again like Adam in paradise: having a will that is free again not to sin but an inherited corruptible body that always tries to drag the will back into sin. This is the life of a christian before "the first death"— the physical death. However, the final state of man and the end of history comes with his inability to sin. This state comes with the death of the mortal body and resurrection in a body dead to deception.

Thomas Aquinas has a more "sensible" outlook that does not dictate a linear progression to its ultimate end: "Everything—whether it has knowledge or not—tends to good."[8] The operative word is "tend." Not everything happens by Epicurean accident and not everything occurs along a divinely dictated linear path.[9] Instead, he suggests Aristotle was right that political science be pursued as the science that will show the ultimate end of human life and that this will show that the general trend to perfection is a road toward complexity.[10]

## CONCLUSIONS AND CONSEQUENCES

Augustine's divinely illuminated polemics were abused by the scholastics that followed him in the medieval period to punish as heretical any disagreements or questioning of his conclusions. However, his reliance on Plato and the classics rescued him from the book burners in the centuries that followed. It is difficult to say whether Augustine would now say his reliance on Plato and the classics was human error or divinely dictated illumination. Thomas Aquinas would arguably claim it was a good tendency on Augustine's part, whether Augustine consciously made the "error."

Both would agree that there is an ultimate end to human existence. History has an end. However, Augustine views the end as arriving in linear fashion with its realization dictated to humans by God. Thomas Aquinas views the end as an idea—a word with senses—that will be achieved by man through his divinely provided ability to think and make (repeated) errors.

As a consequence, their medieval cosmology does not contemplate the earth as a limited resource and history as circular, although they might allow for some limited circularity, with Augustine awaiting divine illumination and Thomas Aquinas looking for logic to reveal our mistakes. Instead, rules and principles were a limited resource and history was (Augustine) or had a tendency to be (Thomas Aquinas) linear. The choices made by individuals were therefore paramount to the community progress, and each of us has a limited time to get as much as we can right.

## NOTES

1. J. J. O'Donnell, *Augustine* (Boston: Twayne, 1985), 1–2.
2. Augustine, "The Confessions," in *Basic Writings of Saint Augustine*, vol. 1, ed. Whitney Oates (New York: Random House, 1948), 21–22; Augustine at 2–3.
3. Ibid., 63–64.
4. Ibid., xxiii.
5. M. T. Clark, ed. *An Aquinas Reader* (New York: Fordham University Press, 1995), 100.
6. "Matter can also be referred to as nonbeing, not so as to mean that it exists in no way at all, but in the sense that it does not exists as being in actuality." Ibid., 196.
7. Augustine, "The Confessions," 192–193.
8. Clark, *An Aquinas Reader*, 257.
9. Ibid., 335.
10. Ibid., 363–364.

# 2.3

# Ibn Khaldun:
# The Strengthening and Weakening of Asabiya

*Sohail Inayatullah*

Writing at a time of the disunity and decline of the Islamic empire, the horrors of the plague, and the conquests of the Mongol Tamerlane, Ibn Khaldun (A.H. 732–802 or A.D. 1332–1406) sought to understand the rise and fall of civilizations. His historiography was neither descriptive or genealogical, nor was it a defense of a particular civilization—it did not seek solely to glorify Islam—rather, Khaldun searched for the causes behind historical actions and movement.

Khaldun distanced himself from contemporary and historical thinkers of the time by rejecting the theory that history was a degeneration from a previous era of perfection. He also rejected the cyclical regression view of the ancients in which prophecy led to caliphate, then to unjust kingship, then finally to a return to prophecy. Rather, Khaldun searched for structure. Most history is simply about how "people settled the earth until they heard the call and their time was up."[1] His aim was to discover "[t]he inner meaning of history, [which] involves speculation and an attempt to get at the truth."[2] Specifically, it involves the "subtle explanation of the causes and origins of existing things, and deep knowledge of the how and why of events."[3]

The pattern of Khaldun's own life is crucial to understanding his theory of change. Indeed, his own life is isomorphic to his historiography. Khaldun moves from political escapades, intrigues, and efforts to maximize power to his own person; to efforts to play the role of learned advisor to kings and potential princes; and then finally to a philosopher concerned with the deeper patterns of life.

Khaldun also does not develop a history of "being," thus distancing himself from the prevalent theological discourses of the time. His is not the project of finding how Allah influences the course of history. God to him is a figure that stands in the background, providing inspiration and individual purpose, used in his text most often to begin a passage—"May God take care of us and of you"—or as an after-the-fact explanation.[4] It is Allah's will. For Khaldun, what is significant about God is that through religion, the sign of God, humans can increase their unity or *asabiya* and thus provide the basis for their rise in power.

## PERSONAL HISTORY: THE RISE AND FALL OF FAMILIES

Ibn Khaldun was born in Tunis on May 27, 1332. He was tutored in the Quran, the Hadith, jurisprudence, and Arabic poetry and grammar. Ibn Khaldun's family played an important part in the civil wars in Seville in the ninth century. In the next four centuries, they successively held "high administrative posts under the Umayyad, Almoravid, and Almohad dynasties; several were killed in the battle of az-Zallaqah in 1086, which temporarily halted the Christian conquest of Spain."[5] In 1248, just before the fall of Seville and Cordoba, they moved to the northern coast of Morocco. In 1349, the Black Death struck Tunis and took away both his father and his mother. This event was not lost on Khaldun. In his *Muqaddimah* (An Introduction to History), he incorporated this dramatic event, writing of the relationship between plagues and cities, arguing that urbanization spreads such diseases and that a decentralized system of civilization was needed. But he did not allow this unprecedented plague to become an all-encompassing external variable; rather, he chose an endogenous one— that of solidarity—with which external variables interact.

Ibn Khaldun's personal life followed the pattern set by his family. Khaldun spent time in government service, but by 1357, the Sultan Abu Inan suspected his loyalties and threw him into prison. Once Abu Inan died, the wazir Al-Hassan ibn Umar reinstated him. The next eight or nine years, which saw strife between dynasties in Northwest Africa, were the most perilous in Ibn Khaldun's restless life journey. With the fall of Abu Abdallah, Ibn Khaldun raised a large force among the desert Arabs and entered the service of the Sultan of Tlemcen. After a few years, he was taken prisoner. Khaldun next entered a monastic establishment, where he wrote the *Muqaddimah*, finishing in 1377 "with words and ideas pouring into my head like cream into a churn and without the use of a library."[6] He moved to Egypt where he served as judge and applied the idea of *asabiya* to Egyptian history. The ups and downs of life did not end, for his family died in a shipwreck in 1384.

Among the most interesting episodes of his life was his meeting with Tamerlane. In 1400, Tamerlane's Tartar armies invaded Syria and, while in Damascus, Tamerlane asked to meet Khaldun. "The latter was thereupon lowered over the city wall by ropes and spent seven weeks in the Tartar camp."[7] Like a good scholar, he proceeded to give a series of lectures on his theory of history to Tamerlane. But as a loyalist, he did not give Tamerlane the information he needed, namely knowledge that could be used to conquer Egypt and the Islamic West.

With Islamic civilization in crisis within and without—in decline and disintegration—it is not surprising that he chose to write about the rise and fall of dynasties. Making a similar point, Mushsin Mahdi concludes, "The picture of the Islamic world during the fourteenth century as depicted by Ibn Khaldun, and for the most part substantiated by other sources, was one of general decline and disintegration.... Western North Africa, where Ibn Khaldun grew up and spent fifty years of his life before going to Egypt, was the worst part of the Islamic world in this respect. It presented him with a spectacle of chaos and desolation."[8]

## THE PRIMITIVE–CIVILIZATION CYCLE

Ibn Khaldun wrote from a unified worldview. Thus, what happens to the individual, happens to the group, happens to a city, and happens to a civilization. Individuals follow a birth, rise, adulthood, and decline cycle as do dynasties, cities, and civilizations. Only God stands above, but although everything is per his will, he does not privilege one group over another. Rather, those groups who remain courageous, whose followers give leaders legitimacy, and who construct themselves as one people, last over time. Others find their fortunes decaying. When fortunes decay, those who have the strongest group feelings, the primitives, come back into control and power, thus continuing the cycle. In addition, Khaldun separates God and the world. Although individuals can attain various levels of spirituality, it is the tension embedded in choice that gives rise to the various alternative futures, not the will of the spirit.

Khaldun begins his historiography with the state of nature. He finds two types of culture: that of the primitive and that of the civilized; the rural and the city. They are near opposites of each other. Bravery, morality, unity, strong kinship ties, and respect for parental authority describe the rural, and cowardice, fragmentation, economic and social ties, and individuality describe the city. But they are not unrelated. Groups start as nomads and as they rise in wealth they construct or conquer cities. But in cities, with increased economic activity and size, new relationships emerge. This leads to a concentration on leisure and sensual pleasures which then leads to the breakdown of the city. Thus, nomads are not genetically more pious, rather the environment creates the context for the different behaviors of city and nomadic life.

*Asabiya* begins with the ideal person in nature, the Bedouin nomad. "Man seeks first the bare necessities. Only after he has obtained [them] does he get to comforts and luxuries. The toughness of nomadic life precedes the softness of sedentary life."[9] The Bedouins are more courageous because they have to be. Living in the desert requires such behavior, while those in the city resort to government laws and regulations and thus destroy their "fortitude and power of resistance."[10] Through environmental adversities, desert people develop increased solidarity. With compassion and the desire to protect those of the family, group feelings—*asabiya*—continues to grow and consolidate. However, intertribal conflict leads to numerous wars and anarchy.

"Once a superior solidarity emerges within a group, it tends to subdue lesser solidarities and bring them under its control. The result is a greater solidarity that unites the conflicting factions and directs their efforts to fight and subdue other groups. This process of expansion and unification continues until a point is reached when the newly formed solidarity is able to conquer the dominions of a civilized state or to establish new cities and the institutions characteristic of a civilized culture."[11] The group with the strongest unity rules other groups. From kinship, kingship emerges. Kingship leads to the desire for more power and the tribe expands its population and size, accumulating power, riches, and leisure. Kingship or royal authority is considered a necessity so as to avoid groups fighting and to give social cohesion. Thus, kings provide a superordinate authority. According to Khaldun, "He [the king] must dominate them and have power and authority over them, so that none of them will be able to attack another. This is the meaning of royal authority."[12] Besides kinship, religion provides *asabiya*. It creates new loyalities and a new solidarity. Indeed, religion mixed with blood loyalty in the context of just royal authority creates a formidable unity of mind and purpose, the ideal civilization.

## RISE AND FALL: UNIFICATION AND FRAGMENTATION

*Asabiya* literally means the fiber or sinew by which a group is held together. It is that which binds people into effective groups. When *asabiya* is strong, there is legitimacy; when it is weak, dynasties fall, empires are conquered, and a new group with a stronger *asabiya* rises.

Dynasties, cities, and civilizations have clear stages. "Through the conditions that are peculiar to a particular stage, the supporters of the dynasty acquire in that stage traits of character such as do not exist in any other stage. Traits of character are the natural result of the peculiar situations in which they are found. . . . The first stage is that of success, the overthrow of all opposition, and the appropriation of royal authority from the preceding dynasty."[13] Thus, the new group does not have to start all over, it has learned from the previous. In this stage, the ruler is benevolent and does not claim all authority for himself. In the second stage, the ruler consolidates power and makes himself the sole executive so as to exclude others from their various claims of royal authority. At this stage, "[There is] kindness to subjects, planned moderation in expenditure, and respect for other people's property. Nothing at this time calls for extravagant expenditures, therefore the dynasty does need much money. Later comes domination and expansion (luxury) caus[ing] increased spending. It calls for the increases in soldiers allowances and in the salaries of the people of the dynasty. Extravagant expenditures mount."[14] But before the decline there is the third stage, wherein "the fruits of royal authority are enjoyed: the things that human nature desires such as acquisition of property, creation of lasting monuments, and fame."[15] It is in this middle stage where the kingdom is prosperous, unity is high, expenditures medium, the army loyal, and the ruler just. In the fourth stage, the ruler imitates the previous ruler and becomes conservative, not departing from tradition and thus making the mistakes of the previous cycle. Then, in the fifth and final stage, there is waste and squandering.

He loses legitimacy. This is the stage of senility and the dynasty is destroyed. "At the end of the dynasty . . . crippling taxes weigh heavily upon the people and crush their incentives. . . . When they compare the costs of their production and the taxes they must pay with their income and see what little profit there is in trade and business they lose all hope."[16] A general apathy and hopelessness, argues Khaldun, "steal over people when they lose control of their own destinies and become dependent on others. Such a dependent people will be conquered by the first fighting tribe they encounter."[17] Also at this time the elites—government officials and private individuals—leave the city with the wealth they have amassed.

Thus, with fights in the inner group, the ruler eliminates and humiliates the contenders—legitimacy is destroyed. What results is a new but much weaker group feeling. This continues the further decline. Eventually, people who do not share in the group feeling of the elite take charge, but their commitment is not that strong and the dynasty is split and can be easily overthrown. In addition, with expansion more funds must be paid out to the masses, and with luxury, group feeling decreases. Thus, to deal with crises rulers pay out more money, which hastens the decline. This is in sharp contrast to the beginning of the dynasty, when it had a desert attitude—no extravagant expenditures, a sense of royal authority, and regular fasting and other spiritual practices by the leaders. "Within the army too there is a struggle for power. . . . [They] 'are caught up in the effeminacy of sedentary culture' and lose their desert toughness, they seek power through assiduous competition for leadership."[18]

But luxury is not always the downfall. Khaldun is far more sophisticated than that. For example, in the beginning of a dynasty luxury actually leads to increased group feeling and royal authority as it brings on more children. The population of the leaderships expands. It is only in subsequent generations that the nonproductive elite become problematic and bring on their own decline, but before the final end there is a temporary rise.

Group feeling has often disappeared (when the dynasty has grown senile) and pomp has taken the place it occupied in the souls of men. Now, when in addition to the weakening of group feeling, pomp, too, is discontinued, the subjects grow audacious vis-à-vis the dynasty. . . . At the end of a dynasty, there often also appears some (show of) power that gives the impression that the senility of the dynasty has been made to disappear. *It lights up brilliantly just before it is extinguished, like a burning wick the flame of which leaps up brilliantly a moment before it goes out, giving the impression it is just starting to burn, when in fact it is going out.*[19]

Thus, dynasties rise, consolidate power, expand, grow old, become senile, and then die. This rise and fall is the rise and fall of unity, identity, and legitimacy, or in one word—*asabiya*. New dynasties emerge at the periphery among provincial governors or among rebels with a stronger group feeling. However, the new dynasty comes to power not through sudden action, but through perseverance. There is battle after battle, until eventually the senility not to mention the pestilences and famines of urban centers bring the old dynasty down. And, of course, the new dynasty will follow the cycle of the previous one; it will rise and fall.

## THE TIME OF DISINTEGRATION

Khaldun also gives us empirical indicators of decline using generational time. Khaldun hypothesis is that the nobility of a family lasts four generations. The first generation knows the value and struggle of work. The son of the second generation was in contact with the father and saw with his eyes how to work, to labor. However, since he did not use his own creative power to learn, the son is inferior to the father. This is even more the case for the third generation, which must "be content with imitation, and, in particular, reliance upon tradition."[20] By the time of the fourth generation, all creativity, practicality, and independent judgment have been lost. The fourth generation "thinks that it was something due his people from the very beginning by virtue of the mere fact of their descent, and not something that resulted from group effort and individual qualities."[21]

The family thus revolts and finds a new leader. The new leader then grows, while the man of the fourth generation continues to decline. Khaldun gives an interesting example of this theory. The children of Israel were told by God to go forth and conquer, but they did not. Thus, they wandered forty years until a generation had passed away, and a new one that had not witnessed the humiliation by Egypt could take over. Moreover, this new generation was strengthened by adverse desert conditions, developed *asabiya*, and thus could accomplish the destined mission ahead.

Dynasties follow a similar pattern, lasting on the average three generations or 120 years (three times forty, the age of maturity). The first generation "retains the desert qualities, desert toughness and desert savagery."[22] They live on basic needs; their unity and their desire for more goods keep them active and vital. But with royal authority and a luxurious life, "the second generation changes from the desert attitude to sedentary culture, from privation to luxury and plenty, from a state in which everybody shared in the glory to one in which one man claims all the glory for himself while the others are too lazy to strive for glory."[23] By the time of the third generation, all memory of the toughness of desert life has been forgotton, "as if it had had never existed."[24] They lose their Bedouin heritage and become like children in need of defense. This last generation continues the show of courage by having contests and shows, but their courage, for the most part, is gone. Often a *Wazir*, an appointed minister, takes power away from the family, especially when a weak member of the family is appointed sucessor. *Wazirs*, however, even as they exercise full authority, disguise their power under the form of a ruler's representative. The dynasty stays under the *Wazir's* control since the "royal princes . . . have forgotton the ways of manliness and have become accustomed to the character traits of wet nurses. . . . They do not desire leadership."[25] Ultimately, royal authority is lost to those with stronger *asibiya*.

The causes of historical change are thus endogenous. What causes the rise, leads to the fall. External factors are important but not essential. The cycle remains: primitivism, civilization, kingship and absolute power, leisure and functional economic relations, disintegration, and primitivism again.

## A LASTING LEGACY

Khaldun, like his personal history of rise and fall and rise, presents us with a history of the rise and fall of civilizations. History is cyclical, moved by endogenous forces. The key to history is social unity and solidarity. It is this and the search for basic needs that lead to royal authority and the development of the state. State power is held as long as the elite are innovative, fair, and unified. But with size and civilization, lethargy, cruelty, impiety, and sensuality develop. Instead of kinship, functional relationships become paramount. Instead of unity, there is fragmentation. Eventually, group feeling breaks apart and those with a stronger group feeling rise and take state power. They then follow the same pattern. While God does not work in history, the notion of God provides unity to the people who have faith. It is this faith that leads to strength and victory.

Khaldun's works form the basis of much of present sociological thought. One can find his thinking in Comte (the creation of a science of society), in Weber (the routinization of charisma and the politics of bureaucracy), in Spengler (the culture/civilization dichotomy and the biological life cycle applied to society), and in Marx (the town and country distinction), among many others. Ibn Khaldun's influence is such that he is rarely credited, yet many grand thinkers use and live his framework.

## NOTES

1. Ibn Khaldun, *The Muqaddimah*, trans. Franz Rosenthal, ed. N. J. Dawood (Princeton, N.J.: Princeton University Press, 1967), 5.
2. Ibid.
3. Ibid.
4. Ibid., 206.
5. *The New Encyclopaedia Britannica—Micropaedia*, 15th ed., s.v. "Ibn Khaldun."
6. Lenn Goodman, "Ibn Khaldun and Thucydides," *Journal of American Oriental Society* 92 (1972): 251.
7. *Brittanica*, 223.
8. Muhsin Mahdi, *Ibn Khaldun's Philosophy of History* (London: George Allen and Unwin, 1957), 26.

9. Khaldun, *Muqaddimah*, 93.
10. Ibid., 95.
11. Mahdi, *Ibn Khaldun's Philosophy*, 199.
12. Khaldun, *Maqaddimah*, 47.
13. Ibid., 141.
14. Irene Brown, "Ibn Khaldun and African Reintegration" (paper presented at the 1971 Universities Social Sciences Council Conference, Makerere, December 1971), 27.
15. Khaldun, *Muqaddimah*, 141.
16. Brown, "Ibn Khaldun and African Reintegration," 32.
17. Ibid., 28.
18. Ibid., 32.
19. Khaldun, *Maqaddimah*, 246 (emphasis added).
20. Ibid., 105–106.
21. Ibid.
22. Ibid., 137.
23. Ibid., 177.
24. Ibid.
25. Khaldun quoted in Ravi Batra, *Muslim Civilization and the Crisis in Iran* (Dallas: Venus Books, 1980), 115.

2.4

# Giambattista Vico: Barbarism and Providence

*Daniela Rocco Minerbi*

## HISTORICAL AND PHILOSOPHICAL CONTEXT

The seventeenth century was a period of intellectual confusion in Europe due to the disintegration of the unity of knowledge and social and political organization. The previous integration had offered a unitary intellectual framework throughout the Medieval Age. The disintegration was brought about by the new discoveries of nature's physical laws, made by Galileo, Copernicus, Kepler, and Leibnitz.

New scientific knowledge of natural phenomena created the need for a new relationship between man and nature, nature and God, and man and God. Scientific knowledge subtracted itself from the authority of Christian theology and became a challenge to it, thus initiating the crisis and degeneration of Christian medieval cosmology.

This crisis, which involved religion, metaphysics, and the natural sciences, also became a crisis of epistemology. The method of knowledge of scholastic thought, which allowed the use of reason only within the dogmas decided by Church authority, was abandoned. This method, concerned mainly with the classification of nature created by God, had been rendered irrelevant by the development of physical science. To this picture one must add the loss of Christian doctrinal unity caused by the Protestant reformation.[1]

The new mathematical, a priori, deductive method of Descartes was the only unifying factor, but this was only a method, not an overall principle of intellectual order. According to Vico, Descartes's method was abstract and could not furnish an understanding of physical reality.[2] The intellectual climate in Naples, where Vico lived, was constituted by skepticism, and the censorship of the Counterreformation.[3] It was this fragmentation of knowledge that created in Vico the need for a universal vision and motivated him to undertake its formulation.

## INTELLECTUAL BIOGRAPHY

Giambattista Vico was born of humble origin in Naples in June 1668. At the age of seven, Vico miraculously survived a fall from a ladder. This event strengthened his conviction that the work and plans of Providence can turn tragic human affairs into good ones. He was an exceptional child for his resolution to learn and study the antiquities and humanities. In Naples, Vico studied law at the university and thereafter taught rhetoric, beginning in 1699. Overall, his was a life of poverty and isolation. The works that he wrote were neither in keeping with the cultural trend of Naples nor understood. Hence, he was perceived as extravagant.[4]

Vico aspired for the chair of civil law all his life. It is thanks to his failure to win the chair that he finally decided not to write for professional advancement. It was then, at the age of over 55 years, that he wrote *La Scienza Nuova* (the New Science), followed later by a new revision called *La Scienza Nuova Seconda* (the Second New Science). It is the latter work that expounds the author's conception of history. Giambattista Vico died in January 1744.

## VICO'S CONCEPT OF HISTORY

Some of the questions Vico addressed were of an epistemological nature and led him to reflect on the great validity of the study of the humanistic disciplines that reveal man's nature and development. Other questions were of a historical nature: They searched for the origin of the construction of civil society and the causes of the development of civilization. The investigation of the origin of mankind led him to inquire into the consistency of Christian theology (the time of creation of man by God) with scientific and historical findings. It was his intuition and his studies of antiquities that brought about the idea of multiple origins of civilizations.

For Vico, the law furnished insights into the origins of civilization. Vico stated that jurisprudence was founded in human nature, and human nature was inspired by eternal principles of justice and rationality. The law, being founded in human nature, is natural law. It is not contingent or relative to a particular society or historical time. Natural law is based on eternal truths and therefore it is law for everybody; it is universal. Natural law is immanent because it is based on the essence of human nature, and it is metaphysical because it is informed by eternal, universal ideals.[5]

Natural law is present in potentiality in every people; it is not imported or imposed by one people to another. But justice is administered by men according to the degree of development of their reason; in a primitive state, the law could not be founded on a fully developed rationality. Vico believed that the true, deeper cause of the origin of social life and law was the essence of justice, goodness, and rationality that resides in human nature.

## VICO'S THEORY OF KNOWLEDGE

Vico's theory of knowledge is based on a new relationship between epistemology (the study of the way in which knowledge takes place) and ontology (the study of the fundamental character, the essence of being). Epistemology and ontology are not viewed as totally separate functions, therefore the ontological distinction between subjectivity and objectivity becomes minimized. For Vico, man was not simply a spectator of reality existing prior and apart from himself. In order to know, the knower/agent cannot be passive, otherwise no act of knowing could happen, no reality and world (made by men) would exist. There would be no history to know, if nobody acted it out. To know, without at the same time making, is impossible. Knowledge, action, and reality are integrated, they are the object of the knower who is the subject of knowing and making. Man performs an activity that is epistemological and ontological at the same time.[6]

True knowledge requires knowing the original causes of phenomena. In order to know the primary causes, to know *"per causas,"* one had to be the originator, the maker of that reality, because only the maker knows and has within himself the causes and reasons of what he has made. Absolute knowledge is the entire truth, because to have knowledge one has to know the causes, and to know the causes is to know the truth. A scientist is able to reach the truth in proportion to the degree to which he is the maker of that reality.[7]

For Vico, the only field in which human thought can create and shape reality is history. History is made by man, therefore man can have true knowledge of it. History is the only field that can constitute a science. By establishing the principle that in order to have true knowledge of something one has to be the maker of it, Vico expresses his skepticism of the power of pure reasoning to understand reality. Vico's fundamental criteria of knowledge holds that *"verum and factum converuntur"* (what is true and what is made coincide).[8]

Vico stated that man cannot have real knowledge of nature since it is not created by man. Nature is made by God. Knowledge of physical sciences can only be attained to the degree that, through experimentation, the physical process is imitated and recreated to analyze the effects derived from its partial causes. Vico was critical of Descartes's rationalistic method because it was not connected to reality; instead, he admired the experimental method of Bacon and wanted to deal with history in the same scientific manner as the new physical sciences were dealing with physical phenomena.

## HISTORY AS CREATIVE HUMAN ACTIVITY

For Vico, history was the manifestation of creative human activity. The causal origin of history resides in man's mind, which is informed and inspired by metaphysical ideals of justice and honesty. History begins with human nature. It is from human nature that custom arises, from custom laws, and from laws governments. These metaphysical ideals are reminiscent of Platonic philosophy, according to which the innate eternal "ideas" represent the universal, noncontingent aspect of reality and constitute the eternal truths and the essence of knowledge. However, the difference between Plato's innate ideas and Vico's metaphysical ones is that the latter are the result of a historical process.

Vico affirmed not only that true knowledge was possible, but that it could be attained through the study of history, because history was the creation of the human mind. Historical truth had to be obtained by understanding each different developmental phase of humanity. He needed to rediscover the mental processes of the first men to find out how the first forms of socialization came into being. Reconstructing the way in which the mind of the first humans worked meant reconstructing the process of history.

Vico concluded that the founders of humanity were poets who thought in terms of poetic imaginative universals, not in terms of abstract rational concepts. The term *poets* had the Greek meaning of makers or creators.[9] This poetic time, the age of gods, could be viewed as the most creative historical phase.

For Vico, mythology and fables constitute real history and a true, though incomplete, form of knowledge; they were the manifestations of minds expressing themselves in poetic and imaginative forms rather than in conceptual ways. The first creation of man's imaginative thought was divinity, by which he explained thunder. It was because of the fear of divinity that man's self-consciousness and control of his instinctual behavior started.

Man's development from a stage of mere consciousness of himself toward intellectual clarity and rationality in the direction of complete knowledge of the truth, is inseparable from his sociopolitical actions and is expressed in the creation of increasingly rational institutions.

## SCIENCE OF HISTORY: *LA SCIENZA NUOVA*

Vico wanted to create a science of history that would be concerned with the universal and eternal elements in it, not the temporary and contingent ones. To achieve this he needed to establish a relationship between philology (the study of the uncertain, the contingent, the relative, and the temporal) and philosophy (the study of truth, the absolute, and the immutable).

This work of synthesis is found in the *Scienza Nuova Seconda*. He started his study of history from the time of the dispersion of man over the earth. Vico discovered that a metaphysical structure could be observed in history; an eternal pattern of birth, development, and decline that was encountered by every civilization independently of any contact or influence with each other. Through history, the social unit will increase in size from the family up to encompass a whole nation, the last social unit. Occasionally, Vico also talks of even larger units, such as "Christian republic," "republic of Europe," and "republic of letters."[10]

## VICO'S CHRONOLOGY OF THE AGES

Vico solves the discrepancy between the origin of humanity and the biblical story of the creation of man by God by isolating the history of the Hebrew people, who have preserved the memories of their history since the beginning of the world, longer than all other nations.[11]

The descendants of Ham and Japheth and the non-Hebrew descendants of Shem, lapsed into a state of bestiality and had to rediscover civil life. They could do so because they had within themselves the seeds of light and justice that are never dead. The New Science deals only with these latter peoples, who are the founders of the "gentile nations." After the universal flood, these primordial men wandered on the Earth for 200 years, acquiring a giant stature because of harsh existential conditions.

The age of gods marks the first age of the development of history. It is called so because the first institution was religion. The passage from bestiality to the first type of society is matrimony. The family constituted the first social unit, with the father as the authority. The family soon included the *famuli*, fugitives seeking protection in exchange for cultivating the land. The government was theocratic. The type of knowledge of this age was sensual, and the rational ability of the mind was not yet developed. This age lasted 900 years, both for the Greek history and for the Latins.[12]

The second age is that of the heroes. The social unit was constituted by a collection of families under the authority of the fathers who formed an aristocracy. The social structure was made up of two groups: the fathers and the *famuli*. The political unit was the city. The passage from the family to the city is explained by the necessity of the fathers to unite, forming an aristocratic commonwealth in order to resist the rebellion of the *famuli* who aspired to freedom and equality and who were ultimately quieted with concessions.[13] The type of knowledge was fantastic, and not yet rational. This age lasted 200 years for the Greek history. The passage from the second age to the human age was accomplished by wars which caused the ruin of the cities of the heroic age.

The third age is that of men. The social structure was made up of two classes: the nobles, as the government; and the plebs, composed of a merger of the *famuli* of the heroic cities.[14] The plebs, grown greatly in number and having reached a greater development of mind, revolted and caused the transformation of the aristocratic commonwealth into a free popular commonwealth. The political unit was the nation. Human reason was fully developed and the type of knowledge was rational.

In the end, the popular commonwealth became corrupted as both the powerful and the free people looked out for their private interests at the expense of the nation's. The plebs, who were at first moved by the desire to be free and equal, were later motivated by the wish for power and the popular commonwealth turned into a commonwealth of the powerful. A monarch was sought to preserve the existence of the nation from civil wars. Monarchy represented for Vico the last form of human government; monarchies were the expression of a free popular government because the people would choose the monarch. The establishment of a monarchy, however, required the absolute development of human reason.[15] However, people would not be capable of establishing this form of government. They would be conquered by an outside nation or would return to a state of barbarism because of corruption and selfishness and through civil wars. This second barbarism would last centuries.

After the second barbarism would follow a new divine age, the age of Christianity in Europe, during which families took refuge with bishops and abbots in ecclesiastical nations. To the second divine age follows the second heroic age, which coincides with the period of feudalism; the vassals represent the *famuli* of the previous heroic time and the barons represent the heroes. It is the period of the great monarchies of Christian Europe ruled by the aristocracies. The third age, the human one, is the contemporary time of Vico. It is the age of the new sciences and, philosophically speaking, the age of reason.

## THE DRIVING FORCE IN HISTORY

The beginning of social life coincided with the establishment of the first institutions (religion and matrimony), and also constituted the very beginning of civilization. Fear, necessity, and utility were the motifs that encouraged man to spring to action, but the inspiration for what direction man's action had to take was derived from the seeds of truth and goodness that man had within. These sources of inspiration constitute the driving force of history: human nature, meant as human mind.

This driving force brings about the development of a civilization from one historical age to the other. Man's mind matures and develops from one historical age to the other in the direction of greater rationality and greater knowledge of the truth. The principles and ideals of truth motivate man toward the making of history. This "reason" is manifested in the making of institutions, governments, and laws, and is a sparkle of Divine Providence. Therefore, Providence is immanent. It is this rational Providence, immanent in human mind, that is the true cause of civilization and socialization. Providence works through the natural means of human reason. Through the course of history, man reaches his true human nature, the full development of his rationality; that is to say, man is truly human when he has fully developed his reason and consciousness.

Through the different ages of civilization, the common good goes from being limited to few to becoming more and more inclusive of men until, in the free popular government of the human age, it is extended to all human beings.[16] As the common good becomes completely extended to every human being, it becomes harder for man to differentiate it from his own individual private good. Man, even after relapsing to a bestial state, does not lose those principles of truth and piety and can, therefore, rediscover religion and law. Man's ascent from barbarism is attributed to a superhuman wisdom, to Divine Providence, which is referred to as a mind that has a design always broader than the particular and narrow plans of men.[17]

## COURSE AND RECOURSE

A course in history develops through three ages: the divine age, the heroic age, and the human age. It ends in a period of barbarism and is followed by a recourse of the same three ages. The third age of the recourse is constituted precisely by Vico's contemporary time. That is the point where Vico's demonstration of the design of history has to stop, but the design of history is unending. The passage of the ages represents the evolution of man's mind, which is synonymous with reason, consciousness, and wisdom.

The recourse is not simply a repetition of history; it implies that the next historical wave will also go through three stages: a divine, a heroic, and a human one. The entire recourse itself constitutes a giant second step in the development of history. The recourse is a historical event, not just a conceptual pattern. It is a new chance given to mankind to attain true humanity; it is the equivalent of a new trial.[18]

## DOES HISTORY END?

History is the continuous evolution, happening in cycles, of mankind toward the actualization of those metaphysical ideas, truths, or principles that are always present in the human mind. In shaping reality according to these principles, man creates institutions, languages, laws, governments, and civilizations; at the same time, man develops himself—develops his mind, broadens his consciousness, and refines his reason. As he reaches a higher degree of refinement, he attains a more refined form of social life with more rational and human institutions.

For Vico, the development of reason coincides with the fulfillment of man's humanity. Vico refuses the concept of the immutability of the human mind and of the mind's eternal rationality since the beginning of history. The human mind possesses specific capacities that are specific of each historical period. Providence reveals itself in and by means of human reason. Providence is the manifestation of the rationality of man throughout history. History never ends; it is the continuing growth of man, slowed down by periods of barbarism. History is the evolution of man's rationality, which is itself the manifestation of Divine Providence.

## NOTES

1. Stuart Hampshire, *The Age of Reason* (New York: New American Library, 1956), 11–18.
2. Thomas Berry, *The Historical Theory of Giambattista Vico* (Washington, D.C.: Catholic University of America Press, 1949), 17–25.
3. Ibid., 21–25.
4. Ibid., 3–11.
5. Alfonsina Albini Grimaldi, *The Universal Humanity of Giambattista Vico* (New York: S. F. Vanni, 1958), 212–283.
6. Tom Rockmore, "Vico, Marx, and Anti-Cartesian Theory of Knowledge," in *Vico and Marx: Affinities and Contrasts*, ed. Giorgio Tagliacozzo (Atlantic Highlands, N.J.: Humanities Press, 1983), 178–191.
7. Richard Manson, *The Theory of Knowledge of Giambattista Vico* (Hamden, Conn.: Archon Books, 1969), 15–28.
8. Rockmore, "Vico, Marx, and Anti-Cartesian Theory of Knowledge," 178–191.
9. Giovanni Battista Vico, *The New Science of Giambattista Vico* (1744 reprint; 3d ed., Ithaca, N.Y.: Cornell University Press, 1968), X–1.
10. Berry, *Historical Theory of Giambattista Vico*, 85.
11. Vico, *New Science*, 68.
12. Ibid., 281.
13. Ibid., 21, 219.
14. Ibid., 217–218.
15. Ibid., 377–378.
16. Robert Caponigri, *Time and Idea: The Theory of History in Giambattista Vico* (London: University of Notre Dame Press, 1968), Chapter XI.
17. Vico, *New Science*, 425.
18. Ibid., 75–76.

## 2.5

# Adam Smith: Self-Love and Love of Others

*Daniel J. Campbell*

Adam Smith wrote the book for capitalism. As capitalism continues to wield influence and order the world over, no understanding of modernity is complete without attention to its effects. However, far from being a capitalist himself, Smith was instead a first-rate intellectual who was working on the utopian-like problem of how tribes, now understood as nations, were to procure their sustenance. Smith saw the problem from a historical perspective that identified previous stages in human socioeconomic organization according to the means through which the people were able to survive and especially flourish. These stages are well known; they are: (1) hunting, fishing, and gathering, (2) pasturage or herding, and (3) agricultural.

Marx made these designations famous. However, where Marx may have given a theory for movement through the stages, Smith never did. For him it is more a matter of happenstance and discovery that gains the new stage, not theoretical necessity. Smith's project was to articulate the perfect fourth stage: the age of commerce, as distinct from the imperfect precursors that include mercantilism and, interestingly enough vis-à-vis Marx, feudalism. However, if all that Smith accomplished was to initiate the real fourth stage, then he ought to be included only as a footnote to the theory of macrohistory and macrohistorians. What makes Smith a macrohistorian is his attention to whether the tribe or nation is in a state of stagnation, decline, or prosperity, and, most of all, his articulation of the active ingredient necessary for success at any stage. This ingredient is to be found in the moral sentiments common to the group. It is Smith's reason or theory for prosperity that both fueled his articulation of the fourth stage and necessitates his inclusion as a seminal macrohistorian.

## BIOGRAPHY

The man who wrote the blueprint for capitalism led a fairly quiet life. Adam Smith devoted much of his life to his masterworks, *The Theory of Moral Sentiments* and *The Wealth of Nations*, revising and republishing each several times before his death in 1790. Since these two works are virtually all he ever published during his lifetime, and because of Smith's devotion to both over this long period, the present interpretation draws the conclusion that both works are of the same project and need to be considered in conjunction.

Smith's intellectual engagement ran deep in many other subjects. The library he left was as extensive as it was varied. Literature, art, and especially philosophy occupied much of his time in his readings and conversation. He shared company with some of the leading intellectuals of the day, those from his native land of Scotland as well as others in England and France. David Hume and he were friends.

Adam Smith was not without a curiously strange side. He suffered from a nervous affliction which caused a shakiness, especially to his head. His speech was often peculiar and difficult to understand. He was not handsome, sometimes appeared in public nearly unpresentably, had an odd gait, and often spoke to himself out loud at length. He was well known to the town commoners for his absentmindedness and propensity to fall into states of reverie, the accounts of which are often hilarious. He never married. Adam Smith was an only child, whose parents both came from propertied families. He never knew his father, who died prior to his birth. His mother did not remarry and the two must have had a close relationship, as he lived with her off and on over the years, including her final years, the last of which came only six years prior to his own death. Once, when he was three, he was kidnapped by a passing band of gypsies only to be soon abandoned and returned to his mother.

At the age of fourteen, Smith began his nine years of study at Oxford. At the age of twenty-seven he accepted the chair of logic at the University of Glasgow and was soon professor of moral philosophy. During these twelve years as a professor, the happiest years of his life as he was to later confide, Smith published *The Theory of Moral Sentiments*. The book won him wide recognition. During this time, Smith also took up an interest in the history of jurisprudence. This endeavor was sparked by Montesquieu's *Spirit of Laws*, which appeared in 1748. In this work, Montesquieu distinguishes between societies subsisting on hunting, on herding or pasturage, and on agriculture. Smith lectured on this topic of jurisprudence but never published. Today, we have two sets of notes from these lectures. These surviving notes contain more development of the stage theory of history than either of his two books. Thus, though he makes use of stage theory in *The Theory of Moral Sentiments* and more so in *The Wealth of Nations*, in no place does he give full attention to this stage theory. It was Smith's student, Professor Millar, who actually first published such a theory. This work, *The Origin of the Distinction of Ranks*, published in 1779, is credited with being the first materialist conception of history.

## STAGE THEORY

Through his study of the origins and growth of government and jurisprudence throughout the ages, Adam Smith discovered an undeniable fact of human history. He saw that the means of subsistence for any given community, tribe, or nation could be derived from one of three primary sources. Furthermore, relative to each given source there applied a range of possible, and thus predictable, social structures and types of government. Working from this historical perspective, Smith came to see that there was an entirely new possibility for the source of human subsistence. *The Wealth of Nations* is the prescription for this new age. He called it the age of commerce. Hence, it was out of a consideration of previous historical types that our modern economy emerged. To the progression that includes hunting, herding, and planting, he added exchanging.

As mentioned earlier, Smith has no theory for the progression from one stage to the next. There are, however, certain requirements that should be mentioned in this regard. Transitions from the hunters to the herders and from this to the planters proceed from the discovery and adoption of a different basis for the means of subsistence for the community. Extenuating circumstances, such as climate, geography, and the availability of domesticatable animals both for food and as beasts of burden, all have an effect on the possibility for achievement of subsequent stages. Currency is necessary for the fourth stage. Prior to Smith's time, there had been movements toward the fourth stage. Currency and trade had existed for centuries, but during these times most people continued to derive their subsistence from the land. The age of commerce replaces its precursor when the populace at large participates in a genuine exchange economy for its sustenance. It was the genius of Smith to articulate the connection between his world and its next stage. At the heart of this insight are the principles of the free market. No previous transition was brought about by the intellectual contributions of one man.

Though the transition to the fourth stage is by far the most complex, there is one aspect in which the three are similar. Just as both the discoveries of animal domestication and husbandry and of farming were pivotal, the fourth stage required the marked increase in manufacturing output that had appeared by Smith's time. In a concise statement of this transition and its effects, Smith writes, "Commerce and manufacturers gradually introduced order and good government, and with them, the liberty and security of individuals, among the inhabitants of the country, who before had lived almost in a continual state of war with their neighbors, and of servile dependency upon their superiors. This though it has been least observed, is by far the most important of all their effects."[1]

Smith is optimistic about the changes brought on at the attainment of each new stage. In fact, the initial period of each new stage is a time of ascendency. The move to herding allows for a more stable means of subsistence, larger communities, and better defense against invasion. The move to agriculture does the same. With time, however, communities of either stage tend to become polarized in terms of wealth, making for a small wealthy class, the servants (broadly construed) of this class, and the rest, who are involved in production. This is what Smith means by "servile dependency," and it most likely also means that the community is either in decline or stagnation. Feudalism, according to Smith, is this state of the agricultural age. The move to the genuine exchange economy breaks the agrarian-based class structure and promises a long period of ascendency because of the fact that free-market trade is built on human creativity of virtually inexhaustible potential. Thus means that the wealthy class is open and changing. It also means there should be a great degree of freedom of employment for the worker. Unlike livestock or land, free trade, by definition, cannot become the property of one class. Because of this fact, Smith had much cause for optimism regarding the plight of individuals during the age of commerce.

If all human societies past and present fit into one of four designations, then it is the differences between them that matter greatly with regard to our understanding. As mentioned, climate, geography, the possibilities for transportation, and the availability of animals for domestication all play a part in the uniqueness of historical communities. In addition, war and natural destruction are causes for reformation within a community, resulting perhaps in changes from decline to ascendency or the opposite.

## THE MORAL COMPONENT AND INDUCTIVE REASONING

In addition to the material causes of history, there is another principle of causation rooted in the attitudes of the humans whose history is under consideration. Smith writes, "The man of the most perfect virtue, the man whom we naturally love and revere the most, is he who joins, to the most perfect command of his own original and selfish feelings, the most exquisite sensibility both to the original and sympathetic feelings of others."[2]

Herein lies a moral driving force of history. In its most simplified formulation, this drive has a two-part function: love of others and self-love. In general, Smith's first book elucidates the former while the latter receives prominence in his second book. In specific passages, he might appear to favor one to the exclusion of the other, but taken as a whole, his theory requires both. Since *The Wealth of Nations* is by far the more popular and influential work, Smith is often misrepresented as believing only in self-love and its contingent manifestations, such as self-betterment, self-interest, and selfishness.

Smith, however, does not use the phrase "love of other" (except incidentally). His term is sympathy, and it is alluded to in the first sentence of *The Theory of Moral Sentiments*: "How selfish so ever man may be supposed, there are evidently some principles in his nature, which interest him in the fortune of others, and render their happiness necessary to him, though he derives nothing from it except the pleasure of seeing it."[3]

Perhaps empathy and compassion come closer to what is meant by sympathy. The highest and fully moral choices arise out of a drive that

Smith calls "the sympathetic feeling of the impartial and well-informed spectator."[4] When the morals of a society are built on these principles, then this society is in a state of ascendence, no matter what its means of subsistence. If self-love and love of others are not working in combination as the moral motivation of individuals at large, then the tribe, community, or nation will ascend no more. It will stagnate and probably decline. Smith describes this idea of moral deliberation as follows:

When I endeavor to examine my own conduct, when I endeavor to pass sentence upon it, and enter to approve or condemn it, it is evident that, in all such cases, I divide myself, as it were into two persons. . . . The first is the spectator, whose sentiments with regard to my own conduct I endeavor to enter into, by placing myself in his situation, and by considering how it would appear to me, when seen from that particular point of view. The second is the agent, the person whom I properly call myself, and of whose conduct, under the character of a spectator, I was endeavoring to form some opinion.[5]

The richness of this passage is worth close attention. First, to examine one's own conduct is no mere luxury. It is a necessity that belongs to self-love because to examine begets proper actions and these in turn bring personal benefits from society. Obviously, unexamined conduct can bring harm to oneself. Second, proper conduct can result from an initially selfish motive so long as it is in agreement with, if not tempered by, the approving perception of others. Third, the standards of approval are arrived at inductively by each person. They are induced from the mores of society and, thus, are unique to each society and ultimately to each member's position within that society. "Well-informed" indicates this inductive knowledge, and as inductive, such knowledge is never fixed, but evolves over time. In this respect, the particular state in which the society exists is suggestive of many general moral principles which attend that society. The society that meets Smith's moral code is one in ascendence; one in which the working class is not in servile dependence to the wealthy class.

In another place, Smith touches upon the mechanism that makes progress (understood here as movement through the stages, thereby realizing the greatest prosperity and liberty for the individuals of society) possible: "As to love our neighbor as we love ourselves is the great law of Christianity, so it is the great precept of nature to love ourselves only as we love our neighbor, or what comes to the same thing, as our neighbor is capable of loving us."[6] Social organization is raised on the foundations of the "great precept of nature" understood as self-love and love of others, inextricably combined. This is the mechanism that drives human history. When its two components operate synchronously within the people of a society, then that society advances; if they do not, then society does not, and is generally drastically worse off.

Induction plays a large role in Smith's thought. In making moral decisions, he relies on the individual to be informed by inductive observations. In addition, this whole theory of moral sentiments is an induction that starts off with the words, "There are some principles in human nature."[7] As A. L. Macfie argues in his book, *The Individual in Society: Papers on Adam Smith*, the most important arguments offered by Smith are inductive.[8] For instance, to determine what stage a community is in, there needs to be an examination of how it provides for its survival. No theory can provide this conclusion.

The famous invisible hand idea of Smith is also an induction. The term itself appears only once in *The Wealth of Nations*, and since its use there is economic, the concept has been interpreted as an economic phenomena. In *The Theory of Moral Sentiments*, however, the invisible hand is put forth to bridge a perceived gap between the shortsighted pursuits of man (including moral ones) and the monumental accomplishments that have generated commercial society from early humankind. The economic version (of the invisible hand) refers to the propitious operation of the free market, where the pursuit of personal well-being benefits society at large. Despite the fact that the invisible hand is used synonymously with God and the "Great Architect of Nature," in times of stagnation and decline the effects of the invisible hand vanish. In the end, it must be that the invisible hand is a principle arrived at inductively, and its existence depends on the harmonious engagement of self-love and love of others. The invisible hand owes its efficacy to the workings of these drives and is thus rather ineffectual in itself; not to mention that it is negated once self-love and love of others no longer function as a unity.

For all the optimism that Adam Smith holds for the initiation into the true age of commerce, he also gives evidence for its decline. This claim by Smith may strike some as erroneous or even absurd, and for this reason some explanation is needed. Even if these principles are human nature, there no claim that they be manifest at all times. This sentiment might, at times, remain latent. Moreover, these two drives are often inimical towards each other. When self-love and love of others fail to combine as the motivation of individuals within a society, then that society will ascend no more. It will stagnate and decline, and perhaps even regress to a lower stage. The healthy and ascending society is a moral one, where morality arises out of the interplay between both drives. The spectator principle harmonizes self-love and love of others, and consequently it is the source of morality.

The age of commerce, although it brings much improvement and progress during the initial ascendent stage, contains within itself the seeds of stagnation. Capitalism lends necessarily to the attenuation of the drive to love others, aggrandizes the drive to self-love and thus results in a people who can no longer act morally. In addition to this miserable condition, it can be added that, in advanced capitalism, the material condition declines as well. The majority is reduced to bare subsistence in an era that mirrors a feudal structure, excepting that the land owners have been replaced by the capital owners. Notice here that, in other terms, Smith's utmost concerns can be phrased as material and spiritual, where spiritual is understood as rooted in morality.

Since Smith induces his main principles, he is not to be faulted when these principles fail or change in some way. When change occurs a new induction must be made, and, in fact, he does offer them as evidenced by his predictions of future circumstances. Similarly, the realization or actualization of the healthy or ascending motives will differ according to the unique and particular circumstances surrounding the action. However, all this discussion of Smith's inductions must not be taken as an exclusion of deduction. The fact is that virtually all the profound insights into capitalism offered in *The Wealth of Nations* are deductions from his main principles, themselves arrived at inductively.

## CONCLUSION

Adam Smith's theory of macrohistory can be characterized as a rise-and-fall version. When self-love and love of others combine as the motivation for a society's individuals, the society rises. When they fail or are absent, the society falls (or at least stagnates). In this respect, there is the same either/or dichotomy at work, expansion and contraction. As for the immense time frame between shifts, Smith is ambiguous.

For Smith's theory, how a society or civilization in decline is able to flip itself around, to pull itself up by its boot-straps and rise again, is unanswered. Yet for all his ambiguities, inconsistencies, and unanswered questions, Adam Smith stands among the tallest of beacons regarding social philosophy of the entire modern age. Today, in the 1990s, with over two hundred years passed since his death, Smith remains unceasingly remarkable for his depth, accuracy, influence, and humanity.

## NOTES

1. Adam Smith, *The Wealth of Nations*, ed. Andrew Skinner (1776; reprint, Middlesex, England: Penguin Books, 1986), 508.
2. Adam Smith, *The Theory of Moral Sentiments*, ed. D. D. Raphael and A. L. Macfie (Oxford: Clarendon Press, 1976), 152.
3. Ibid., 9.
4. Ibid., 294.
5. Ibid., 113.
6. Ibid., 25.
7. Ibid., 9.
8. A. L. Macfie, *The Individual in Society: Papers on Adam Smith* (London: George Allen and Unwin, 1967).

## 2.6

# George Wilhelm Friedrich Hegel: Dialectics and the World Spirit

*Brian Shetler*

George Wilhelm Friedrich Hegel[1] was born on August 27, 1770, to a Lutheran family at Stuttgart, on the edge of the Black Forest.[2] Driven out of Austria during the sixteenth-century Austrian persecution of Protestants, his "quiet bourgeois household" has been characterized as governed by a spirit of honesty, economy, and industry, where education was the most important concern.[3] Many of his relatives served in the civil service, including his father, who was a fiscal officer.[4]

Despite this peaceful start, Hegel's life was far from uneventful. On a personal level, he faced many obstacles: His mother died when he was thirteen years old; his first son, Ludwig, was born out of wedlock to a woman he was seeing in the war-torn city of Jena; his brother, Louis, died as a soldier for Napoleon in his Russian Campaign of 1812; his sister, Christiane, with whom he became very close, had incapacitating emotional breakdowns.[5]

The world surrounding him was also awash with change. War across Europe followed soon after the Americans declared their independence. For much of Hegel's adult life, the West was at war in the name of reason.[6] German literature at the time was arguably in its "great age."[7] The philosophers were busy trying to rationalize what was occurring and speculating about what it meant for the future. An apocalyptic note was in the air.[8]

Schooling, under these circumstances, had to be of the highest concern for a family if a child was to receive any. At age five, Hegel attended a Latin school and at age seven he was sent to a gymnasium. He proved himself to be ready to learn everything about anything, but had no one direction or interest. He was known as the kind of uninteresting character who takes prizes in every class, including one for good conduct.[9]

At the direction of his father, Hegel left the gymnasium for the theological seminary of Tübingen when he was eighteen. It was "an institution in which some show of monastic discipline was kept up. The members of the 'Stift' wore a peculiar dress, and were subjected to a somewhat petty system of punishments—generally by deprivation of the customary portion of wine at dinner—for all offenses against the regular order of the place."[10] At Tübingen, Hegel's conduct was not so good. With no teachers trained in Kant or Rousseau, he took the course work as a routine to be completed with minimal attention. He frequently incurred penalties for absences from lectures. In addition, he befriended Friedrich Wilhelm Joseph

Schelling, five years his junior, and with Schelling formed a political club to discuss the ideas of the Revolution rapidly advancing in France.[11]

He also formed a strong bond of friendship with a poet named Friedrich Holderlin.[12] With Holderlin, Hegel shared a great interest in classical Greek philosophy. But in his later years at Tübingen, he devoted much of his time to studying Kant.[13] However, these studies were apparently hidden from the authorities at Tübingen. In 1793, he left Tübingen with a certificate stating that he was "a man of good parts and character, somewhat fitful in his work, and little gift of speech"; and that he was "fairly well acquainted with theology and philology, but had bestowed no attention whatever on philosophy."[14]

Following his schooling, he went into private tutoring in Switzerland and then Germany from 1793 to 1800.[15] From 1801 to 1806 he worked as a university lecturer in Jena, Prussia, and when the Napoleonic wars disrupted life at the University of Jena, he worked as an editor.[16] During this time, his ideals of reforming Christianity to its primitive folk form were transformed into an extreme realism, a philosophy of logic, nature, and spirit breaking with Schelling's philosophy of identity.[17]

In 1808, he was named director of a gymnasium in Nuremberg, and three years later married Marie von Tucher from an old aristocratic family, with whom he had two sons, Karl and Immanuel. From 1812 to 1816 he published his *Science of Logic*, enabling him to take a position as a professor at Heidelberg University in 1816.[18] Two years later he succeeded Fichte at the Berlin University.[19] A year later his assistant was imprisoned on suspicion of demagoguery.

His relationship with the arrested assistant, however, did not prevent him from becoming the state examiner in Brandenberg in 1820. However, he was refused admission to the Prussian Academy of Sciences in 1826.[20] In 1830, Hegel became rector of Berlin University.[21] In 1831, he died there suddenly, presumably from cholera.[22]

## HEGEL'S THEORY OF KNOWLEDGE

For Hegel, knowledge is a phenomenon among people: "[K]nowledge is only actual."[23] It is a practice and by this practice a concept—itself a part of its practice. In his *Phenomenology of Spirit*, Hegel undertakes "an exposition of how knowledge makes its appearance." Knowledge as phenomenon "can be regarded as the path of the natural consciousness which presses forward to true knowledge; or as the way of the Soul which journeys through the series of its own configurations as though they were the stations appointed for it by its own nature, so that it may purify itself for the life of the Spirit, and achieve finally, through a completed experience of itself, the awareness of what it really is in itself."[24]

But in philosophy—the discipline accorded by Hegel to be the highest state knowledge has attained among people—there is a dilemma regarding knowledge, and a "certain uneasiness seems justified." As an "instrument to get hold of the Absolute," knowledge or cognition (depending on the translator) comes in different types with different limits in kind and scope.[25] In addition, Hegel points out, "If cognition is the instrument for getting hold of the absolute being, it is obvious that the use of an instrument on a thing certainly does not let it be what it is for itself, but rather sets out to reshape and alter it. If, on the other hand, cognition is not an instrument of our activity but a more or less passive medium through which the light of truth reaches us, then again we do not receive the truth as it is in itself, but only as it exists through and in this medium."[26]

In other words, an absolute, as it is known, cannot be separated from its contextual practices without altering the way it is known or what is known. Therefore, any absolute is subject to its context, making its pursuit apparently absurd. However, Hegel does not conclude with this dispairing result. Instead, he sets off to his studies with the resolution that if it is not present in particulars, it cannot be universal nor absolute. This resolution is compelled on Hegel by his consciousness, not chosen.[27]

Knowledge, pursuing self-knowledge, reflects on itself to finally realize itself in the negation of its negation, according to Hegel. For knowledge, however, the goal is fixed just as necessarily as the sequence of progression. It is that point where knowledge no longer has need to go out beyond itself where it finds itself and where the Concept corresponds to the object and the object to the Concept. The progression toward this goal is consequently without halt and at no earlier stage is satisfaction to be found. Although what is limited to a natural life is by itself powerless to transcend its immediate existence, it is driven out by another power— thus to be uprooted in its death. But since consciousness is for itself its own Concept, it immediately transcends what is limited, and, because this limitedness is its own, its transcends itself. With the positing of something individual, the beyond is also established for consciousness, even when it is only next to what is limited, as in special intuition. Consciousness, therefore, suffers violence at its own hands, a violence through which it destroys for itself any limited satisfaction. "Under the influence of this violence, anxiety may well retreat from the truth and try to conserve what is in danger of being lost. But it can find no rest. Should it wish to remain in thoughtless indolence, thought will trouble the thoughtlessness and its restlessness will disturb that indolence."[28]

This violence is summed up by Hegel as a dialectical progression from acceptance of a truth, to its negation and destruction, to a new understanding, to another destruction, and so on without interruption until the definite synthesis of both particular and universal knowledge: total Reality, total correspondence between the concept and its realization. As an example, Hegel employs this dialectic in arguing the logic of fearing error in scientific knowledge:

If concern about falling into error makes one in the meanwhile distrustful of science, which takes up its work and actually knows without any such hesitations, then one should not overlook the possibility of reversing this procedure by placing distrust in this very distrust and becoming concerned about another question: Is not this fear of erring already the error itself? . . . [I]t assumes that knowledge may be true despite its presuppositions that knowledge is outside the absolute and therewith outside the truth as well. By taking this position, what calls itself the fear of error reveals itself as a fear of the truth.[29]

Therefore, total or true, absolute knowledge is not revealed in just pursuing an objective true reality and nothing more. Total knowledge is revealed in pursuit of the pursuit itself, in reflecting on the pursuit and thereby reaching beyond it—beyond differentiating objective and subjective to realization of this differentiation as both an object and subject itself. For Hegel, then, the medium itself is the message, the practice itself the purpose, the context itself the content. The realization of something from nothing, for him, is the cosmic realization of the creative spirit. "In fact, it is only when the nothingness is taken as the nothingness of what it comes from that it is the true result; for then nothingness itself is a determinate nothingness and has a content . . . the result is comprehended as it truly is, as determinate negation, a new form has thereby immediately arisen, and in negation the transition is made by which the progression through the complete sequence of Shapes takes place of its own accord."[30]

This theory of knowledge for Hegel is central to his conception of history. "The aim of world history . . . is that the Spirit should attain knowledge of its own true nature, that it should objectivise this knowledge and transform it into a real world, and give itself an objective existence."[31] This, for Hegel would result in absolute freedom for the universal Spirit that moves history.

## MACROHISTORY

The medium, instrument, and fuel of history, for Hegel, is Spirit in process. History is the process of Spirit working out that which it is potentially through a dialectic resolution of theses and antitheses. In his *Lectures on the Philosophy of World History*, Hegel is kind enough to set out the stages of this dialectic.

The first, childlike stage he found to be exemplified by the civilizations in China and India. He called this the "Oriental World" stage. It is characterized as largely agrarian with a unity of Spirit with nature.[32] The processes of freedom have not been established, although the society has organized under the patriarchal figure with the potential for the history-making steps toward self-realizing freedom. The few steps taken toward freedom leave these civilizations with little in the way of history, in Hegel's opinion.

The second, youthful stage he found to be exemplified by the "Greek World." It is a stage of separation, "in which the Spirit is reflected within

itself and in which it emerges from a position of mere obedience and trust."[33]
"If nations are impelled merely by desires, their deeds are lost without trace (as with all fanaticism), and no enduring achievement remains. In this way, the Greeks speak of the rule of Chronos or Time, who devours his own children (i.e., the deeds he has himself produced); this was the Golden Age, which produced no ethical works. Only Zeus, the political god from whose head Pallas Athene sprang and to whose circle Apollo and the Muses belong, was able to check the power of time; he did so by creating a conscious ethical institution, i.e. by producing the state."[34]

The third, manhood stage he found to be exemplified by the "Roman World," in which "the individual has his own ends for himself, but can only attain them in the service of a universal, of the state."[35]

The fourth, "German" (of course) stage he found to be exemplified by the "Christian World," which he likened to old age. In this age, the divine—as distinguished from the natural—spirit "has come into the world and taken up its abode in the individual, who is now completely free and endowed with substantial freedom.... This is the realization of the subjective with the objective spirit."[36]

The future stage, according to Hegel, was likely to lay in the form of the state and its actions in America, possibly involving a North–South conflict. Based on the ennui that he quotes Napoleon voicing with regard to old-man Europe, Hegel states that "America is ... the country of the future, and its world-historical importance has yet to be revealed in the ages which lie ahead—perhaps in a conflict between North and South America."[37]

The course of development through these stages is dictated by "spirit's consciousness of its own freedom and of the consequent realization of this freedom."[38] History is full of plateaus, no matter what they are named by historians, when realignments or revolutions in our self-consciousness lead to periods of harmony, bloom, virtue, and vigor; periods in which the state's or people's common interest seems one with the private interest of its citizens or members.

The final synthesis resulting from this history-making pursuit, according to Hegel, is achieved when the Idea (universal abstract existence, objectivity, necessity) synthesizes with human passions (individual, subjectivity, freedom) as liberty under conditions of morality in the state.

Two elements, therefore, enter into the object of our investigation; the first the Idea, the second the complex of human passions; the one the warp, the other the woof of the vast arras web of Universal History. The concrete mean and union of the two is Liberty, under the conditions of morality in a State.... Without the state, this union is not achievable.

But in a state many institutions must be adopted, much political machinery invented, accompanied by appropriate political arrangements—necessitating long struggles of the understanding before what is really appropriate can be discovered—involving moreover, contentions with private interests and passions, and a tedious discipline of these latter, in order to bring about the desired harmony.[39]

## CONCLUSIONS AND CONSEQUENCES

In Hegel's construction of history, the road of progress, as opposed to stagnation, is paved in a spiraling route of negation. In his conception of this dialectic, the driving force of Spirit within people worked through this negation to realize itself. All other forms realizing themselves in this dialectic would go beyond themselves, but finally the realization of Spirit, which is beyond all and in all absolutely and therefore is uncontained and beyond going beyond itself, emerges and we arrive at the end of history.

However, the path of negation to negation of that negation and so on, if taken without Hegel's aesthetic appreciation of abstract spiritual beauty, is a road to annihilation; the pursuit of negation is not the same pursuit as that of Spirit seeking self-realization and freedom, but a pointless perversion of that pursuit. As Albert Camus points out,

The nihilist revolution, which is expressed historically in the Hitlerian religion, thus only aroused an insensate passion for nothingness which ended by turning against itself. Negation, this time at any rate, and despite Hegel, has not been creative.... Neither efficacious nor exemplary, they consecrate the blood-thirsty vanity of nihilism. 'They thought they were free,' Frank cries hysterically; 'didn't they know that no one escapes from Hitlerism?' They did not know; nor did they know that the negation of everything is in itself a form of servitude and that real freedom is an inner submission to a value which defies history and its successes.[40]

However, with Hegel's dialectic pointing to the foundation of society, its thoughts, and its functions, in practices and the dialectic realization of them—leading to going beyond those practices—where else could Hegelianism lead but to emptying of all values? If all ideas, including religious ones, are at base functional or mediums, what is left to believe? History as the story of man progressively making himself into God is not inspiring but instead engulfing. Virtue and vice are no longer distinguishable. Immanent success determines what is now considered transcendent. Everything changes and there is no value, institutional or otherwise, that defies history and its negative successes.

Hegel's history of humanity (as the preeminent product of the universe) endogenously realizing itself (an act of the universe realizing itself) is doomed to faithlessness and violence to itself if one forgets the boundless spirit moving history. If one does not subscribe to this boundless spirit but follows the process of negation for its own sake, the self-correcting dialectic will leave the small acts of negation for its own sake in the dustbin of history as acts with little or no historical substance other than the act of the exercise of the will.

## NOTES

1. "Misconceptions about Hegel begin with his very name." Walter Kaufmann, *Hegel: Reinterpretation, Texts, and Commentary* (New York: Doubleday, 1965), 31.
2. Edward Caird, *Hegel* (Edinburgh and London: William Blackwood & Sons, 1883), 3, 17; Also see Clark Butler, *G. W. F. Hegel*, (Boston: Twayne [Twayne's World Authors Series 461], 1977), 19.
3. Caird, *Hegel*, 4–5.
4. Ibid., 3.
5. Ibid., 3–4; Kaufmann, *Hegel*, 33, 112, 187.
6. Kaufmann, *Hegel*, 33. The French Revolution started when he was nineteen; four years later he saw the abolition of Christianity (replaced by the cult of reason) in France during the same year that Immanuel Kant came out with his *Religion within the Bounds of Mere Reason*.
7. Ibid., 32. Works of the time include those of Lessing (*Nathan*), Goethe (*Meister, Iphegenia, Faust: A Fragment*, etc.), the German romantics, Fichte, Schelling, and Holderlin (the latter two were among Hegel's closest friends).
8. Ibid., 33.
9. Caird, *Hegel*, 4–5. Much of the information about Hegel's schooling is from a diary he kept. At age fourteen he started this diary, a common practice. He chronicled the progress of his readings and appreciation for one of his teachers, Loffler, who had given him extracurricular instruction.
10. Ibid., 13.
11. Ibid., 10.
12. Ibid, 11.
13. Hegel had a particular affinity for Greek poetry, especially the tragedies of Sophocles. Later in his life he would declare to his students, "At the name of Greece the cultivated German feels himself at home. Europeans have their religion—what is transcendant and distant—from a further source, from the East, and especially from Syria; but what is here, what is present, science and art—all that makes life satisfying, and elevates and adorns it—we derive, directly or indirectly, from Greece." Ibid., 13.
14. Ibid., 12.
15. Ibid., 13, 42.
16. Ibid., 45–68.
17. Ibid., 45–64.
18. Ibid., 69–76.
19. Ibid., 89.
20. Butler, *G. W. F. Hegel*, 16.
21. Caird, *Hegel*, 103.
22. Butler, *G. W. F. Hegel*, 17.
23. George Wilhelm Friedrich Hegel, *Phenomenology of Spirit*, trans. A. V. Miller (Oxford: Clarendon Press, 1977), 13.
24. Ibid., 49.
25. Ibid., 46; "knowledge" was used interchangeably with "cognition" in an earlier translation by Kenley Royce Dove, quoted in Martin Heidegger, *Hegel's Concept of Experience* (New York: Harper and Row, 1970), 8.
26. Hegel, *Phenomenology*, 46.

27. Ibid., 47, 51.
28. Heidegger, *Hegel's Concept of Experience*, 16–17.
29. Ibid., 9–10.
30. Ibid., 16.
31. Hegel, *Phenomenology*, 64.
32. George Wilhelm Friedrich Hegel, *Lectures on the Philosophy of World History*, trans. J. Sibree (London: George Bell and Sons, 1888), 130.
33. Ibid.
34. Ibid., 145.
35. Ibid., 130.
36. Ibid., 131.
37. Ibid., 170.
38. Ibid., 138.
39. Hegel, *Lectures*, 24–26.
40. Albert Camus, *The Rebel*, trans. A. Bower (New York: Vintage Books, 1958), 185–186.

## 2.7

## *Auguste Comte: The Law of the Three Stages*

*Claus Otto Scharmer*

### BIOGRAPHY

Auguste Comte was born in Montpellier, France, on January 19, 1798. Louis Comte, his father, a tax official, and Rosalie Boyer, his mother, were strongly royalists and deeply sincere Roman Catholics. The leanings of his parents severely conflicted with the republicanism and skepticism that were sweeping through France in those days. Comte felt this contradiction deeply and resolved it at a very early age by rejecting both Catholicism and royalism.

In October 1814, Comte, at the age of sixteen, moved to Paris to study at the École Polytechnique. The Polytechnique routine was very strict: A drumbeat opened the day at 5:30 A.M. and ended it at 9:15 P.M. The whole day was completely organized. Comte often escaped the school at night, wandering among the prostitutes and Paris crowds. In school, one of the tutors used to question pupils while slouching on a chair with his feet up on a table. When Comte's turn to answer came, he positioned himself in the same casual manner. Comte was sent back to Montpellier under police supervision and thus never gained a college-level degree.

Before the end of 1816, he returned to Paris in order to experience the disorder of society as well as to understand it and to help in the task of social reconstruction. At the age of twenty he became a secretary and was adopted by Claude Henry Saint-Simon (1760–1825), a well-known philosopher and one of the founders of socialism. For almost seven years Comte worked for the utopian social reformist and became familiar with the worlds of industry, finance, and politics, which he happened to know beforehand only through reading.

In May 1821, on one of his evening walks, the twenty-three-year-old Comte met Caroline Massin, a young prostitute, whom he lived with briefly and then married.

In 1822, Comte wrote *Opuscule fondamental*, a first version of his thought which was published by Saint-Simon with the title, *Prospectus des Travaux Scientifiques Nécessaires Pour Reorganiser La Société*. With this writing, Comte, for the first time in his life, became conscious of the novelty of his thought. Because he felt that Saint-Simon had not given him adequate credit for his academic contributions, he left his employer and teacher in 1824.

In 1826, the twenty-eight-year-old Comte developed a scheme by which he would present a series of seventy-two public lectures on his philosophy of life. The lectures were held at his house in Paris for a private audience composed of many of the most distinguished thinkers of his time. After the first two lectures, Comte suffered a nervous breakdown that prevented him from continuing his schedule. Continuing to suffer from depression, he sought to commit suicide by throwing himself into the Seine. He was rescued by a soldier of the municipal guard who happened to be passing by. In 1829 and 1830, he managed to take up his projected lecture series. The following twelve years were devoted to their publication (in six volumes).

In 1830, Comte was jailed for three days for refusing to enroll in the National Guard. From this year to 1848, he delivered annually, without fees, a course of lectures to the working man. Meanwhile, he failed several times to get a regular position at the École Polytechnique in Paris. But he did get a minor position as lecturer in 1832. In 1837, Comte was given the additional post of admissions examiner, and for the first time, an adequate income.

In 1842, Comte published his *Cours de Philosophie Positive* (The Positive Philosophy), in which he was the first to use the term *sociology*. He outlined his view that sociology is the ultimate science. He also attacked the École Polytechnique, with the result that in 1844, his lectureship was not renewed.

In October 1844, the happiest, saddest, and most influential relationship of Comte's life began. The unhappy philosopher, separated from his wife, met the also unhappy Madame Clotilde de Vaux and instantly fell in love with her. In the spring of 1845, he revealed his feelings to her. For one year he wrote to her twice a day and met her twice a week. Clotilde deeply shared Comte's idealistic motives, but the young lady, who suffered from tuberculosis, did not respond to his feelings with more than "affection." She insisted on the platonic nature of their relationship. In 1846, Madame de Vaux died and left a fundamentally changed Comte. The notion of love in its highest mode, as voluntary devotion and submission, became an essential part of his writing and teaching. "On ne peut pas toujours penser, mais on peut toujour aimer" (you cannot always think but you can always love) he is reported to have said on the day when he declared his love.[1]

The next eight years were devoted to the completion of his second major work, the four-volume *Systeme de Politique Positive* (published 1851 to 1854), which had a practical intent of offering a grand plan for the reorganization of society. Comte saw himself as the high priest of a new religion of humanity. He believed in a world that eventually would be led by sociologist-priests.

Another idiosyncratic idea of Comte was his belief in "cerebral hygiene," that is, he avoided reading the work of other people in order not to be "polluted." As a consequence, Comte eventually became hopelessly out of touch with the intellectual developments of his own time. In spite of (or partly because of) these strange ideas, Comte developed a considerable following in France as well as in other countries. Today he is celebrated as one of the founders of sociology. August Comte died on September 5, 1857.

## THE LAW OF THE THREE STAGES

The work of Comte can be seen as a reaction against the French Revolution and the Enlightenment. In order to combat the negative and destructive philosophy of the Enlightenment, he developed his concept of "positivism," or "positive philosophy."

The cornerstone of his approach is what he calls the "law of the three stages." The theory proposes that there are three epistemological stages through which human intellectual development has moved throughout history: "We have indicated the general direction of the human evolution, its rate of progress, and its necessary order. We may now proceed at once to investigate the natural laws by which the advance of the human mind proceeds. The scientific principle of the theory appears to me to consist in the great philosophical law of the succession or the three stages:—the primitive theological state, the transient metaphysical, and the final positive state—through which the human mind has to pass, in every kind of speculation."[2]

The first stage, the *theological stage* (until A.D. 1300), was characterized by major idea systems that emphasized the supernatural as the cause of natural and social events. The physical and social world was seen as ruled by gods or God, respectively. The first stage subdivides itself into three periods: The beginning is characterized by fetishism (e.g., the unity of matter and mind); later on people assumed a wide variety of gods in order to explain the physical and social world; finally, the plurality of gods became monotheistic, gods were substituted by God. The concept of a single God and a set of divine laws which has been created by Him reveals again an increased level of abstraction.

This development from personal beings toward abstract forces as cause and explanation was enlarged by the influence of Arabic scientific thought towards Europe in the eleventh and twelfth centuries. Thus, the second stage, the *metaphysical stage* (1300 to 1800), was characterized by the belief in abstract forces such as "nature," "essence," or "final causes," rather than in personalized gods. These abstract forces were seen as cause for natural and social worlds and events. The metaphysical stage is described as a transitional period between the theological and the positivistic state. It is characterized by the parallelism of both interpretations: divine beings or natural laws, respectively. Although many singular phenomena are already viewed in a positive mode, the more complex phenomena, like organic and social life, remain in the theological mode of interpretation. Only when the last and highest science (sociology) has reached the positive state would history have moved from this to the next stage.

The third stage, the *positivistic stage*, which the world entered around 1800, is characterized by the belief in science. People have given up looking for absolute causes (God or nature), and concentrated instead on observation of reality in the search for the laws that govern the world. Comte claims universal validity for this law. Individuals, groups, nations, and civilizations (Western as well as non-Western) are going through these three stages. Even the development of science can, according to Comte, be seen in this pattern.

## THE LAW OF THE HIERARCHY OF SCIENCES

In his *Law of the Hierarchy of the Sciences*, Comte develops a logical and historical order of the six major sciences. The order begins with the most abstract science (mathematics) and ends with the most concrete one (sociology). In-between are astronomy, physics, chemistry, and biology. The sciences have attained their positivistic stage in precisely the order which is given with the law of the hierarchy of the sciences. Thus, sociology is the last science to achieve the positivistic stage. According to Comte, "Social Science has, with all its complexity, passed through the theological state, and has almost everywhere fully attained the metaphysical; while it has nowhere yet risen the positive, except in this book."[3] Similar to Hegel and other macrohistorians, Comte regards his own work as a major leap forward in human evolution.

The hierarchy of sciences and their succession in history reflect an ongoing methodological progress. Mathematics developed deduction and logical arguments; astronomy required additional observation; physics introduced the experiment; chemistry, classification; biology, comparison; and, sociology, historical analyses. The law of the hierarchy of sciences is an important addition to the law of the three stages because it explains why some sciences have reached the positivistic stage and some have not. It also offers some elementary principles for education and teaching, which should, according to Comte, be based on a profound knowledge of all six fundamental disciplines.

We can summarize that the positive stage is the final stage of history in which people believe not in gods but in sciences. The final stage of sciences is the positive stage, which has been realized—in the case of social science—by nobody except Comte himself.

## COMTE ON EUROPEAN HISTORY

Comte claimed universal validity for his law of the three stages. In the case of Europe, the theological–military stage was succeeded by a metaphysical–legal and eventually a scientific–industrial period.

The theological–military period was ruled by the goal of conquering ("polytheistic period") and defending ("monotheistic period") territory. Every society in history is, according to Comte, a kind of theological–military society because the metaphysical–legal period is essentially a theological–military society which has been modified by scientific–industrial progress. The goal of this society is both military and industrial, finally aiming at industrial production as a major end, even in the case of war.

Comte was very much against the contradictory metaphysical period, which he regarded as incapable of providing inner balance and stability. Instead, he argued in favor of his scientific–industrial stage, which is ruled by the single goal of production. Like the theological–military, the scientific–industrial is again an "organic" epoch. Comte viewed the attempt to build a society on negative, critical principles, such as freedom of conscience, sovereignty of people, and democratic elections, as the major error of his time.[4]

His vision, as in the Middle Ages, was based on the balance between spiritual and worldly power. The single possible intellectual power in Europe which could play this role (which was performed by the Catholic Church in the Middle Ages) was that of the European scientists. Just as people have confidence in scientists regarding physical and chemical matters, Comte believed that scientists should be put in positions where they could develop solutions for social and political problems as well. Comte hoped for the emergence of a new elite based on positive science, which could organize itself like a church, with a kind of religious hierarchy and spiritual leadership at the top.

## CRITICISM

To Comte's law of the three stages, four objections can be made. First, there is no parallelism between intellectual states (theological, metaphysical, scientific) and political organization (military, feudal, industrial society).[5] Priests and warriors do not necessarily always cooperate, as they did after the French Revolution, with the reactionary alliance between church and aristocracy. In addition, there is no strong correlation between monotheistic religion and defensive military behavior. Rather, it might turn out the other way around.[6] Finally, the history of the twentieth century has definitely proved that the thesis that industrial societies are most likely to be peaceful is wrong.

Second, there are not identical, but different intentions between religion, metaphysics, and positive science.[7] Opposed to positive science, which aims at objective structures of reality, religious knowledge aims primarily at salvation and metaphysical knowledge; toward the essence and meaning of reality. Positive science, focused on control, cannot give answers to questions of religion and metaphysics.

Thus, religion, metaphysics, and science are equal original modes of human knowledge. None of them can adequately substitute for each other. As religions and metaphysics are unable to serve the purpose of rational command over reality—which is the core of Comte's criticism—science is incapable of substituting for religion and metaphysics. In spite of this, wherever science tries to expand into the extrascientific domain, as in the case of Comte's scientific religion, science stops being science. It becomes a pseudoscientific dogmatic *Weltanschauung* (worldview).

Third, Comte's positivism does not meet its own criteria. If Comte had truly worked on strict positive evidence, he could never have "discovered" the law of progress nor could he have understood the ultimate structure of scientific–industrial society. Although Comte was against religion, his intention with his positive science was towards a religious goal. As a consequence, his science became a kind of religion with Comte as its founder. This change of his positive science—from a substitute of religion to a religion itself—should not be regarded as accidental, but as a predictable result. A similar result in the twentieth century can be observed in orthodox Marxism.

Last, Comte does not reflect the cultural assumptions of his historical view. Like many other Western macrohistorians, Comte refers only to Western experience and intellectual concepts but nevertheless claims universal validity for his theory. The notion of God (as creator), the alliance between priests and aristocracy (the European Middle Ages), the idea of linear progress (a largely Western time perspective), and the concept of rational science all refer to the same underlying "cosmology," that of Western civilization. Among the various non-Western civilizations, several quite different cosmologies can be found. Not only did Comte not discuss his fundamental assumptions—the knowledge boundaries that he existed under—but, in fact, believed that he was not even making any assumptions. Otherwise, he would have written an explanation as to why he opted against a (predominant) immanent notion of God, against a cyclical concept of time, and against an extended rationality in our concept of science.

## COMTE AND HEGEL

In some important respects, Comte's view resembles that of Hegel. Although neither of them knew much about the other, their historical views show four parallels and one important difference.

First, both of them conceptualize history as a process progressing toward a well-defined final stage (*Zusichselbstkommen des Weltgeistes* [self-reflection and self-awareness of world spirit] for Hegel; positive state for Comte). Second, both of them referred to all periods of human history. Third, both of them use an explicit measure for historical progress (progress in consciousness of freedom or proximity toward scientific positivism, respectively). Last, the major leaders of history, "important men," are tools of progress of mankind. Just as the Hegelian *Weltgeist* (world spirit) uses historical leaders of major importance in order to steer history toward the correct direction, the scientific progress of Comte uses major inventors and scientists for the same purpose.

Looking at the key notions of Hegel and Comte, *Weltgeist* and mankind, respectively, we see both of them serving as subjects of history. The *Weltgeist* is realized history according to its prehistorical essence, whereas the (prehistorical) essence of mankind by Comte is less clear because it can be recognized only by way of positive observation and comparison with animals.

Summarizing, we can conclude that Comte's macrohistory is clearcut linear. What then is the driving force of history? Obviously, the mind of the people. Thus, the cause for social disorder is, according to Comte, intellectual disorder. Intellectual disorder is basically to be seen as a state of the mind from past stages that continues to exist in the positive age. Only when positivism and its representatives ("high priests") gain total control over the society will social disorder disappear and history fulfill itself by realizing the final positivistic stage.

Although the religious elements of Comte's work tend to sound strange from today's perspective, the problem to which Comte addressed his work—the crisis and disintegration of the modern scientific–industrial society—remains unresolved and, at the end of the twentieth century, is even more important than ever before.

## NOTES

1. Auguste Comte, *Rede über den Geist des Positivismus* (Talk about the essence of Positivism), trans. and ed. Iring Fetscher (Hamburg: F. Meiner Verlag, 1956), 19.

2. Auguste Comte, *The Positive Philosophy*, trans. Harriet Martineau (London: Trubner, 1875), 131.

3. Ibid., 132.

4. Auguste Comte, *Systeme de Politique Positive ou Traité de Sociologie Instituant La Religion de L'Humanité*, vol. 4 (Paris: Georges Cres, 1912), 368.

5. Gaetano Mosca, *Die herrschende Klasse* (The ruling class) (Bern: A. Francke Verlag, 1950), 81.
6. See Johan Galtung, *Peace by Peaceful Means* (London: Polity Press, 1996), 213.
7. See Max Scheler, *Über die Positivistische Geschichtsphilosphie des Wissens* (Positivistic philosophy of knowledge), in Moralia, *Schriften zur Soziologie und Weltanschauungslehre* (Leipzig: Reclam, 1923), 26.

## 2.8

## Karl Marx: Techno-Economic Stages

*Johan Galtung*

### BIOGRAPHY

Son of a lawyer, Karl Heinrich Marx was born in Trier, Prussia, in 1818, and died in London in 1883. He first studied law at the University of Bonn, and, from 1836 to 1838, law, philosophy, and history, in addition to English and Italian, in Berlin. As Hegelian philosophy dominated at the time, he gave up law and turned to philosophy. His doctoral dissertation from the University of Jena was entitled "The Difference between the Democritean and Epicurean Philosophies of Nature." For some years, he edited the newspaper *Rheinische Zeitung*, a radical opposition paper which was suppressed in 1843. Marx then moved to Paris, from where he was expelled (by Guizot) in 1845. He then moved on to Brussels. The same year he had to renounce Prussian citizenship. His friendship with Engels (born 1820 in Wuppertal) was a major factor in making England and London his residence. He moved there in 1849 with his wife Jenny, and worked mainly in the British Museum. From 1851 to 1862 he was a regular contributor to the *New York Daily Tribune*. Marx and Engels also participated in the German revolution of 1848 and 1849, and they coedited the newspaper *Neue Rheinische Zeitung* in Köln.

His major works are numerous, but our concern here is not the enormous and impressive totality of Marx's writings and other activities but his theory of macrohistory. The following quote from the preface to *A Contribution to the Critique of Political Economy* provides a useful overview:

In the social production which men carry on they enter into definite relations that are indispensable and independent of their will; these relations of production correspond to a definite stage of development of their material powers of production. The totality of these relations of production constitutes the economic structure of society—the real foundation, on which legal and political superstructures arise and to which definite forms of social consciousness correspond. The mode of production of material life determines the general character of the social, political and spiritual processes of life. It is not the consciousness of men that determines their being, but, on the contrary, their social being determines their consciousness. At a certain stage of their development, the material forces of production in society come in conflict with the existing relations of production, or—what is but a legal expression for the same thing—with the property relations within which they have been at work before. From forms of development of the forces of production these relations turn into their fetters. Then occurs a period of social revolution. With the change of the economic foundation the entire immense superstructure is more or less rapidly transformed.[1]

What Marx describes as "definite relations that are indispensable and independent of their will," a sociologist today might refer to as an "economic structure," since the focus is on material production. Marx actually does so himself, going on to say that "the totality of these relations of production" is "the real foundation" of society. Here lies, of course, the strength and weakness of the whole construct: strong in making transparent how such structures operate, weak in making opaque other mechanisms that could be nominated as "real foundation" mechanisms.

Then come the "material forces of production," and without getting into an abyss of controversies, including in Marx himself, let us simplify and translate this as "technical structure," or "technology," also using the latter word for the social relations induced by a certain technique.[2] We now have

relations of production = mode of production = economic structure

forces of production = means of production = technical structure

Then come the two basic propositions on which the whole Marxian construction rests:

Thesis #1: "*The mode of production of material life determines the general character of social, political and spiritual process of life.... Their social being determines their consciousness.*"

Thesis #2: "*At a certain stage of their development the material forces of production in society come in conflict with the existing relations of production—from forms of development of the forces of production these relations turn into their fetters.*"

We get a three-tier construction with a causal flow upwards: in the basement, the forces of production (means); on the ground, or basis floor, the relations of production (mode); and at the higher levels, the superstructure of Marx's construction—social processes, political processes (including law and state), arts, spiritual life, and consciousness in general.

The most interesting part is how Marx sees the relation between means and modes, forces and relations of production: as asymmetric one-way, with means having an impact on mode, and as dialectic in the special sense that there is an accumulation of changes in means within an existing mode, that first is productive in the development, then becomes counterproductive (their fetters), and finally has to yield, to burst. There is a rupture between means and modes, with the means liberating themselves from the existing mode, in search of a new mode compatible with the new means.[3]

What has happened once can happen again, and we ultimately end up with the four famous modes: "In broad outline, the Asiatic, ancient, fedual and modern modes of production may be designated as epochs marking progress in the economic development of society."[4] In another version, "primitive communism" replaces the Asiatic mode of production.[5]

However, parallel to this discourse runs another which is less abstract. There are still relations of production, but now they are expressed in terms of ownership of the means of production: collective ownership, slavery, serfdom (feudalism), capitalism, and in recent Marxist discourses with socialism and communism on top of that. The ownership then passes from collective ownership via slave owners, serf owners (feudal vassals and lords), labor-force buyers (capitalists), the proletariat (expressed as the dictatorship by the Communist Party), and back to collective ownership again.[6]

The modes are now seen in terms of classes, not only the more abstract "relations": those who possess and those who do not possess the means of production. At that point, it becomes very concrete; the class that possesses the means of production fighting for the old mode—theirs—and the proletariat, with the "enlightened section of the bourgeoisie" (including those who might become the owners of the new means in a new mode), fighting for a change. In addition, at the end of its useful life every mode starts deteriorating, the proletariat is more exploited than ever to compensate for deterioration while in reality contributing to it, and the net result is a new era.

The audacity in the whole construction consists in postulating the dialectical formula from quantity (the development of the means of production within the old mode) to quality (the quantum jump to a new mode) all over in space and time, for all economic formations, for all transitions, and, by and large, in the same order. As has been pointed out rather often, the more audacious and sweeping, the more counterexamples can be cited. But maybe Marx, like Sarkar, did not intend correspondence to be perfect. Maybe he was pointing to the basic mechanism and the major thrust of history, and less concerned with details.

However that may be, it is certainly a discourse that shaped the twentieth century in a major way; for good and for bad, improving the condition of the working classes in many countries, but also leading to extremes of violence in the names of revolution and counterrevolution.[7] The discourse kept hundreds of thousands of intellectuals busy exploring its foundations and implications, and became the bread and butter of countless party functionaries, members, and others, including the millions who believed the Soviet Union and its satellites would last forever.

## CRITIQUE

Leaving that aside, let us begin a critique by postulating another way of relating means, modes, superstructure, and consciousness: by seeing them at the same level. There is no denial of interrelations. But with four bundles of variables ("syndromes"), twenty-four causal chains can be constructed. Of these, twenty-four Marx gambles on one: means–modes–superstructure–consciousness.

How about Marx himself? The son of a lawyer, why did he develop a consciousness different from what was to be expected given his position in the economic structure, or as any "social being" in that mode of production? Is this law valid for everyone but Marx; is he the *Übermensch* (superman or overman), not only capable of coming up with a bright theory, something many have done during history, but of transcending the limitations induced by the social forces impinging upon him? Then, and more crucial, how did the forces or means of production change? To the extent there are techniques involved, was there not one or more innovators somewhere, singly or combined? Let us call them engineers. Did their ideas, however inspired by laws of nature, observation/inspiration, or economic necessities not at least gestate in the consciousness? Did the consciousness not come before the new means of production? And in that case, was Marx really a materialist? To give the role to the forces of production as the *force motrice* in history is at the same time to give to the engineer the role as *primus motor*, one reason why technicians and engineers had so much power in the ex-socialist countries, like businessmen and lawyers in capitalist countries, and more particularly to their position close to the moving center of the social universe.

For Marx, it was not the world spirit but the innovative, creative engineering spirit that moved the world. Marx was an idealist from this point of view, in that he, more than others, traced the impact of such innovations not only on the daily lives of so many, but also on the whole social construction, indeed the whole history of social constructions everywhere.

But how about social engineers, to use that infelicitous term? Imagine that enough people want a new way of relating to each other. For instance, they might want to relate less, preferring working at home, using what is usually the most expensive part of their livelihood, whether privately owned or rented, not only for reproduction but also for production—perhaps like people in the "free professions" often do? In that case, there would be a clear effort to put the cart before the horse from the dogmatic Marxist point of view. But why not put the mode before the means, ordering some new horse/means?

One answer today would be fax machines or e-mail for (practically instant) communication of not only oral (telephone) but even written messages. Another would be excellent delivery systems for parts and the like for material production, having small offices and workshops at home.[8]

Later on, much more imaginative techniques could be imagined for moving objects, closer to telekinesis. But leaving such speculations aside, the point is that Marx directs our thinking in the opposite direction. The engineer's consciousness steers the change of the mode through the change of the means; steering the change of the means by changing the mode becomes a subjugated discourse.

Marx also underestimates how much can be done by changing the superstructure, including the laws and how the state is operating, as seen by social democratic countries and others. For the Soviet Union, this became catastrophic: Instead of designing new social relations and then searching for the appropriate technology, they just imported or invented the technology and put it into their socially, state, or collectively owned mode of production. Of course, there was a predilection for technologies that fitted that mode: large combines of factories, huge collective farms, and gigantic transportation systems. Leaving aside the ubiquitous critique of the rigidities of that type of system, the point in this connection was the emergence of technologies for the micro level of social organization. The privately owned television made consumption at home of home movies preferable to the movie house; the private car was preferable to the metro and bus system, and so on. Then came the personal computer (PC), a technology that created a potential rupture with the large-scale enterprise in the Soviet Union.

In other words, Marx brought the Soviet Union into being, but was also its undoing. New means of production were as catastrophic to the old mode in a socialist society as in a feudal society; both formations underestimated the flexibility of the capitalist formation (there is always some way of making some money on something new). Marxian thinking can also be blamed for conditioning them away from thinking more in terms of microsocialism and less state planning. And perhaps the PCs and other techniques would then have provided welcome answers.

## WHAT BROUGHT IT DOWN?

An additional way of gaining some insight into Marxist thinking would be to ask what brought it down. The Maoist challenge was not gladly accepted by state Marxism in the Soviet Union. That challenge was probably not so much in terms of the vision of landless peasants as the proletariat (rather than industrial workers in countries with an abundance of the former and very few of the latter), but much deeper differences between Marx and Mao. Marx's consciousness was Occidental and Judeo-Christian; Mao's was Oriental and Daoist–Confucian–Buddhist (both of them might have denied this vehemently). To Marx, the communist society was the final state of history, whether referred to as the end or the beginning of (real) history.[9] To Mao, there would at any time be contradictions to be overcome, some antagonistic (requiring violence) and some not. Socialist, even communist, society would be no exception to this rule; only that from the 1920s to the 1940s the contradictions of feudalism–capitalism–imperialism were the primary contradiction to receive major attention (as indeed they did).

Thus, the Maoist view opens for the possibility of political struggle after the socialist revolution. In the Marxist–Leninist view, the major problem should have been overcome with a socialist revolution and a tough initial period of dictatorship of the proletariat. Nevertheless, when major problems showed up, the leadership must have been overtaken by a feeling of despair: They had changed the mode, so where were the fruits to be enjoyed as a result of all the violence and hard work?

The point here is not sovietology, but how Marxist thinking contributed to its own undoing by having certain rigidities, possibly unconscious to Marx, built into it. And there were other shortcomings, some of them of equal significance, to the Marxist tradition, perhaps more in nonsocialist, liberal countries with strong Marxist currents among intellectuals.

First, where is Nature? Marx mentions Nature, but in a rather skimpy way. The capitalist countries, however, were in the throes of major ecological crises; a thinker oblivious to that discourse would not easily be taken seriously. Second, where was the human individual, the person, the self, the religious longing—indeed craving—to be united with some self? Marx is not without psychology; his theory of alienation in capitalist society is a major contribution. But the self detached from the means and modes of production interface and its possible pathologies receives very scant attention. Third, without denying class struggle as a major aspect of the "modern bourgeois" condition, where is Djilas's "New Class"? The PMP–BCI class of Party–Military–Police and then Bureaucrats (state)–Capitalists–Intelligentsia? Can they be seen only as close to ownership of the means of production, or is the relation more complex? What if they are all "socialists," yet behave very much like the old feudal/capitalist upper classes? Fourth, and even more important, where are gender relations as a major focus? Where is patriarchy and its alternative, partnership? Very few people experience the contradiction between means and modes of production directly. As a consequence, Marx risks becoming abstract. Fifth, where is the world?[10] Where in Marx does one find a peace theory that could be used to explain hostile relations among socialist states, where the struggle for raw materials and markets was reduced almost to zero, yet there was still conflict?

In the 1970s and beyond, to leave out the environmental, spiritual, participation, feminist, and pacifist discourses was, of course, a guarantee of sounding the death knell of a proud tradition. Thus, out Marx went and Marxist professors in the West all of a sudden became professors of Marxist studies, a safe niche compatible with a certain distance to the man himself. He, of course, has been cast in the Occidental tradition of one god, History, with its workings made transparent by one prophet,

Karl Marx, one redeemer, Lenin, and finally one theologian, Stalin. It is not so easy to be both macrohistorian and the ideological basis of a movement that shook the world.

## A REVIVAL

Marx will live on and probably have a revival, for his dialectical, rupture-oriented methods and for his critique of capitalist society.[11] Moreover, the many who today enthusiastically embrace the term "sustainability" are Marxists without knowing it. Marx's term was much better: reproducibility. This can be applied to nature, to the human self, to the working class, and to the countries in the periphery of the system: Could it be that they are made use of to the extent that they can no longer reproduce themselves? If yes, they are exploited—nature wilting, people dying, countries unable to sustain themselves. Marx explained how this happened: not by stealing, but by invisible transfers from low to high that are built into the structure of relations. Those on top did not like that. They still do not.

## NOTES

1. Karl Marx, *Karl Marx: The Essential Writings*, ed. and Intro. by Frederick Bender (New York: Harper and Row, 1972), 161–162.

2. See Johan Galtung, *Development, Environment and Technology* (New York: United Nations, 1979), 1, for an elaboration of the equation whereby technology = techniques + structure.

3. For a use of this as a general perspective in social change, see Alain Gras, *Sociologie des Ruptures* (Sociology of ruptures) (Paris: Presses Universitaires de France, 1979).

4. Karl Marx, *A Contribution to the Critique of Political Economy*, trans. S. W. Ryazanskaya, ed. Maurice Dobb (New York: International Publishers, 1970), 21.

5. The whole idea of such stages is, of course, Hegelian, even if the mechanism of transition is very different. Moreover, Hegel had pre-history, Oriental, Antiquity, Medieval Christian, and German Christian. The latter three translate into antiquity, feudal, and modern bourgeois in the quote. The first two Hegelian phases are reflected in Marx's ambivalence, with "primitive communism" reflecting "pre-history" and "Asiatic mode" representing "Oriental." One basic difference between Hegel and Marx, however, is that, to Hegel, change is in space with the world spirit moving from one place to the other; to Marx, change is in time with societies having to change by their own dialectic.

6. To the disrespectful comment "do we really have to pass through all of that only to end up where we started" there is, of course, the answer that other things have changed in the meantime, since each mode permits further development of the means up to the limits.

7. Thus, Marxist historiography with such stages as feudalism–capitalism–socialism, all relevant for Eastern Europe during the Cold War period, shaped the thinking of very many to the point of becoming a self-fulfilling prophecy. Those who wanted the transition to socialism did their best to prevent the sys-

tems from "sliding back" into capitalism (Hungary, 1956; Czechoslovakia, 1968). Those who resisted it seemed almost to have given up hope. Europe in 1989 was a great surprise for the latter more than for the former.

8. One way of doing this would combine reliable and frequent public communication with cargo delivery systems. When the present author was a little boy in the 1930s, the trams of Oslo operated an excellent cargo service for foodstuffs, spare parts, and the like, with pick-up points, in principle, at every stop. In Spain today, bus services have the same function. In Germany and a number of other countries there is a *Kurierdienst* for rapid delivery of small parcels all over the country, and there is, of course, federal express services. Some of this becomes expensive, though, and when operated between countries, customs formalities may wipe out whatever gain has been made (one factor motivating the formation of the European Community).

9. That particular perspective is more because of Engels.

10. The world exists, but Marx comes across as strangely friendly to Western imperialism: "England has to fulfill a double mission in India: one destructive, the other regenerating—the annihilation of old Asiatic society, and the laying of the material foundation of Western society in Asia." Karl Marx, *Essential Writings*, 413.

11. See, for instance, G. A. Cohen, *Karl Marx's Theory of History: A Defence* (Oxford: Clarendon, 1979).

# 2.9

# Herbert Spencer: Progress and Evolution

*Sohail Inayatullah*

## BIOGRAPHY

No history of the idea of progress can be complete without a reading of Herbert Spencer. His theory of social evolution has become the ground plan of the modern world. As much as Adam Smith, it is Spencer that provides the metaphorical backbone of capitalism—the concept of "survival of the fittest."[1] While the rest of his efforts might be forgotten in the centuries ahead, his social Darwinism will not.

Herbert Spencer was born in a lower-middle-class family in Derby, England, in 1820. As an only child, Spencer grew up introverted and highly reflective—in fact, he spent most of his early years daydreaming. His father was a teacher and businessman who owned thirteen houses in Derby. After his businesses failed, he took to teaching his son full time. More important in shaping Spencer's worldview was his parents' dissenting views on religion, which inspired Spencer's own non-conformist views; for example, he advocated the abolishment of the church. From

1837 to 1846, Spencer was a railway engineer, a profession that his utilitarian and technical education had well prepared him for.

After leaving the railways, he continued his engineering skills, but this time as an inventor. He also worked on various writing projects leading up to his grand theory, his *Synthetic Philosophy*. Until 1857, Spencer worked as a writer and an editor for the *Economist*. In 1851, he published *Social Statics*, which contained the essence of most of his future writings. By 1869, he had suffered a serious nervous breakdown, the first of many. From 1860 to 1896, while Spencer worked on *Synthetic Philosophy*, he experienced financial difficulties. John Stuart Mill offered to cover all the losses from the third volume of his *Biology*, but Spencer turned him down. Other notable friends included Darwin and Huxley. Fortunately for Spencer, his American admirers underwrote many of his costs, though this clashed severely with his personal code of self-help. By the late 1890s, Spencer had become a renowned philosopher, and, in 1896, he finished his *Synthetic Philosophy*. However, by 1903, when he died, he had outlived his fame. While early on he might have believed that "always toward perfection is the mighty movement—toward a complete development and a more unmixed good," Spencer's last years were spent in disillusionment as Britain moved away from individualism to concerns for state intervention for the sake of distributive justice.[2] But while Britain might have moved away from laissez-faire individualism, it was in America that his ideas flourished so much that, even at the end of the twentieth century, progress and evolution remain central to economic thinking (although now under the language of development and growth).

In Spencer's time, it was comments like those of Edward Youmans to Spencer that were characteristic of the day: "I am an ultra and thoroughgoing American. I believe that there is great work to be done here for civilization. What we want are ideas—large, organizing ideas—and I believe there is no other man whose thoughts are so valuable for our needs as yours are."[3]

Spencer should be seen in the context of the industrial revolution, the West's sense of optimism in science, man, and progress. In retrospect, Spencer placed the spirit of this era in a giant sweeping law, his theory of evolution.

## UNIFIED THEORY

Spencer concentrated his efforts on developing a unified theory of reality. For Spencer, it was philosophy that could unify knowledge. "Knowledge of the lowest kind is *un-unified knowledge*, science is *partially-unified* knowledge, philosophy is *completely-unified* knowledge."[4] Central to this theory was a general law of evolution. Evolution is characterized by increased differentiation and increased heterogeneity: "There is habitually a passage from homogeneity to heterogeneity, along with the passage from diffusion to concentration. . . . In the course of its advance from a germ to a mass of relatively great bulk, every plant and animal also advances from simplicity to complexity. The increase of a society in numbers and consolidation has for it concomitant an increased heterogeneity both of its political and its industrial organization. And the like hold for all super-organic products—Language, Science, Art and Literature."[5]

Spencer's law of evolution was a universal law, applicable to individuals, societies, and galaxies. Central to his theory was the law of persistence of force, in which he argued that a thing cannot remain homogenous if it is acted upon; that is, things go from homogeneity to heterogeneity. Moreover, each further differentiation becomes a parent of future differentiations. "Multiplication of effects advances in a geometrical progression along with advancing heterogeneity."[6] But the prime mover in all this is the unknowable. While Spencer was a positivist, he believed that the Ultimate Cause of being could not be known or demonstrated by science; it was to remain a mystery. And yet it is this unknowable that provides a teleological purpose to evolution and moves man to perfection. Thus, Spencer's evolution was not value free, but had a moral purpose.

In Spencer's unified philosophy, there are deep similarities between the biological and the social. For example, Spencer writes that "societies, like living bodies, begin as germs—originally from masses which are extremely minute in comparison with the masses some of them eventually reach."[7] Spencer further compares nerves with telegraph wires, arteries with railways, and the body with society:

The life blood of the developing organism acquires an unequivocally commercial character as the circulating mass of commodities in the body politic. The flow of both is stimulated by demand, limited by supply. Profit is the excess of nutrition over waste; over-exercise followed by inability to supply the deficiency results in slump. Railways become arteries, their branch lines blood vessels. The regulating structure of society becomes its nervous system, its cephalic ganglion (king) emerging from among the *minor ganglia* (aristocracy) to assert (his) authority. Meanwhile the cerebral agency (parliament) coordinating stimuli from all parts of the organism, rises to challenge for supremacy.[8]

To some degree, Spencer furthers Comte's scientific positivism, arguing that the fading of the ancient world and Platonic ideas of essences constitute evidence of scientific progress. Science is the leader in unifying all thought into a grand scheme. But underlying the entire scheme is the Unknown Reality: unknowable by science or religion, put forth by philosophy.

The key metaphor for Spencer was biological, derived from evolutionary theory. While initially Spencer believed evolution was entirely progressive in its thrust, in his later writings Spencer argued that there were stages of equilibrium and even oscillation. "The pattern of universal rhythm comes into play; dissolution follows evolution, disintegration follows integration. In an organism this phase is represented by death and decay, but in society by the establishment of a stable, harmonious, completely adapted state."[9]

Still, evolution could only end in perfection and the greatest state of happiness for the many. It was the ability of humans to adapt to changing conditions that would continue the onward march of progress until man became perfect:

> Progress ... is not an accident, but a necessity. Instead of civilization being artificial it is a part of nature; all of a piece with the development of an embryo or the unfolding of a flower. The modifications mankind have undergone, and are still undergoing, result from a law underlying the whole organic creation. ... As surely as the tree becomes bulky when it stands alone, and slender if one of a group ... as surely as there is any meaning in such terms as habit, custom, practice; so surely must the human faculties be moulded into complete fitness for a social state; so surely must evil and immorality disappear; so surely must man become perfect.[10]

But in this adaption only the fittest could survive. Despite the glorious language of evolution, ultimately Spencer was ultraconservative. For Spencer, the poor were unfit and were to be eliminated. State interference would only hamper evolution. In Spencer's words, "The whole effort of nature is to get rid of them, and make room for better. ... If they are sufficiently complete to live, they *do* live, and it is well they should live. If they are not sufficiently complete to live, they die, and it is best they should die."[11] Only voluntary charity to the poor was appropriate, since it helped develop the nature of the donor, quickening the development of altruism. "Society advances where its fittest members are allowed to assert their fitness ... and where the least fitted are not artificially prevented from dying out."[12] But the poor and the biologically handicapped should be left to themselves. This was true for individuals and, as one might expect given the unity of thought in his model, for societies and other aggregates as well. In this way, "each generation will contain a higher proportion of the fittest and a smaller proportion of the unfit, a process of racial purification which continues until unfitness is bred out altogether, and the superior inherit the earth."[13]

Much of this comes directly from his biological metaphor, which is not merely descriptive, for it justifies a society of rulers and ruled, a center and periphery. "As the embryo develops two distinct layers for its satisfaction of its needs, the mucous (ectoderm) to provide nutrition, and the serous (esoderm) to coordinate its actions, so the emergent society produces two distinct classes, the lower producing nourishment, the higher controlling the functions of both."[14]

This metaphor provides a biological justification for a lower and higher class of people and nations: some to provide raw materials, others to provide rulership. Along with his notion of the survival of the fittest, Spencer's metaphor of the body politic has (through the vehicle of development theory) justified structural inequity at the social and global interstate level. However, Spencer does allow for a third class that mediates the other two. "The two-tier embryo, furthermore, gradually develops a third, or vascular layer, responsible for the distribution of commodities, just as society develops a middle class."[15] But it is still the higher-level class which controls the other classes.

Societies also follow the same pattern as organisms: the process of growth, differentiation (into functions and classes), and integration. Central to societies and organisms is the struggle for existence. It is this struggle which leads to progress and to evolution.

## SOCIETAL STAGES

Spencer developed a stage theory of societies based on two ideal types: the militant and the industrial. The chief difference between them is that the former is based on compulsory cooperation and the latter on voluntary cooperation. The militant phase precedes the industrial. However, prior to both there is an initial period of barbarism. In this period there is little differentiation and heterogeneity except in differences between sex. There is no social aggregation per se; rather, every family is self-sufficient except for the purposes of aggression and defense. It is, however, the difference between the governing and the governed that constitutes the first important social differentiation. Power first passes on from family to family; eventually, certain members are deified, the most ancient of which is the supreme god. However, the civil and religious remain closely linked. Over time, these two arenas becomes differentiated and the king is no longer the chief priest. While there has been a change among the governing there has also been a change among the governed. A division of labor and class develops. This division of labor exists at all levels, from the factory to the nation.

As society moves from the barbarous, it enters the militant and is organized around survival and domination. "It bristles with military weapons, trains its people for warfare, relies upon a despotic state, submerges the individual. . . . In contests among societies those best exemplifying these militant traits will survive; and individuals best adapted to the militant community will be the dominating type."[16]

The social structure in the militant society is hierarchical and rigid. There is little upward movement, with emphasis placed on obedience and order instead of innovation and change. Patriotism, bravery, and strength are all attributes of the militant type.Continuing with his biological metaphor, Spencer remarks, "The social structure adapted for dealing with surrounding hostile societies is under a centralized regulating system to which all the parts are completely subject; just as in the individual organism the outer organs are completely subject to the chief nervous center."[17]

As the militant society expands, it reaches a stage of equilibrium. Through social evolution the peaceful industrial society develops. Based on social contact, this society places the individual at the center. Natural selection produces an individual, the industrial type, who is independent, kind, and honest. Instead of domination of others, industrial cooperation follows. This was Spencer's obvious hope for England and the Western world. However, Spencer did not apply his analysis to present societies; he remained, as an anthropologist, discussing the other nations of the Asias and Africas. They remained as examples of militant and even barbarous states, while it was Europe that exhibited the industrial and America that would pass everyone by.

Civilization does not end with the industrial. A possible future type might emerge, "different as much from the industrial as this does from the militant—a type which, having a sustaining system more fully developed than any we know at present, will use the products of industry neither for maintaining a militant organization nor exclusively for material aggrandizement; but will devote them to the carrying on of higher activities."[18] Spencer does not detail the contours of this new society. He merely writes, "As the contrast between the militant and the industrial types is indicated by inversion of the belief that individuals exist for the benefit of the State into the belief that the State exists for individuals; so the contrast between the industrial type and the type likely to be evolved from it is indicated by inversion of the belief that life is for work into the belief that work is for life."[19] In this vision, it would be the individual businessman that would lead society onward. According to economist Robert Nelson, "In social Darwinism, the successful businessman was among the chosen, now the central agent in the evolutionary progress of mankind. Herbert Spencer believed that the end result of progress would be a world without government, marked by altruism in individual behavior."[20]

It was not this new society that Spencer saw emerging in his later years, but the rebarbarization of civilization. He saw a conflation of industrial and military with the rise of Imperial Germany. The antagonism between industry and war was an evolutionary step that Nature had yet to work out. But even though the social conditions of Spencer's late nineteenth century were disturbing, evolutionary theory remained optimistic: "Social evolution throughout the future, like social evolution throughout the past, must, while producing step after step higher societies, leave outstanding many lower.... But ... in time to come, a federation of the highest action, exercising supreme authority, may, by forbidding wars between any of its constituent nations, put an end to the re-barbarization which is continually undoing civilization."[21] Of course, the nations to enforce this new superordinate authority would be ones with the least vestiges of the nonmodern: ones with the highest degree of differentiation, the greatest level of capitalist development, and who embraced the ideology of individualism.

But change to the future had to be incremental. As a Darwinian, Spencer was a gradualist, critical of revolutions and attempts for massive social transformation. Nature would select the highest and the best. States would do best not to intervene. For Spencer, "the great task of sociology was to chart 'the normal course of social evolution,' to show how it will be affected by any given policy, and to condemn all types of behavior that interfere with it."[22] Social theory could then aid in evolution but it could not change the forward movement of progress. "Any adequate theory of society will recognize the general truths of biology and will refrain from violating the selection principle by 'artificial preservation' of those least able to take care of themselves."[23]

What Spencer did not understand was the ability of the modern state to both provide social support to the individual (within the confines of the nation-state) and enlarge its own. Nor did he understand the complimentary role of military and industry. The ideology of individualism and a strong state could coexist; indeed, it was the state that provided the evolutionary thrust to help particular businesses from one nation-state (and within nations) compete against other businesses from another nation-state.

## COMPARISONS AND CONCLUSIONS

We can make many useful comparisons to other macrohistorians examined in this book. The debt to Comte is there. Indeed, it is only in the role of the unknowable—God as immanence—that Spencer significantly differs from the general thrust of Comte. It is this that made him palatable to Americans: positivism and God all in one. Otherwise, both assert the onward march of society from the primitive to the religious to the positive scientific. Both theories are clearly linear in shape. Even when there is barbarism, it is not the beginning of a new cycle, as with Vico; rather, it is backward movement in the forward steps of evolution.[24]

While Comte focused on stages of knowledge (the theological, the metaphysical, and the positive), Spencer articulates social types and stages, specifically the militant and industrial stages of society. Moreover, their understanding of societal laws was quite different. "Comte wanted to argue from history that progressive stages could be discerned, and that one could infer from this an invariance which was lawful. Spencer, in contrast, found by induction an *abstract principle*, which for him governed every possible system, from astral to cellular, from psychological to cultural."[25]

Like Marx, Spencer believed that the state would wither away—the individual would be victorious—but unlike Marx, Spencer did not believe that class gave unequal privileges or rights to a particular group. Class had no functional role in his system.

In sharp contrast to Spencer is Spengler, who saw not evolution and progress in the march of history but degeneration from culture to civilization; not the rise of the West but the decline of the West.

There are clear similarities between Sarkar's theory of struggle and progress and Spencer's theory of evolution. However, while Sarkar develops his theory for the happiness of all, Spencer believes that evolution is for the happiness of the many. The few—those who cannot adapt—should not be helped by the many. Rather, those nations, societies, and individuals impede the march of man toward perfection. For Sarkar, society is not a contract or a mere aggregation of individuals but a family moving toward the sublime. Each member helps the other; it is especially the duty of the strong to help the weak. For Spencer, society is moving forward, but those individuals who cannot continue the march should not slow down society as a whole.

Spencer also differs from cyclical theorists such as Spengler and Vico in that even though both use biological metaphors, Spengler uses the life cycle (birth, maturation, and then death) while Spencer focuses on differentiation and integration, the linear dimension. However, like the ancients, such as Ssu-Ma Ch'ien, a complete philosophy of the real must be unified—what is true for the cosmic and the individual should be true for the social.

While Spencer wished for the happiness of the many, it is his theory that today justifies the happiness of the few. Spencer gives us social evolution. While there might be some backsliding in history, there is no escape in the historical march upward. Even though humanity is interdependent and integrated—an organic whole—the differences between states and between individuals was not seen as a call for transformation but rather as justification for privilege.

## NOTES

1. For the latest reading on this, see Robert Henry Nelson, *Reaching for Heaven on Earth: The Theological Meaning of Economics* (Lanham, Md.: Rowman and Littlefield, 1991), 5.

2. Quoted in David Wiltshire, *The Social and Political Thought of Herbert Spencer* (Oxford: Oxford University Press, 1978), 104.

3. Richard Hofstadter, *Social Darwinism in American Thought* (New York: Brazilla, 1959), 31.

4. Quoted in Wiltshire, *Social and Political Thought*, 195.

5. Herbert Spencer, *First Principles* (1862; reprint, Osnabruck: Otto Zeller, 1966), 487.

6. Ibid., 440.

7. Herbert Spencer, *Structure, Function and Evolution* (London: Michael Joseph, 1971), 120.

8. Wiltshire, *Social and Political Thought*, 233–234.

9. Hofstadter, *Social Darwinism*, 37.
10. Quoted in Peter Manicas, *A History and Philosophy of the Social Sciences* (New York: Basil Blackwell, 1987), 70.
11. Quoted in Hofstadter, *Social Darwinism*, 41.
12. Quoted in Wiltshire, *Social and Political Thought*, 195.
13. Ibid., 197.
14. Ibid., 233.
15. Ibid.
16. Hofstadter, *Social Darwinism*, 42.
17. Spencer, *Structure, Function and Evolution*, 161.
18. Ibid., 169.
19. Ibid.
20. Robert Nelson, "Why Capitalism Hasn't Won Yet," *Forbes*, 25 November 1991, 106.
21. Spencer, *Structure, Function and Evolution*, 214.
22. Hofstadter, *Social Darwinism*, 43.
23. Ibid., 44.
24. Spencer is not very clear about this, as he also posits an osicillation between evolution and dissolution. The problem with this approach is that it contradicts his evolutionary approach, his assertion of homogeneity to heterogeneity. But these metaphysical problems are not what Spencer is remembered for; rather, it is for the survival of the fittest, the limited role of the state, and the belief in unabated progress.
25. Manicas, *History and Philosophy*, 69.

*2.10*

## *Vilfredo Pareto: The Unbreakable Cycle*

*Daniela Rocco Minerbi*

### BIOGRAPHY

The second part of the nineteenth century showed a transformation in Europe toward unified nation-states. In Italy, unification was preceded by internal revolutionary movements aiming at democratization and nationalism. The conflict between industrial capitalism and the working mass had its theoretical expression in economic liberalism and socialism. Philosophically, there was a shift from metaphysical speculation to natural sciences and social sciences; from the a priori and deductive method to the inductive and the logico-experimental method. The use of pure reason no longer appeared adequate to represent and understand reality. This is the context in which Pareto lived. English liberalism and the philosophies of Comte, Spencer, and Darwin were among the main influences on his thought. His studies of system analysis and mathematics and his disillusionment at the sight of the incompetence and corruption of politicians were the other main factors that shaped his views.

The Marquis Vilfredo Pareto was born in Paris in 1848. His mother was French, his father an Italian in voluntary exile because of his antimonarchic views and support of Mazzini and the republican movement. Thanks to a political amnesty, his family moved back to Italy in 1858 and settled in Turin. After attending secondary school in classic studies, he entered the Polytechnic, from which he graduated with a doctorate in engineering. These studies had a powerful influence on Pareto's economical and sociological ideas. Scholarly studies of humanities and the classics provided him with a vast store of historical evidence which proved of great value in the demonstration of his historico-sociological theory.

His professional life from 1870 to 1882, in Rome and in Florence as director of the *Societa' Ferriere d'Italia*, was fundamental to the evolution of Pareto's political and economic views. While he was a believer in liberal economic policies and free trade, he was disillusioned with the Mazzinian ideals of democracy, humanitarianism, and perfectibility of human nature. He was consumed with bitterness as he observed the government's economic policy of protectionism and military adventures on the one hand, and the necessity in his job to negotiate "deals" with politicians on the other.[1]

These were the conditions that led Pareto to retire in 1882. During the next eleven years he wrote a great number of articles on economics in the hope of receiving a professorship. By the beginning of 1900, he expressed his most severe criticism of the political situation, as he was completely disillusioned by the corruption and incompetence of the governing class and by the politicians' pursuit of self-interest under the guise of parliamentary democracy and humanitarianism.

He realized his academic aspiration in 1893, when he was offered the Chair of Economics at the University of Lausanna. His main research interest was now to investigate his conviction that people's conduct is not the result of logical reasoning. This conception is expounded in his *Trattato di Sociologia Generale* (The Mind and Society), written between 1907 and 1912. Pareto died on August 19, 1923, the year of the Fascists' march on Rome.[2]

## PARETO'S CONCEPT OF HISTORY

### Logical and Non-Logical Actions

Human behavior is in part logical, yet mostly non-logical. In economics, the non-logical element has been taken into consideration using the variable "tastes."[3] But Pareto considers the economic sciences insufficient in analyzing the complexity of social behavior in human organization.

Logical reasoning that originates logical conduct occurs in the dominion of science. Logical actions are those that use means appropriate to ends and logically link means with ends.[4] They do so not only according to the judgment of the doer, but also according to the objective judgment of an expert competent observer. Logical actions are, at least in large part, results of processes of reasoning. "Non-logical actions originate chiefly in definite psychic states, sentiments, subconscious feeling, and the like."[5]

Pareto, using the inductive logico-experimental method based on observations of uniformities, examined a large number of historical examples of human actions, theories, and belief systems which sought to explain such events. But he concluded that what appears as logical theories are only rationalizations of psychic needs and feelings. Such logical rationalizations make historical events or human conduct look like the result of a set of beliefs. Rationalization in logic form is itself the result of a deep-seated human need. Neither economic science nor theories, doctrines, and beliefs are able to sufficiently explain the elements that constitute social behavior, since there is no logical connection between them and behavior.

## Residues and Derivations

To come to grips with this problem, Pareto introduced the concepts of deep-seated subconscious feelings and logifications. Psychic needs, subconscious feelings, and propensities are called "residues" (the common denominator of actions and rationalization). Residues are innate to the human psyche. They are grouped in six classes. Two of these classes, opposite in their characteristics, contain psychic needs that are fundamental to the survival and progress of a social organization.

Class 1 residues are comprised of desires and propensities for innovation, inventiveness, and enterprise, while Class 2 is made up of psychic needs for stability, order, morals, and religion. Two other classes, Class 4, which contains needs of sociability and uniformity, and Class 5, which seeks individualism and integrity, are not taken directly into account, but Class 4 seems to be absorbed by Class 2, and Class 5 seems to be absorbed by Class 1. The remaining classes are Class 3, which includes desire to manifest sentiments by external acts, and Class 6, sex residue. These two classes do not appear to be fundamental to the development of Pareto's sociological theory.

Residues cannot be known directly, but they can be inferred from man's behavior and the rationalizations manifesting them. Throughout history, men have acted in analogous ways even if their behavior has been attributed to the effects of a variety of different doctrines, which Pareto calls "pseudo-doctrines." Uniformities of human conduct imply the existence of a hidden, specific, and constant psychic need.

Logical rationalizations are *a posteriori* statements about behavior; they do not cause and do not explain it, however they may influence conduct indirectly by means of reinforcing or weakening the psychic need at its root. Although logifications are thought activities, they are pseudo-logical or non-logical. Pareto calls them "derivations" and divides them into four classes according to the type of argument on the basis of which they are sustained. The classes are affirmations, authority, accord with sentiments or principles, and verbal proofs. To derivations belong philosophies, theologies, and doctrines, called by him non-logical experimental sciences because of the lack of connection between their claims to effect changes in the social system and their actual effectiveness. Observations show that residues originate behavior.

### Social System, Equilibrium, and Utility

Pareto also introduced the concept of "system," drawing on his earlier studies in physics. Human organization is conceived as a system. A system is constituted by a set of variables in a relationship of mutual dependence. Each variable has a different degree of variability; some vary lightly over a long period of time, some vary considerably over a short time. The variable that is more constant can be seen as determining the other; in other words, it can be considered the independent variable.

In the social system, variables can be equated to forces. These forces are in equilibrium. However, since the forces are not immutable, they cause the equilibrium to have different shapes over time. The length of the interval of time required to establish a new (i.e., a differently shaped equilibrium) depends on the amount of time required by the forces in it to complete the particular actions necessary to reach a new balance.[6]

Society is a system of forces in changing equilibrium over time, that acquires different shapes of organization. Any type of organization has to be justified by its goal, which Pareto calls "utility." It follows that the equilibrium, and a particular shape, is related to the utility to be achieved. In fact, the elements acting in a system are not interdependent at random, but aim toward a certain goal and toward a certain organization that best provides the attainment of the goal.

The determination of the goal, that is the utility, is an almost impossible task since it reflects the arbitrary judgment of whoever makes the determination.[7] Pareto makes the distinction between the satisfaction of the needs of each individual, the utility of the individuals, and the satisfaction of the goals of the system as a whole (i.e., utility for the system). But even if the definition of the goal, or utility, could be approximated, it would never be permanent, since new and different elements support different goals over time. The result is a moving equilibrium of ever-changing forces aiming at a continually redefined utility.

### Heterogeneity and Elite Circulation

Society is heterogeneous; people differ physically as well as in their abilities, psychic needs, and propensities. Some men are more gifted than others, and also some men have different gifts from others; that is, man's residues vary in intensity and in type. Pareto uses only Class 1 residues, called "combination residues," and Class 2 ones, called "persistence of aggregates residues," as the main ones accountable for the differentiation of individuals. Those individuals with higher degrees of either Class 1 or Class 2 residues—those with a greater capability to improve their welfare and those with a greater capability to rule and use authority—form the elite; all other men constitute the mass. Residues are accountable for the formation of the elite. Society is schematically comprised only of two classes.

At this point, another element crucial to the analysis of societal change is introduced. The new variable is called the "circulation of the elite," and its value increases or decreases depending on how open or closed the elite is to the assimilation of new members. An open elite begets the circulation faster, and thus the integration of those individuals most capable to increase the prosperity of society and the stability of the system is greater.

### Degeneration of Elites and Societal Change

The proportion of Class 1 and Class 2 residues in the elite and degree of circulation of the elite are related to the utility of the system and to its equilibrium. If the mixture of the two classes of residues were not unbalanced, and if circulation to and from the elite were flowing such that the most capable were always in control of the government, that elite and its government organization would endure; in fact, it would be the ideal state. The social utility, that is, the maintenance of public order, national independence, flexibility to adjust to crises, and increase of national wealth, would be assured.[8] There would be enough Class 2 residue individuals endowed with the capacity to maintain internal order and the independence of the country as well as sufficient individuals able to achieve scientific progress and economic prosperity.

But elites are not fixed; since the distribution of residues and their circulation is not constant, they degenerate. When circulation is blocked, the stimulus for struggle is lacking. Moreover, the children of the elite remain part of the elite even if they have not inherited talents for leadership. Thus, the elite become decadent and are no longer comprised of the most gifted individuals. The subjected masses, on the other hand, are made rich by the presence of individuals with a high degree of Class 1 and/or Class 2 residues who have not been assimilated by the elite.

Even if circulation flows, another phenomenon endangers the stability of the system's equilibrium. In fact, the proportion of the two classes of residues tends to move in the direction of Class 1 residues. Usually the men endowed with Class 1 residues, that is, with the spirit of enterprise, innovation, and invention, have the drive and ability to move upward and join the elite, so that the elite, as time passes, has a tendency to become predominantly rich in Class 1 residues. Besides, the Class 1 residue individuals, in assimilating those elements of the mass gifted with the same talents they have, leave the mass without leadership. Also, by acquiring Class 1 residue elements, which bring scientific progress and prosperity, the elite requires less Class 2 residue individuals (those individuals willing and capable to use the power of authority and force in governing), because it can maintain its power through special concessions and compromise rather than through use of authority.

As the elite becomes less willing and competent in the use of power for its internal order (although it may camouflage such a situation under a facade of humanitarianism) and is more inclined to use deceit and fraud, it reaches its decadence. It becomes vulnerable to the use of force from below, from the subjected masses, and from the outside in the form of foreign domination. Even the new governing class rich in Class 2 residues, which will take over, will not last forever. It will become rigid, bureaucratic, and petrified; unable to produce wealth, it will have to be open to individuals with Class 1 combination residues.

## CIRCULATION OF ELITES AND THEIR CORRESPONDING GOVERNMENTS

Pareto interprets history as an endless fluctuation between two limits, between two types of elites and government organizations; that is, between an elite rich of Class 1 residues or combination residues, governing through democracy, and an elite comprised of Class 2 residues or residues of persistence of aggregates, governed by a bureaucratic autocracy.

An elite is formed with individuals endowed with both classes of residues. Individuals with combination residues prevail, decadence starts, and the elite is overthrown by the mass, which is rich with residues of Class 2. The old government is replaced with a new authoritarian one based on the use of force. As time passes, new men with combination residues will join the elite, in part because of their abilities and in part because they are needed for the growth of prosperity which they necessarily bring about. The cycle starts again.[9]

During a democratic government, the economy grows, industrial and commercial interests grows, and, in turn, this phenomenon increases the circulation of the elite so that Class 1 residue individuals predominate and are better suited for these activities. The government is very expensive but very productive. Speculators, those who venture in economic and financial enterprises to increase their income, thrive. Generally, the social atmosphere is that of immediate gratification, of short-term planning, and of individualism. Intellectually, skepticism prevails over faith; that is, derivations express intellectual religion.

As the pendulum swings toward the opposite direction, which happens, as already mentioned, through an internal revolution or a foreign conquest, the elite becomes dominated by Class 2 residues. In this era the government is despotic, bureaucratic, and autocratic; circulation in and out of the elite is slow; the economy grows little; and owners of savings, men with fixed income, and "rentiers" prevail. Government is inexpensive and produces little. The social climate fosters deferred gratification, long-term planning, and sacrifice of individual interests for community ones. Derivations are expressed in the form of metaphysical religions and faith.

Pareto insists on showing the interrelatedness of government, political, economic, and intellectual cycles. Each elite type not only corresponds to a government form, but also a certain economic, political, and intellectual activity; all these phenomena are mutually related.

Pareto sees history as a never ending fluctuation between democracy and bureaucratic autocracy. His observations cover the last few thousand years of Western history; they start with the Athenian democracy at one end of the pendulum and the Greek tyrannies at the other end. The second cycle of democratic government is represented by the Roman republic at one pole, and the despotic lower Roman empire at the other. The feudal states and medieval republics at one end, and the absolute monarchies of nineteenth-century Europe at the opposite end, constitute the third cycle. Modern pluto-democracy constitutes the first half of the fourth and latest cycle, and correspond to the contemporary time of Pareto.

## CONCLUSION

Pareto lived at a time when Britain was on an ascending economic and industrial growth curve. The British parliamentary system seemed to be the model political institution for social reform. Such an example had a strong impact on Pareto's conviction that economic liberalism and democracy, together, provide the most desirable socioeconomic system. But as he observed the Italian political system approach a plutocratic structure, a phenomenon happening at the same time throughout Europe, he lost his trust that politicians and government people (i.e., the leadership) were willing and capable to act according to any scientific, logical reasoning or any experimental evidence, as well as the conviction that scientific proof may, in any way, effect political decision making and action.

The governing elite, therefore, must act according to instinctual or subconscious psychological motivations and drives (i.e., residues) that cannot be known directly but are manifested through man's logical rationalizations and theorizing, and can hence be inducted. Pareto's effort was to produce a logico-experimental analysis, based on the inductive method and past and current historical events, to discover the real forces behind historical facts. Pareto is influenced by positivistic thought, thought that has focused on the research of the law of natural phenomena for the purpose of making predictions. His conception of society as a system of mutually interrelated variables seems to derive both from his study of physics and economics and from that part of evolutionistic thinking that had abandoned the determinism of the environment—be it natural, such as in Lamarck, or social, such as in Spencer—for the idea of "mutuality" among variables.[10]

Pareto, at variance with determinism, does not explain sociohistorical changes by means of cause–effect relationships. One system is explanatory of the next one and vice versa. Shared with evolutionistic thought is the acknowledgment of "adaptation." Residues, those innate psychic forces, have an adaptive value: "In a given society of a certain stability, the residues that we find operative will for the most part be residues favorable to its preservation."[11]

Derivations, which have the purpose of logifying and confirming the residues, also have an adaptive function. This adaptation also applies to utility, whose goal is to preserve society, and to the elite that, having Class 1 and Class 2 residues, has the capability to give stability and prosperity to the social system. When certain residues become predominant to the point that they are not adaptive to the preservation of the social system, as in the case of the degeneration of the elites, they are substituted by others, those of a new elite brought about by the revolting mass in order to establish a new form of adaptation to life.

Pareto acknowledges a prevailing of Class 1 residues in art, science, and economic production in the course of the centuries. In the latter two fields, the findings of logico-experimental sciences have contributed to their great predominance, particularly in modern life. Human activity seems more and more directed by reason. But Pareto also states that this observation does not apply to the political and social activities.

In conclusion, man has a precultural (instinctual) psychological biogram which has adaptive value. Such a biogram, which is constituted by the residues, interacts with culture (i.e., derivations) and is responsible for social life and class formation which, in turn, determines the organization of the system by mutual relationship with other variables.

Pareto observes progress in the realm of natural and physical sciences, but he states that passions and sentiments are unchangeable. To the extent that Pareto believes in the adaptive value of sociopolitical behavior, he could be considered a social evolutionist; in fact, the undulatory movement between the two types of social organizations is not, in itself, in contrast with evolutionism. But from one pluto-democracy to the next and from one bureaucratic autocracy to the next, the ratio between Class 1 and Class 2 residues does not change on average. No progress happens. For this reason, Pareto does not appear to believe in linear sociohistorical evolution and is more of a cyclical macrohistorian.

## NOTES

1. Lewis Coser, *Master of Sociological Thought* (New York: Harcourt Brace Jovanovich, 1971), 403–404.

2. S. E. Finer, introduction to *Vilfredo Pareto: Sociological Writing* (New York: Frederick A. Praeger, 1966), 3–8.

3. Vilfredo Pareto, *The Mind and Society: Trattato di Sociologia Generale*, vol. 4 (New York: Harcourt, Brace and Company, 1935), 1442.
4. Ibid., vol. 1, 77.
5. Ibid., vol. 1, 88.
6. Giulio Farina, *Vilfredo Pareto: Compendium of General Sociology* (Minneapolis: University of Minnesota Press, 1980), 357.
7. Lawrence Henderson, *Pareto's General Sociology: A Physiologist's Interpretation* (Cambridge: Harvard University Press, 1935), 50.
8. Coser, *Master of Sociological Thought*, 400.
9. Finer, *Vilfredo Pareto*, 257–258.
10. Coser, *Master of Sociological Thought*, 410.
11. Pareto, *The Mind and Society*, vol. 3, 1344.

# 2.11

## Max Weber: History as Interplay and Dichotomy of Rationalization and Charisma

*Claus Otto Scharmer*

### BIOGRAPHY

Max Weber was born in Erfurt, Germany, on April 21, 1864. The differences and contradictions between his mother and his father can be seen as a basic pattern of his life.[1] His father was a bureaucrat who rose to a relatively important political position. As a representative of the political establishment, his father avoided any kind of action or sacrifice that could have threatened his position in the system. In addition, he greatly enjoyed various kinds of earthly pleasures. This stood in sharp contrast to his wife, Marianne Weber. She was a deeply religious woman, much more concerned with other worlds than with earthly pleasures and trying to live a Calvinist ascetic life. The tension between these two poles deeply influenced Weber's psyche. He first opted in favor of the lifestyle of his father. Later in his life he turned more to the way of life of his mother.

At the age of eighteen, Max Weber left home to attend the University of Heidelberg. After three terms he left Heidelberg for military service, and in 1884 returned to Berlin to his parents' home in order to take courses at the University of Berlin. He remained in Berlin for eight years, completed his studies, earned his Ph.D., became a lawyer, and started teaching at the University of Berlin.

In 1896, he became professor of economics at the University of Heidelberg. In the midst of the first blossoming of his career, in 1897, his father died after a violent argument between the two of them. The thirty-three-year-old Weber was shaken by this event and eventually had a nervous breakdown. Over the next seven years Weber was mostly unable to sleep or to work, and was always near a total collapse. After this extended time of suffering, he finally regained his physical and mental powers.

In 1904, he delivered his first public lecture in six-and-a-half years, and in 1905 published one of his most famous works, *The Protestant Ethic and the Spirit of Capitalism*. Although he still suffered from serious psychological problems after 1904, Weber had, at this time, a second blossoming of his academic work and career. He published his studies of world religions in a world historical perspective. When he died in 1920, Weber was working on *Economy and Society*, and although it was published, it remained unfinished.

## DISCOURSE OF INTELLECTUAL GIANTS: WEBER, MARX, NIETZSCHE

The Weberian approach to macrohistory, his way of conceptualizing the course of universal history, is shaped by a dichotomy which reflects his exposition and argument with two giants of nineteenth-century European thought: Karl Marx and Friedrich Nietzsche. "The world we live in, is a world which is largely imprinted by Nietzsche and Marx," Weber is reported to have remarked.[2] We can see the influence of Karl Marx on Weber in his entire work on religion. As opposed to Karl Marx, who focused on material conditions (means and modes of production), Weber saw cultural conditions as important in understanding the development of history. However, while Weber focused primarily on cultural conditions he never denied the importance of other perspectives. In 1920, he expressed the interplay of both clusters of factors as follows: "Not ideas, but material and ideal interests directly govern men's conduct. Yet very frequently the world images that have been created by ideas have, like switchmen, determined the tracks along which action has been pushed by the dynamics of interests."[3]

Weber, who was referred to as "Marx of the middle class," was also opposed to Marx with respect to methodology and to predictions of the future of capitalism (and socialism respectively).[4] Weber foresaw that the lives of workers would not improve if private property and the means of production became state property. His other important insight was the warning of an increasing degree of rationalization and bureaucratization, especially for the Western countries. Both can be regarded, from the point of view of the end of the twentieth century, as excellent predictions by the liberal sociologist, especially when compared with those of his socialist counterpart.

The influence of Nietzschean thinking on Weber can be seen throughout his works. As Eugene Fleischmann and Martin Albrow have pointed out, there is a list of elementary features in Weber's thought which were part of the Nietzschean framework: the multiplicity of values; the impossibility of making a rational choice between them; the emphasis on power and structures of domination; radical ethical individualism; the rejection of happiness as an appropriate goal for human beings; and relentless intellectual integrity and asceticism.[5] And yet, Mommsen is right to underline some substantial differences between Weber and Nietzsche: Weber did not share the Nietzschean notion of a superman who rules the "herd" for the sake of his own qualities; the Weberian charismatic leader was "filled with a sense of responsibility for the people he led rather than with contempt for the herd."[6]

Nevertheless, one of the few values that has continued to exist is that of the nation-state, which always served as a frame of reference in Weber's thought. As Weber wrote, "We are not going to endow our descendents with peace and happiness, but with eternal struggle for the maintenance and upgrading of our national stock."[7]

## FORCES OF RATIONALIZATION AND CHARISMA AS POLES OF UNIVERSAL HISTORY

The Weberian conceptualization of macrohistory is based on two major pillars which reveal the imprints of (anti) Marxian and Nietzschean thought: his objectivity-based concept of (cultural) rationalization on the one hand and his stress on subjectivity-based charismatic leadership on the other. However, Weber himself changed his attitude toward the essence of universal history throughout his life, and his final position envisioned a dialectic between the forces of rationality (and the process of rationalization) and charisma.[8]

According to previous research on how Weber was received, rationalization has been seen as a single axis through his work. History has been reconstructed as a process of rationalization of (1) world views and (2) social relations which have led to disenchantment, in which all world views become devalued, and finally resulting in the famous "iron cage":

The puritan *wanted* to follow his calling—we *have* to become professionals. As the asceticism of the monastery cells had been carried over in the life of the calling and started to dominate the moral life of the inner person, it helped to contribute to build the economic system of the powerful modern cosmos with its technical and economic conditions for a mechanical machine oriented production, a basis for economic life which today conditions the lifestyle of everybody who is born into the machinery and not only those who are employed by it, with overpowering force until the last gallon of fossil fuel has been burnt.[9]

Later he also says: "The concern for material goods should only rest 'like a thin cloak' on the shoulder of the saints that you can throw away any time.... But fate wanted this cloak to become an iron cage. As asceticism undertook the task of rebuilding the world in order to unfold itself in the world, the material goods of this world got increasing and finally unavoidable power over people like never before in history."[10]

The Weber reception offered two different strategies for interpretation of the process of rationalization. First, the teleological view reconstructed Occidental history as a linear process of disenchantment and as rationalization according to the predominant worldview. Second, the evolutionist interpretation, which regards the present order of the world as one among many other types of rationalization, by chance happened to become realized.[11] However, more recent studies tend to emphasize a third position, which stresses, on the one hand, the distinctness of Western rationalization of world views and social relations without, on the other hand, falling in the trap of postulating a linear concept of history with only one (Western) type of rationalization and one type of final outcome (iron cage).[12] Mommsen is correct in emphasizing the hypothetical status of much of Weber's writing about the future, aiming with his own predictions at some kind of self-denying prophecy. "No one knows as yet ... whether, at the end of this vast development, totally new prophets will emerge or will there be a powerful revival of old ideas and ideals, or, of neither of these, whether there will be a state of mechanized petrification, embellished by a kind of frenzied self-importance. In that case it might indeed become true to say of the 'last man' of this cultural development [that he is a]: 'specialist without soul, hedonist without heart: this cipher flatters itself that it has reached a stage of humanity never before attained.'"[13] As to the variable which enables these scenarios to occur or not, Weber provided a clear answer: Individual charisma as a source of value-oriented and creative action and leadership.

Weber's model of historic change is based on the antinomic poles of rationalization and charisma. Also important were his dichotomies of inner-worldly versus outer-worldly orientation/motivation and material interests versus value-based, individual action.

The Weberian distinction between traditional, rational, and charismatic types of domination reflects the polarity of historical forces that has been spelled out: the latter serving as the source for value-based acting, the former as types of routinization or rationalization, respectively. At the end of the systematic presentation of the types of domination, Weber notes with regard to the charismatic type, "In traditionalist periods charisma is *the* great revolutionary force, in contrast to the equally revolutionary force of 'ratio' which works from *without*, either by changing the conditions of life and daily problems and so changing men's attitudes to those conditions, or else through intellectualization."[14] Charisma is effective since it works from within, changing an individual's basic convictions leading to a complete reorientation of the self towards others and the world.

Whereas Weber used his typology of domination in his early writings more towards a historic succession (charismatic–traditional–rational), he later turned toward a less linear and more open and even cyclical interpretation.[15] Charisma was seen as the source which not only served at the origin of the world religions but which, after periods of routinization and rationalization, could also have a powerful comeback through the superior power of fresh charismatic leadership and domination.

## SWIMMING AGAINST THE STREAM

According to Schluchter, the historical analysis in Weber's work operates on three different levels: sociological, historical, and situational.[16] All three levels are historical in a general sense, but in Weber's terminology the first is the domain of sociology and makes use of ideal type or model construction. The second level is labeled by him "historical" in the more narrow sense, or sometimes "evolutionist" (*entwicklungsgeschichtlich*). Here we find causal explanations of past events; for instance, his secular theories (rationalization). The third level is what he occasionally calls analysis of general social and political situations, which refers to the contemporary play and struggle of forces.

Weber rejected any kind of clearcut, general model of development in human history or of stages of history. As Weber expert Wolfgang Mommsen summarizes his research, "All the same the type of charismatic rule due to personal dedication, to extraordinary value-ideals, or 'gifts of grace' and the type of legal rulership with its formal rationalization of all areas of life together represent the antinomic basic principles of society. Actual history takes place in the area of conflict between these two poles. It is a constant competition between the originally charismatically induced movements and the existing political, economic and religious institutions, the latter having formal rationality on their side."[17]

Weber's view on macrohistory is actually much less linear than is often thought. In spite of all the rationalization and bureaucratization of the Western world, Weber already sees the arrival and the return of ancient gods: "The old, numerous gods deprived of their magic and so in the form of impersonal powers risen again from their graves, strive for power over our lives and recommence their eternal battle with each other."[18]

There is no real final stage in Weber's writing, no *Endzustand*, apart from pessimistic predictions, which possibly serve primarily as self-denying prophecies. What then is the *force motrice*? Certainly the conflict between charisma and rationalization. More precise, social and rational institutions can be interpreted both as counterpart to and effect of previous charismatic, value-based actions. For instance, modern rational capitalism is both a counterpart for today's charismatic actions as well as a result of previous charismatic/religious movements. Thus, the *force motrice* has two aspects: first, it is constituted by the conflict of both poles as mentioned above; second, there is an underlying primacy of the charismatic value-based action over the material conditions and its institutions. For Weber, charismatic power is based on religious belief in religion. This belief leads to an inner revolution which then shapes the external world.

The interplay of the two poles in Weberian thought reflects both the impact of Marx (rationalization as objectivistic law of history) and the impact of Nietzsche (the revolutionary potential of the human subject). In addition, it is surprisingly similar to Sorokin's interplay of ideational and sensate state. The difference is that Sorokin based his analysis on the macrolevel of society, whereas Weber focuses on the individual and its charismatic capability for leadership as prime mover in history.

On the one hand, Weber's intellectual honesty saved him from drawing a simplistic synthesis between the two fundamental forces. On the other hand, he also failed to overcome this very dichotomy. The political solution he offers aims towards a democracy of plebiscitary domination, *plebiszitäre Führerdemokratie*. After the rise of Hitler and Nazi Germany just a few years later, this vision is certainly problematic.

Weber failed to construct a synthesis between objective rationalization and subjective creativity, between outside-driven and inside-driven social action, precisely because this is the way it is. There is no mediation between the two of them, neither in Weberian theory or in historical reality.

Weber essentially fails to realize the third metacategory next to objectivity and subjectivity: intersubjectivity. Jürgen Habermas, for example, criticizes the Weberian notion of rationality, which refers merely to instrumental but not to communicative (intersubjective) action. With the intersubjectivistic extension of the concept of rationality and action theory, Habermas fulfills the necessary condition to meet the very challenge of twentieth-century sociological thought: to link and mediate micro- and macrolevel, inside-driven and outside-driven social action or action theory, and system theory, respectively.[19] In other words, there is no *tertium non datur* (excluded middle) between Marxian (objectivity-based) laws of history and Nietzschean (subjectivity-based) freedom of a unique superman. There does exist a third way: creative freedom for all members of society. This, of course, presupposes a notion of freedom which refers to other humans not as boundary but as necessary, enabling conditions for advanced (intersubjective-based) freedom and collaborative social action.

## NOTES

1. Georg Ritzer, *Sociological Theory* (New York: Knopf, 1988), 26–27.
2. Wolfgang Mommsen, *Max Weber: Gesellschaft, Politik und Geschichte* (Society, politics and history) (Frankfurt: Suhrkamp Verlag, 1982), 146.
3. Wolfgang Mommsen, "Personal Conduct and Societal Change," in *Max Weber, Rationality and Modernity*, ed. S. Whimster and S. Lash (Boston: George Allen and Unwin, 1987), 48; H. H. Gerth and C. Wright Mills, eds., *From Max Weber: Essays in Sociology* (London: Routledge, 1948), 280.

4. Mommsen, *Max Weber*, 145; "I am a member of the bourgeois class, and feel myself to be so and have been brought up in its views and ideal." Quoted in Martin Albrow, *Max Weber's Construction of Social Theory* (London: Macmillan Education, 1990), 58.
5. Albrow, *Max Weber's Construction of Social Theory*, 57.
6. Ibid.
7. Ibid., 59.
8. Whimster and Lash, eds., *Max Weber*, 13.
9. Max Weber, *Gesammelte Aufsätze zur Religionssoziologie I* (Selected essays about sociology of religion) (Tübingen: J. C. G. Mohr, 1988), 203–204.
10. Ibid.
11. Mommsen, "Personal Conduct," 37.
12. Ibid., 37–41.
13. Ibid.
14. Ibid., 48–49.
15. "The continuum of Mediterranean–European civilizational development has known neither an end closed cyclical movement, nor an unequivocally monolinear evolution." Ibid., 46, quoting Max Weber, *The Agrarian Sociology of Ancient Civilizations*, trans. R. I. Frank (London: NLB, 1976), 366.
16. Gunther Roth and Wolfgang Schluchter, *Max Weber's Vision of History, Ethics and Methods* (Berkeley and Los Angeles: University of California Press, 1979), 195–201.
17. Mommsen, "Personal Conduct," 50.
18. Ibid.
19. Jürgen Habermas, *Theorie des kommunikativen Handelns* (Theory of communicative action) (Frankfurt: Suhrkamp Verlag, 1981); and Jürgen Habermas, *Erläuterungen zur Diskursethik* (Explanations about *Diskursethik*) (Frankfurt: Suhrkamp Verlag, 1991).

*2.12*

# Rudolf Steiner: History as Development toward Emancipation and Freedom

*Claus Otto Scharmer*

## BIOGRAPHY

Rudolf Steiner was born in Kraljevec, Hungary (today former Yugoslavia), on February 27, 1861. His parents came from Austria and he was the first of three children. His father was an official at the Austrian Railway Corporation. In his childhood and youth, Steiner lived in several small villages in Hungary and Austria. Having passed the final examination at school with honors in 1879, Steiner moved to Vienna and studied mathematics, physics, chemistry, and biology at the Technische Universität Wien.

In 1883, the twenty-two-year-old Steiner was appointed to edit the natural science branch of Goethe's writings for *Kürschners Nationalliteratur* (Kürschner's National Literature). In 1890, Steiner moved from Vienna to Weimar, where he worked at the *Goethe-Schiller-Archiv*. During this time he got to know, among others, Ernst Haekel and Friedrich Nietzsche. In 1891, he earned a Ph.D. at the University of Rostock with a thesis on epistemology with special reference to the work of the German philosopher J. G. Fichte.

In 1897, Steiner left Weimar and went to Berlin. He became a teacher of rhetoric and history at the *Arbeiterbildungsschule* (School for Workers), founded by Wilhelm Liebknecht, and he worked for the *Magazin der Literatur* (Journal of Literature). He moved in the circles of intellectuals and artists of those days and got to know, among others, Rosa Luxemburg, Else Lasker-Schüler, and Stefan Zweig. Steiner, however, not only got recognition for his work and ideas; in fact, he had to face strong opposition among the intellectual circles he moved in.

The basic idea of his approach was already pointed out in his *Philosophy of Freedom*, published 1894, and referred to as the "principal work" by Steiner himself throughout his life. This approach is based on the epistemological distinction between observance and thinking as the two elementary components of cognition. The very first step towards such a *Geisteswissenschaft* (humanities) is the observation of one's own thinking. The basic difference between the observation of one's own thinking and the observation of all other perceptions is that normal perceptions are based on things that already exist, whereas one's own thinking is produced by the individual himself. In the former case it is only possible to get an outside perspective, in the latter case we can have both an outside and an inside perspective because our thinking is part of the observation; that is, produced by ourselves. This is the keystone in Steiner's philosophy: The claim that (scientific) cognition is not only based on sensual perceptions, but also on nonsensual perceptions with the observance of the thinking ("thinking of the thinking") as the point of departure.

Of course, this type of *Geisteswissenschaft* is "nonscientific" from the viewpoint of today's science in one very important respect: You cannot prove the results of your research by referring to data based on sense perceptions. The only way to verify or falsify the results from Steiner's *Geisteswissenschaft* is to go the way of inner development (of thinking) that enables the individual to have the kind of supersensory perceptions Steiner was talking about. According to Steiner, this way of development is possible for everybody who exercises the necessary training of thinking. Taking this into account, plus the fact that Steiner did basic studies in all cultural branches of his time—natural sciences, math, philosophy, literature, history, and cultural history—it is not surprising that Steiner encountered resistance to his approach.

In 1904, Steiner was fired from the school, very much to the regret of his numerous students, because his teaching of history did not fit at all into the mainstream of Marxist thinking in the institution. Having faced this resistance against his approach in many intellectual groups, Steiner turned away from these circles and addressed himself to new audiences more open to his ideas at the beginning of the twentieth century, such as the Theosophical Society (founded by H. P. Blavatsky in 1875). Steiner joined this organization in 1902 and was appointed head of the German section of the organization in the same year. After increasing differences between Steiner and the international representatives of the Theosophical Society, Steiner and his second wife to be, Marie von Sivers, left the Theosophical Society and founded the Anthroposophical Society in 1913.

In 1902, Steiner started to give an increasing number of lectures each year all over Europe. It was calculated that he gave a total of 6,000 lectures throughout his life.

Having originated several new approaches in architecture and art from 1907 to 1913, Steiner, as an outcome of his anthroposophic research, founded numerous movements for the restructuring of economical, political, and cultural life between 1917 and 1924. These include the following: politics (the threefold social organism, 1917), education (foundation of the Waldorf School movement, 1919), medicine (fundamentals for an extended medicine, 1920), religion (assistance to the foundation of the "Christian Community," 1922), therapeutic pedagogy (foundation of a new therapeutical pedagogic movement, 1924), and agriculture (foundation of the biologic-dynamic way of agriculture, 1924). Each of these movements can be seen as a response to the disenchantment (*Entzauberung*) with our world and an attempt to reverse the general shift of increasing rationalization by developing a fundamentally new culture of working and living with a move towards a more human-based perspective of development.

Each of these movements is based on the principle that appropriate action and performance in each field of society is impossible without the consideration of the sensual reality as well as the conditions of the spiritual reality. Thus, he tried to make spiritual knowledge practical and useful for daily life.

Today, it can be said that each of these movements has been developed with increasing success throughout the twentieth century except for one: the movement for the restructuring of society—politics as the threefold social organism. This very first movement was a total failure. But it should be seen as by far the most important one, because only the idea of the threefold social organism gives the total picture of a social organism inside of which the others are referred to as elements. In fact, it might even be said that the foundation of the other movements by Steiner was partly a reaction to the fact that the first one had failed.

Steiner developed the idea of the threefold social organism during World War I in 1917. He proposed to stop the war with a peace proposal combined with a total reconstruction of the German nation-state in the direction of functional decentralization. He said that in modern society three partly autonomous subsystems can be distinguished: culture (including sciences, arts, and religions), politics, and economy. For each of these subsystems he demanded self-governance according to principles that are adequate for this particular system (freedom in culture, equality and democracy in politics, responsiveness and brotherhood in economy).

After two unsuccessful attempts to convince key politicians, Steiner and a small group of supporters started a large political campaign for his ideas of social restructuring. This third attempt also failed. Having realized this, Steiner switched his activities toward the founding of the movements for education, medicine, therapeutic pedagogy, arts, and agriculture.

In 1923, he founded the *Freie Hochschule für Geisteswissenschaft* (Free University of Humanities) in Dornach, Switzerland, an international center for research and education in the various branches of anthroposophic *Geisteswissenschaft*. Steiner died on March 30, 1925 in Dornach.

## THE UNITY OF THE WORLD AS BASIC DOCTRINE

The major doctrine in Steiner's philosophical approach is his monistic view of the world. As opposed to all dualistic approaches, which claim the independent existence of a spiritual world besides the sensual world, as can be seen in the Occidental tradition since Plato (reality and ideas, body and mind), Steiner sees the world as one holistic unit in which material and spiritual reality are mutually interwoven modes of existence that can be transformed into one another.

One point of departure for Steiner's approach is the separation of recognizing the subject and the recognized object as a fundamental experience of man found in the Occident. He saw this alienation between individual and world as a basic fact of modern history. Religion (in latin, *religare*, meaning "to relink") is in his view the attempt to overcome this separation. Anthroposophy (wisdom about Man) is tilling in the same field. The difference is, according to Steiner, that it is not based on belief and faith, as religion is, but on the development of consciousness and thinking. Thus, the individual has the capacity to overcome the separation by way of entering the world with the subject-based thinking in order to complete both outside perspective (reality) and inside perspective (idea) to a new unity.

## THE STAGES OF MACROEVOLUTION

Steiner sees the evolution of the universe, men, and nature as one unified process that is divided into four major periods. In the first planetary stage of evolution, every being, today divided into minerals, plants, animals, and human beings, had the same level of development. Within this first period some beings separated themselves from further development. The outcome of this stage of development is what today (in the fourth period) we see as the physical world (in nature) and as the physical body (of man). Those beings which separated themselves within the first period appear in the fourth period only with one body on earth: their "physical body." These beings are referred to as (the world of) minerals.

In the second planetary stage, beings developed a second body, which was added to the first one they had developed in the previous stage. In this stage too, some beings separated themselves from further development. The outcome of this period is (from today's perspective) in nature the living, and in man the "body of life" ("etheric body"). Those beings which separated themselves in the second period exist today only with two bodies on earth: their physical and their life-body. These beings are referred to as (the world of) plants.

In the third planetary stage of evolution, beings developed a third body. Again, some beings separated themselves from the rest. Today's outcome of this period is the mental world in nature and the mental body ("body of soul") in man. Those beings who separated in the third period exist today with three bodies on earth: a physical body, a body of life, and a mental body. These beings are referred to as (the world of) animals.

In the fourth planetary stage of evolution, human beings developed a fourth body: the "I" (self, *Ich*). As mentioned, besides the humans there also exist beings with three bodies (animals), two (plants), and one in the physical world, together referred to as nature.

Thus, we can summarize Steiner's perspective as follows. Until today the macroevolution consisted of four stages. In each stage, beings developed an additional form of what is called the human body. Thus, today the human being is defined as having four different, integrated bodies. Nature is the existence of beings that were, in former stages, at the same level of development with those beings that mankind is today. Because they separated themselves during one of the former stages of evolution (which was, so to speak, a sacrifice for further human development), their conscience today is not in the physical world (as a human's is) but somewhere in the spiritual world.

For the future, Steiner sees three further stages of evolution. In these stages human beings (may) develop a fifth (*manas*, mind), sixth (*buddhi*, intuitive), and seventh (*atma*, soul) body. These bodies are transformations from the first three bodies of man. The actor who (may) perform this transformation is the fourth body of man: the I.

Thus, the total picture of Steiner's concept of macroevolution is seven stages of development, seven stages of consciousness, and seven bodies of men. Three of them were developed in the past, the fourth one is developing in the present, and three more will be developed in the future (as transformations of the first three stages or bodies). In each stage of development, human beings have special tasks to cooperate in a sort of coevolutionary process with the beings that are referred to as nature.

## REINCARNATION AND KARMA

The core concept for the understanding of Steiner's view on evolution and history is the doctrine of reincarnation and karma. This concept is fundamental because it links the history of the individual (biography) with the history of humankind (macrohistory) with the history of the earth (macroevolution).

Reincarnation means rebirth and karma means (in Steiner's concept) fate, which is built by the higher I (self), on the basis of former actions and future destinies, in such a way that it is open for possibilities. Due to his freedom, man can ignore these possibilities or use them. Here lies a slight difference from some Oriental karma concepts, which may come closer to the idea that former actions determine present life. An often-used comparison says that reincarnation and karma link the different lives of a human being much like the days of a lifetime are linked by sleep during the night. One obvious consequence of this concept is that humankind today is partly the same as the humankind of former times. Studying history does not mean studying the history of somebody else, but studying the history of ourselves, of our previous lives.

Steiner uses the concept of reincarnation not only for humans, but also for our planet, the earth, and our planetary system. According to his writings, our current planetary system has existed only since the fourth period of evolution. In each previous stage, this system had a completely different existence, and between each of these periods there was a time in which the system had no physical existence ("eternity"). Thus, the concept of reincarnation is applied to the individual (history) as well as to the planetary system (macro- or cosmic evolution).

## THE STAGES OF MACROHISTORY

The Steinerian concept of evolution is, as mentioned, based on seven planetary or consciousness stages. Each of this stages consists of seven "rounds," which each consist of seven "globes," which each consist of seven "ages," which each consist of seven "cultural periods." In other words, evolution of mankind includes $7^1$ (7) planetary stages, $7^2$ (49) rounds, $7^3$ (343) globes, $7^4$ (2,401) ages, and $7^5$ (16,807) cultural periods.

The development of the present stage (earth) has included mainly a kind of repetition of the former stages. Within the fourth age (atlantic age), the human beings developed their fourth body (I). The fifth age (postatlantic age) is the present one. Like all other ages it is divided into seven cultural periods. It began with the ancient Indian period (around 7000 B.C.), followed by the ancient Persian period (around 5000 B.C.), the Egypt–Chaldean period (around 3000 B.C.), and the Greco–Roman period (around 750 B.C.). The current period began in the fifteenth century. In each of these periods, development of mankind focuses on a particular quality of mind, and in each time period there exists one civilization which plays a leading role in this development.

In terms of figures, we can express the whole macroevolution as a development from (1.1.1.1.1), the beginning of the first stage, to (7.7.7.7.7), the very end of the seventh stage. Talking about the current macro stage (earth) means talking about a period from (4.1.1.1.1) until (4.7.7.7.7). The current position within this system is (4.4.4.5.5).

## HISTORY AS A DEVELOPMENT TOWARD EMANCIPATION AND FREEDOM

The Steinerian system of macroevolution dwarfs other gigantic schemes, such as that of Karl Marx. One aspect, for example, is the role of the different spiritual beings of the universe. These beings, to put it simply, go through a similar development as human beings do in the whole process and their development is highly interwoven with the human development.

This leads us to a question: What is the wide goal for the "project mankind?" Steiner says, "Those who are Gods today were once human beings, and man will develop towards divine nature in the future. The human being is a God to be and the Gods are nothing but men, which have reached perfection."[1]

The major difference between other spiritual hierarchies and the human being is, according to Steiner, that the latter have become emancipated so far from the spiritual world that they have reached freedom of choice in where they want to direct their further development. This makes the human being unique in the whole evolutionary process. As a consequence, the perspective for future development described is only one possible path that exists for mankind.

Steiner is consistent in his approach. The individual human being is the center of the universe. He is the smallest spiritual unit in the universe; at the same time, as an independent variable of development and history, he is endowed with the potential to become the highest.

## DEVELOPMENT PERSPECTIVE: REVOLUTION FROM INSIDE

The development perspective given by Steiner is based on the spiritually enabled individual; on the capacity to transform reality—the reality of the self as well as the reality of the world. Like Mahatma Gandhi, who developed a new theory of power based on power over oneself (as opposed to power over others), Steiner tried to overcome the iron cage of modernity (Max Weber) by giving a methodology for inner, self-transforming development of man as a point of departure for the foundation of a new culture.

If we look at the activities of the anthroposophical movement today (Waldorf Schools, biodynamic farms, etc.), one may say that they are good at "processes" and at the micro level (projects), but they are weak at "structure" and at the macro level. This is a difficult point, but it does not necessarily count for Steiner, who made major efforts in the political field, and got little support from the anthroposophists.

## THE SYMPTOMATOLOGIC APPROACH: STEINER'S HISTORIC METHOD

Steiner referred to his methodology for historic cognition as a "symptomatologic" approach. Historic facts are not history but just the dead body of history. The symptomatologic approach tries to perceive the underlying stream of the evolution of world history. He saw matter-oriented history as an external perspective on world history and the symptomatologic approach as inner perspective to world history. Thus, the symptomatologic methodology looks at events and actions of groups or individuals, asking what kind of deeper shifts and flows are speaking with the voice of the actions, mostly without the conscious knowledge of the performing actors.

Symptomatologic history is comparable with the idealistic and the morphologic approaches in the sense that all of them talk about an evolution of spirit and mind through history. But unlike those two, the symptomatologic approach focuses on individuals and their connection to certain spiritual impulses or underlying flows.

Thus, we can conclude that Steiner's perspective on the macrohistoric process was linearly based, although there exist numerous cyclical components within his generally linear perspective. The existence of both, the idea of progress and the idea of a final aim and stage (which can be reached by humankind), fulfills both criteria of our definition for a macrohistorian with a basically linear perspective.

## NOTE

1. Kurt E. Becker, *Anthroposophie—Revolution von Innen, Leitlinien im Denken Rudolf Steiner's* (Anthroposophie—Revolution from within, guidelines in thinking of Rudolf Steiner's thinking) (Frankfurt: Verlag Freies Geistesleben, 1988), 30.

## 2.13

## Oswald Spengler: The Maturation and Decay of Cultures

Sohail Inayatullah

### BIOGRAPHY

Oswald Spengler (1880–1936) was born in Blankenburg, Germany. He was the son of a postal official and attended Munich, Berlin, and Halle Universities. His primary training was in mathematics, but he also had a vast understanding of the natural sciences. He first worked as a school teacher, but by 1911, gave up teaching to study and write history. In general, little is known of Spengler; indeed, according to Edwin Franden Dakin, Spengler obscured all facts about his life, stating only that his family was engaged in the mining business.[1]

Spengler was thirty-eight when the first volume of *The Decline of the West* was published, although he began thinking about the idea of the book seven years earlier. With few public records to describe his life, there are only the conflicting words of acquaintances. One shows him "carrying his precious manuscript around with him even while in war service, adding to it slowly."[2] Others deny he was in the service. Others remember him living "in a cold, dark tenement, eating in cheap restaurants frequented by laborers, trying to find a publisher."[3] In general, he lived the life of an artist and intellectual. Spengler's work was not that of a revolutionary; rather, it was a text that laid bare the truth of history and the rise and fall of cultures.

Spengler wrote at a time when progress, democracy, and causality were not to be questioned. The West was civilization. To assert that the West had reached its completion, that it had finished the life history of its soul, was a radical statement. Moreover, to state that different cultures where equal in their history and followed a similar pattern directly confronted the highly Eurocentric views of the day. Spengler was a cultural relativist at the time when the West was unquestionably supreme. There was no Third World movement, no deconstruction of reality, no quantum physics. Yet, at the same time, in German academic and bourgeois circles there was a sense of cultural despair, a sense that something was wrong with industrialism and rationality, that somehow the nobler part of the past had been lost with modernity. From this conflicting environment, Spengler produced a new theory of history that developed a science of history while simultaneously arguing that history was art, interpretation, and poetry.

Spengler's contribution was a new perspective on history, the use of a new unit of analysis, and the placement of this unit in a lifecycle (again echoing the "evolutionary" spirit of the time). Spengler also had stages: Once a culture was born, it went from its cultural phase to its civilization phase; from city to megalopolis; from feudalism to aristocracy to the bourgeois to the mass and then to the rise of the new Caesars. This unfolding of culture was isomorphic with the unfolding of the individual. "Morphologically, the immense history of a ... culture is the exact equivalent of the petty history of the individual man, or of the animal, or of the tree, or the flower.... In the destinies of the several Cultures that follow upon one another is compressed the whole content of human history."[4]

In Spengler's theory, each of the world's great cultures—Egyptian, Chinese, Semitic, Indian, Magian (Muslim), Classical, and Western—underwent a similar life cycle that could be understood from the life cycle of the natural world. The pattern of the cultures, their history, and their soul could be intuited by the sensitive historian.

## TYPES OF HISTORY

Borrowing from Goethe, Spengler raises the key problem of the twentieth century as that of exploring "the inner structure of the organic units through and in which world history fulfils itself, to separate the morphologically necessary from the accidental, and, by seizing the purpose of events, to ascertain the languages in which they speak."[5]

As with other macrohistorians, Spengler wished to find the causes of historical change—"a metaphysical structure of historical humanity"—that was independent of outward social, political, and economic forms; the unchanging that could make sense of the changing.[6] Spengler searched for a "science" of society but not a science as Comte would define it, for the source of culture would always remain a metaphysical mystery. The true meaning of the culture could by understood by its corresponding mystical soul. While Comte rejected the search for a metaphysical interpretation of history, Spengler specifically rejected the positivistic notion of a science of history. For Spengler, science must be free of Darwinian causal and systematic influence.

Like other macrohistorians, Spengler tells us that his revelation is unprecedented. "The 'world-as-history' ... here is a new aspect of human existence on this earth [that] has not been realized, still less presented."[7] Still, the history of Spengler is not based on truth or falsity, but on levels of insights: superficial and deep. Spengler is not the scientist but the artist. According to him, "We must not lose sight of the fact that at bottom the wish to write history *scientifically* involves a contradiction. True science reaches just as far as the notion of truth and falsity have validity.... But real historical vision belongs to the domain of significances, in which the

crucial words are not 'correct' and 'erroneous,' but 'deep' and 'shallow.'
... Nature is to be handled scientifically. History poetically."[8]

This is similar to the Oriental notion of truth, such as that expressed by Ssu-Ma Ch'ien. In this view, there are levels of truth: The seer can see the more profound levels of history and thus illumine the past so that it can teach the people of the present. In addition, truth for Spengler is closer to *understanding* in the hermeneutic sense rather then *explanation* in the positive-empirical sense. For Spengler, "it is the method of living into (*erfülen*) the object as opposed to dissecting it."[9]

Spengler continues this notion of history as insight by dividing history into two types. The first is the Ptolemaic system of history, which is primarily linear and causal and divides history into three phases: ancient, medieval, and modern. This history is Eurocentered, and even when European philosophers moved out of the explanatory scientific model (Herder, Kant, and Hegel), they remained within the threefold division.

However, Spengler presents an alternative Copernican view. He writes, "I see, in place of that empty figment of one linear history ... the drama of a number of mighty Cultures, each springing with primitive strength from the soil of a mother-region to which it remains firmly bound through its whole life-cycle; ... each having its own idea, its own passions, its own life, will and feeling, its own death. Here the Cultures, people, languages, truths, gods, landscapes bloom and age as the oaks and the stonepines, the blossoms, twigs and leaves."[10]

But there is no aging of humankind. This macro unit of analysis does not exist for Spengler. Spengler then asserts, again, countering Eurocentric thought (or any universalizing thought), "Each Culture has its own new possibilities of self-expression which arise, ripen, decay and die to never return. There is *not* one sculpture, one painting, one mathematics, one physics, but many, each in its deepest essence different from the others, each limited in duration and self-contained, just as each species of plant has its peculiar blossoms or fruit, its special type of growth and decline."[11]

## THE LIFECYCLE OF CULTURES

In this sense, each culture is a separate person with its own equally valid view of the real. For Spengler, culture truly is his unit. And there are many cultures, each with its own pattern, each following a general overall pattern—birth, growth, maturity, and death.

These stages are also analogous to the seasons. Spring is the beginning (birth and infancy), followed by summer (youth), then autumn (maturity), and finally winter (old age and decay). This is the classic Hindu pattern of the decline of culture from the golden age (spring), to the silver (summer), to the copper (autumn), and finally to the iron (winter). History then degenerates. While at one level this is cultural pessimism, at the same time it depends which culture one is in, the rising culture or the declining culture. Spengler would even object to the use of the word decline; rather it is the maturation of the culture, the setting of the sun, the arrival of winter—a natural but not necessarily depressing event.

Thus, Spengler does not see one grand culture, nor does he write about the development of a unified human culture or the history of being in search of itself like other mystical spiritual writers. Spengler is Western. This is not transcendental history. Just as there are many individual souls there are individual cultures. For the Chinese, the dynasty is replicated in the heavens and in the world; for the Indian, there is eventually one grand soul that unites existence; but for the Westerner—Spengler—there are many separate souls and thus separate cultures.

The crucial distinction for Spengler is between culture and "civilization." For Spengler culture is a unique creation of various cosmic forces which eventually degenerates into civilization, meaning big-city life dominated by the desire for money. Once this stage is reached, then death will certainly follow. Culture begins not with struggle or unity, as with Khaldun, but with the awakening of a great soul. In Spengler's words, "A culture is born in the moment when a great soul awakens out of the protospirituality of ever-childish humanity and detaches itself, a form from the formless, a bounded and mortal thing from the boundless and enduring. It blooms on the soil of an exactly definable landscape, to which plant-wise it remains bound. It dies when this soul has actualized the full sum of its possibilities in the shape of the peoples, languages, dogmas, arts, states, sciences and reverts into the protosoul."[12]

Thus, as with Hegel, the relationship between history and the great individual is central. But whereas Hegel chooses the state as the unit of history, Spengler remains with culture (although the state is important). However, for both, the passionate struggle for existence and the movement toward the ideas is central. As Spengler writes, "Its living existence, the sequence of great epochs which define and display the stages of fulfillment, is an inner passionate struggle to maintain the Idea against the powers of chaos without and the unconscious muttering deep down within."[13]

Each culture has a prime characteristic symbol. The classical Greek culture is represented by the body, the Chinese culture by the tao (the indefinable way), and Western culture by pure and limitless space (expansion). In addition, there are specific types of art, music, and literature that reflect each culture. These are the works that define the formative and climax phases of the culture and capture its spirit. It is through art, the unconscious, and the myths that create our dramas that we can understand history, not through a scientific objectification of history.

Each culture is a vast system in which the parts relate and can only be understood by the larger pattern. Each culture then exists in its own cosmology. Culture understood in this way follows the ordering of the classic episteme, wherein the universe is symmetrically balanced: as above as below, as within as without. The person, the social, and the cosmic can be understood as parts of the larger whole. When one dimension is perfectly understood, the whole reveals itself.

## STAGES OF HISTORY

Like many other macrohistorians, Spengler gives us stages for his scheme. The first is preculture, the second is culture (which is divided into early and late), and the third is civilization. In the preculture stage, "there are no classes, no mass, no state, no politics"; an existence of tribes and peoples without politics and the state.[14] This is obviously Khaldun's early Bedouin stage, Sarkar's early worker phase, and Marx's early communism. These precultures are the basis from which cultures can develop. Why some develop and others do not Spengler leaves to cosmic forces, in contrast to Toynbee, who argues for the right mix of challenge and response. The development of culture is characterized by the emergence of two classes, the nobility and the priests (A.D. 900 to 1500 for the West).

However, over time, the culture passes into its late culture phase, wherein the idea of the state and national government are realized. At this point, the next class emerges: the bourgeois, or the capitalist class. In the late period, the idea of the state is actualized and the bourgeoisie emerge (1500–1800). According to Sorokin in his interpretation of Spengler, "urban values replace agricultural ones. Money emerges victorious over landed property and values."[15] Also at this time, money and democracy are destroyed from within. At the beginning, democracy is controlled by the intellect; soon, however, money buys votes. In Spengler's words, "Through money, democracy becomes its own destroyer, after money has destroyed intellect."[16]

It is this money spirit that leads directly to overextension, to an overweighted central unproductive superstructure. This money spirit does not distinguish between capitalism and socialism; for Spengler, both were dominated by a materialistic, money-oriented interpretation of life. This money spirit leads to imperialism (the need to extract further material and cultural wealth) and is harbinger of the decline of culture. It was the decline of the Egyptian, Greco-Roman, Indian, and Chinese cultures.

Mass civilization—people without spirit, individuality, and inner life—emerges where the money spirit is triumphant. For the West, this started in the eighteenth century and will continue for another 400 years, with the last two hundred dominated by Caesars, the strong force that can conquer money.

Civilization thus emerges from culture. This emergence is inevitable just as decay is inevitable. Spengler places this simple pattern of degeneration onto the landscape of history such that with Western culture, for example, the Romans become the natural successors of the Greeks (the decline of the Greek soul to the Roman intellect). By the twentieth century, culture has become civilization. There is only death to look forward to. In this late stage, the balanced state ends, as Mosca writes.[17] No longer are the nobility, clergy, and bourgeoisie in a unified state. At this stage of civilization, the fourth class develops, the mass. There is no cycle nor spiral, only death.

Spengler does not relate this, however, to prehistory as cyclical theorists would. The city develops into the megalopolis. In these world cities, there is no home. Instead of folk, there is mob. In Spengler's words,

> Its [the mass'] uncomprehending hostility to all the traditions representative of the Culture (nobility, church, privileges, dynasties, convention in art and limits of knowledge in science), the keen and cold intelligence that confounds the wisdom of the peasant, the new found naturalism that in relation to all matters of sex and society goes back far to quite primitive instincts and conditions, the reappearance of the *panem et circenses* in the form of wage disputes and sports stadia—all these things betoken the definite closing down of the Culture and the opening of quite a new phase of human existence.[18]

With this grand size, there is a revolution and anarchy. Clearly, Sarkar's workers' revolution is Marx's proletarian revolution or Sorokin's stage of chaos. In Sorokin's interpretation, "Just as in the late period of culture, money becomes victorious over aristocratic politics and values, so now the politics of rude force triumphs over money and the money policies of the bourgeoisie."[19] Once power is consolidated in a Caesar-like rule (Toynbee's Universal State), a new religiosity develops (Toynbee's Universal Church). For Sarkar, this is the next cyclical transition from the warrior era to the intellectual era. For Spengler, this is already the end—there is no cycle, simply the last breath of a dying culture—although, as with Khaldun, there is often a brilliant moment in which it appears that all is well and the culture is in bloom, but, in fact, death is near.

Thus, World War I became not an event to be understood by economic discourse or a strategic viewpoint, rather it is "the type of *historical change of phase* occurring with a great historical organism of definable compass at the time preordained for it hundreds of years ago."[20]

## FINAL COMPARISONS

Khaldun, like Spengler, sees city life and civilization as part of decline and not part of progress, but he is not concerned with art and the biological metaphor but with unity, power, and legitimacy. The group with *asabiya* grows and eventually the dominant group takes over and establishes a dynasty, but over time there is degeneration. It is inevitable. The links to Toynbee are also obvious: both use civilizations/cultures as their units of analysis; both see the arrival of the universal state (the Caesars) not as the culmination of civilization, as many do, but as an indicator of the coming decline. While the similarities with Sarkar's work are striking, Sarkar does not use culture as his key variable. It is not culture which rises and falls. Moreover, no civilization must necessarily die by itself. Civilizations can be regenerated by spiritual forces, or they can be vanquished by external forces if they are weak in some major areas (a universal social outlook, for example).

The importance of Spengler is in his placing history in a life cycle, his use of culture as his unit (thus allowing a cultural relativity), his questioning of progress, his critique of the classic order of history of ancient, medieval, and modern, and his questioning of democracy as the final political structure. While his predictions appear possible (depending on one's reading of the West and other cultures), Dakin sums up his work as follows: "Whatever may be the final reputation of Oswald Spengler, whatever the fate of his philosophy or predictions, ... whether or not his theories correspond to reality, he painted a world panorama that, like a great play or a great symphony, is its own justification for existence."[21]

Spengler's influence on modern social thinking is considerable, so much so that the discourse of decline, especially of the West, has become a common phrase in our language, used and reused at popular and scholarly levels. What Spengler perhaps did not see is the possibility of cultural synthesis in the next century in the development of a global human culture, but given his metaphor of the individual soul and the cultural soul, we should not be surprised. His method does not allow for it. But his method does reveal to us the differences and similarities in cultures and the patterns that they tend to follow through time.

## NOTES

1. Oswald Spengler, *Today and Destiny*, intro. Edwin Franden Dakin (New York: Alfred A. Knopf, 1940), 353.
2. Ibid., 354.
3. Ibid.
4. Oswald Spengler, *The Decline of the West*, trans. Charles Atkinson (New York: Alfred A. Knopf, 1962), 104.
5. Ibid., 105.
6. Ibid., 3.
7. Ibid., 7.
8. Quoted in Patrick Gardner, ed., *Theories of History* (Glencoe, Ill.: The Free Press, 1959), 198.
9. Quoted in Amitai Etzioni and Eva Etzioni-Halevy, eds., *Social Change* (New York: Basic Books, 1973), 20.
10. Gardner, *Theories of History*, 194.
11. Ibid.
12. Etzioni and Etzioni-Halevy, *Social Change*, 21.
13. Ibid.
14. Pitirim Sorokin, *Sociological Theories of Today* (New York: Harper and Row, 1966), 192.
15. Ibid., 193.
16. Ibid., 196.

17. Gaetano Mosca, *The Ruling Class*, trans. Hannah Kahn, intro. Arthur Livingston (New York: McGraw-Hill, 1939).
18. Spengler, *Decline of the West*, 25–26.
19. Sorokin, *Sociological Theories*, 194.
20. Spengler, *Decline of the West*, 37.
21. Spengler, *Today and Destiny*, 364.

## 2.14

## *Pierre Teilhard de Chardin: Universal Personalization*

*Daniela Rocco Minerbi*

### BIOGRAPHY

Pierre Teilhard de Chardin was born on May 1, 1881, in Orcines, France. The son of a noble and the great grandniece of Voltaire, he loved nature, particularly minerals and stars, and was tutored at home in a very religious Catholic family. As a child, he showed an unusual awareness of the corruptibility and nondurability of things. He studied with the Jesuits and became a member of the order in 1918. Even as a young pupil, his interest in rocks was very pronounced.[1]

Teilhard focused his attention on the natural sciences throughout his education. In England, he became acquainted with the thoughts of Henri Bergson. Back in France, after serving as a stretcher bearer in World War I, he obtained a doctorate in paleontology at the Sorbonne. Aside from a few visits elsewhere, he stayed in China from 1923 to 1945. The Catholic church authorities were suspicious of Teilhard's heretic evolutionistic ideas, so they did not allow most of his work to be published. In spite of that, he did not leave the church, and his secretary published his works after his death.[2] It was during his Chinese exile that he was involved in the project that led to the discovery of the "Peking Man" skull. Teilhard spent the last years of his life in the United States, where he met scientists with whom he was able to discuss his holistic ideas. He died in New York on Easter Sunday, April 10, 1955, at the age of seventy-four.

### INTELLECTUAL CONTEXT

Teilhard's contribution to knowledge is his research for a synthesis overcoming the dualism between matter and spirit. This dualism is reflected in all areas of knowledge: between science and religion, ontology and phenomenology, and space and time. Although he had been educated by the Jesuits in the dualistic philosophy of Thomism, he was committed to resolving this dichotomy. It was because of his departure from the scholasticism of Thomas Aquinas that the Catholic church banished his philosophical works.

Teilhard's philosophical predecessors were French spiritualists and idealists, derived from the German idealists Schopenhauer and Schelling. Teilhard was also well acquainted with Bergson's creative evolutionism. Teilhard integrated both Darwin's and Lamarck's evolutionistic views of adaptation and natural selection in his philosophy.[3] Teilhard's thought developed at the time in which quantum physics, Einstein's theory of relativity, and Abbe George Lamaitre's theory of an initial explosion causing the beginning of the universe were being formulated.

Teilhard was both a scientist and a priest, who could explain one field in terms of the other, and he searched for a unity of knowledge that could provide a key to the meaning of all reality. While science had brought the understanding of nature, religion provided a path toward spirituality, and biological science and the social sciences had deepened for him the understanding of humankind. But how could these separate truths, each in its own field, contribute to the understanding of each other, to the whole of knowledge, to the meaning of existence?

## TEILHARD'S THEORY OF KNOWLEDGE

Teilhard does not base his epistemology on deductive speculation, as is characteristic of the scholastic philosophy which aims at explaining reality through logical reasoning within the boundaries of preexisting dogmas. For Teilhard, the key to the comprehension of the universe consists in approaching it as an evolutionistic process. His view of the universe is not an ontological study of a static reality. By introducing the time dimension and conceiving the reality of the universe as a process, the reference point for all knowledge and the meaning of the universe must be found in the realization that the universe is engaged in a process of becoming. The future represents reality, being, truth, and the Omega point; the present represents a state of becoming and of reality in the making. Omega is the essence, the truth, and the absolute. The future, therefore, cannot be a becoming toward nothingness or toward extinction. This would make the universe, and man's existence in it, meaningless. So, the future must already exist; the Omega point, the fulfillment of the universe, must exist potentially.[4]

This dynamic view of the universe as a process allows Teilhard to develop a unitarian and teleological conception of reality. What resolves all the dichotomies and ties everything together is evolution. What gives meaning to the whole universe, to matter, to life, to human existence, and to the spirit is evolution. Teilhard's inquiry is then about the goal and the direction along which the universe moves. In conclusion, the meaning of human existence requires the understanding of the whole history of the universe. Teilhard explains the direction of evolution by means of phenomenological observations of the process and by a reference to a teleological point, the Omega point.[5]

## TEILHARD'S METHODOLOGY

Teilhard's methodology consists of a retrogressive phenomenological study observing how, throughout the whole time span of evolution, certain laws have been at work. His study goes backward to the beginning of the universe by projecting a film of the past, from the origin to the present, that shows the form and direction of evolution so as to anticipate the trend for the future.

Evolution happens according to a dialectic that Teilhard refers to as the law of recurrence. The moments of the dialectic show up as "divergence," arrangements of few elements into a multitude of different new combinations; as "convergence," the union of diverse elements on the same level of evolution; and as "emergence," new elements which are more complex than their components.

A law of increasing complexity and centricity applies to each stage of the process of evolution, and each particular stage is unrepeatable. Evolution tends toward the spirit, toward a maximum point of complex matter. Complexification is the condition for spiritualization of matter; in fact, there is a correlation between complexification, organization of matter around its center, and cerebration; between cerebration and development of consciousness; between consciousness and reflection; and between reflection and spirit. This process of transformation requires energy, which acts both externally as a force of necessity, and internally as a sense of affinity or sympathy. The two aspects of energy Teilhard refers to are "tangential" energy, which is physical, and "radial" energy, which is psychic and spiritual.[6]

## HISTORY OF THE UNIVERSE: EVOLUTION AND ITS STAGES

The origin of the universe consists in its materialization, or condensation of a self-subsistent potentiality. Teilhard assumes the existence of a force of attraction in the universe. There is a center which is also the origin, because it provides the impetus and the goal, and because it is the point of attraction of everything else. It is also a force, an energy. This center exists through the process of creation which also means condensing, unifying, and organizing. Being itself means creating, and to create is the dynamic aspect of being. To be and to create are not two distinct moments. The opposite of existing–creating–unifying is nonexistence–dissociation–disaggregation and multiplicity.

To say that the universe is created from nothingness (*ex nihilo*) means that it started from a state of infinite and infinitely disassociated multiplicity, having within itself the potential and the desire (the force of attraction) for being created; the precreational universe seems to have been an unstable nothingness—a plea for being. *Welstoff*, the stuff of the universe, is simultaneously spirit and matter; it is spiritual matter or material spirit. Pure matter does not exist; the moment it appears it is already spiritual because of the spirit, or force of attraction, which allows the creatable multiplicity–nothingness to condense.[7]

The observation of the stages of development of the universe, from the formation of inorganic matter (geogenesis), to the appearance of life (biogenesis), to the birth of reflective consciousness (noogenesis), and to the spirit (Christogenesis), has relevance for the understanding of the phenomenon of human life within the context of evolution, and an indication of what the future of humanity will be. However, since humanity constitutes that point at which evolution has acquired reflective consciousness, it follows that human beings have acquired free will. That is, from now on the future of evolution lies in our own hands, because human beings are the makers of their own future. Their freedom will allow them to choose to act consonant with the trend evolution has exhibited up to the appearance of human beings; that is, in the direction of complexity–centricity–union or not. If this is the choice, then humanity will be heading toward a loving union of all humankind where the personality of each individual is enhanced and grows through the interaction with others. But if the individual, misinterpreting the concept of being human, confusing personal growth with individualism, and misinterpreting himself or herself as the final point of evolution chooses to pursue self-centered, individualistic aims—both in the form of individual and/or collective egotism, and avoiding or refusing the path toward greater complexity and union (the challenge entailed by the relationship with the rest of humankind)—then he will follow the path toward divergence, multiplicity, and simplicity; the path opposite from evolution, toward disintegration, entropy, and death.[8]

### Geogenesis

Geogenesis is the explanation of the initial materialization of the cosmos. After the condensation of the initial matter, atoms of the different chemical elements are formed according to the stated process of diversification, complexity, and inner organization. Formation of matter implies a growth in diversification, spread, and complexity; then, under certain unrepeatable conditions when the elements of the geosphere cannot grow anymore along those three parameters, evolution continues by taking up a new dimension.

### Biogenesis

The origin of life is not due to greater agglomeration of matter or growth of size. It is a function of growth of complexity. Biogenesis starts when the cell appears, marking the beginning of the biosphere. By the law of recurrence, life first proliferates, covering the geosphere; then it branches off in increasingly differentiated and complex organisms. Life is a tree, from the trunk of which the different types develop, more and more complex and organized.

When individual organisms have reached their definite form (at the end of their ramification), they tend toward each other and socialized life. A branch whose living elements have reached their ultimate identity may become extinct because of internal or external causes, or may branch out in a new organism that is more complex and organized. Any successive evolving ramification is characterized by a deeper and deeper degree of consciousness. In the zoological realm, evolution is manifested in the degree of cerebration and complexity of the nervous system. The brain is the material sign of consciousness.[9]

With anthropogenesis, a new branch shoots out from the tree of life, from the very beginning already qualitatively different because of the new acquisition: reflection; that is, consciousness of itself as a separate object. Reflection is not a change of degree, but a change of state. The law of recurrence is evident: Even consciousness cannot grow forever without changing state and becoming reflection.

## Noogenesis

Man's evolution is no longer in the biological and anatomical direction and proceeds, instead, in the growth of spontaneity, socialization, and culture. Besides biological inheritance, genetically transmitted at the individual level, another inheritance of collective nature is now bestowed upon man: culture, the accumulation of successive intelligences and memories. Noogenesis represents both the shift of evolution from the individual man to the whole human reality, and the shift from the anonymity of the individual creature to personalization. The personality is the unique way in which an individual organizes and unifies all experiences, all reflective activities, all perceptions, and all memories. Like all other species, mankind also goes through the stages of divergence: first, differentiation; second, individualization of the human being; and third, convergence, during which the growth in number and expansion of each individual entity within the finite space of the planet increases the pressure that brings about the necessity for a new synthesis and a new social arrangement. The last stage is the emergence of a new community which constitutes a new synthesis qualitatively different from the previous stage.[10]

The danger for society is the formation of a human mass neither harmonized nor in union, but depersonalized in a totalitarian sociopolitical system that acts as a mechanizing factor, in which the value of the individual is subordinated to the programming of the mass imposed from the outside. Totalitarianism is counterrevolutionary because it depersonalizes the human being to ensure social order. Personalization instead leads to socialization, both by bringing one individual in contact with another, and by spontaneously creating in the individual the desire for the encounter with the other. The two processes—growth of the individual (so that it becomes a person), and of socialization (so that it becomes part of a community)—are interdependent. Each personality becomes more itself and more distinct by the encounter with the other, not in spite of it. Two people in love become more whole the more they are lost in each other, but the higher the level of the union the greater their personal growth. "Union differentiates," and "union personalizes."[11]

### Christogenesis: The Omega Point

In the end, evolution will become a movement toward a harmonious and complex humanization of the earth. Omega, being the point of maximum centricity and union, is the point of complete personalization of all and each of the elements. The individual being becomes personal when it universalizes itself, and becomes fully human through the process of socialization when in true communication with others.

Evolution is eternal, or else what sense would it have? How could it be justified if the end is merely extinction? Moreover, since the trend of evolution is toward increasing spiritualization of matter, then the focus must also be spiritual; because the trend is toward union of all humanity and not toward individualism, and, at the same time, toward personality, it must be transpersonal and superpersonal. It must be a point which is personal, but transcending individual personality; it must be a focus completely loving, because love is the greatest expression of socialization; it must be completely spiritualized matter; and it must be already existing, immanent in man.[12]

The ultimate point or final state of the universe is called Omega. Omega has the characteristics of Christ. It will be a new emergence, unpredictable and undeductible because qualitatively different from what precedes it. For Teilhard, time is instrumental to a new emergence; time is convergent. This concept represents Teilhard's fundamental contribution to philosophical and scientific thought.[13]

## EVIL, SUFFERING, DEATH, AND IMPERFECTION IN AN EVOLUTION TOWARD LOVE

Evil is the trend toward disassociation, toward multiplicity, and toward matter. It is the trend in the opposite direction of evolution. The danger of branching off, rather than associating and organizing, is present at each level of evolution. The pull toward the two opposite directions of unity and multiplicity causes anguish. Teilhard believes that the temptation toward individualism, disassociation, and multiplicity, and the temptation to revolt against union and growth, increases with consciousness. As multiplicity is evolutionary evil, suffering is the experiencing of evil, and sin is the moral aspect of evil.[14] In an evolutionary sense, evil is destined to disappear because being antievolutionary it is on the path toward its own extinction.

Suffering is not useless: It has the role of motivating toward growth; it forces the human being out of his egocentrism; it can make the human being one with others; and it can super-center him or her on God. "Suffering stimulates, spiritualizes and purifies."[15]

The victims of suffering are those who pay the price for the evolution of all. Although they might appear inactive, they are the most active and most entrusted agents of human growth, spiritualization, and transformation, both because they compensate and pay for evolutionary imperfection and, unable to partake of the enjoyment of prevailing life, they have to participate in it by relying on higher forms of joy and love. There is enormous potential energy of growth in suffering. In order to harness and utilize this energy, sufferers must achieve consciousness of their suffering and channel it into a desire for global, social, and human transformation, "so that the world's pain might become a great and unique act of consciousness, elevation and union."[16]

Moral evil is counterevolution at the personal level, it is not acting in the direction of growth and unity; it is individualistic pursuit at the expense of the other. In evolutionary terms, evil is a steering toward multiplicity, nothingness, and extinction rather than association and union. Moral evil derives from man's misunderstanding of his highest position in evolution, which leads him to conceive of himself as an end rather than as the spearhead of evolution in whose hands lies the responsibility of evolution itself.

Suffering manifests itself in three modes corresponding to the three aspects of evolution: pain of plurality, pain of differentiation, and pain of metamorphosis. The pain of plurality is caused internally, within the human being, by the incompletedness of the internal physical order, and externally, among human beings, by the incompletedness of the union with others. The pain of differentiation results from the labor to resist entropy; it is the price of growth. The pain of metamorphosis is represented by death. Even the personality cannot grow indefinitely without changing state. Death is not the ultimate evil; it is transformation from a state of incomplete human evolution and incomplete union with the "other" to a state of spiritual union with others and with God. It obliges one to surrender all the results and conquests of one's whole lifetime.[17] Death is an ahistorical, transcendent change of state toward spiritual union, whereas the Omega point is a historical and evolutionary transformation.

## CONCLUSION

The evolution of the universe will end in Omega; the point of convergence of time, space, and energy. At the ultimate point of centricity, when no other syntheses are possible, the noosphere will be fully constituted by energy. At this point of synthesis, the convergence of time and space will take place; that is the end of time. Omega, involving time, space, and energy, is the point of super complexity, of super organization, and of complete centricity. Because of this convergence, in Omega occurs the release of an immense spiritual energy of love.

The "end of time" is the point at which the universe enters eternity, a fifth dimension whose advent can be predicted because of the recurrent working of the law of complexity and centricity, but whose characteristics cannot be foreseen. Although, according to the laws of thermodynamics, the universe has a tendency toward inertia, multiplicity, and states of higher entropy, and although a dissipation of energy occurs at each level of transformation in evolution, still the universe is not going toward extinction, but is evolving. On one side the universe tends toward increasing entropy, but on the other side the universe moves in the direction of complexification–centricity. It moves toward two opposite directions: entropy and life.

The trend toward life and consciousness is irreversible. Such irreversibility is obvious in the noosphere, where evolution becomes self-conscious and therefore cannot be acting incongruently toward self-extinction. Therefore, the noosphere must be eternal as Omega must be eternal. The term eternal refers to the new dimension that the universe acquires in converging into Omega. The end of the history of the universe implies the entrance of the universe into a new dimension, beyond the concept of time as known to the human being.[18]

In his writing, "Comment Je Vois" (As I see it), Teilhard expresses in four statements his entire belief system and philosophical conception:

> I believe that the evolution is toward the Spirit.
>
> I believe that the Spirit fulfills itself in a personal God.
>
> I believe that the supreme personality is the Universal Christ.
>
> I believe that the universe is in evolution.[19]

## NOTES

1. Claude Cuenot, *Teilhard de Chardin* (London: Collins, 1970), 3–4.
2. Sheila Marie Scheirer, *The World View of Pierre Teilhard de Chardin* (Ann Arbor, Mich.: University Microfilms International, 1980), 65–109.
3. Paul Maroky, ed., *Convergence* (Kerala, India: C. M. S. Press, 1981), 119–133.
4. Pierre Teilhard de Chardin, *The Future of Man* (New York: Harper and Row, 1964), 58, 228–231.
5. Eulalio Baltazar, *Teilhard and the Supernatural* (Baltimore: Helicon Press, 1966), 149–155.
6. Pierre Teilhard de Chardin, *The Phenomenon of Man* (New York: Harper and Row, 1961), 42–45, 254–263.
7. Pierre Teilhard de Chardin, *Writing in Time of War* (New York: Harper and Row, 1968), 93–114.

8. Teilhard de Chardin, *Phenomenon of Man*, 237–238, 263.
9. Ibid., 117–159.
10. Ibid., 178–277; Teilhard de Chardin, *Future of Man*, 262–274.
11. Teilhard de Chardin, *Phenomenon of Man*, 238–269.
12. Teilhard de Chardin, *Future of Man*, 119, 180–207.
13. Teilhard de Chardin, *Phenomenon of Man*, 259.
14. Teilhard de Chardin, *Writing in Time of War*, 92–102.
15. Ibid., 43, 68–71; Teilhard de Chardin, *Activation of Energy* (London: Collins, 1970), 248.
16. Teilhard de Chardin, *Human Energy* (New York: Harcourt Brace Jovanovich, 1969), 51.
17. Ibid., 50–88.
18. Teilhard de Chardin, *Phenomenon of Man*, 271, 237–303; Pierre Teilhard de Chardin, *The Vision of the Past* (New York: Harper and Row, 1966), 149; Teilhard de Chardin, *Future of Man*, 48, 65–66, 82–96, 155–184, 196–213.
19. George Magloire, *Teilhard de Chardin* (Paris: Nouvel Office D'edition, 1994), 222.

## 2.15

## Pitirim Sorokin: The Principle of Limits

*Johan Galtung*

### BIOGRAPHY

Pitirim Sorokin (1889–1968) was technically a Russian but actually a Komi from the vast part of Siberia east of the Urals. At the time of the October 1917 "socialist" revolution he was secretary to Kerenski, the head of the March 1917 "bourgeois" revolution. He was sentenced to death by the Bolsheviks, released, went to the United States (like Kerenski), and ultimately became a professor at Harvard University. There, he headed the Harvard Research Center in Creative Altruism, founded by the Lilly Endowment.

An extremely prolific writer, his major work in macrohistory remains his *Social and Cultural Dynamics*, published in four volumes, but also in a one-volume edition, which is cited here.[1] The following section summarizes the key concepts in his theory.

### CULTURAL MENTALITIES

Sorokin's unit of analysis is a system of culture, as opposed to what he calls "congeries," a mere hodge-podge of elements taken from anywhere and not expressing any coherent theme. He is interested in integrated systems, and more particularly in what he calls "types of culture mentality." What he does is to identify some types, asking thirteen questions of these cultural mentalities, characterizing them, and comparing them with each other. Sorokin's cultural mentalities, however, do not carry geohistorically identifiable names. They are "ideal types" in a Weberian sense, referred to as "ideational," "idealistic," and "sensate." Possible translations might be "spiritual," "eclectic/integrated," and "materialist," but only as a first approximation for the reader. Here, Sorokin's terms will be used. The following is a table of Sorokin's basic paradigms:[2]

| Cultural Mentality | Ideational (Ascetic) | Sensate (Active) | Idealistic |
|---|---|---|---|
| 1. Reality | transcendental | empirical | both |
| 2. Needs, ends | spiritual | manifold | both |
| 3. Satisfaction | maximum | maximum | great, balanced |
| 4. Methodology | self-modification | external modification | both ways |
| 5. *Weltanschauung* | being (*sein*) | becoming (*werden*) | both |
| 6. Power-object | self-control | external control | both |
| 7. Activity | introvert | extrovert | both |
| 8. Self | integrated spiritual | integrated materialist | both |
| 9. Knowledge | transcendental knowledge | empirical knowledge | both |
| 10. Truth | inner experience meditation intuition | observation, senses measurement inductive/deductive | both |
| 11. Moral values | absolute transcendental | relativistic utilitarian | both |
| 12. Aesthetic values | sacred art | secular art | both |
| 13. Social, practical values | those leading to ultimate reality: transcendental salvation | those leading to ultimate reality: wealth, comfort, prestige | both |

This is a very rich system, to be read vertically, horizontally, and in totality. Read vertically, the table communicates the content of the cultural mentalities along the thirteen dimensions. Read horizontally, the focus is on the considerable differences. As a totality, the table communicates deep perspectives in terms easily understood and recognized but more clearly put together by Sorokin than by most others.

The two types, the Ideational and the Sensate, stand forth clearly. I used the ideational–sensate dimensions as an explanatory variable in a study of early 1960s Sicily, a society divided between the two cultural mentalities.[3] Of course, asking respondents in three modest villages where they stood on these classical dimensions, taken by Sorokin from philosophical and sociological discourses, would make little sense. But the basic mentalities were expressed in terms of occupation and spheres of allegiance, with "priest/religious activities" being ideational and "engineer/improve village conditions" being sensate. In-between were "lawyer/family life" (more ideational) and "physician/oneself" (more sensate). Occupations were then presented in pairs, as were the spheres of allegiance, to make for all possible comparisons; in the end, two indices were constructed.

Even with such simple indicators it was possible to reproduce many of Sorokin's thirteen dimensions. Thus, most basically, the sensates wanted changes of the system in which they lived, and not only for themselves. In addition, the sensates had a much more developed social perspective, space perspective, and time perspective. The ideationals were more limited in the here and now, which is logical given their more transcendental orientation. The sensates see alternatives in this world, possibilities for themselves and for the villages. The ideationals assume external stability in the rhythms of the centuries and millennia (typically expecting as many children as God wants, while sensates want two).

From this description, one might believe the sensates to be the agents of change and the ideationals the reactionaries, one more variation of the theme of modern versus traditional. But it was not that simple, as underlined by some points in Sorokin's analysis.[4] As a matter of fact, there were two types of sensates: one located in the tertiary-high professional strata of the villages, and one in the primary-low, the landless labor. One might wonder about such a powerful potential alliance. But then the more egoistic aspects of the sensate orientation showed up: the sensates in tertiary-high wanted to migrate out of the villages to improve their personal conditions or that of the family, whereas those in primary-low were migrating into their own families and staying in the villages with the same goal in mind. Who identified with the village level? The ideational, not necessarily in the sense that they wanted to "improve the conditions," but in the sense that this was the place they were born and were going to spend their life energies of various kinds before the afterlife. The conclusion is ultrastability, among other reasons because tertiary-low and primary-high had no difficulty cooperating, as opposed to the others.

One is reminded of Arthur Koestler and the distinctions drawn in his essay, *The Yogi and the Commissar*.[5] There is the problem of applicability outside Western philosophies. The ideationals remind us of the Middle Ages, with many aristocrats trying to enact idealistic roles, and the sensates remind us of Antiquity and Modernity. But we can let that problem sleep. Sorokin provides sufficient similarity with non-Western philosophy to claim some kind of universality.

## DYNAMICS

What we have seen so far is a typology of cultural mentalities, recognizable and identifiable beyond Sorokin's terminology. But how does dynamism enter this typology? The answer is, of course, by conceiving of them as phases or stages in a historical diachrony. Like Marx before him or Sarkar after him, Sorokin postulates the order of the stages:

*Thesis #1,* The general sequence of social and cultural dynamics is ideational–idealistic–sensate–chaos, and back to ideational.

The dynamism is brought about as a result of

*Thesis #2, The principle of limits* Human beings have richer spectrums of needs than any sociocultural formation built around coherent themes can satisfy; their limits are their undoing.

A brief summary of the historical sequence according to Sorokin would run as follows. Humanity starts at a high pitch, ideational. This is the ascetic and spiritual heading for the transcendental. From Sorokin's writings, it looks like his sympathies were with this stage, or perhaps the next, the idealistic. However, human beings are too complex for the simplicity, however spiritually manifold, of this formation to give sufficient satisfaction to a sufficient number to ensure stability. For exceptional people there is no problem; for the majority, except for exceptional periods, this is a problem. And for the exceptionals there is a simple solution: the society within the society, the monastic order.

The result is a sliding movement, downhill from the spiritual heights of the ideational. Popes start putting on weight and everything becomes more material—more rounded, as it were. On the way down, there is the idealistic phase, but people may have the same problem as Sorokin in identifying that phase. Strictly speaking, it is not a stage but an eclectic/integrated in-between, in which both are approximately equally represented.

If we now assume that this phase is the "best of both worlds," then why does the idealistic phase not constitute a stable anchoring point for humanity? Probably because by that time the downward slide has come too far. Freud's superego–ego–id scheme is very useful here. In the ideational stage, superego dominates, ego is at its service, and id is suppressed. But id announces itself, superego weakens, and ego emerges as a synthesis, even transcending both in the idealistic phase, leading to strong, highly individualistic people with remarkably distinct profiles.

But the id appetites have been awakened. The ego is no longer steered by a strong superego and may want more. In the ensuing sensate stage, we then get the opposite of the ideational profile: id has the upper hand, ego is its obedient servant, and the superego control is disappearing. People become less individualistic and more similar, this time not striving for salvation in the transcendental but for satisfaction here and now.

The reason for the idealistic phase not being the permanent abode for humankind may be located exactly in its eclecticism. There will be strong forces in both directions, heading for the more consistent formations more dear to the logical mind. But the memories of the limits encountered in the ideational phase may still be vivid, deposited in the collective subconscious but easily retrieved. The sensate style of life remains to be tested; it is, literally speaking, alluring.

So down society goes, even quickly, into the materialism of the sensate "gutter," as Sorokin sometimes describes it. In the ideational phase there may certainly have been violent conflicts over which ideational orientation is valid. But in the sensate phase there is this problem plus the obvious problem of scarcity. If everybody is out to satisfy material needs there may not be enough to go around, and particularly not if nature's needs are to be respected (a less prominent perspective in Sorokin).

So society sinks even deeper, into chaos. The coherence and the residues of ideational–idealistic controls disappear and a grab-what-you-can mentality emerges—like people storming into supermarkets in the United States during a New York blackout or a Los Angeles riot, precisely grabbing what they can. Or, at a more personal level, what occurs is drinking and eating, fooling around and cheating on spouses, *carpe diem*, and respecting moral rules and laws only if the consequences of being caught are too unpleasant. From this position of utter depravity, with no dignity left, humanity arises again like a Phoenix from the ashes and reaches the spiritual heights of the ideational mentalities: energized again, ready to start afresh, and fully redeemed.

The question is, of course, where does the energy for that quantum jump, upward, against forces of moral gravity and depravity, come from?[6] A push and pull discourse can be used here, as for studies of migration between countries. Migration from one cultural mentality to the other, and, more particularly, the jump from chaos to ideational, would be motivated by disgust with oneself and with how the human condition has degenerated into nonhuman and even antihuman absurdities. There are also the pull forces, the longing for steering and guidance. Saul on the road to Damascus, in other words, only this time as a collectively shared experience. So up it goes, initiating the downhill slide again; only the last time may have been too long ago to serve as a reminder. The appropriate myth, then, is Sisyphus, not only the Phoenix.

## PROBLEMS

As usual with macrohistorians, the problems are numerous. The major problem seems to lie with the definition of a mentality which is not supposed to be a mere congerie: it must have logical consistency. The schemes in Sorokin's basic paradigms are admirably consistent. But who worries about that? According to the Laws of Thought in the Aristotelian tradition, contradiction is a "sin," or at least an error. A or non-A; *tertium non datur* (the excluded middle). But this is a dominant characteristic of the Occident; it is not found in the Daoist–Buddhist traditions so prominent in the Orient. To live with contradiction is considered a more normal human condition because all life is filled with contradictions. To search for the contradiction-free is to search for something nonexistent or bound to have limits. Consequently, Sorokin's principle of limits, a brilliant idea in its simplicity, certainly applies, but particularly well because Sorokin uses it on his own, to a large extent Western, constructs.[7]

Those interested in macrohistory not only to make sense of an enormous amount of historical data, but also for theories or for creating a better future, could draw a very simple conclusion from Sorokin's principle of limits. If each cultural mentality is too limited, and if there are good reasons for postulating a need for consistency, why not have several cultural mentalities inside the same society? In the present era of states, some of them even narrowing down to nation-states, this would mean inside the same country, with international borders.[8] When a person feels his or her personal limits have been reached, the time has come to move on to a new cultural mentality, in this life and in this country; in other words, a country with not only pluralism of ideas within the same culture and/or cultural pluralism within the same country, but structural pluralism within the same country. And that means structures so different that very different cultural mentalities can be lived within them, not only believed in.[9]

Sorokin seems to assume that everybody reaches the limit at the same time and that society can harbor only one sociocultural mentality. In that case, there are only two possibilities: migration to another country (Sorokin's own solution), or a convulsive transformation from one stage to the next.

Historical data seem to indicate that Sorokin is right: we did, indeed, have these transitions from sensate Antiquity to a more ideational Middle Ages, and from that period to a more sensate Modern Period. But the problem is that the finding is not easily replicated in the Orient, one interpretation being that it has a more eclectic, both and orientation. The Orient has more ability, in other words, to live both mentalities in the same life and within the same person, not only within the same country by migrating from one place to the other.[10]

## WORLD MACROHISTORY

There is a question which Sorokin does not seem to answer: What would a world macrohistory look like from his perspective? If all societies around the world are in synchrony, the same stage at the same time, then there is no problem. But what if the relation is asynchronic? How would ideational and sensate societies relate to each other? In the answer hides a tragedy masked as a riddle: How can such different mentalities relate at all, except by the sensate simply absorbing or crushing the ideational? There is an exception, of course: the ideational converting the sensates. While conversion is possible, it is not likely. Ideationals, fighting the temptation of the flesh all the time, know the sensates better than the other way round. The sensates do not listen to inner and remote voices until the sensate agenda has been exhausted, probably with a bang more than a whimper.

Unlike Marx, Sorokin did not have vast amounts of followers. But admirers may be found, not only for his gigantic intellectual sweep and erudition, but also for images of creative altruism. He has not suffered distortions from countless "Sorokinites" like Marx did, even in his lifetime. And yet he was also a prophet, like Marx. His message in the 1930s was doom and gloom, visioning not only a major war but also the extreme cruelty and the genocide that went with it. He lost to Talcott Parsons as the leading sociologist at Harvard, possibly the major blow in his eventful life. But then Parsons had a much more optimistic message than Sorokin: as a structural-functionalist, integration was not only a theoretical category but a practical possibility, with only small incremental adjustments needed. Sorokin was right, of course, but the world often demands hope, not only truth.

## NOTES

1. Pitirim Sorokin, *Social and Cultural Dynamics* (Boston: Porter and Sargent, 1970).

2. Ibid., 38–39; adapted from Table 1. The clearest, most extreme types of ideational and sensate are presented here; the formulations are abbreviations in order to be able to highlight the main points. The reader will benefit from consulting the original.

3. The results are reported in Johan Galtung, *Members of Two Worlds: A Development Study of Three Villages in Western Sicily* (Oslo: Universitetsforlaget, 1971). The data collection was carried out in 1960.

4. The author actually had the occasion to visit and discuss the findings with Sorokin at his home in Massachusetts in 1961.

5. "The Commissar believes in Change from Without. He believes that all the pests of humanity . . . can and will be cured by Revolution. . . . [The Yogi] believes that nothing can be improved by exterior organization and everything by individual effort from within; and that whosoever believes in anything else is an escapist." Arthur Koestler, *The Yogi and the Commissar* (New York: Macmillan, 1946), 3–4. Sorokin's categories are more general than Koestler's; there is no assumption that sensate human beings are Marxist and/or violent or that ideational human beings are Gandhian and/or nonviolent.

6. In the research seminar underlying this book this was known as "the Brian question," posed by Brian Shetler. The question applies not only to Sorokin but also to other cyclical macrohistorians who postulate transitions not only from high to low, but also from low to high. Maybe this looks problematic because of metaphors, such as "it is easier to go downhill than uphill," which anybody only modestly acquainted with mountains will know not to be necessarily true. However, the problem derives from observations and intuitions about moral more

than physical behavior. It is easy to break moral rules, not so easy to keep them, and very difficult to set and practice even more exacting standards.

7. For an elaboration of this, see Johan Galtung, "Back to the Origins: On Christian and Buddhist Epistemology," chapter 1.1 in *Methodology and Development* (Copenhagen: Ejlers, 1988), 15–26; see also chapter 4.4, "Contradictory Reality and Mathematics: A Contradiction?" 162–175.

8. I am reminded of a Romanian dissident, the late Pavel Apostol, who organized the Third World Futures Studies Federation conference in Bucuresti in 1972 and his thesis, not dear to the authorities, of "several roads to socialism within the same country."

9. This is the theme of Johan Galtung, "Structural Pluralism and the Future of Human Society," in *Challenges from the Future: Proceedings*, vol. 3 (Tokyo: Kodansha, 1971), 271–308. The vision is of a society with a maximum of "sociotopes" within its borders.

10. The reader might find the discussion of a Hindu life scheme in Chapter 5 interesting from this point of view because it provides for more focus on the sensate elements in certain phases of life, and on the ideational elements in other. However, all four phases actually integrate Sorokin's two cultural mentalities, but with different emphasis.

## 2.16

# *Arnold Toynbee: Challenge and Response*

*Johan Galtung*

### BIOGRAPHY

Arnold Toynbee was born in London in 1889. He studied Greek and Latin at Oxford University, where he later taught ancient history. During World War I he worked on Turkish affairs in the Political Intelligence Department of the Foreign Office, and during World War II he was director of the Research Department of the Foreign Office. He participated in Versailles in 1919, and from 1925 was Director of Studies in the Royal Institute of International Affairs. In addition to such establishment positions, illustrating a not atypical Foreign Office career starting with Greek and Latin, he wrote the nine volumes of *A Study of History*, of which the first six volumes were published from 1934 to 1939.[1] There is also the much referred to one-volume edition.[2] He died in 1975 at the age of 86, a celebrated sage. But, like most great people, he has drawn his fair share of criticism. There is no consensus about his works.[3]

His general theory of history must have been summarized thousands of times by now, some of it in writing, most of it by lecturers in history and in social sciences. Like Marx, and unlike Sorokin, his terms have become almost indelible parts of Western culture. I received such a summary for the first time from a history professor at the University of Oslo, Norway, in 1953.[4] Sorokin found Toynbee wanting, not only for the usual "his theory does not fit my particular subject of study" reasons, but also because of vagueness and generality. As an example of Toynbee's lack of precision, Sorokin chose his theory of the appropriate environment for civilizational growth as an environment that preferably should be "neither too friendly, nor too unfriendly," similar to cooking books recommending "neither too much, nor too little" salt.

Admittedly, this is not very precise, either for elites in search of challenges or for aspiring cooks, except if one adopts a more generous view, a macrohistorical view. Thus, when Toynbee or any other macrohistorian says anything so grand, most often they are announcing a central dimension of their discourse. They ask us to focus on the level of friendliness of the environment when considering the rise or fall of civilizations. Thus, if the minority fails to creatively pick up the challenge the environment may have been too extreme in either direction. To the "it does not fit my case" argument there is an obvious response: Why not? Perhaps it is best to assume, as a point of departure, Toynbee's "historical laws" as a heuristic, and then identify other factors that may also have been operating and causing deviations. Research in this direction may lead to new hypotheses and insights.

In any case, we should not blame Toynbee for his grandness—nobody else has done such a thorough job on twenty-six civilizations.[5] He developed his insights, formulated them as testable hypotheses, and ventured ahead, even though a social scientist might have wished he had more training in the social sciences and less in classics. His penchant for metaphors and Greek mythology does not communicate well with people outside the arts. Some simple social science concepts might have been useful in making his theory more rigorous. But Toynbee is the only Toynbee we have; we should be grateful, and if he is found wanting, try ourselves to do better.

The present summary, influenced by a critique made by Sorokin, consists of ten points.[6] These points should probably be seen like laws of mechanics—for instance, for falling bodies—abstractions from reality that are only approximated in empirical reality far from laboratory conditions. If this is permissible in physics, then why not in history? Why do we tolerate $s = 1/2gt^2$ in physics textbooks and remain so skeptical of, for instance, Toynbee?[7]

## ANALYSIS

*Point #1* The unit of analysis is a civilization, "the smallest unit of historical study at which one arrives when one tries to understand the history of one's own country."[8] He also mentions, as "intelligible fields of study," that there are "societies which have a greater extension in both Space and Time, than national states or city-states, or any other political communities," and then sees civilization as a "species of society."[9] Thus, as Sorokin points out, there is a mix of religious, territorial, and political traits. Sorokin vehemently criticizes this as leading to analyses of congeries, not of types of cultural mentality, believing his own approach to be more meaningful.[10]

*Point #2* The focus of analysis is the genesis or emergence of a civilization, how civilizations are reproduced (kept operating), and how they decline in the end.

*Point #3* The mechanism of genesis or emergence of a civilization is the challenge and response cycle, in the context of an environment (all external conditions) neither too favorable (no response necessary), nor too unfavorable (no response available).

*Point #4* The carrier of the genesis or emergence is a creative minority, capable of perceiving the challenge and generating an adequate and creative, not merely ritualistic and routine, response.

*Point #5* The conditions for growth of a civilization are repeated application of the challenge and response cycle, "withdrawal and return" of the creative minority with ever new responses to ever new challenges, and expansion of this to a challenge–response–mimesis (CRM) cycle, with responses freely imitated and followed by a mimetic majority, both by the Internal Proletariat of the society and by the External Proletariat of its "barbarian neighbors." There will be no "fratricidal struggle, no hard and fast division. It is a solidary body."[11] Under such conditions, the civilization can unfold its dominant potentials, differentiating it from other civilizations in the same process. But, to stave off decline, the civilization has to continue growing, so the challenge–response–mimesis cycles have to be operating all the time.

*Point #6* The decline of a civilization sets in when the challenge–response–mimesis cycle is arrested. The decline has three phases: breakdown, disintegration, and dissolution.

*Point #7* In the breakdown phase, the civilization is no longer creative, and both Internal and External Proletariat withdraw their mimesis; unity breaks down. But the civilization may still continue as "petrified life in death," or fossilized.[12]

*Point #8* In the disintegration phase, the Creative Minority becomes a Dominant Minority trying to control the Internal and External Proletariat by force, to prevent their takeover in internal class wars and external wars. This phase may last long, and may take the shape of a Universal State, which is little more than the shell within which a civilization is dying.[13] The reaction of the Inner Proletariat may take the form of a Universal Church, which may then serve as the basis for a new civilization.[14] Thus, one civilization gives birth to another.

*Point #9* In the dissolution phase of a civilization, the External Proletariat starts attacking instead of trying to integrate, although it is one of Toynbee's basic tenets that a civilization dies from suicide (failure to be creative), rather than from murder. There is total disunity with a sense of drift, sin begins to grow, and promiscuity and syncretism become dominant. Vulgarization and proletarization invade arts and sciences, philosophy and language, religion and ethics, and manners and institutions. The final conquest by the External Proletariat becomes more like a coup de grace.

*Point #10* In this phase, there is only one possibility left: transfiguration, possibly brought about by a Transfigured Religious Savior.[15] There is a transfer of the process to the supersensory Kingdom of God, a step forward in the eternal process of elevation of Man to Superman, and of "the City of Man to the City of God."

This adds up to a flowchart with branching-off processes at all points (see Appendix B), considerably more complex than some of the other macrohistorians. We start at point zero and time zero. There is neither unity nor disunity, but a creative minority capable of running some challenge-response–mimesis that can be identified. A civilization emerges, growing with each successive and successful cycle with increasing unity.

This process lasts as long as it lasts, until the minority is no longer creative. Obviously, some failures do not count; it is the lasting, institutionalized failure to be creative that is disastrous. The withdrawal of support from the proletariats, crucial for the survival of the civilization, not to mention the elites, follows. Disunity and strife set in. The elite tries to control them through the mechanisms of an all-embracing, universal state, maybe an empire. If they succeed they might be able to get the CRM cycles going again in sufficient numbers for a new takeoff or a return to what, at this point, no doubt are "the good old days." If not, the slope downward will become steeper until the External Proletariat or nature gives the civilization its final blow, with a bang (conquest), or a whimper (ecological erasure).

But could these processes not be precisely the challenges that might have an invigorating effect on the elites and test their mettle, bringing out the creative potential? Certainly, but the challenge may also be too much; the elites may "rest on the oars," and produce too little response too late to be able to turn the tide.[16]

## COMPARISONS

There is much similarity to Khaldun here, but Khaldun sees the renewal from the External Proletariat, whereas Toynbee, like Marx, sees it as coming from the Internal Proletariat. The similarity to Marx comes in by mentioning the proletariat at all. There is even an intimation of Lenin in the reference to External Proletariats. At the same time, there is a similarity to Sorokin and Spengler in the focus on cultural creativity as opposed to the gutter of materialism and sensualism. There are also elements of Augustine (the City of Man, City of God), and of Hegel (the creative spirit, the magic touch). But, as Sorokin points out important sociologists are either not known to Toynbee or not used: Durkheim, Weber, Pareto, not to mention Tarde, with his *Laws of Imitation* located in the very center of Toynbee's theory.[17]

However, a look at the twenty macrohistorians that form the substance of this book brings out a basic point: No one is so central and covers so much of the discourses of the others as Toynbee, whether deliberate or not. So many of the others are classless, and unambiguously elite centered. While partly true for Toynbee, he does mention class. His culturalism actually brings him quite close to Gramsci.

What to many is a vice is also a virtue: his high level of generality. Toynbee works with "challenge" as a key concept but he does not specify what type of challenge. Smith might think in terms of economic challenge, Comte epistemological challenge, Spencer evolutionary challenge, but Toynbee covers them all with his overarching concepts. If audacity is a mark of the genius, Toynbee certainly has it.

## INSIGHTS AND FLAWS

To gain more insight into his thinking, let us try to test him out on Western civilization today—which means Western imperialism, of which he quite often wrote very critically. Thus, consider this:

The entrepreneurs of mechanized industry secured "growth" at the expense of their own employees, of the "natives" of still unmechanized countries, and of nonhuman Nature. The wages originally paid to the workers in mechanized industry were low; the unmechanized industries of Asia, such as spinning and weaving, were put out of action by the competition of mechanically produced Western manufactures. Asian, African and Latin American countries were compelled to admit such Western goods at low customs rates. And the limited reserves of the planet's irreplaceable natural resources of fuels and raw materials (such as coal, metals, and mineral oil) were consumed on a scale and at a pace that were unprecedented.[18]

He then goes on to predict that the developed countries will soon be living in a permanent siege economy, in a struggle for the control of their diminished resources. Clearly, this has not yet happened, but certainly may. Writing in 1974, he was no doubt influenced by the impact of the OPEC action to improve the terms of trade for crude oil. But the basic point is the view of the total world system as exactly that, a system, where the parts have an impact on each other.

That also shows the flaw in his civilization definition: If one should really go to the limit of what is relevant for one's own society, starting almost anywhere in the world today, one ends up with the whole world. Toynbee, had he still been alive, might have agreed and certainly posed this question: Is the small minority running this world creative enough? His own prediction of authoritarian outcomes would be indicative of a resounding no, since, in the long run, authoritarianism does not assure the support of the Internal and External Proletariats.[19]

For Toynbee, the elites of the Western world, increasingly identical with the elites of the entire world, are in a squeeze. Either they keep their economic growth going by exploiting the Internal Proletariat, the External Proletariat, and Nature (in which case, all three may turn against these elites), or they exploit less and build relations of care and caring, but may not be able to keep their economic growth operating. The solution the elites and the Internal Proletariat found is not to exploit less but to pursue economic growth even more relentlessly (as this is the only way to meet the continual demands for higher wages without losing profits). Obviously, this will be at the expense of the External Proletariat and Nature, however, "'natives' and Nature have now worked together to bring the growth of the mechanized countries' GNP to a halt."[20]

Skimming Western history, we see how an Internal Proletariat went West and brought about the American Revolution, and an exploited External Proletariat in the East brought about the Russian revolution. What happened? Is Toynbee relevant?

A Toynbee-type analysis of these two civilizations, whether he sees them as part of Western civilization or not, brings out some interesting points. After the genocide in the Western Hemisphere the environment might have been too friendly and too easy to meet the challenges.[21] But the Americans overcame that by seeking new challenges, and assured a constant supply of immigrants more than willing to imitate if the Internal and External Proletariats of Native Americans, black slaves, and their successors grew restless. Essentially, that is still the situation, since the Universal State was consummated by Eisenhower when he brought the number of states up to the present fifty. There is still mimesis around the world of the American way of life, maybe even to a point that Toynbee's original perspectives did not foresee: The CRM cycle is kept alive by the mimesis more than by creative response.

In the East, the process was very different, but again Toynbee's perspective is useful. The challenge was a devastated country after World War I. Interventions and hunger all over, combined with the urge to build a totally new system, was probably more than any minority, however creative, could have responded to in a satisfactory manner. As a result, the minority went from creative to dominant very quickly. The Soviet

Union became the Universal State as described by Toynbee. The imitation was not entered freely; the Internal Proletariat was forced to imitate and the repression was so total that they were not able to form a Universal Church as a response to the Universal State.

The External Proletariat, however, and not only members of Communist Parties, for a long time maintained the illusion that there was something to imitate. The hypothesis might be that the Soviet system was to some extent kept alive on the inside partly because of the expectations from the outside; that is, we cannot let the Third World masses down. There was, with the nuclear threat to the Soviet Union from the West and the only serious war, with Nazi Germany, the type of challenge to which the dominant minority in some stages responded creatively (such as with Sputnik).

The Soviet Union is the story of a civilization declining before it emerged, unable to sustain itself through challenge–response–mimesis cycles entered into freely. The symptoms of breakdown and disintegration were usually more evident than signs of something emerging. And the end was exactly as predicted by Toynbee's paradigm: suicide rather than murder. The Soviet Union collapsed with a whimper—an implosion.

But what of the larger Western civilization whence they both came? Toynbee's prediction is for a repressive phase for the West, reminiscent of his universal state. In that case, there will almost certainly arise some kind of Universal Church, maybe built around what today is called "green values," essentially values of reproducibility, against exploitation. Will the elites respond creatively even to that challenge, or will it give birth to a new kind of Western civilization? This also depends on whether the External Proletariat hopes for integration or turns against the West in an all-out challenge; for instance, uniting today's Third World with remnants of the ex-socialist Universal State. All of these are questions that emerge from Toynbee's macrohistory, a proof of its lasting value.

## NOTES

1. Arnold Toynbee, *A Study of History*, 12 vols. (Oxford: Oxford University Press, 1934–1961). Volumes 1 to 3 were published in 1934, volumes 4 to 6 in 1939, volumes 7 to 10 in 1954, and volumes 11 and 12 in 1961.

2. Arnold Toynbee, *A Study of History* (Oxford: Oxford University Press, 1947). Also, Arnold Toynbee, *A Study of History*, illustrated (Oxford: Oxford University Press, 1971).

3. For a very unfriendly comment, see H. Trevor-Roper, "The Prophet," review of *Arnold J. Toynbee: A Life*, by William McNeill, *New York Review of Books*, 12 October 1989, 28–34: "His grand historical scheme is now as dead as a dodo; a monument of wasted erudition. His egotism, his self-dramatization, his inflated biblical style, and his subordination of world history to his own per-

sonal circumstances make him ridiculous." This is too harsh. Maybe Toynbee will actually outlive Trevor-Roper, and that is what the latter fears? Less unfriendly is the commentary by George Kennan, "The History of Arnold Toynbee," *New York Review of Books*, 1 June 1989. Kennan has difficulties with the impersonal nature of Toynbee's history—a history without names. Of course, this is macrohistory; maybe Kennan did not understand that.

4. The brilliant late Jens Arup Seip.

5. The civilizations are Western, two Orthodox Christian, the Iranic, the Arabic, the Hindu, two Far Eastern, the Hellenic, the Syriac, the Indic, the Sinic, the Minoan, the Sumeric, the Hittite, the Babylonic, the Andean, the Mexic, the Yucatec, the Mayan, the Egyptiac, and the five "arrested" ones: Polynesian, Eskimo, Nomadic, Ottoman, and Spartan. This list can be read focusing on what is missing: Where is Africa? North America? Why did he focus on those eliminated by the Spaniards and not on the many eliminated by the British? If Polynesian, how about Micronesian and Melanesian? But it can also be read more generously: Who else has had this erudition?

6. Pitirim Sorokin, "Sorokin's Briefing on Toynbee" (Harvard University, Cambridge, 1957–1958, mimeographed).

7. One answer is, of course, that the mechanical laws may be verified under laboratory conditions (vacuum, no dissipating forces of any kind). But social psychological experiments and simulation exercises under laboratory conditions can also be devised that might replicate Toynbee's abstract and generalized processes.

8. Pitirim Sorokin, *Social Philosophies of an Age of Crisis* (Boston: Beacon Press, 1951), 214.

9. Toynbee, *Study of History* (1971), 45, 48, 114.

10. Ibid., 209–217.

11. Ibid., 116.

12. Among the examples are the Egyptiac civilization between the sixteenth century B.C. and the fifth century A.D.; and Far Eastern civilization in China from the ninth century A.D. until today. In other words, there may be very long periods when the civilization persists on the basis of routine only.

13. One example given by Toynbee is the Roman Empire, controlled by the Hellenic dominant minority.

14. Medieval Christianity as a reaction to the excesses of the Roman Empire, or Buddhism as a reaction to the excesses of Hinduism would be good examples here. Sorokin, *Social Philosophies*, 118. But what about Marxism under capitalism?

15. Toynbee's Christianity shines through here: Jesus the Christ.

16. A very Oxford–Cambridge type of expression; Americans might tend to say "be the victims of their own success."

17. Sorokin, "Sorokin's Briefing," 5.

18. Arnold Toynbee, "After the Age of Influence," *Observer*, 14 April 1974.

19. For a good insight into how Toynbee thought about most issues, see his dialogue in Daisaku Ikeda, *Choose Life* (London: Oxford University Press, 1976).

20. Toynbee, "After the Age of Influence."

21. See David Stannard, *American Holocaust* (Oxford: Oxford University Press, 1992).

## 2.17

# Antonio Gramsci: Hegemony and the Materialist Conception of History

*Marsha Hansen*

### BIOGRAPHY

Antonio Gramsci was born in Sardinia on January 23, 1891. The Italy of his day was plagued by complex economic, social, and political problems which were exacerbated by the division of the country into an industrialized north and an agrarian south. This division more than smacked of colonialism, with the southern Sardinians suffering the weight of the imbalance. Gramsci was a southerner.

Gramsci's family's economic situation required that he go to work as a young boy. Sickly and bearing the effects of an early accident, young Gramsci worked under arduous conditions. Despite such hardships, Gramsci was intellectually precocious and won a place at the university in Turin. He established himself as a brilliant philologist, but was compelled to turn his energies and intellectual gifts to political activism and social analyses.

Gramsci's political activism lead to imprisonment under Mussolini's fascist regime from 1926 until 1937. In 1937, his deteriorating health required that he be hospitalized. He died shortly after his release from prison.

Despite the fact that he was certainly the major force in the development of Italian communism, Gramsci's works have only recently become readily available to English-speaking audiences. Self-dubbed a "critical communist," Gramsci has quickly gained recognition as one of the seminal minds of his era. This reputation is not based solely on the political activism for which Gramsci is noted, but on the import his writings have for historiography and political inquiry in general.

### GRAMSCI AND MARX

While his name is inevitably linked to Marx, it is erroneous to consider Gramsci a derivative thinker. His contributions to socialist thought and his refinement of elements of Marxism point to an intellect more than able to give genesis to ideas that shape worlds. Highly critical of the respective mechanistic and economic models of Marxism being expounded in the late nineteenth and early twentieth centuries, Gramsci's interpretation of Marxism appears to remain true to Marx's own philosophic and conceptual themes while not evidencing dogmatic slavishness.

Gramsci looked to Marxism for what he viewed as its potential for creating milieux for social change. His version of Marxism is one that addresses the problems of historical change and of history's failure to change. Gramsci does not dodge ontological questions, and succeeds in substituting an ethical imperative in place of the teleological element underlying Marx's cosmology.

Gramsci reacted strongly against the determinist and fatalist aspects of Marxism. Even though Marx himself was sometimes guilty of nodding off to the dialectical nature of the organic connections in a society's life, Gramsci attributed the reduction of Marx's system to economic determinism to a misunderstanding of the concept of historical materialism. He traces this in part to F. A. Lange's *History of Materialism*. Of Lange, he writes, "They studied what traditional materialism was and its concepts were taken as the concepts of historical materialism. So it can be said that for the greater part of the body of concepts put forward under the label of historical materialism, the principal teacher and founder was none other than Lange."[1]

Gramsci observed that a whole series of followers of historical materialism "started out with the dogmatic pre-supposition that historical materialism is undoubtedly traditional materialism somewhat revised and amended . . . by the dialectic."[2] Gramsci understood the dialectic to be a doctrine of consciousness and the inner substance of history and the science of politics, not a subspecies of formal logic or elementary scholasticism. As a very able philologist, Gramsci certainly understood the origins of the dialectic in classical antiquity. Still, he was able to reject the idea of the dialectic as a subspecies of formal logic, as were both Marx and Hegel. Gramsci writes in *The Modern Prince*

It is the problem of the relations between structure and superstructures which needs to be posed exactly and resolved in order to reach a correct analysis of the forces working in the history of a certain period and determine their relationship. One must keep within the bounds of two principles: (1) that no society sets itself tasks for whose solution the necessary and sufficient conditions do not already exist or are not at least in process of emergence and development; (2) that no society dissolves and can be replaced unless it has first developed all the forms of life implicit in its relations.[3]

By reflecting on these two canons, Gramsci believed that one could successfully develop a whole series of other principles of historical methodology. However, in studying a structure, Gramsci distinguished between relatively permanent organic movements and occasional "incidental" movements. While incidental phenomena are dependent on organic movements, their significance has no great historical importance. For Gramsci,

The error often committed in historico-political analyses consists in having been unable to find the correct relationship between what is organic and what is occasional: thus one succeeds in either expounding as directly operative causes which instead operate indirectly, or in asserting that direct causes are the only effective causes; in one case there is an excess of "economism" or pedantic doctrinarism, in the other an excess of "ideologism," in the one case an overestimation of mechanical causes, in the other an exaltation of the voluntarist and individual elements.... The dialectical nexus between the two kinds of movement and therefore, of research, is difficult to establish; and if the error is serious in historiography, it is still more serious in the art of politics, where we are dealing not with reconstructing past history but with building present and future history; one's own inferior and immediate desires and passions are the cause of error, in so far as they are substituted for objective and impartial analysis, and this happens not as conscious "means" to stimulate action but as self-deceit. Here also, the snake bites the charlatan, or rather the demagogue is the first victim of his demagogy.[4]

As for "economism," Gramsci saw it as originating in syndicalism and liberalism, with very little relationship to Marxism. He believed that historical economism was confused with historical materialism, even writing that it was necessary to "fight against economism not only in the theory of historiography, but also and especially in the theory and practice of politics."[5]

During his incarceration, Gramsci kept his intellectual skills honed. He left copious notes, though the system of prison censorship, failing health, and limited resources were barriers to a truly systematic presentation of his ideas. Among the extant papers are insightful analyses of social, political, and historical issues, as well as discussions of methods for philosophical, historical, and political inquiry. The creative output during the years of his confinement is a testament to the triumph of the human will and to the social ethic which underlies Gramsci's political and social analyses.

Like Marx, Gramsci never set out specifically to write history; however, also like Marx, Gramsci did set out to offer a systematic methodological expression of the entire life of a society. Gramsci considered a scientific approach to the study of history as a vital constituent part of such a system. He believed that politics and economics could never be separated from history.

## THE RELATIONS OF FORCES

Gramsci wrote that giving a canon of research and interpretation as an historical cause leads to a theoretical error. In discussing the problem of the relations of forces, Gramsci identifies three different stages or levels. These are (1) a relation of social forces tied to the structure that is objective and independent of man's will; (2) the relation of political forces (i.e., an estimation of the degree of homogeneity, self-consciousness, and organization reached by various social groups); and (3) the relations of military forces, often immediately decisive.[6] Gramsci describes these stages as reciprocally mixed both horizontally and vertically, depending on economic and social activities and territory.

Gramsci saw historical development as continuously oscillating between the first and third stages, with the mediation of the second stage. He writes that in the development of history, two levels of the third stage are presented in a great variety of combinations. These two levels are the technicomilitary and the politicomilitary. The relevance of the concept of hegemony to historical development becomes clear in discussing interplay among these stages.

The most valuable tool elucidated by Gramsci for the examination of history is the concept of hegemony. Simply put, hegemony means ideological control by one class or group over others to the extent that structures of particular social systems are viewed as "natural." The active consent of major groups in a society to such moral and philosophical leadership is implicit. Hegemony differs significantly from totalitarianism in that consensual, voluntary, and legitimate elements are central to the former. Totalitarianism amounts to failure to achieve hegemony.

In looking at a society, Gramsci found it helpful to describe its superstructure as being divisible into two great floors: civil society and political society or the state. Civil society consists of private organisms like schools, churches, clubs, and parties which contribute to the formation of political and social consciousness. Political society consists of public institutions, such as the government, army, courts, and police. The latter is the source of coercive power, while the former represents the locus of hegemonic or cultural leadership. Gramsci goes on to describe what he calls the "integral state": political society interwoven with civil society in such a way that hegemony is protected by means of coercion.

Hegemony is important to Gramsci in analyzing historical development. Rather than conclude that fundamental historical crises are directly caused by economic crises, Gramsci offers that economic crises "can only create a more favorable ground for the propagation of certain ways of thinking, of posing and solving questions which involve the whole future development of State life."[7] Such a conceptualization allows room for the iniative of human will but does not reflect the "fateful" element associated with Marxism. Gramsci cites a proposition of Marx that is often overlooked: "Popular beliefs" or beliefs of the same kind as popular beliefs have the validity of material forces.[8]

Gramsci saw much of his work as providing correctives for Marxism, but not of Marx himself. Perhaps Gramsci succeeds in bridging the gap between nineteenth- and twentieth-century Marxism, representing the philosophy of praxis as an independent and complete structure of thought. Unfortunately, there is little anyone, including Gramsci, can do to deliver Marxism from its unilinearity.

## NOTES

1. Antonio Gramsci, *The Modern Prince and Other Writings*, trans. Louis Marks (New York: International Publishers, 1957), 116.
2. Ibid.
3. Ibid., 165–167.
4. Ibid.
5. Ibid., 158.
6. Ibid., 169–171.
7. Ibid., 152.
8. Ibid., 158.

## 2.18

# *Prabhat Rainjan Sarkar: Agency, Structure, and Transcendence*

Sohail Inayatullah

### PERSONAL HISTORY

Prabhat Rainjan Sarkar was born in May 1921, in Bihar, to an old and respected family that had its roots in regional leadership and in ancient spiritual traditions. Sarkar's early life was dominated by fantastic events, spiritual miracles, and brushes with death. He was nearly killed in his early years by a religious sect who believed that Sarkar was destined to destroy their religion. Surviving this event and many similar ones, by the 1950s he had become a guru with many followers. In 1955, he founded the sociospiritual organization *Ananda Marga*. Soon after, he articulated a new socioeconomic theory and social movement called the Progressive Utilization Theory, or PROUT.

Until his death on October 21, 1990, Sarkar remained active in Calcutta, composing nearly 5,000 songs, called *Prabhat Samgiit* (songs of the new dawn), giving spiritual talks, lecturing on society and economy, managing his organizations, and teaching meditation to his numerous disciples, especially his senior monks and nuns, *avadhutas* and *avadhutikas*.

### THE PERSONAL AND SOCIAL

Sarkar places the rise, fall, and rise of his movement in the same language that he uses to explain aspects of history. For him, whenever truth is stated in spiritual or material areas of life, there is resistance. This resistance eventually is destroyed by the very forces it uses to destroy truth. "Remember, by an unalterable decree of history, the evil forces are destined to meet their doomsday."[1]

For Sarkar, movements follow a dialectical path: thesis, antithesis, and synthesis. A movement is born, it is suppressed and oppressed (if it truly challenges the distribution of meanings of power), and if it survives these challenges it will be victorious. The strength of the movement can be measured by its ability to withstand these challenges.

Sarkar's own life and the life of his organizations (having been banned during the 1975 Indian Emergency) follow this pattern, although at this point the success of the PROUT movement has yet to be determined.[2] In our interpretation, it is this mythic language that is also perhaps the best way to understand his theory of history, for it is myth that gives meaning to reality, makes understandable the moments and monuments of our daily lives, and gives a call to sacrifice the moment so as to create a better tomorrow.

Sarkar's universe is the habitat of grand struggles between *vidya* and *avidya*: introversion and extroversion, contraction and expansion, compassion and passion. This duality is an eternal part of the very metaphysic of the physical and social universe. Unlike the Western model, where social history can end with the perfect marketplace or the conflict-free communist state, for the Indian—for Sarkar—social history will always continue. Only for the individual, through spiritual enlightenment, can time cease and the "mind" itself (and thus duality) be transcended.

## SARKAR'S LARGER CIVILIZATIONAL PROJECT

Sarkar's intent was and is (his organizations continue his work) to create a global spiritual socialist revolution; a renaissance in thought, language, music, art, and culture. His goal was to infuse individuals with a spiritual presence, the necessary first step in changing the way that we know and order our world. Unlike the socialists of the past, who merely sought to capture state power, forgetting that the economy was global and thus, in the long run, strengthening the world capitalist system; or utopian idealists, who wished for perfect places that could not practically exist; or spiritualists, who only sought individual transformation at the expense of the wider community, Sarkar has a far more comprehensive view of transformation.

Theoretically, this included a range of new approaches to understanding social reality, of which the social cycle is the key structure. His theory of neo-humanism aims to relocate the self from ego (and the pursuit of individual maximization), from family (and the pride of genealogy), from geo-sentiments (attachments to land and nation), from socio-sentiments (attachments to class, race, and community), and from humanism (man as the center of the universe), to neo-humanism (love and devotion for all inanimate and animate beings of the universe). Paramount here is the construction of self in an ecology of reverence for life, not a modern secular politics of cynicism. Spiritual devotion to the universe is ultimately the greatest treasure that humans have; it is this treasure that must be discovered and shared by all living beings. Only from this basis can a new universalism emerge which can challenge the national, religious, and class sentiments of history.

The first step, then, is liberating the intellect from its own boundaries and placing it in an alternative discourse. Sarkar then seeks to make accessible an alternative way of knowing the world that includes, yet steps beyond, traditional knowledge points: reason, sense-inference, authority, and intuition.

The central framework for his neo-humanistic perspective is his Progressive Utilization Theory. PROUT encompasses Sarkar's theory of history and change, his theory of leadership and the vanguard of the new world he envisions, as well as his alternative political economy.

## THEORY OF HISTORY

Sarkar's theory of history consists of four classes: workers, warriors, intellectuals, and accumulators of capital. Each class can be perceived not merely as a power configuration, but as a way of knowing the world; as a paradigm, episteme, or deep structure. In Sarkar's language, this is collective psychology or *varna* (here, dramatically reinterpreting caste). Each *varna* comes into power bringing in positive necessary changes, but over time exploits and then dialectically creates the conditions for the next *varna*. This cycle continues through history, and for Sarkar is indeed an iron law of history, true irrespective of space/time and observer conditions. It is a law because it has developed historically through evolution and because the cycle represents a universal social structure. For Sarkar, there are only four ways of dealing with the environment: being dominated by it, dominating it through the body, dominating it through the mind, or dominating it through the environment itself.

While the parallel to caste is there (*shudra, ksattriya, brahmin,* and *vaeshya*), Sarkar redefines them, locating the four as broader social categories that have historically evolved through interaction with the environment. Caste, on the other hand, developed with the conquest of the local Indians by the Aryans and was later reinscribed by the Vedic priestly classes.[3]

Sarkar believes that while the social cycle must always move through these four classes, it is possible to accelerate the stages of history and remove the periods of exploitation. Thus, Sarkar would place the *sadvipra,* the compassionate servant leader, at the center of the cycle and at the center of society (not necessarily at the center of the state). In his life,

Sarkar's efforts were to create this type of leadership instead of building large bureaucratic organizations. He sought to create a new type of leadership that was humble and could serve, that was courageous and could protect, that was insightful and could learn and teach, and that was innovative and could use wealth—in a word, the *sadvipra*.

These leaders would, in effect, attempt to create a permanent revolution: a worker revolution when the capitalists begin to move from innovation to commodification; a warrior revolution when the worker era moved from societal transformation to political anarchy; an intellectual revolution when the warrior era expanded too far, becoming overly centralized and stagnating culturally; and an economic revolution when intellectuals use their normative power to create a universe in which knowledge is only available to the select few, favoring nonmaterial production at the expense of material production. Through the intervention of the *sadvipra*, Sarkar's social cycle becomes a spiral: The cycle of the stages remains, but one era is transformed into its antithesis when exploitation increases. This leads to the new synthesis and the possibility of social progress within the structural confines of the four basic classes.

Sarkar's theory allows for a future that, while patterned, can still dramatically change. For Sarkar, there are long periods of rest and then periods of dramatic social and biological revolution. Sarkar's theoretical framework is not only spiritual or only concerned with the material world; rather, his perspective argues that the real is physical, mental, and spiritual. Concomitantly, the motives for historical change are struggle with the environment (the move from the worker era to the warrior era), struggle with ideas (the move from the warrior to the intellectual), struggle with the environment and ideas (the move from the intellectual era to the capitalist era), and the spiritual attraction of the Great, the call of the infinite. Thus, physical, mental, and spiritual challenges create change.

### The Stages of the Social Cycle

| | | |
|---|---|---|
| Shudra | Worker | Dominated by Environment |
| Ksattriya | Warrior | Struggles with and dominates Environment |
| Vipra | Intellectual | Struggles with and dominates Ideas |
| Vaeshya | Capitalist | Struggles with and dominates Environment/Ideas |

The key to Sarkar's theory of history, thus, is that there are four structures and four epochs in history. Each epoch exhibits a certain mentality, a *varna*. This *varna* is similar to the concept of episteme, paradigm, ideal type, class, stage, era, and a host of other words that have been used to describe stage theory. Sarkar himself alternatively uses *varna* and collective psychology to describe his basic concept. Collective psychology reflects group desire, social desire. There are four basic desire systems, which are historically developed. First the *shudra*, then the *ksattriya*, then the *vipra*, then the *vaeshya*. The last era is followed either by a revolution by the *shudras* or an evolution into the *shudra* era.

The order is cyclical, but there are reversals. There can be a counterrevolution in any era or a counterevolution. Both are short-lived in terms of the natural cycle, since both move counter to the natural developmental flow. But in the long run, the order must be followed.

Significantly—and this is important in terms of theories of macrohistory—Sarkar does not resort to external variables to explain the transition into the next era. It is not new technologies that create a new wealthy elite that can control the *vipras*; rather, it is a fault within the *viprans* themselves. Moreover, it is not that they did not meet a new challenge or respond appropriately, as Toynbee would argue. Rather, Sarkar's reasoning is closer to Ibn Khaldun's and other classical philosophers. They create a privileged ideological world or conquer a material world and use this expansion to take care of their needs, but when changes come they are unprepared, for they themselves have degenerated. While changes are often technological (new inventions and discoveries of new resources), it is not the significant variable; rather, it is the mindset of the *vipran*, individually and as a class, that leads to their downfall.

## THE INDIAN EPISTEME AND CONSTRUCTION OF HISTORY

Following the classic Indian episteme, reality has many levels. Most ideologies only have accentuated the spiritual (*Vedanta*), the material (liberalism), the individual (capitalism), the collective (communism), the community (Gandhism), race (Hitlerism), or the nation (fascism), but Sarkar seeks an alternative balance of self, community, ecology, and globe. Yet the spiritual is his base. In his view, Consciousness from pure existence transforms to awareness and to succeeding material factors (the Big Bang onwards) until it becomes matter. From matter, there is dialectical evolution to humans. Humans finally can devolve back to the inanimate or evolve as cocreators with consciousness. For humans, there is structure and choice, nature and will. There is both creation and there is evolution. With this epistemic background, we should then not be surprised at his dual interests in the material and spiritual worlds and their dynamic balance.

Placing Sarkar in an alternative construction of the real is central to understanding his social theory. Sarkar wrote from India, from the poverty that is Calcutta. The centrality of the cycle, then, can partially be understood by its physical location. The cycle promises a better future ahead; it promises that the powerful will be made weak and the weak powerful, the rich will be humbled and the poor enabled. The cycle also comes directly from the classic Indian episteme. In this ordering of knowledge, the real has many levels and is thus pluralistic; the inner mental world is isomorphic with the external material world, there are numerous ways of knowing the real, and time is grand. According to Romila Thapar, "Hindu thinkers had evolved a cyclic theory of time. The cycle was called the *kalpa* and was equivalent to 4320 million earthly years. The *kalpa* is divided into 14 periods and at the end of each of these the universe is recreated and once again *Manu* (primeval man) gives birth to the human race."[4]

In this classical model (from the *Gita*), the universe is created, it degenerates, and then is recreated. The pattern is eternal. This pattern has clear phases; the golden era of *Krta* or *Satya*, the silver era of *Treta*, the copper era of *Dvapara*, and the iron age of *Kali*. At the end of *Kali*, however, the great redeemer, whether Vishnu or Shiva or Krishna, is reborn, the universe is set straight, *dharma* or truth is restored, and the cycle begins again.

Is there a way out, an escape from the cycle? Classically, it has been through an alchemical ontological transformation of the self: the self realizing its real nature and thus achieving timelessness—the archetype of the yogi. Concretely, in social reality this has meant the transformation of a person engrossed in fear to a mental state where nothing is feared, neither king nor priest; all is embraced, lust and greed are transcended, and individual inner peace is achieved. To this archetype, Sarkar has added a collective level asserting that individual liberation must exist parallel to and in the context of social liberation. Spirituality is impossible in the context of the social body suffering in pain. For him, the world has a "defective social order. . . . This state of affairs cannot be allowed to continue. This structure of inequality and injustice must be destroyed and powdered down for the collective interest of the human beings. Then and then alone, humans may be able to lead the society on the path of virtue. Without that only a handful of persons can possibly attain the Supreme Perfection."[5]

But Sarkar uses the redeemer concept to provide the way out of cyclical history, too. This is his *Taraka Brahma*. The first was Shiva, who transformed the chaos of primitive life to the orderliness of humanity. Next was Krishna, who restored the notion of national community. For Sarkar, another redeemer is needed to transform the fragmented nation-states into a planetary community. However, paradoxically, the concept of the redeemer for Sarkar is metaphorical; it is meant to elicit devotion by making the impersonal nature of Consciousness touchable in the form of a personal guru.

Sarkar thus develops ways out of the cycle: individual and social. In contrast, Orientalist interpreters like Mircea Eliade believe that the theory of eternal cycles is "invigorating and consoling for man under the terror of history," as now man knows under which eras he must suffer and he knows that the only escape is spiritual salvation.[6] Sarkar finds this view repugnant, for people suffer differently and differentially in each era; those at the center of power do better than those at the outskirts and laborers always do poorly. Indeed, throughout history different classes have done better than other classes, but the elite managed quite well. "Oftentimes, some people have lagged behind, exhausted and collapsed on the ground, their hands and knees bruised and their clothes stained with mud. Such people have been thrown aside with hatred and have become the outcast society. They have been forced to remain isolated from the mainstream of social life. This is the kind of treatment they have received. Few have cared enough to lift up those who lagged behind, to help them forward."[7]

The hope is not resignation, but transformation of the cycle. It is here that Sarkar moves away from the classic Hindu model of the real—of caste, fatalism, and mentalism—most likely influenced by fraternal Islamic concepts, liberal notions of individual will, and Marxist notions of class struggle.

For Sarkar, there are different types of time. There is cosmic time, the degeneration and regeneration of *dharma*; there is individual liberation from time through entrance into infinite time; and there is the social level of time, wherein the times of exploitation are reduced through social transformation, thus creating a time of dynamic balance, a balance between the physical, social, and spiritual.

This differs significantly from other views of Indian history. In the idealistic view, history is but the play or sport of Consciousness.[8] In this view, the individual has no agency and suffering is an illusion. In the dynastic view, history is but the succeeding rise and falls of dynasties and kings and queens; it is only the grand that have agency. This is in contrast with Aurobindo's interpretation, influenced by Hegel, in which instrumentality is assigned to historical world leaders and to nations.[9] For Sarkar, making nationalism into a spiritual necessity is an unnecessary reading. God does not prefer any particular structure over another.

Following Aurobindo, Buddha Prakash has taken the classic Hindu stages of gold, silver, copper, and iron and applied them concretely to modern history. For Prakash, India, with nationhood and industrialism, has now awakened to a golden age that "reveals the jazz and buzz of a new age of activity."[10] But for Sarkar, the present is not an age of awakening, but an age "where on the basis of various arguments a handful of parasites have gorged themselves on the blood of millions of people, while countless people have been reduced to living skeletons."[11]

Sarkar also rejects the modern linear view of history, in which history is divided into ancient (Hindu), medieval (Muslim), and modern (British–Nationalistic) periods. In this view, England is modern and India is backward. Only if India can adopt rational, secular, and capitalist or socialist perspectives and institutions—that is, modern policies—can it too join the Western world. India, then, has to move from prehistorical society—people lost in spiritual fantasy and caste but without state—to modern society.[12] Sarkar's views are closer to Jawaharlal Nehru, for whom history is about how humans have overcome challenges and struggled against the elements and inequity.[13] Sarkar's views are also similar to the recent "Subaltern" project, in which the aim is to write history from the view of the dominated classes, not the elite or the colonial.[14] However, unlike the Subaltern project, which eschews metanarratives, Sarkar's social cycle provides a new grand theory.

Sarkar's own historiography is meant to show the challenges humans faced: the defeats and the victories. His history shows how humans were dominated by particular eras; how they struggled and developed new technologies and ideas; and how they realized the *atman*. It is an attempt to write a history that is true to the victims but does not oppress them again by providing no escape from history and no vision of the future. His history is clearly ideological, not in the sense of supporting a particular class, but rather giving weight to all classes and attempting to move them outside of class and ego and toward neo-humanism.

## FRESH BREATH OF AIR

History is the natural evolutionary flow of this cycle. At every point, there are a range of choices; once made, the choice becomes a habit, a structure of the collective or group mind. Each mentality comes into power with an associated leadership class, makes changes, and administers government, but eventually pursues its own class ends and exploits the other groups. This has continued throughout history.

Sarkar's unit of analysis begins with all of humanity—it is a history of humanity—but he often refers to countries and nations. The relationship to the previous era is a dialectical one; each new era emerges out of an old era. History moves, not because of external reasons, although the environment certainly is a factor, but because of internal organic reasons. Each era gains power—military, normative, economic, or chaotic—and then accumulates power until the next group dislodges the previous elite. The metaphysic behind this movement is, for Sarkar, the wave motion. There is a rise and then a fall. In addition, this wave motion is pulsative; that is, the speed of change fluctuates over time. The driving force for this change is first the dialectical interaction with the environment, second the dialectical interaction in the mind and in ideologies, and third the dialectical interaction between both ideas and the environment. But there is also another motivation: the attraction toward the Great; the individual attraction toward the supreme. This is the ultimate desire that frees humans of all desires.

While clash, conflict, and cohesion with the natural and social environment drive the cycle, it is the attraction to the Great, the infinite, that is the solution or the answer to the problem of history. It results in progress. For Sarkar, the cycle must continue, for it is a basic structure in mind, but exploitation is not a necessity. Through the *sadvipra*, exploitation can be minimized.

To conclude, Sarkar's theory uses the metaphors of the human life cycle and the ancient wheel; that is, technology. There is the natural and there is human intervention. There is a structure and there is choice. It is Sarkar's theory that provides this intervention; an intervention that, for Sarkar, will lead to humanity as a whole finally taking its first deep breath of fresh air.

## NOTES

1. Ananda Marga, *Ananda Vaniis* (Bangkok: Ananda Marga, 1982).
2. See Vimala Schneider, *The Politics of Prejudice* (Denver: Ananda Marga, 1983). See also Tim Anderson, *Free Alister, Dunn and Anderson* (Sidney: Wild and Wolley, 1985); and Anandamitra Avadhutika, *Tales of Torture* (Hong Kong: Ananda Marga, 1981).
3. For various interpretations of caste in Indian history and politics, see Nicholas Dirks, *The Hollow Crown* (Cambridge: Cambridge University Press, 1987); Rajni Kothari, *Caste in Indian Politics* (New Delhi: Orient Longman, 1970); Louis Dumont, *Homo Hierarchicus* (Chicago: University of Chicago Press, 1979).
4. Romila Thapar, *A History of India* (Baltimore: Penguin Books, 1966), 161.
5. Prabhat Rainjan Sarkar, *Supreme Expression*, vols. 1–2 (Den Bosch, The Netherlands: Nirvikalpa Press, 1978), 17.
6. Mircea Eliade, *The Myth of the Eternal Return* (Princeton, N.J.: Princeton University Press, 1971), 118.
7. Prabhat Rainjan Sarkar, *The Liberation of Intellect—Neo-Humanism* (Calcutta: Ananda Marga, 1983).
8. See Sarvepalli Radhakrishnan, "History: An Idealist's View," in *Readings in Indian History, Philosophy and Politics*, ed. K. Satchidananda Murti (Dehli: Motilal Banarsidass, 1974).
9. Sri Aurobindo, "The Spirituality and Symmetric Character of Indian Culture," and "The Triune Reality," in Murty, *Readings*, 361.
10. See Buddha Prakash, "The Hindu Philosophy of History," *Journal of the History of Ideas* 16 (1958): 494–505.
11. Shrii Anandamurti (P. R. Sarkar), *Namah Shivaya Shantaya* (Calcutta: Ananda Marga, 1982), 165.
12. See Ronald Inden, "Orientalist Constructions of India," *Modern Asian Studies* 20 (1986): 401–446; See also Edward Said, *Orientalism* (New York: Vintage Books, 1979); and Ashis Nandy, *Traditions, Tyranny, and Utopias* (New Delhi: Oxford University Press, 1987).
13. See Jawaharlal Nehru, "History: A Scientific Humanist's View," in Murti, *Readings*.
14. Ranajit Guha and Gayatri Chakravorty Spivak, *Selected Subaltern Studies* (New York: Oxford University Press, 1988). See also D. D. Kosambit, "A Marxist Interpretation of Indian History," in Murty, *Readings*, 40.

## 2.19

### Riane Eisler: Dominator and Partnership Shifts

*Riane Eisler*

Cultural transformation theory proposes that we can better understand our past, our present, and the possibilities for our future by charting the dynamic interaction of two movements. The first is the tendency of social systems to move toward greater complexity, largely because of technological breakthroughs or phase changes. The second is the movement of cultural shifts between two basic organizational forms or "attractors": the dominator and partnership models.

This theory derives from a multidisciplinary study of history (including folklore and myth). Like nonlinear dynamics and chaos theory, it is nonlinear, focusing on both systems maintenance and transformative change. It includes the full span of human evolution, beginning with protohistory. Unlike conventional approaches that focus almost exclusively on what has accurately been called "the story of man," it draws from a database that includes the whole of humanity, both its female and male halves.

Cultural transformation theory proposes that the emergence of our species initiates the age of coevolution or cocreation. Now, because of ever more powerful human technologies, cultural, rather than biological, evolution begins to play an ever greater role. At each decisive technological juncture, the principle of templating determines the choices for technological applications. For example, the templating of the dominator model gives high priority to technologies for domination and destruction, whereas the templating of the partnership model gives high priority to technologies that sustain and enhance life. The principle of cumulation then amplifies this templating, driving the social system and history in one direction and against each other.

Cultural transformation theory thus proposes a multilinear rather than unilinear course for human cultural evolution. While the mainstream in the early development of civilization oriented more to a partnership model, during a chaotic period in our prehistory there was a shift in a dominator direction.[1] In our time of systems disequilibrium, we see a powerful thrust toward a partnership model, countered by strong dominator systems resistance—with our future depending on the outcome.

### SOCIAL SYSTEMS: TWO BASIC MODELS

Looking at human cultures from this new perspective makes it possible to see patterns that are otherwise invisible. It also makes it possible to see that the virtual omission of half of our species from the study of society has created severe distortions and inaccuracies. It has obscured the fact that how a society structures the roles and relations of the female and male halves of humanity is of critical importance for the structure of all institutions—from the family, religion, and education, to politics and economics. It has obscured the fact that the social construction of gender roles and relations affects, and is in turn affected by, a society's guiding system of values and cognitive cultural maps. And it has made it impossible to see striking commonalities in societies that, on the surface, seem completely different.

## The Dominator Model

The samurai of medieval Japan, Hitler's Germany, the Masai of nineteenth-century East Africa, and Khomeini's Iran are generally considered to have nothing in common. But underneath their radically different surfaces is a distinctive pattern that only becomes visible when information about women and traits and activities in these societies associated with femininity or masculinity are taken into account.

The samurai culture arose from a swing not only toward rigid male dominance, but also toward a highly stratified and authoritarian system in which the samurai or warriors—as well as the fighting of wars—were accorded high value.[2] Similarly, the rise of fascism in Germany was characterized not only by a shift toward warfare and other forms of institutionalized social violence, such as the Nazi's infamous death camps, but also by the reinstitutionalization of rigid male dominance and the reidealization of the male as warrior.[3] Male socialization for the highly warlike Masai likewise hinged on the identification of masculine identity with dominance and aggression: in other words, with strongman rule, be it in intimate or intertribal relations. The idealization of the male as "holy" warrior and the return of women to their "traditional" place in a rigidly male-dominated family was also central to Khomeini's authoritarian and violent regime in Iran.

In short, the common feature of all these seemingly diverse social systems is that they primarily orient to the same basic model of social organization. This is the androcratic version of the dominator model. Depending on which basic human type—the female or the male—is ranked over the other, this model can take two forms. One is the ranking of women over men in a matriarchal or gynocratic form of social organization. The second, which has prevailed over most of recorded history, is a patriarchal or androcratic social structure based on the ranking of men over women in a domination hierarchy ultimately backed up by force or the threat of force.

Like earlier examples of this model, such as the theocracies of ancient Babylon and Judaea, and the Aryans, Dorians, and other Indo-European tribes, such societies have a characteristic and mutually reinforcing social and ideological configuration: rigid male dominance and the devaluation of anything considered "soft" or "feminine," a generally hierarchic and authoritarian social organization, and a high degree of institutionalized social violence, ranging from child and wife beating to chronic warfare.

The more closely a system approximates this model, the more highly such stereotypically "masculine" values as aggression, dominance, and conquest tend to be idealized and accorded social governance. Qualities such as caring, compassion, and peacefulness may be given lip service by both women and men. However, they are generally considered appropriate only for women and "weak" or "effeminate" men; in other words, for those who are in both social structure and cognition automatically excluded from social governance.

Here, two points are crucial. First, every society will have some violence, but in the dominator model violence is institutionalized to maintain rigid rankings of domination and idealized as "heroic masculinity." Second, we are dealing with stereotypes based primarily on gender-specific socialization, and not innate biological differences between women and men.[4]

### The Partnership Model

In the model of partnership or *gylany*, neither half of humanity is permanently ranked over the other.[5] This is a way of structuring human relations—be they of men and women, or of different races, religions, and nations—in which diversity is not automatically equated with inferiority or superiority.[6] Here, we find a different core configuration: a more equal partnership between women and men in both the so-called private and public spheres, a more generally democratic political and economic structure, and (since it is not required to maintain rigid rankings of domination) abuse and violence are neither idealized nor institutionalized. Stereotypically "feminine" values can be integrated into the social guidance system.

Today there is a strong movement toward a partnership social organization (most notably in the Scandinavian world).[7] However, until recently, societies approximating this configuration were believed to exist only at the most technologically primitive level, among tribes such as the Ba-Mbuti, Tiruray, and !Kung.[8] In the nineteenth century, archaeologists found evidence of prehistoric societies that were not androcratic or patriarchal, which they termed matriarchal.[9] But more recent archaeological findings, as well as closer reexaminations of earlier discoveries, indicate that these earlier societies oriented to a partnership model.

These findings are congruent with myths about an earlier, more harmonious and peaceful age. The Judeo-Christian Bible tells of a garden where woman and man lived in harmony with each other and nature—a time before a male god decreed that woman should henceforth be subservient to man. The Chinese Tao Te Ching recounts a time when the yin or feminine principle was not yet ruled by the male principle or yang—a more peaceful and just time when, we are told, the wisdom of the mother was still honored. The ancient writings of the Greek poet Hesiod tell of a "golden race" who lived in peaceful ease before a "lesser race" brought in Ares, the Greek god of war.

While these stories were undoubtedly over-idealized, they are congruent with archaeological findings.[10] There is evidence of stable Neolithic societies, going back approximately 8,000 years, where the arts flourished and differences in status and wealth, as the British archaeologist James Mellaart writes, were not extreme. There are also strong indications that these were not male-dominant societies. Their anthropomorphic religious imagery was primarily female. Women were priestesses and important craftspeople. As the archaeologist Marija Gimbutas wrote, before Old Europe was overrun by Indo-European hordes, the female was seen as "creative and active," with neither the female nor the male "subordinate to the other."[11] There is a paucity of fortifications and signs of destruction through war, and their extensive and advanced art does not glorify warriors and wars.[12]

In sum, while these were not ideal or even violence-free societies, there is archaeological and mythical evidence that the original direction of Western civilization was more peaceful and socially and ecologically balanced. That is, it oriented primarily to the partnership model. But there is also evidence that during a chaotic period of disequilibrium there was a shift to the dominator model, bringing into sharp relief the interaction between cultural shifts and technological phase changes.

## TECHNOLOGICAL PHASE CHANGES AND CULTURAL SHIFTS

As noted earlier, the emergence of our species initiated the age of human coevolution or cocreation. In its initial phase, it brought with it the first human-made tools and artifacts, as well as that most fundamental conceptual tool: language.[13] It is also in this initial phase that the two basic forms of social organization first appeared.

The traditional assumption has been that the development of androcratic social organization—the interactive configuration of rigid male dominance, strongman rule, and institutionalized violence—and the development of human society are one and the same. Accordingly, "man the hunter" is generally presented as the sole protagonist of our early technological evolution. However, fossil remains indicate that (like apes, monkeys, and most contemporary foraging tribes) early hominids survived primarily on a vegetarian diet. Moreover, as the paleoanthropologist Adrienne Zihlman and the anthropologist Nancy Tanner note, "woman the gatherer" seems to have played a major part in the evolution of human technology.

Zihlman and Tanner cite data indicating that chimpanzee females, who, like human mothers, share food with their offspring, are among the most adept nonhuman tool users, often using sticks to more effectively dig up roots and small forms of animal protein.[14] They argue that the hominid mothers who shared food with their offspring (and therefore had to gather extra food) followed this practice, and that they probably also fashioned the first containers to carry and store food.

By developing these technologies and by using stones and mortars to soften vegetable fibers for their babies, these females improved their offsprings' chances of survival. Moreover, this may have facilitated the gradual substitution of smaller jaws and teeth for the large jaws and mandibles with which most other primates soften vegetable foods—a cocreative process that facilitated the evolution of a species with room in its cranium for our large human brain and the larynx box needed for the vocalizations we call language.

### The Agrarian Age

The next major technological phase change is our shift from technologies to merely forage for food to our cocreation of food with nature through the technology of farming. This phase begins approximately 10,000 B.C., at the onset of the Neolithic or first agrarian age (although the first use of seeds probably goes back thousands of years earlier). Indeed, rather than being discrete developments, each phase change is a gradual process, in which at first isolated new nucleations eventually culminate in qualitative systems change.

Again, traditional accounts of this phase have been male-centered—even though Neolithic art centered on female anthropomorphic images.[15] These religious images offer important information about the cognitive maps of Çatal Hüyük and other early Neolithic sites. As Mellaart writes, they also provide the "missing link" between the Paleolithic so-called Venus figurines (25,000-year-old full-bodied, often pregnant, female images) and the veneration in historic times of a Great Goddess from whose womb all life is born and to whose womb all life returns at death, like the cycles of vegetation, to be reborn.

As noted, in these more egalitarian and peaceful early farming societies women and men seem to have lived and worked in partnership. Flowing from a more reliable supply of food and other natural resources, they bequeathed us most of the life-supporting and life-enhancing technologies on which later civilizations are founded: from the manufacture of fibers into sophisticated rugs, wall hangings, and clothing and the use of clay and wood for increasingly complex housing and furniture to the building of seaworthy boats for transportation and trade and the first mining and smelting of metals for both jewelry and tools. It is also here that, through the cumulation of partnership templating, we see the first great expansion of humanity's mental powers through the creation of complex cultural systems, including intricate systems of religion, government, and the arts.

Agriculture (and, with this, the concentration of larger settled populations) could only develop in relatively fertile areas. In less hospitable regions, there was a different technological development: nomadic pastoralism. The mass migrations of nomadic herders from their homelands during times of prolonged drought and gradual desertification brought cataclysmic changes in the mainstream of Western cultural and technological evolution.[16]

In Europe, as the Indo-Europeanist J. P. Mallory writes, nomadic incursions displaced and destroyed previous cultures. Gimbutas dates the beginning of these incursions between the fifth and fourth millennia B.C. These invaders (who as Gimbutas writes, were "ruled by priestly and warrior classes who had mastered the horse and weapons of war") brought with them a different technological emphasis.[17]

In more partnership-oriented societies, the emphasis had been on technologies to create: technologies to sustain and enhance human life, guided by the life-giving image of a Great Mother. The emphasis after the shift to an androcratic direction—as one might predict from a culture that in its more technologically primitive stages, as Gimbutas notes, deified the lethal power of the blade—focused on technologies to destroy: technologies to enable men to dominate and conquer.[18] Now we begin to find such seemingly diverse, but essentially related, gods of war as the Greek Ares and the Hebrew Yahweh or Jehovah. Even female deities like Ishtar and Athene, through the process of cooption, became identified with warfare—an ideological metamorphosis, as the religious historian E. O. James notes.[19]

This is not to imply that natural and human resources were no longer channeled into technologies to support and, at least for those on top, enhance life. But, as noted earlier, in societies orienting primarily to a partnership or dominator model there is a different system of cultural templating.

In dominator-oriented societies, priority is given to the power symbolized by the blade: the power to dominate and destroy. As a consequence, in most Bronze Age civilizations, with the notable exception of Minoan Crete, the character of Western civilization became profoundly altered. Nonetheless—and this is of critical importance for the revision of our cognitive maps of history—even after this cultural transformation, gylany remained in the cultural substratum, coopted and exploited.

The partnership model also acted as a "periodic attractor." As we enter recorded history, we see oscillations between periods of partnership resurgence followed, until now, by androcratic regression. For example, the rise of early Christianity, inspired by the partnership teachings of Jesus, was followed by the rigidly male-dominant, authoritarian, and highly violent (as in its inquisitions and witchburnings) "orthodox" Church. Thus, the dominator and partnership models as periodic attractors provide new insight into the dynamics underlying seemingly random workings of history, including the extreme violence of medieval "men of God."

Moving forward into the next technological phase change, the underlying tension between the partnership and dominator configurations becomes progressively greater. While the attractor of the partnership model becomes stronger, the scale of violence of androcratic regressions vastly increases—mainly due to larger populations and more "advanced" techniques of destruction.

### The Industrial Age

This next major phase change is the modern industrial or machine age. With the rise of capitalism, machines began to be used for other purposes than the aggrandizement and entertainment of ruling elites (like the ingenious hydraulically powered fountains at the Villa d'Este near Rome). Nonetheless, their uses were still largely guided by the cognitive maps of a dominator rather than partnership model.

There is no inherent reason manufacturing plants during the earlier phases of industrialization had to be designed as assembly lines in which humans themselves became cogs in giant machines. This is demonstrated by a Swedish Volvo plant's switch in the 1960s to work teams that made many of their own decisions about how to best build a car, rather than themselves becoming automatons. Neither was there anything inherent in industrial technology to make sweatshops, mines, and other business enterprises exploit and dehumanize men, women, and children in dangerous workplaces. Nor is a worldview that sees nature's life-giving and sustaining capacities (like woman's life-giving and sustaining capacities) as no more than man's natural due inherent in industrial technology.

The idealization of "man's conquest of Nature" was not introduced by Newtonian science or Cartesian rationalism. It is articulated in religious passages such as Genesis 1:28, where we read that God gave man dominion "over every living thing that moveth upon the earth." Bacon's often-quoted pronouncement that science must "torture nature's secrets from her" is not a function of modern thinking, much less modern science.[20] It stems from entrenched dominator cognitive maps going back all the way to the Babylonian *Enuma Elish*, where (in another mythical clue to a fundamental cultural shift) the god Marduk creates the world by dismembering the body of the Mother Goddess Tiamat.[21] But, through the cumulation of dominator cultural templating, the environmental damage caused by ever more powerful technologies now begins to reach critical proportions.

### The Nuclear/Electronic/Biochemical Age

The next major phase change, the nuclear/electronic/biochemical age, starts in the second half of the twentieth century. Now, our species possesses technologies as powerful as the processes of nature, including unprecedentedly powerful technologies to take life through ever more exorbitantly expensive weaponry—the kind of power to destroy all life on this planet formerly attributed only to a supreme Father God. This has fueled an intensifying movement to complete the shift from a dominator to a partnership model.

The organized modern challenge to entrenched traditions of domination already began with the post-Enlightenment political rebellions against the "divinely ordained" rule of kings in Europe and the Americas during the eighteenth and nineteenth centuries. It continued in the twentieth century with ever more intensive challenges to the dominator rankings of racism, colonialism, and, through the resurgence of feminism with the twentieth-century women's movement, the male half of humanity's control over the female half. Most recently, the domination and conquest of nature has been challenged by the environmental movement. At the same time, the challenge to the third major component of androcracy, a high degree of institutionalized violence, has also become progressively stronger—not only in the growing rejection of war as a means of conflict resolution, but also in the growing exposure of institutionalized forms of intimate violence such as wife battering, child beating, and rape.

But this mounting global partnership movement has, in turn, sparked intensified dominator systems-maintenance pressures. One manifestation, which we see all around us, is the reidealization of "masculine" aggression and conquest. As the works of social psychologists David Winter and David McClelland show, such manifestations predict what we, in fact, are seeing worldwide: a backlash of repression and the escalation of violence in intertribal and international, as well as intimate, relations.[22] Another manifestation is the concentration in mammoth transnational corporations of enormous economic and political power, leading governments and international agencies such as the World Bank and the International Monetary Fund to formulate policies that further widen the gap between haves and have nots—including "structural adjustment" policies that curtail social funding for such stereotypically "feminine" priorities as feeding children and caring for people's health.[23] Still another manifestation is the pressure by dominator religious elites to reinstate strongman rule in both home and state (a phenomenon occurring worldwide through the rise of Christian, Muslim, Hindu, and other forms of so-called religious fundamentalism, which is actually dominator fundamentalism) and efforts to again confine women to their traditional mothering roles[24] (even though every year 90 million more people swell our numbers, exacerbating already severe economic, ecological, and social problems).[25]

### The Human Actualization or Extinction Phase

Today we stand at an evolutionary crossroads. Guided by a partnership cognitive cultural map, the cumulating result of human creativity and technology could be the realization of our unique human potentials. Guided by a dominator cognitive cultural map, our level of technological development could lead to the end of our human adventure on Earth.

In charting the dynamics of cultural shifts and technological phase changes sketched in this chapter, I have become convinced that we can shift from a dominator to a partnership direction during this time of global systems disequilibrium. We need to address many interlocking forms of domination and exploitation, from the economic domination and exploitation of "inferior" races to the unbridled exploitation and domination of nature. But only when we consciously focus on the critical importance of how the roles and relations of the female and male halves of humanity are structured will we have the foundation we have lacked until now: a solid base on which to build a more equitable, peaceful, and ecologically sustainable world.

Let us develop new cognitive maps that take into account the whole of our history and the whole of humanity. Then we can make more conscious and humane choices for our future—before the cumulation of dominator cultural templating cuts short the age of human cocreation.

### NOTES

1. Although my work focuses on Western civilization, there are indications of this shift in other major world regions, such as Meso-America and Asia. See June Nash, "The Aztecs and the Ideology of Male Dominance," *Signs* 4 (1978): 349–362.

2. See, for example, I. Takamure, *Joshi no Rekishi*, vols. 1–2 (Tokyo: Kodansha Bunko, 1975).

3. Claudia Koonz, "Mothers in the Fatherland: Women in Nazi Germany," in *Becoming Visible: Women in European History*, ed. Renate Bridenthal and Claudia Koonz (Boston: Houghton Mifflin, 1977).

4. See, for example, R. C. Lewontin, Steven Rose, and Leon J. Kamin, *Not in Our Genes* (New York: Pantheon Books, 1984); Anne Fausto-Sterling, *Myths of Gender: Biological Theories about Women and Men* (New York: Pergamon Press, 1984); Ruth Hubbard, *The Politics of Women's Biology* (New York: Rutgers University Press, 1990).

5. *Gylany* is a neologism composed of *gy* (from the Greek *gyne* or woman) and *an* (from the Greek *andros* or man), with the linking letter *l* between them standing for the Greek verbs *lyein* (to resolve) or *lyo* (to set free).

6. I distinguish between hierarchies of domination and actualization. Riane Eisler and David Loye, *The Partnership Way* (San Francisco: HarperSanFrancisco, 1990), particularly charts and discussion on 179.

7. Riane Eisler, David Loye, and Kari Norgaard, *Women, Men, and the Global Quality of Life* (Pacific Grove, Calif.: Center for Partnership Studies, 1995).

8. Colin Turnbull, *The Forest People: A Study of the Pygmies of the Congo* (New York: Simon and Schuster, 1961); P. Draper, "!Kung Women: Contrasts in Sexual Egalitarianism in Foraging and Sedentary Contexts," in *Toward an Anthropology of Women*, ed. R. Reiter (New York: Monthly Review Press, 1975); Stuart Schlegel, *Tiruray Justice: Traditional Tiruray Law and Morality* (Berkeley and Los Angeles: University of California Press, 1970).

9. See, for example, J. J. Bachofen, *Myth, Religion, and Mother Right* (Princeton, N.J.: Princeton University Press, 1967).

10. See, for example, James Mellaart, *Çatal Hüyük* (New York: McGraw-Hill, 1967); Marija Gimbutas, *The Goddesses and Gods of Old Europe* (Berkeley and Los Angeles: University of California Press, 1982); Nicolas Platon, *Crete* (Geneva: Nagel, 1966).

11. Marija Gimbutas, "The First Wave of Eurasian Steppe Pastoralists into Copper Age Europe," *Journal of Indo-European Studies* 5, 4 (1977): 277–338.

12. Jaquetta Hawkes, *Dawn of the Gods* (New York: Random House, 1968); Platon, *Crete*; Mellaart, *Çatal Hüyük*; Gimbutas, *The Goddesses and Gods of Old Europe*.

13. Riane Eisler, "Technology at the Turning Point," *International Synergy* 2, 1 (1987): 54–63.

14. Nancy Tanner, *On Becoming Human* (Boston: Cambridge University Press, 1981); Adrienne Zihlman, "Women in Evolution, Part II: Subsistence and Social Organization among Early Hominids," *Signs* 4, 1 (1978): 4–20.

15. Eric Neumann, *The Great Mother* (Princeton, N.J.: Princeton University Press, 1955).

16. James DeMeo, "The Origins and Diffusion of Patrism in Saharasia, c. 4000 B.C.E.: Evidence for a Worldwide, Climate-Linked Geographical Pattern in Human Behavior," *World Futures* 30, 2 (1991): 247–271.

17. J. P. Mallory, *In Search of the Indo-Europeans* (New York: Thames and Hudson, 1989), 238; Marija Gimbutas, *The Civilization of the Goddess* (San Francisco: HarperSanFrancisco, 1991).

18. Gimbutas, "The First Wave," 281.

19. E. O. James, *The Cult of the Mother Goddess* (London: Thames & Hudson, 1959). The dominator shift is reflected in symbology idealizing a masculinity of "heroic warfare" and "strong-man rule," which, along with feminine subservience, is basic to the gendered subtext of dominator cognitive maps.

20. Bacon, quoted in Fritjof Capra, *The Turning Point* (New York: Bantam Books, 1983), 56.

21. For how biological and social systems replicate themselves, see Vilmos Csanyi, *Evolutionary Systems and Society: A General Theory* (Durham, N.C., and London: Duke University Press, 1989).

22. David McClelland, *Power: The Inner Experience* (New York: Irvington, 1975); David Winter, *The Power Motive* (New York: The Free Press, 1973).
23. This pattern templates the 1995 U.S. Congressional cutbacks of social programs. The rationale was federal deficit reduction, but Congress voted $7 billion for obsolete aircraft the military did not even want and proposed a $425 billion tax break for upper-income taxpayers.
24. For example, in Bangladesh, Muslim fundamentalists staged a demonstration demanding the government ban nongovernmental organizations that educate women and provide health care for them or face a religious war—even though Bangladesh has never been a particularly orthodox Islamic country—because, as one Bangladesh politician put it, "they have challenged the authority of the husband." Joe Klein, "Mothers vs. Mullahs," *Newsweek*, 17 April 1995, 56.
25. "1994 World Population Data Sheet," *World Population News Service POPLINE* 16 (May–June 1994), 1.

## 2.20

# *Cosmic Gaia:*
# *Homeostasis and Planetary Evolution*

Christopher B. Jones

Cosmic Gaia is a biography of the planet Earth's evolution that combines macrohistory with geology, climatology, geochemistry, and biology. The Gaia hypothesis was not originally conceived as an exploration of the past, present, and future of human history, but as bold planetary history. Furthermore, the story of Gaia and biography of planet Earth told by maverick British scientist James Lovelock has significant implications for the macrohistory of humanity. Lovelock's hypothesis is significant, not because it looks at a broad scope of planetary events and developments, but because it looks at these in a new and different way. What sets Lovelock's conception apart is that, unlike most scientists who study the ancient Earth (e.g., geologists, paleobiologists), he conceives of the Earth as a living organism.

The study of macrohistory and the study of Gaia (called geophysiology) are similar. While macrohistory looks at the underlying forces and energies that move history and civilizations, geophysiology looks at the whole history of life on Earth that includes human history. If macrohistory is a broad framework of analysis to help us better understand the past, present, and future of humanity, then geophysiology (i.e., the study of the health of Gaia) is a broad framework to understand the future of the planet and our place in the planetary scheme of things.

## GAIA AS HYPOTHESIS

Geophysiology and the Gaia hypothesis have been widely publicized and hotly debated in the scientific community. Gaia's emerging biography is at least partly tied to Lovelock's own biography. It is no mistake that such a theory should come from an independent scientist, a self-described maverick.[1] Lovelock, inventor of the electron capture device (the instrument that allows us to measure quantities of gas and pollutants in parts per million or smaller), has managed to remain outside large, bureaucratic, scientific organizations (although occasionally consulting for them). In defiance of conventional wisdom that the Earth is essentially dead and that the gross planetary mechanisms are either chemically or physically based, he proposes that the Earth is like a living organism whose parts maintain optimal conditions for life.

The Gaia hypothesis evolved as an idea during Lovelock's consulting work with the National Aeronautics and Space Administration (NASA) Jet Propulsion Laboratory. Discussions on the possibility of life on Mars led Lovelock to look at the long-term history of the atmosphere, oceans, and biosphere and their roles in the evolution of life on this planet. There were some curious aspects of the Earth's history, such as the roles of oxygen and carbon dioxide, temperature, and ocean salinity, that suggested that conditions favorable to life were being manipulated by life. Life has existed on the planet a large fraction of the time since its formation—despite the incredible odds against it. Lovelock and his collaborators formulated a hypothesis: Life maintains conditions favorable to the existence of life on Earth.

## COSMIC PROPORTIONS

Lovelock's biography of Gaia is of truly cosmic proportions. Geological evidence points to the emergence of life some 3.5 billion years ago. From the radioactivity of rocks, we can deduce that the Earth itself formed roughly a billion years (an eon) before that. Lovelock has reasoned that the first billion years of microscopic life laid the foundation for the emergence of Gaia. Part of the transition from earliest life to a planetary regulatory system—Gaia—was the accumulation of oxygen in the atmosphere. The accumulation of this gas led to the first major crisis of the biosphere, and mass extinction (of prokaryote bacteria) roughly 2.5 billion years ago. The period of the last 2.5 billion years constitutes Gaia's life as a "social organism," and the period in which life has blossomed and bloomed into a tightly coupled complex of interactions between plants, animals, insects, microbes, atmosphere, soil, and water.

The unit of measurement for human macrohistory is either a stage of human development or a period of civilization. The unit of analysis for Gaian macrohistory is the lifetime of an entire planet's 2.5-billion-year-old symbiotic life system. While primitive microbial life existed for an eon before that, Lovelock traces Gaia's genesis from the transition of an anaerobic to an aerobic atmosphere (i.e., oxygen rich), and from the dominance of prokaryote to eukaryotic bacteria. Lovelock is clear, however, that Gaia is more than just the biosphere. She is the whole of the oceans, atmosphere, lifeforms, and land surface that are tightly coupled in their interactions with one another.

Lovelock has his share of critics who see various elements of Gaia (e.g., geology) as processes independent of life's processes. His theory bucks the mainstream paradigm operating in much of biology, geology, and geochemistry. The paradigm is that the Earth has been formed primarily through physical and chemical processes, and the biota has had only a minor role, not a decisive one. Lovelock continues to look for evidence that it is the biological sphere that has driven and regulated the physical realm.

One indicator that Gaia has had a hand in regulating the planet's environment is the constancy of the amounts of oxygen in the atmosphere. As improbable as it might seem, the level of oxygen in the atmosphere has remained fairly constant over eons, neither so low nor so high that aerobic life has died out. For example, had the percentage of oxygen ever been over 24 percent, lightning strikes would have set the world afire. At 24 percent oxygen, even damp vegetation would burn. Lovelock cites evidence of the existence of charcoal in the geological record that suggests that there has been enough oxygen available for forest fires, but not so much oxygen to produce a dramatic global conflagration.

Another aspect of the planet's past that Lovelock cites as evidence of Gaia's regulatory process is the constancy of the salinity of the world's oceans. The evidence suggests that there has been a near steady-state condition for ocean salt, although salt continues to run off the land and into the oceans. According to Lovelock, the runoff from land surfaces and mid-oceanic creation of salts would raise the oceans to their current level of salinity (3.5%) in only 60 million years. Yet evidence suggests that the Earth's oceans have rarely exceeded this percentage in 4 billion years.

The third major element that stands out as a stable factor in the Earth's environment is the atmospheric temperature. The surface temperature of the Earth appears to have been relatively constant since the very dawn of life on the planet. Earth's temperature has remained somewhere between the freezing and boiling points of water, although in the 2.5-billion-year life of Gaia the solar output has increased by roughly 30 percent. Lovelock explains that this feature is due to the production of greenhouse gases and/or their regulation by the planet's biological communities. More than any other factor, the regulation of temperature within a narrow range has been crucial to the existence of life as we know it.

Among the biggest criticisms of the Gaia hypothesis is that it is teleological. The objection has been that species are not altruistic and do not purposely decide to evolve in certain ways (or evolve to serve certain regulatory planetary functions) to maintain optimal conditions for life. Lovelock, however, has never argued that life had foresight or planned developments to maintain optimal conditions. In *Gaia: A New Look at Life on Earth*, Lovelock used cybernetics as a way of trying to explain how specific biological mechanisms could function as negative (or positive) feedback mechanisms in regulating the planetary environment. Like the thermostat in a heating system or the governor in an engine, there are biological feedback processes that dampen or regulate changes in the planetary environment.

A key concept related to the Gaian cybernetic system is homeostasis, or "that remarkable state of constancy" that organisms maintain when the environment around them is changing. Particularly because of the mechanical connotation of the word "cybernetic," homeostasis describes the Gaian tendency for the atmosphere, oceans, soil, and biosphere to sustain moderate environmental conditions by active control.

Following the publication of Lovelock's first book, he and a colleague developed a simple computer model called the "Daisyworld" model. In this simulation, black and white daisies were used to populate a hypothetical world. Lovelock and coauthor Andrew Watson designed this world populated only by daisies to model what would happen to the planet's temperature over time as the solar output changed. In the early life of this planet, dark daisies predominated and warmed the planet. As the solar output from its hypothetical sun grew, the proportion of white daisies also grew and effectively cooled the planet. This simple model illustrated—with nothing more than two colors of daisies—the natural tendency toward homeostasis and stability. The model also illustrated that perturbations to the system are homeostatically dampened and resisted, when the authors simulated the effects of planetesimal impacts on Daisyworld's surface.

In his second book, Lovelock adapted the model to explore the homeostatic influences of a variety of environmental features, including Daisyworlds populated by three colors of daisies, twenty colors of daisies, and then daisies, rabbits, and foxes. The results strongly suggest that the more variables (i.e., species), the more robust and viable the system becomes. Put simplistically, the more species, the more inclined the Gaian system is to maintain homeostatic conditions. This has led Lovelock to defend the species diversity of the tropical rainforest as a critical resource for the maintenance of the long-term stability of planetary environmental regulation.

Lovelock takes pains to be absolutely clear that, to him, Gaia is more than just biosphere; Gaia is the synthesis of life, atmosphere, ocean, and soil. Gaia is a living organism whose life depends on all these features. Metaphorically, the oceans and rivers are like the circulatory system, atmosphere like the feathers or fur (as well as a kind of circulatory system), and soil the medium out of which life springs. For Gaia, all these elements are inseparable, and have been for eons. Even those processes which we think of as purely physical, such as earthquakes and oceanic volcanoes, may have Gaian origins and Gaian "purposes." The processes of life extend deep into the planet and have become intrinsic to life as we know it, evolution as it is, and our future as a global species. Failure to recognize and act on that knowledge may be our undoing as a species.

## GAIA AS SYNTHESIS

In contrast to other macrohistory constructions in which the patterns of human civilization are characterized as linear, cyclical, and spiral, Gaia shares all those characteristics to some extent. Thus, to characterize Gaian development and future history simply as linear or cyclical might miss the point that Gaia has compounded many dimensions of biological and material environment developments. Metaphorically, in contrast to the two-dimensional patterns of human history, the patterns of Gaian history might be thought of as three dimensional. If human macrohistory has linear or cyclical qualities, then Gaian development has a "symbiotic" quality, because different stages of development have been compounded and synthesized. For example, even after the prokaryote cells fell from their global position of dominance, they became an indispensable part of other organisms and processes.

It seems almost inescapably the case that there is a unidirectional aspect to cosmic history. While the universe may expand and collapse in eternal cycles (as Buddhism and some Big Bang theories maintain), the life of stars, planets, and lifeforms are caught in a stream of space-time which flows only in one direction. Thus, Gaia is bound in a solar system whose star is reaching middle age and will ultimately die of old age. Gaia is generally at the mercy of universal processes of radioactive decay and Newton's law of thermodynamics. Gaia, whose age is a large fraction of that of the universe itself (based on estimates from astrophysics), is nevertheless a creature of the universal flow of time, energy, and entropy.

One example of Gaia's linear progress is the slow but steady decrease in the total atmospheric amount of the greenhouse gas carbon dioxide since the planet was first formed. Lovelock argues that this decrease is a mechanism which has compensated for the growing solar luminosity, some 30 percent greater now since the beginning of life on Earth. Gaia in an evolutionary sense is notable for her "development" and progression in forms and patterns of life which have grown ever more complex. The development of sensory organs and nervous systems is one example of patterns of linear planetary history.

Equally inescapable is the cyclical nature of the Gaian system, which has been subject to periodic mass extinctions and cosmic catastrophes, such as planetesimal, asteroid, and comet impacts, ice ages and glacial cycles, and other recurring astrophysical patterns. Some cyclical periods are diminishing, such as impacts with planetesimals, while others, such as ice cycles, appear to be increasing in frequency. Some cycles are as regular as clockwork, such as the galactic "year," the time it takes to revolve around the galactic center, approximately 250 million years.

Within the Gaian system, changes are produced by both endogenous (internal) and exogenous (external) forces. The byproducts of life itself (i.e., pollution) are sources of internal contradiction within the system which force individuals and species to adapt to new conditions. Forces external to the system, such as solar and cosmic radiation, also have an impact directly on individuals and indirectly on the local environment.

Endogenous factors include pollution (oxygen was the first major global contaminant), climate changes, volcanism, plate tectonics, local background radiation, and others. These factors have precipitated major stresses on the biotic community, such as ice ages and mass extinctions. The emergence of free oxygen around 2.5 billion years ago was nothing short of a global catastrophe which precipitated a dramatic transition from the dominance of one type of bacteria (anaerobic) to another (aerobic). As a result, anaerobic bacteria were effectively pushed into oxygen-free environments, such as marshes and sediment beds.

Exogenous forces have been no less instrumental in manifesting lifeform changes in the biosphere, and in many ways cosmic catastrophes have been even more dramatic in their effects. The impact of large planetesimals during the early phases of life on the planet created searing thermal shock waves and produced "nuclear winter" effects which lasted for years. Some major impact is still widely believed to have occurred roughly 65 million years ago, coinciding with the demise of the dinosaurs. Increasing solar radiation has had just as significant an impact on the evolution of life, although one far more gradual than sudden impacts.

The linear and cyclical aspects of Gaia's behavior and environment have influenced Gaian stages of growth by means of synthesis. Synthesis as a strategy of developing greater complexity is exemplified by the origin of multicellular organisms. The first forms of life on Earth were the prokaryote cells, a kind of primitive bacteria. One type of prokaryote was an ancestor of modern cyanobacteria, the first type of cell capable of photosynthesis. Some of these early bacteria evolved into endosymbionts—integrated parts (like organs) of larger, more complex cells. The eukaryotic cells, which dominated the Earth after the emergence of abundant oxygen, integrated these bacteria, as chloroplasts, into their cell structures in a symbiotic fashion.

That is not the end of the story of the cyanobacteria. The successors of other early prokaryote cells, the methanogens, found homes a few billion years later inside the intestines of large multicellular organisms. Not only are they found in insects, fish, and birds, but also in so-called "higher forms," such as mammals—including humans. As assistants in the process of our digestion, they also serve us symbiotically. In fact, it has been suggested that without these "lowly" forms of life the "higher" forms simply would not exist. They are the basic building blocks in Gaia's regulatory processes.

## GAIAN FUTURES

One lesson from astrophysics and its implications for geophysiology is the linear nature of change in the planet's thermodynamic balance (i.e., the sun is heating up). We are being reminded of this fact indirectly via the scientific debate on global warming and an accelerated greenhouse effect. The bottom line is that the external warming trend will continue. How Gaia responds to that, and how our species responds, is a major issue for future geophysiology.

The buildup of carbon dioxide ($CO_2$) in the last century from industrial production and deforestation has not created the "greenhouse effect." In fact, ($CO_2$) has served as a kind of thermal blanket (or greenhouse gas) for hundreds of millions of years to keep all life from freezing. Lovelock has pointed out, however, that the total amount of $CO_2$ necessary for that effect has decreased over time (since the sun keeps warming). Eventually, $CO_2$ will need to be "phased out" by Gaia if this regulatory process is to keep pace with a warming sun. When (or before) we reach the point where our $CO_2$ thermal blanket is no longer needed—in a few million years—one of two things must happen. Either a mechanism must evolve which would serve as an "icehouse effect," or Gaia will seek out a higher thermal steady state. If Gaia opts for a higher steady state, nearly all life on Earth will need to adapt to a much higher average surface temperature.

Technology now has become the vanguard of planetary change. Our use of technology for most of the last million or so years had little effect on Gaia. In the last century, this relationship has changed. Lovelock has cautioned that our industrial technologies may, in fact, be a catalyst to bring about the next (higher) thermal steady state. In other words, our production of carbon dioxide and the other dozen or so greenhouse gases may give us more than just a slightly higher global temperature; we may be seeing the onset of a new stage of life on Earth. One question is how or whether our species can adapt.

## COSMIC GAIANS

The relevance of geophysiology to macrohistory, more than anything else, is that it represents a new paradigm in science and social discourse in the West. It is, as the subtitle of Lovelock's first book announces, "a new view of life on Earth." As a holistic theory of our planet as a living organism, it presents a fundamental challenge to the conventional wisdom, and, as such, promises fundamental changes in science and technology. While it now represents hardly more than a peripheral challenge to the dominant paradigm, its potential as a threat to the scientific status quo should not be underestimated. Exactly what the implications are if it is able to supplant the dominant reductionist paradigm is yet to be determined. However, given the widespread environmental degradation and destruction, it may be that the Gaia hypothesis will receive even greater attention, both within the scientific community and elsewhere.

On the other hand, geophysiology is not enough to ensure the survival of our species and countless others. While understanding the past of Earth is important, the past of the planet is not necessarily a guide to where Gaia is headed in the future. Nor is geophysiology a substitute for the loss of meaning—the purpose and significance of daily life which has been trampled, along with the tropical forests and unwary species, under our feet in the name of progress.

Lovelock's original intention was not to promote a mythic conception of the Earth, but to describe this homeostatic self-regulating system. He borrowed the term Gaia, as suggested by his friend William Golding, in lieu of "the creation of barbarous acronyms, such as Biocybernetic Universal System Tendency/Homeostasis."[2] While Gaia was perhaps apt as a description of a global self-regulating system, it did indeed strike a mythic chord in theological and other spiritual circles fairly far afield from planetary ecology, biochemistry, and geology. From a Gaian perspective on planetary history, the evolution of more complex lifeforms is by no means indicative of their superiority. We are, in fact, all interdependent, regardless of the complexity of our nervous systems.

We humans are engaged in a grand planetary experiment. That is one reason why it does not seem to make much sense to talk about history anymore without considering our relations with Nature and the planetary context in which events and actions occur. Furthermore, we are at a nexus of technological, environmental, and social change unparalleled in the entirety of human experience. For macrohistory to be considered as an area of study or discourse, it must include the Big Picture of planetary history in which we are embedded.

## NOTES

1. James Lovelock, "The Independent Practice of Science," *CoEvolution Quarterly* 26 (Spring 1980): 22–30.
2. James Lovelock, *Gaia: A New Look at Life on Earth* (Oxford: Oxford University Press, 1979), 10.

# Chapter 3

# *Macrohistorians Compared: Toward a Theory of Macrohistory*

## Sohail Inayatullah

This chapter compares the selected macrohistorians to each other by using a series of defining factors of macrohistory. These factors are not exhaustive, nor does every macrohistory exhibit all these points; however, our own viewpoint is that the more of these points that are touched on, the more complete a theory of macrohistory. These factors are both theoretically inferred from analyzing macrohistory and empirically derived from a reading of numerous macrohistorians, mostly those from Chapter 2 (see Appendix A for a chart summarizing key perspectives and Appendix B for diagrams illustrating their theories). Perspectives from important thinkers such as Gaetano Mosca, Eric Voegelin, Michel Foucault, Fred Polak, and Elise Boulding are also introduced so as to gain additional insight into macrohistory and the selected macrohistorians.

Drawing from the introductory chapter, we can assert that macrohistory is about the trajectory of a unit through space and time. Macrohistory is the study of a unit through time (diachronic) and the study of noncontiguous points, neighborhoods, and contexts (nomothetic). Macrohistory, then, surveys history across various units of analysis, searching for patterns, regularities, and change.

By stepping back from this tapestry, we derive our first defining factor. The macrohistorian is part of this tapestry of space, time, and history existing in a certain context—a knowledge frame, a worldview, an episteme, or a cosmology.

If we move to the work itself, we can ask what the causes and mechanisms of change and the theory of change are. This is our second factor.

Is there an initial agent that disappears, or is change embedded in the model of macrohistory itself? What are the metaphysics of change? How does change occur? What are the specific mechanics of transformation? Finally, what changes and what is stable?

From this factor, we can then ask what the continuities and discontinuities within the trajectory are. What is the shape of change? This is our third factor: the stages of history and patterns of change. Without stages and patterns, time becomes muted and change invisible; the work would no longer be macrohistory.

But these stages need to be explained and the variance accounted for. From the notion of stages, the next logical point is this: In analyzing the causes or mechanisms of change, if we take this view, we see that the crux of the macrohistorian's theory rests on metaphysical choices in terms of what is immutable and what is changing in their theory. Related to this is a specific cause of change—the transcendental. This is our fourth factor. While many definitions are possible (the first cause, the prime mover, superagency), it is often considered the nonnegotiable dimension of history: that which is not relational, which exists by itself. Our question, however, is not theological but sociological; that is, how does the transcendental function in macrohistory?

All these causes and choices must concretely refer to something that is changing, the datapoints. The question then becomes, what exactly is changing through history? What is the unit of space that moves across time? This is our fifth factor. What is the range of possible units? And how does the choice of the unit relate to the episteme, the stages of history, the causes of change, and the role of the transcendental?

The stages, patterns, causes, and units are explained in a particular language. This language is given to the macrohistorian by the particular episteme. Language is constitutive of the data of history, not a neutral describer of data. To go deeper into the work of the macrohistorian, we can ask what metaphors each author uses. This is our sixth factor. How do these metaphors enlighten and darken particular stages of history or units of analysis? Metaphors create worlds: They fix stages, entrances, and exits. Then we can ask if there are ways to transcend these worlds our words have created. In particular, we focus on how each macrohistorian creates different metaphors of time.

Not only are there ways to transcend the metaphors of history, but macrohistorians also articulate concrete ways to transcend the stages of history to create a new future. How will the new future be brought about and who will bring about this new future? Who are the vanguards of change? This is our seventh factor.

The eighth factor relates to the earlier question, but asks not who will bring on the next stage of history, but if there are ways out of the entire project itself. That is, is there an exit from the grand narratives created by the macrohistorical project? Once entered, are there escapes? This is a question of how seriously the macrohistorian and believers see history—as a guiding light for inquiry and action or a totalizing truth empirically based on some "objective" account of the past. This is a question and an analysis of the politics engendered by the theory. Sensitivity to the long-range social and human implications of the theory is another important way to analyze the macrohistory.

Macrohistory not only has value in terms of understanding the past but also in understanding the future. While the two previous points are contextualized by the stages of history (the vanguard and the politics of exit), we can also generally ask what the theory says about the future. Can the pattern of the past be applied to the future? In addition, what is the view of the future from the particular macrotheory? This is our ninth factor. Is the future bright for all, or only for a few? Will the future be but a recapitulation of some ancient time? Is there a difference between the desired future and the future predicted by the theory? Can anything be done to bridge this gap, if it exists?

Finally, given that each macrohistorian, by necessity, has a perspective on the writing of history—on historiography—we need to understand these views to better appreciate their macrohistory and to understand their own location in the writing of history. What is the relationship between the macrohistorian's own text and other texts? For example, does the author believe that previous histories have been fundamentally flawed and his or her macrohistory provides the correct approach? This is our tenth and last point, thus completing our theory of macrohistory and macrohistorians.

In summary, these factors are as follows:

1. The episteme and context of macrohistories and macrohistorians
2. The causes and mechanisms of change
3. The stages of history and patterns of change
4. Metaphysical choices and the role of the transcendental
5. The units of analysis and their weight or role in creating change
6. The metaphors of time used to illustrate the theory
7. The role of the vanguard of change (Who will create the new order?)
8. The exits or escapes from their theoretical constructs
9. Perspectives on the future
10. Perspectives on historiography

The first factor encircles the theory, placing it in a broader epistemological framework. The second to fifth factors examine the dynamics and shape of change, asking what is changeable and what is immutable. The sixth factor builds on the previous five and explores the language—the metaphors—of the earlier factors. The seventh to ninth factors examine the implication of the macrohistorians' theories, especially as they relate to the future. The last factor again locates the author, not so much in the very broad episteme or the less broad analysis of metaphor, but in the more specific perspectives on historiography, especially in relation to their own historical writings.

Most theories of history do not include all these factors. Some might have basic stages of history, but the reasons why one stage leads to the next are lacking; the causes and mechanisms of change are missing. A political theorist might have a theory of leadership, but the role of leadership in bringing about new societal stages is not explored. Historians might have detailed accounts of particular eras, but from these empirical observations general hypotheses as to the shape of history and the direction of change are not developed—a theory of history is not articulated. A macrohistorian might have stages of history and causes, but he or she does not then reflect on how history should be written. A complete theory of macrohistory is difficult to achieve when viewed in the context of these criteria.

## 3.1 EPISTEME AND CONTEXT

Each person who writes a macrohistory evokes the universal and the transcendental, but their grand efforts also spring from the dust and the mud of the particular and the mundane. For example, Ibn Khaldun asserts that his sociology is time, space, and culture invariant, yet the bases for his theory emerged from the primacy of unity in Islamic thought. His theory of history and his comments on historiography can be located within the current thinking of the fourteenth century. Given his knowledge of Bedouins, personal participation in various coups and assorted palace intrigues, and the centrality of unity in Islamic cosmology, it is not surprising that what emerges is a history of dynastic change with Bedouin challenges to "civilization" leading to unity employed as the key explanatory variable.

But using the life history of an individual to infer the nature of his theory simply personalizes a series of events. While remembering the subjective, it does not place the subjective in the historical economic and language practices that surround that person; in other words, the episteme. As we will develop in Chapter 5, on macro and micro, the personal discourse is useful for comparison, but there is more than that to understanding theories of macrohistory.

For example, Chinese macrohistorian Ssu-Ma Ch'ien had to write within his episteme before he could change it. To be intelligible, he had to write in the context of Confucian history. There were various problems to be addressed, such as the periodicity of history, the causes of the rise and fall of dynasties, the role of the tao, the importance of morality in giving meaning to history, and the centrality of the golden past. However unique and revolutionary his writing was, it still existed within a particular sea of knowledge.

While the contextual nature of knowledge is obvious to us when we (as modernists, the expanded West) examine the past, when we examine our present, following Comte, we tend locate it as the rational and the scientific. The past is constructed as relative and ideological (that is, not objective), and the future is the fulfillment of truth, the final stage of history once the last vestiges, the remnants, of the religious or philosophical past have been modernized, that is, vanquished. Thus, we submit our own "present" as outside of history and outside of a metaphysic.

But this is so for all grand thinkers: cyclical and linear. Indian interpreters of Sarkar's writings, for instance, locate him outside of history, even outside the Indian tradition. For them, Sarkar's knowledge is not contextual but universal. They forget that Sarkar uses the Indian tradition as a point of departure. And yet, as he moves away and attempts to articulate a new cosmology, the isomorphism to Indian thinking is marked. His stage theory, social cycle, and role of the transcendental are clearly reflective of Indian philosophy, albeit transformed, since Sarkar borrows from liberalism, Marxism, and other traditions.

Every writer emerges from a discourse, a way of knowing and constructing the world. This is not only true for Islamic, Chinese, and Indian historiography, but for Western thinkers as well, even as they often claim empirical objectivity. Hegel's conception of history was a direct response to the third antinomy and Kant's problematic solution to it. Hegel accepts Kant's antinomy and makes it his dialectic, with Spirit as one variable and the State as his other variable.

Although Marx attempted to create a perfect new world realizable through an objective understanding of the real, he was responding to a tradition as well—the concerns of nineteenth-century Europe. His thinking was contextualized by the rationality of the Enlightenment and its German response (the idealistic perspective of Kant and Hegel). Given the idealistic nature of the philosophical nexus around him and the recent Christian past, he claimed that his work was a science of the objective of the material world, and not a speculation on the idealistic or religious world of the medieval era.

Our perspective, then, is that every thinker and every thought exists within boundaries of what is considered intelligible. There is no place from which one can speak objectively. Epistemological boundaries—languages, structures, and practices—define the significant and the trivial, the negotiable and immutable, and the real. These boundaries are also subjects of different discourses.

History is the creator and is created by new discourses. These new discourses are what some of our macrohistorians have created, such as Ssu-Ma Ch'ien, Khaldun, Marx, and Sarkar. These new discourses are also the historical ruptures, to use Michel Foucault's language, that end the old and begin the new.[1] They are the periods when the future ceases to be an image or a vision, and becomes a present. These are the points of transformation that are the central tools for our macrohistorians.

Consider Vico. In his theory, there are four stages: the Age of Gods, the Age of Heros, the Age of Men, and the Age of Barbarians (from which we return to the Age of Gods). Central to his theory is the notion of *corsi-ricorsi* (movement on a path or course, and then a return), which functions as the larger metaphor and the deeper pattern that gives us the stages themselves. Without these contributions, Vico would have remained significant to social history, but merely as someone who moved toward a new science, not someone who gave us a true vision of an alternative science, one that had with it clear demarcations of the ages of time. However, Vico's own work did not usher in a new discourse; instead, the empirical social science perspective of Comte and others did. These new discourses break the ground of previous ways of knowing. They create a new history, a macrohistory. They rearrange the relative placements of self, nature, and god; space is turned over, time is reestablished, and suddenly the world is new again. But these new discourses never emerge *ex nihilo*. To function, the evernew must be intelligible to the old and the aging. Without this intelligibility, only those who exist outside of contemporary notions of the natural and the rational can participate in the new discourse. Often, the new discourse remains only in the mind of a few, if at all, as was the case with Vico.

Each thinker emerges from a particular discourse and, in the case of most macrohistorians, attempts to create new categories of the social and the transcendental that create the possibilities of new discourses. In this sense, their new categories cease to belong to the original thinker. Rather, they become part of the historical collective intellectual space, so much so that, over time, their remarkable original observations become commonplace.

Within this framework, we are not attempting to ascertain which macrohistorian's theory is true in the sense of correspondence with historical "facts." This is not our question. To begin with, the problems of ascertaining what is true are both numerous and complex. We take the perspective that a theory's contribution to humanity is not whether it corresponds to that which has been preselected as "facts," but if it changes the way the world is socially constructed. But what then of the relationship between the empirical and the theoretical? For us, the theoretical gives us the empirical and, indeed, the empirical gives the theoretical. They exist in a dialectical relationship; one is not an immutable benchmark for the other.

The modern world makes fidelity to the empirical world as understood as the material, as primarily real, and the mental and spiritual as less real, either as derivative of the material or as imaginary. In other epochs this was not as important. In our preferred epistemological view, Marx's theory is important because it rearranged social and political relationships by restructuring ways of viewing them; it gave new assets to a new class of people. It made revolution by the peasants and workers against the bourgeois, aristocrats, and church both natural, normal, and evolutionary. Marx was important because the economic was placed in the context of the political. He was not important because of his empirical predictions. They have been largely incorrect within the empirical discourse.

Sarkar's work is central because he articulates a structural theory of history, which includes the spiritual and attempts to give assets to all classes: capitalists, warriors, intellectuals (church and university), and workers at different times in history.

Spencer, borrowing from Darwin, provided the intellectual model which legitimated the conquest of the Third World, the colonies. He developed a theory of social evolution in which the powerful nations had a right to rule the poor, who were but evolutionary mistakes. He applied the biological "survival of the fittest" metaphor to the social arena. Within Spencer's linear framework, backward countries looked to developed countries for their vision of the future.

The linear model—which divides history into ancient, medieval, and modern—moves away from the traditional Christian readings of the trinity by bringing the transcendental back to Earth. In comparison, Sarkar keeps the transcendental at the level of the individual (as is expected from the Indian episteme), while the Chinese keep the tao metaphorical (its traces are noticeable but it can never be seen, speak, or be spoken to—it is illusive). The Gnostic Christians, however, link the spirit with the State. Within this Christian background, Hegel created a new theory of history, in which nations can claim that the spirit of God has entered them. As illustrated by the preceeding examples, *it is the creation of new categories of meaning that make a theory significant.* By seeing the world anew, a new world is created. But this world must be intelligible as well. Feminist visionaries use reality as presented (where the voices heard are male and the objectively real is constructed as male), but then they reconstitute these voices and create spaces for either female voices (Boulding's women's history) or for partnership voices, as Eisler would have us do. However, if they are totally divorced from the empirical, however constituted—when there are too few agreed-upon empirical facts to hang their hypotheses on—then consumption by others becomes difficult and their works return to where most scholarship terminates: the garbage heap of intellectual history.

## 3.2 CAUSES AND MECHANISMS

The critical questions for this section are as follows: What are the particular stages of history, and how does the old stage end and the new stage begin? The stages can be concrete historical periods or larger social patterns. Comte had his theological, metaphysical, and positive (the similarity to ancient, medieval, and modern should be obvious). Sorokin has his three ages of the ideational, dualistic, and sensate, but with a fourth stage as the transition, the age of skepticism and chaos. Spencer relates his societal types to phases in history: barbarism, militant, industrial, and a fourth yet to emerge. For macrohistorians, these stages are central to the theory, they are not merely historical eras gleaned from history textbooks.

Most of the grand thinkers we are concerned with believe they are writing a science of the past, present, and future which functions irrespective of the observer. It is not a humble enterprise, analyzing, for example, the history of a particular village or even one nation; rather, it is an analysis of totalities, an attempt to move to an all-encompassing theory of social space and time.

According to John Barrow, macrohistory is a Platonic enterprise concerned with finding the universal laws that explain change. It is an effort to find a theory of everything, of which a theory of history is the key axial point. Unlike art, which remains open to interpretation, a science of society calls for closure and a placement of the theory within the site of the objective (a stable world which exists outside of our knowing of it and for which verifiable laws can be derived). From this view, the social universe is not random or messy; rather, there are patterns that the careful eye can discern. Macrohistory stands in stark contrast to the Aristotelian approach, which stays at the level of the data, eschewing the search for universal laws of the physical and social universes. In the Aristotelian view, the universe is too messy to be compressed into universal physical or social laws.[2]

In dissimilarity is the view of Vico. Although patterned, history and the future are not predetermined—there are laws, but these are soft. As Attila Faj writes, "The famous *corsi* and *ricorsi* are both rheological and chorological, that is, circling 'softly,' round dancing. The softness of the law means that the successive figures of this roundelay are not necessarily unavoidable and are not independent of any condition and circumstance. Each historical stage streams into the following one and gets mixed with it, so we cannot distinguish them sharply. For a long stretch, the stages and everything that belongs to them are mingled like the sweet water of an estuary with the salt water of the sea."[3]

Siding, however, with the Aristotelian perspective are critics of macrohistory, such as Karl Popper.[4] He points out that (1) the macro

Platonic view misses too many significant details, (2) it removes choice and contingency, and (3) it privileges structure over human agency.

But this is not necessarily the case. the Platonic/Aristotelian dichotomy is far too simplistic for most macrohistorians. While the structure/agency dilemma is central within the linear/developmentalist model or the cyclical/fatalistic model, Sarkar (*varna*), Galtung (cosmology), Foucault (discourse), and Sorokin (supersystems) give us ways out of these dilemmas. For example, for Sarkar there is historical structure (evolutionarily derived), but there is individual will and there is a cosmic will, a grander intelligence. These exist in dialectical tension. Choosing structure over agency would be a mistake, as would choosing agency over structure. Keeping divinity and other mysterious factors out of the macroanalysis would also be a mistake. It is not necessary to make a decision which privileges a particular way of understanding; all levels of interpretation must be held onto simultaneously. As with Spengler, there can be shallow and deep levels of understanding.

Privileging one perspective (agency) results in individualism or liberalism (Smith, for example). Privileging another (structure), results in structuralism (Marx, for example). If one moves toward the third, then divinity results (Augustine, for example). The real has different levels; the diamond has many facets. The task is to exist in them simultaneously, to develop a theory that has linear, cyclical, and transcendental dimensions as it basic shape, and has agency, structure, and superagency (the transcendental) as to what causes movement through history.

Anthony Giddens has also attempted to develop a complex sociological alternative, called structuralism, but his theory ultimately privileges one over the other instead of allowing for both; or, alternatively, asking how it is that the categories in question (structure and agency) have come to gain currency, and now are problems that must be solved.[5]

While some macrohistorians find ways to balance the individual and the social (the structural), most focus on the processes in the structure and the system as a whole. In the macro view, size, structure (for example, vertical/horizontal or feudal/bureaucratic arrangements), and relations (person to person, person to nature, and person to society) are significant and primary over individual choices and hopes. Transcendental theories, in general, focus on the individual and his (and sometimes her) relationship to the transcendental and less on the social structures in question, as, for example, in the case of Teilhard's work.

Domination, that is, power, has been categorized as a key variable in explaining the difference between dialectical and equilibrium theories of social change, and in understanding the causes and mechanisms of change. In dialectical theories, change is normal and opposites exist in dynamic tension in every stage. Power and domination are often central to dialectical theories. Dialectical theories can be materialistic (Marx) or idealistic (Hegel) in their orientation, or some combination of both (Sarkar).

In equilibrium theories, stasis is natural and change is incremental. In this volume, we have placed these categories in the larger category of cyclical and linear (and transcendental). A cyclical theory privileges perpetual change, while a linear theory privileges equilibrium, although it could be an evolutionary equilibrium as in the case of Spencer. In cyclical theories, change is endemic to the system: through dialectics, the principle of limits, the Chinese yin–yang principle, or the Indian Tantric *vidya/avidya* (introversion and extroversion) principle.

Ssu-Ma Ch'ien links the yin–yang principle with the rise and fall of the dynasty. Sarkar links *vidya/avidya* with his stages of history and with an individual's own spiritual struggle to gain *moksa* (enlightenment). In contrast, in linear theories change is often due to external causes. Cyclical historians examine the rise and fall of civilizations. Linear historians, on the other hand, believe the fall problem applies to other civilizations (Oriental civilization, for example) while their own civilization (the West) is destined for eternal rise and progress. The formula for progress has been found; the problem now is merely staying the course. Khaldun, writing during the decline of Islamic civilization, could see that the cause of history had to be strengthening and weakening of unity, not just the former or the latter.

While cyclical theorists have linear dimensions (they move up or down), it is the return to a previous stage—however modified—that does not allow for an unbridled theory of progress. Linear theorists also have cyclical dimension to their theories. Within the narrative of linear stages, linear theorists often postulate ups and downs of lesser unit of analysis (for example, within human evolution or the evolution of capital there might be a rise and fall of nations, firms, or dynasties), but in general the larger pattern is progress. Humans might have contradictions (based on the Augustinian good/evil pattern), but society marches on, either through technology, capital accumulation, innovation, or the intervention or pull of God. Spiral theorists attempt to include both, having certain dimensions which move forward and certain dimensions that repeat. Spiral theories are fundamentally about a dynamic balance.

Macro thinkers are rarely useful to any status quo of the present, as they represent change. Cyclical theories, in particular, are seen as pessimistic by the elite of the core nation and the core civilization. From the view of the individual, cyclical theorists are seen as disempowering, since structure and process prevail over agency. Transcendental theories are empowering in that they inspire individuals to act, but they also lead to fatalism since all is in the hands of the transcendental.

Taking a different tact, Braudel believes that physical geography, or the *longue durée* (the long time), plays a role in history and the future.

For Braudel, history must be divided into three levels. There is (1) the history of events (the traditional individual level of history), (2) the history of civilizations and economic systems (processes), and (3) geo-history (geography). This last perspective, according to Braudel, is "history whose passage is almost imperceptible . . . a history of constant repetition, ever-recurring cycles."[6] Braudel is equally interested in the relationship between the physical and social.

This macro environmental view of Gaia is the temporal frame of history. Individual and structural time are but minor aspects of Earth or Gaia time. Humans are inputs and outputs in the rhythms of Gaia. They may or may not be necessary. This view markedly shifts the human-centered view of our macrothinkers. It reminds us that our definitions, categories, and attempts to create a history of humanity are narrowly human centered, and even as we posit universals for all space and time, we fail to see that humans are but one minor dimension of the universe. While one might expect spiritual views to be more sensitive to the Gaian perspective—Chardin, Steiner, Khaldun, or even Spencer—it is still the individual and his or her transcendental that is the key, not the Gaian environmental context.

Reminding us that the causes of historical change are fundamentally based on a problematic frame of historical reference is critical theorist Richard Ashley (as well as Jose Ortega y Gasset). He argues that grand theory articulates a voice, "a central interpretive orientation, a coherent sovereign voice . . . that supplies a unified rational meaning and direction to the interpretation of the spatial and temporal direction of history."[7] Thus, there is a voice (usually from the dominant species, civilization, worldview, class, gender) that interprets history but does not take a critical stance of itself: It does not explain where it stands and how it has come to stand there. This voice then claims to be outside of history and have a special vantage point of seeing history as it is. This writing of history controls the ambiguity of history and imposes various stages (Vico, Marx, Smith, Eisler, and others) and ideal types (Sarkar, Khaldun, Sorokin, Teilhard de Chardin, Spengler, and others).

For Comte, "Social science has with all its complexity passed through the theological state, and has almost everywhere fully attained the metaphysical; while it is nowhere yet risen to the positive, except in this book."[8] For Comte, the truth has been discovered (by Comte); now science can continue to refine it. As Spengler writes, "In this book [*The Decline of the West*] is attempted for the first time the venture of predetermining history."[9] Spencer writes of his work, "We shall find that in their ensemble the general truths reached exhibit, under certain aspects, a oneness not hitherto observed."[10] And, in Marx's words of his own theory, "The premises from which we begin are not arbitrary ones, not dogmas, but real premises."[11]

While this critique of the "coherent voice of history" is true of all grand theorists, there are clear differences as to the level of singularity. For Sarkar and Steiner, both man and God exist in accord with each other and they evolve dialectically, man becoming God and God becoming man. Both make the world in an evolutionary dialectic. For the Chinese too, the tao, the state, and the individual exist. The aim is not total or exclusive knowledge or power, but rather harmony between the different worlds and the different ways of knowing. This is true for Khaldun and other ancient philosophers as well. Balance, not total power; harmony, not epistemological exclusivity is the goal.

But for modern "man," knowledge, power, and the state are intimately linked. The sovereignty of the State will end when history ends, when man has achieved total knowledge and freedom, when history is subordinated to man's will, either as the victory of communism, the victory of the *Geist*, the victory of the perfect marketplace, or the final site of rationality where all needs are met. The goal is the control of society and the development of a model of history which explains the past and posits the end state in the near future or as the culmination of the present (as with Spencer and Comte).

The Gaian view is an attempt to move away from the problem of the voice that stands outside of history. But Gaia must still be interpreted: What is her or his standpoint? Why privilege the environment as data?

Given this critical view of efforts to write a science of history—with concrete stages and patterns of change—how can we understand and explain these attempts to develop general theories that are space, time, and person invariant? Does the act of writing a grand theory eliminate exits from one's theory? Have these social theorists truly discovered the real, or a dimension of the real? Inasmuch as the real is a social construct, are they inventing positions that are different to the present yet sufficiently intelligible from the present to gain currency?

For Wallerstein, one answer to this dilemma is to see grand theory as myth making. These myths play an important function in keeping people optimistic in struggles to transform society. "Myths are an essential element in the organizing process, and in sustaining the troops during the long political battle."[12] But, of course, Wallerstein does not see his economic history as myth; rather, he sees it as an objective account of what has happened.

The question remains: Why not call a theory a myth, a way of seeing, instead of the new truth, the new real? But would it then have potency? For example, would Marxism have potency without the promise of a classless society, the final historical stage? Would capitalism have potency without the promise of the ideal magical marketplace, where hard work is perfectly rewarded? Could liberalism have transformed the world into consumers without the mythology of the invisible hand, of divine self-interest, and of the philosophical division of the world into ancient, medieval, and modern (making the future the perfect, the present the good, the past the bad, and the ancient the wise from which there was a "fall")? Would humanism be successful without creating the sovereignty of man and a hierarchy of needs, indicative of ever higher levels of self-realization? Can sustained transformation be possible without some essentialism, with solely a will to transform, a politicization of all, and a mythification of nothing? Is truth possible without lies? Perhaps we need to rethink our notion of truth and falsehood, moving from *rta* (truth as fidelity to a referent) to *satya* (truth as benevolence, truth for transformation).

We suggest that, with regard to various grand theories—Marx's stages, Hegel's history of the spirit, Khaldun's primitive–civilization–primitive pattern, Sorokin's see-saw pendulum, Vico's cycles of knowing, Spengler's culture–civilization–death life cycle, Eisler's partnership society, and other macro theoretical assertions—while the empirical–applied perspective is important in searching for contradictions, anomalies, deviations from conventional truth, and historical data, these conventions change. Solely placing grand macrotheory within the empirical perspective might tell us more about the context of the present modern episteme than about a fatal flaw in the particular macrohistory. The theory in question might get a better response and more insightful critique at a time when grand theory is more acceptable in the social sciences, and when a good theory is not defined by whether it can be easily operationalized or how well it predicts the future.

More important is the theory's ability to make voices heard that previously could not speak, to find previous pockets of darkness and illuminate them, to pierce through silences. Also important is the ability to remove the future from the limitations of predetermined history and the cycle. Instead, it should create the possibility for the spiral, an acceptance of structure, but a willingness to transform the suffering associated with history.

For many macrohistorians, the attempt to create a science is an attempt at closure for a discovery kept forever open, which while useful in theoretical debate, does not lead to social activism or to the recreation of the world at the level of the material. Critiques based on epistemological skepticism are the type one tends to get toward the end of particular social formations—the present end of the modern capitalist system, for example. Social, political, and economic chaos evident in society is also evident at the level of intellectual theory. Society and truth become decentered; knowledge becomes totally relational. There is no ground for belief and action, and social theory becomes void of content and concerned only with the interpretations of interpretations.

For the macrohistorian, while the poststructural epistemological critique is useful, it remains at the level of mentalities; it does not lead to the creation of new societies, it does not aid in creating new forms of leadership, it does not aid in reconstructing history or in revisioning the future. To be useful to the human condition, macrohistory must begin within an alternative epistemology, but it must end with a transformation of material and social conditions. Views that criticize all perspectives are necessary but not sufficient, as they do not give temporal and spatial direction to self and society.

## 3.3 STAGES AND PATTERNS OF HISTORY

Returning to the issue of the pattern of macrohistory, systems thinker Erwin Laszlo adds a direction vector to our linear and cyclical division.[13] Linear movement can be either negative or positive and cyclical movement can either ascend or descend. In addition, linear and cyclical patterns need not be smooth. There can be jagged movement, with stops and starts; forward leaps and backward falls.

The linear model is expressed in the classic Western model of increased rationality, economic progress, urbanization, secularization, national integration, and modernization. Comte, Spencer, Durkheim, and Weber have been the modern proponents of this perspective. But there are also spiritual linear perspectives. The fall of humanity from Heaven to Earth without redemption is one example. But history can also be constructed with humanity ascending. For example, Teilhard de Chardin saw history as a movement toward God. God pulled all toward Him. Postmodernity accelerates this process as technological changes are leading toward a compression of information; a noosphere, a place of shared spiritual information and insight making it easier to reach the Omega point. Sarkar, as well, argues that the spiritual level can assimilate other levels of existence. The differentiation of the real can be transformed into the unity of *Parama Purusa* (Cosmic Consciousness), thus allowing higher and higher levels of progress. Spiritual writers, in general, emphasize that it is at this third level that the duality of existence can be transcended.

But Laszlo's ideal pattern is the systems science perspective, which attempts to combine the cycle with linear direction. The long-term trend is toward complexity, differentiation, increased size, improved use of energies, and the ability to store and access various energies: material and intellectual progress. This has been the pattern from the Stone Age to the modern period, with only the Middle Ages as a reversal in the long-term trend. The trend is directional, but there are periods of pause and periods of movement. These long periods, however, are increasingly punctuated by frequent periods of revolutionary transformation. These trends become disrupted by chaos. It is not a mere cycle or spiral; rather, there are disjunctions. At the biological level, this perspective is isomorphic to Eldrege's and Gould's theory of punctuated equilibrium, wherein species evolve relatively quickly followed by long periods of stability.[14] After millions of years of equilibrium, the stability is punctuated or interpreted by periods of revolutionary change. This is Eisler's model as well. She argues that we are at a disjunction where we have the possibility to move into a partnership society, thus ending the long history of andocracy.

With Laszlo (and Eisler) and other systems theorists, these periods of change or chaos, however, do not lead to the reoccurrence of the past as with cyclical theories; rather, a new order comes in. What results are new levels of complex structured systems, greater in size and with an improved capacity to access, store, and utilize energies to maintain themselves. While for cyclical theorists these chaotic periods bring on the cycle again, albeit at a new dialectical level (for Sarkar and Marx, but not for Khaldun and Ssu-Ma Ch'ien), for Laszlo (and other systems thinkers) the coming information age will lead to a societal transformation, a new era, outside of the historical cycle.

For Galtung, what is missing in the systems view is the expansion/contraction dynamic. The Middle Ages were not a reversal (as for Laszlo), but an integral dimension of Occidental cosmology: the West in its contraction mode. In addition, systems theorists and biological theory remain oblivious to human needs and desires and the structures of power that are embedded and proceed from these needs. They remain apolitical. Thus, the problem of power, governance, and the relations of production are not explained in most evolutionary theories. When these variables are included, the result often returns to the cyclical: *Plus ca change, plus c'est la meme chose* (the more things change, the more they stay the same).

Besides the shape of the model (linear or cyclical), there is a range of theoretical and political moves that are possible consequences from a theory of macrohistory. One can use the model to predict the future and post-dict the past (the modern scientific position). Or one can use the model to create the ideal person or the ideal state (the communist position). Or one can also attempt to find ways in which the individual and/or collective can harmoniously move with the discovered pattern (the taoist or classical position).

For the modern systems thinker, however, once the pattern of change is discovered, then, like the stock market (where theories to explain market prices move quickly from explaining to influencing the market), it will change, since there is now more information. As humans now are influencing the model, the future will change. The model will no longer work, as the model itself is participating in creating the future. In the short run, information can help predict the future, but in the long run it serves to create the future. For cyclical theorists, the only advantage information can give is humility in the face of the cycle (of dynasty, ecology, virtue, dharma, asabiya, and spirit). The cycle cannot be changed, only honored. The task for humans is to gain harmony with the cycle.

This is the great division between linear and cyclical theorists. For linear theorists, however, there are ways out of the human predicament; for example, through a revolutionary vanguard, through following their natural self-interest and reducing the role of the State (through individuals for Smith and corporations for Spencer), through increased information and organization, through State intervention, or through allegiance to a particular religion. Somehow, history can be improved upon. Progress is possible. Humility is for the ancients.

In our view, the task for the future is in developing social theories that are both cyclical and linear; that is, spiral. To some extent, Sorokin does this by arguing that it is not the periodicity of the cycle that repeats itself but the themes of history that recur. Of course, the events, trends, and individuals change.

Teilhard de Chardin, too, while cognizant of the hubris of humans, argues that there is evolution toward the spiritual. Sarkar makes the division within his cycle of administration and exploitation. With ideal leadership, the cycle can be maneuvered, but as it is fixed (either as a law, or, as Sheldrake would argue, a morphogenetic field, a pattern of behavior, repeated so much over time that it organizes life) it cannot be changed.[15]

Following Khaldun, Weber, in some of his writings, has a cyclical dimension. Once a historical structure is exhausted, "a charismatic leader emerges outside the structure and gives it its *coup de grâce*."[16] As charisma becomes routinized, the new structure will also face declining legitimacy and charismatic transformation. But it is Weber's linear theory that he is most remembered for. Weber saw the development of culture as a process of constantly increasing rationalization, of growing inner consistency and coherence. This is most evident in the transition from magic to science; the development of religion from polytheism to monotheism is also viewed in this light.[17]

Thus, for Weber there are both cyclical and linear elements. There is progress at one level but there is a cycle of charisma–routinization–charisma as well. But it is not only Weber who has traces of both. Adam Smith also includes cyclical elements within his linear march of economic stages. For Smith, there are four stages: the era of hunting—the era of pasturage and herding, the era of agriculture, and the era of commercial and exchange economy. The forces that move society are self-love and the love of others. When these combine, a society rises; but when they are absent, a society declines. Smith, aware of Gibbon's "rise and fall" theoretical framework, argued that nations do not necessarily rise; there is stagnation as well.

However, as with Weber, the deeper pattern is linear—the stages are clearly progressive and there is no return to a time of less bureaucracy or back to the age of hunters. Rather, within the overall framework and at another level of analysis it is leadership for Weber and the nation for Smith that rises and falls. Thus, while they attempt to combine the two, it is a combination of two different levels, not an overall theoretical synthesis, as in the case of Sorokin.

Merely remaining in the cyclical view and not accepting any theory of progress leads one to a pessimistic view of the future and justifies, as in the case of the theories of Pareto and Mosca, elite rule. If history is but a circulation of elites, a rotation of power from one type of elite to another type of elite, then any revolutionary movement, whether democratic or communist, is a sham. Power will centralize irrespective of who gains it. Democracy legitimizes rule of one class, the military another.

For twentieth-century writers like Pareto and Mosca, the cycle operates at the level of governance. Each new elite makes a claim to represent the people, however, it privileges itself or its own class. What hope does this analysis have for efforts to increase participation in governance and public support? Pareto and Mosca would argue that this the wrong question. For Pareto, the circulation of elites shows that, for the realization of the good, society elite rotation must be regular and often. For Mosca, there should be a balance of the various social forces, the different powers of society—military, peasants, landlords, priests, bureaucrats, and so forth.

Cyclical views of history privilege structure over human agency. In contrast, revolutionary movements promise a break of structure, an escape from history. It is this rupture that leads to individual dedication. The practical implications of grand theories which relocate individual action to determinism is that they lead to a politics of cynicism. This is the usefulness of theoretical approaches which attempt to acknowledge the cyclical, the linear, and the transcendental.

From the macro view, history written only at the individual level is essentially devoid of meaning. Individual events are important (e.g., how the vision of a certain person created a dynasty), but events exist within larger patterns, such as the birth and death of dynasties.

Even attempts to move beyond structure and individual agency create new structures. Foucault, for example, argues that he is deconstructing grand historical narratives, showing them to be particular and not universal. He aims to search for the power relations that lie hidden in grand theories, such as Marx's. His interest in not the unities of history but the particular differences. Unities create Kantian categories that structure a world which is, in fact, practice and process. There are no a priori stages or patterns, merely differences which inform our constructions of the real.

Yet, paradoxically, Foucault's own theory can be seen as a grand theory, albeit without a clear driving force of history (the causes and mechanisms of history). In Foucault's history of rationality and punishment, what emerges is the dispersion of different types of power similar to Galtung's, Sorokin's, or Sarkar's theory of power. In the long run, even while Foucault deconstructs he creates a pattern of history (the four epistemes—ancient, classical, modern, and postmodern) which is equally universal in its claims.

## 3.4 METAPHYSICAL CHOICES AND THE ROLE OF THE TRANSCENDENT

In analyzing each historical thinker, the crux of their theory often rests on the metaphysical choices they make in terms of deciding, within their own theory, what is immutable and what is modifiable, or what is contestable and what is given. In each thinker's language, these are not choices, but truths.

From the view of most macrohistorians, once there is a pattern then laws can be derived. These can be based on a cosmic order, on a theory of order where the natural is waiting to be discovered by humans, or on a revelation by a transcendent. But, once a transcendent is created in history, it must have a way to speak. Hegel's transcendent spoke through the great leader and the perfect State; Spencer's Unknowable begins the drama of creation, providing a teleological purpose to evolution; Ssu-Ma Ch'ien's tao spoke through the sage-king and the balanced State; while Khaldun manages to keep the transcendent more as a sign of textual respect, even though Allah is not neutral, preferring virtuous individuals and nations. For Khaldun, Allah gives his blessing to successful projects, but only after the fact.

In the *Vedas*, history is evolutionary and speaks not just through one figure but through the many who are enlightened. These many are then placed in a system of hierarchy from the *avatar* (God descending to Earth as world teacher) to the guru (humans realizing God). Significantly, the prophet is not the sole source of prophecy. For Sarkar, history is spoken through the collective mind of the particular group, and history is reharmonized through the great spiritual leader.

The metaphysical choices are then the following:

1. All historical actions are a result of a transcendental will (this is the idealistic position).

2. Only those actions at points of civilizational crises are transcendental actions (fall of virtue, *dharma*, righteousness). This is the view that God begins history, then disappears, but reappears in a variety of forms when things get worse. God reappears because of His omniscient knowledge or because of the call of the masses or their heightened suffering.

3. Real history occurs despite one's own apparent free will. There is a deeper agency happening behind one's back; in other words, all actions appear to be done by humans, but God uses humans to bring about the larger will of God (Hegel).

4. History occurs through the individual leader or through the family of leadership (Khaldun and Ssu-Ma Ch'ien). For a variety of reasons, the leader or group of leaders (family, dynasty) is more creative or conscious of the transcendental (Toynbee's creative minority). The leader is thus somehow more in touch, harmonious, or reflective of the real than others.

5. History acts not through a religious transcendent nor through royalty, but through the magic of the marketplace, through the natural and rational meeting of the needs of various individuals (Smith).
6. History acts through the most developed State or the most developed empire (Hegel or Marx), or through the contending or rising States (the post-colonial Third World for Sri Aurobindo).
7. History acts through world figures (Hegel), the great women or men (either as sages, kings, capitalists, warriors, or other configurations).
8. Historical acts can be understood through natural physical and social laws. These laws can be eternal, epoch contingent, or derivative from previous laws: linear, dialectical, idealistic, materialistic, or dualistic. The transcendent can be understood through patterns, its material traces, and what is empirically intelligible. A corollary of this view is that history, or the future, can be understood specifically through intellectuals.
9. History moves through the image of the future, the ideal state that draws and attracts people to act (Polak).
10. History occurs through the call of the divine or the attraction of the great (as with Teilhard de Chardin and Sarkar).
11. History begins because of the Prime Mover. But the Prime Mover is a mystery even though it provides a teleological purpose to evolution, moving man to perfection (Spencer).

The transcendental is then the unproblematic. The transcendent or the driving force in history is often seen as that which cannot be challenged or contested. The transcendental has many uses. The key tension with respect to the transcendental is its relationship to the immanent.

Fred Polak attempts to relate the transcendental to the temporal dimension by associating the transcendental with the image of the future. Visions of the future serve to integrate society. The ideal vision or social type is the balance between the transcendent and the immanent, what Sorokin calls the idealistic, mixed type of society.

Philosopher Eric Voegelin is instructive in articulating the tension between the spiritual and its presence in world history. According to Voegelin, this has been the crisis of the West in the past few centuries. By accentuating the material immanent factor too far, Western civilization has become caught in the paradox of rising (technology and better material conditions) and falling (wars, colonialism, imperialism, moral decay). The victory of immanence has been the death of the spirit. For Voegelin, history is the struggle of truth and its fall, of the spiritual and its immanentization.[18] Clearly, this is an approach more similar to Vico than Comte.

For Sorokin, it is not so much the rise and fall of truth but the backward and forward movement of the pendulum. The real is partially sensate and partially ideational. If it was only sensate then there would have been no historical ideational cultures. The same if it had been only ideational. Each society only expresses part of what is possible, and as it changes over time it exaggerates that dimension until the other aspects are suppressed. Eventually, truth is so distorted that the civilization no longer can survive; only through crises is there transformation. There is a rise and fall of truth or the fluctuation of systems of truth. For Voegelin, the immanentization of history is the cause of the decline of Western civilization. Immanentization leads to a position where history has a final epoch and where "truth" is certain. For Voegelin, Christianity stands in opposition to this view, for the essential Christian belief is in the uncertainty of truth, not the dogma of history.

History to Voegelin is best understood as spiritual decline: a downward linear pattern. From spiritual faith to enlightenment to humanism to secularism has been the pattern of decline. The modern period can thus be characterized as a belief in the end of the cycle and the irreversibility of the path of linear history and progress.

Voegelin's contribution is in showing the descent of the spirit into history, wherein history could not have a finality; a finality for which humans could be sacrificed. As Voegelin writes, "Specifically, the Gnostic fallacy destroys the oldest wisdom of [hu]mankind concerning the rhythm of growth and decay which is the fate of all things under the sun.... To every thing there is a season, and a time to every purpose under heaven: A time to be born and a time to die."[19]

Once again, this is the classical view of the cycle, of the acceptance of the natural, of the self-evident good and evil of humans, and of the limits placed by the physical environment. But from the spiritual view the cycle ends outside of history, in the transcendent, in either individual enlightenment (the individual utopia or eupsychia) or through the Grace and redemption of God.

For Voegelin—as with Ssu-Ma Ch'ien and Sarkar—individual perfection should not be confused with the perfection of society. Society cannot be perfect and thus these two arenas must remain distinct. But for Polak, Voegelin's view is only one perspective of the tension between the spiritual and the immanent. There are others that have been historically used. He distills five major orientations toward the Other:

1. Life cannot be purely transitory: There must be something more enduring. Man hopes for future grace.
2. Life cannot simply end in imperfection. There must be an Other realm which man can enter.
3. Life should not be transitory and imperfect. Man rebels out of despair, but without hope.
4. Life is not as it appears to be. This world is an illusion and the essential reality is veiled from man.
5. Life does not have to be the way it is. Man can reform and recreate the world after any image he chooses.[20]

While useful, this is a less elegant model of Sorokin's ideational, idealistic, and sensate types. Moreover, the macrohistorians we are comparing cannot be captured by Polak's five orientations. For example, for Sarkar, the world is perfect (from the level of the Absolute) and it must be reformed by humans, and it is transitory, and there is future grace or transcendence. Sarkar moves from Polak's first image to the fifth, mixing the transcendental and the human agency/creation and providing a metaphysic (as do Steiner and Teilhard de Chardin) wherein humans become cocreators with the force of Life. Also difficult to classify is Ssu-Ma Ch'ien's perspective. He argues that the sage can do what is natural and balanced while allowing the tao to work with him and through him (both transcendental and individual can be balanced within society and State).

From Polak's typology, Elise Boulding develops four historical patterns:

1. Essence optimism combined with influence optimism—the world is good and we can make it better.

2. Essence optimism combined with influence pessimism—the world is good but it goes of itself and we cannot alter the course of events.

3. Essence pessimism combined with influence optimism—the world is bad but we can make it better.

4. Essence pessimism combined with influence pessimism—the world is bad and there isn't a damn thing we can do about it.[21]

Again, while useful as a beginning point of analysis, it does not capture the perspective of our macrohistorians (especially non-Western thinkers). For the world can be neither good nor bad; there can be divinity and there can be choice. And there are many different levels at which one can speak to this. The Indian episteme, especially the richness of Jain and Buddhist epistemology, allows various both/and and neither/nor choices at the individual level. Moreover, there are stages of history where there are mixed societies in which the real is seen as both material and spiritual—fixed and changeable—wherein optimism and pessimism can both exist.

The contribution of Polak and Boulding that is of great significance to macrohistory is the centrality of the image of the future. The society with a rich image of the future rises; without a vision of the future a civilization is doomed, argues Polak. We will return to this dimension later in this chapter.

## 3.5 UNITS OF ANALYSIS

If we focus on the episteme, we enter a theory that primarily can be understood only by privileged intellectuals. One cannot create a social movement based on an epistemic analysis, although one can understand the politics of knowledge better.

Foucault's episteme, Sorokin's mentalities, Galtung's cosmology, Spengler's culture, or Toynbee's civilization, even if not politically revolutionary, are culturally revolutionary in that they relativize macrohistory. They allow comparisons between eras and between cultures. They show that the universal (as championed by a particular culture) is universal only to that culture. Cultures universalize their own categories onto other cultures; their success is based on political, technological, and economic factors, not a priori universal factors.

This tension in history is central to Spengler. He moves out of the linear division of ancient, medieval, and modern by making culture his variable. And while cultures follow a life cycle of birth, maturation, and death, humankind does not age. There is a circulation of cultures in history, to paraphrase Pareto. For Spengler, each culture in this sense is a separate person with its own equally valid view of the real. There are many cultures, each with their own pattern within an general overall pattern—birth, growth, decay, and death.

Cosmologies can be compared as well; one can analyze how, within each agency, structure and transcendence are constructed. From this, social implications for each cosmology are discernable. One can, as Galtung does, examine social formation (vertical and horizontal relationships), structural violence, and other variables.

But while each macrohistorian has his or her unit of analysis, Sorokin best discusses the problem of the appropriate unit of analysis. After a critique of others, he develops his own mentalities. For Sorokin, Toynbee's civilization or Spengler's culture are too functional in their approach. Their units of analysis are not causally related. Their units are not unified systems. For Sorokin, a unit of analysis must be essentially causally integrated like an episteme, *varna*, or cosmology. "It is the identity (or similarity) of central meaning, idea or mental bias that permeates all the logically related fragments."[22]

From this approach, Sorokin develops his macrohistory. He borrows Comte's theological, metaphysical, and positivistic classification scheme but takes it out of its linear structure. For Sorokin, history is rhythmic. History does not end with the positivistic or the sensate. The first description of reality is supersensory, and the third is sensory, with the in-between a "both and" type. He bases these descriptions on three answers to the basic question of the nature of the real. The first results in the ideational system, the second in the sensate, and the third in the mixed idealistic. Besides the similarity to Comte there is also a similarity to Sarkar. The ideational is the *Vipran* era. The sensate is the *Vaeshyan*, and the mixed is the *Ksattriyan*, where both types are present (the struggle with the physical environment and the worship or study of the world of ideas). However, Sarkar adds a fourth stage which Sorokin hints at but does not make explicit. This is the *Shudra* era (or time of chaos), the transitional phase between eras.

In contrast, for Pareto and Mosca these systems are not super-knowledge systems or collective psychologies. Rather, they represent different types of social forces and different types of elites. Pareto uses neither social forces, societies, nor mentalities. Rather, his interest is in leadership and in elites. Again, this leads to a theory of struggle and politics as conflict between elites. For Pareto's, as one elite rises, another descends.

For Mosca, these ways of seeing the world and these different powers must be balanced to create a good society: History is a battle of social forces. For Pareto, it is not the social forces but the elites that embody them that are important. These social forces include money, land, labor, military power, and religion. When these forces are balanced, human potentiality can grow. Indeed, history is the history of the rise and fall of social forces.

Using this as a unit of analysis, what emerges is a theory of politics. The stability of a regime is measured by how many of these forces it controls and how many it does not control. With social forces as a unit of analysis, struggle or conflict becomes central to one's theory, not the nature of the real, as with Sorokin.

In addition, Mosca's stages are similar to Sarkar's. For example, Mosca's theory shows how the warrior class was transformed into the wealthy class as the former gained exclusive ownership of land. At the same time, Mosca includes the Weberian model. Along with this change is the transformation of the feudal state to the bureaucratic state wherein public authority is used to protect private interests. However, he does not specifically develop a theory of normative power—the power of the priests and intellectuals in the ideational stage, or the age of gods or the *Vipran* era. He does mention, however, that, "in societies in which religious beliefs are strong and ministers of faith form a special class, a priestly aristocracy almost always rises and gains possession of a more or less important share of the wealth and the political power."[23] While Mosca hopes for a balance of social forces, Sarkar takes an asymmetrical view to power, believing that one social force will always be stronger (until the next rotation of the cycle) and that balance is possible in the creative minority but not in the entire social structure.

For Ssu-Ma Ch'ien, in contrast to Pareto, it is not the power of the elite but virtue which is the key. With correct leadership, virtue rises; with improper leadership it falls. But what, then, is the unit of analysis? For Ssu-Ma Ch'ien, it is the dynasty. With this as his unit of analysis, his task as a historian was simply to arrange the accounts of dynasties and feudal states in such a way that this pattern of virtue, of growth and decay, could be most readily perceived. His task was to reinterpret history so as to make it easier for individuals, especially monarchs, to follow virtue. There was a natural order.

For feminists, the unit of analysis is not the episteme, rulers, dynasties, or power configurations. The unit is gender. Given this unit, we are not surprised that Eisler emerges with a theory of stages where one gender dominates and stages where the genders exist in dynamic partnership.

Boulding's interest in the problem of units of analysis lies in showing how these units themselves have removed women's voices from history.

Finally, for Steiner, individuals are the unit of analysis, as they alone have choice in their evolution. Life reincarnates from minerals to plants to animals to humans and then onward to divinity. It is this transcendental process as embedded in the self, this supermacro view, that is the key to understanding the complexity of macrohistory.

## 3.6 THE METAPHORS OF TIME

The metaphor of time is just as important as the unit of analysis (the metaphor of space) to illustrate particular theories. The cycle, helix, arrow or line, pendulum, and spiral describe the shape of macrohistory, yet these descriptions are themselves metaphors. These metaphors are not outside our analysis, rather they too constitute history. Specifically, we need to ask what temporal metaphors different macrohistorians use. What is the relationship between the metaphor of time and the theory of history? What can be said about their preferred metaphor of time? Time itself is seen as a central variable in understanding history. However, for most writers it is the unexpressed variable that remains hidden, untouched, and unexplained. Like language, it is used to describe the real world but it is not appropriate for critical examination. Time is considered universal, existing outside of language and culture. But time is construed differently by various cultures.

The Chinese perspective of time is considered astronomical and is related to "a series of cycles based upon the movements of the planets and stars."[24] These cycles extend indefinitely into past and future. "The dates, then, of human history are recorded in terms of the years of rulers, who are the moral counterparts of the Heavenly governors."[25] For the classical Chinese thinker, there is no recognizable date to human history. Heavenly and worldly time are interrelated. They are endless. In contrast, in the Indian tradition dates of importance are assigned by the Vedas; in Islamic thought, history begins with the *Hegira* (when Muhammed left Mecca for Medina); and in Christian history, with the birth of Jesus Christ.

By using the model of the stars, Chinese history easily lends itself to a science of society that is not distinct from a science of the stars or a science of the self. History that is based on the stars can never have any real beginning or end, for the stars appear eternal, continuously moving forward and backward. Society too must follow this pattern: Everything has its place and there is a place for everything. In this model, the tao is the unseen force that provides the cohesiveness for the natural and human universes.

Indian history, however, has different dimensions of time. There is meditation time or transcendental time; that is, timeless time. In this time, consciousness *qua* ego-awareness does not exist. But this spiritual time is individually based and cannot be abstracted or applied to society as a whole. While there is individual enlightenment in spiritual time (where suffering does not exist), there is no condition of utopia where there is social timelessness (with a perfect society). But Indian time also has some similarities with Western time, as time does begin with great personalities or gurus. But, unlike Islam or Christianity, there is not simply one redeemer; there can be many.

Indian time also has a cosmic/cyclical dimension (with one cycle equivalent to 4,320 million years). Mircea Eliade, in his *The Myth of Eternal Return*, writes, "We are confronted with the infinite repetition of the same phenomenon (creation–destruction–new creation), adumbrated in each *yuga* (dawn and twilight) but completely realized by a *Mahayuga*. The life of Brahma thus comprises 2,560,000 of these *Mahayuga*, each repeating the same phases *Krta* (gold), *Treta* (silver), *Dvapara* (copper), *Kali* (iron) and ending with a *Pralaya*, a *Ragnarok* ('final' destruction, in the sense of a retrogression of all forms to an amorphous mass, occurring at the end of each *kalpa* at the time of the *Mahapralaya*)."[26] When society degenerates to its lowest peak, a redeemer is born that regenerates society and begins the next cycle. Vishnu, Krishna, or some other god takes birth to terminate the inequities of *kali yuga* (the Age of Darkness). But while the redeemer is central to the Indian system, he functions differently in comparison to the Judeo-Christian tradition, as evidenced by the lack of millennial movements in Indian history. Even for Sarkar, the redeemer's importance is symbolic (but central to the devotee) and should not be confused with empirical history.

Time, then, decreases in value from the golden era characterized by unity and spiritual development to the iron age characterized by materialism, chaos, and confusion. At the end of the dark iron age, the redeemer sets the world right and the golden era begins again. But the golden era declines, since "the fundamental rhythm of the cosmos is its periodic destruction and re-creation."[27]

What then is the way out? The first way is to patiently wait for the redeemer and, at the same time, to increase one's chances for success by following one's inner destiny and doing good works: *dharma* and karma. The second strategy is to escape the whole cycle of cosmic time and move the ego to a point outside of time: liberation or *moksa*. This can be at the ontological level of the self actually undergoing a sort of alchemical transformation and becoming eternal, or a type of perceptual change in which nothing is feared, all is embraced, and thus liberation while still in this world is achieved.

Buddhist time has various dimensions. Buddhist time has a beginning, the death, the *Mahaparinirvana*, of the Buddha. "Because of the claim to the historicity of the Buddha there is a single, central point to which all events relate chronologically."[28] At the same time, the Buddha is an eternal symbol. Buddhist time in this sense has no beginning and no end. Buddhist time is also spiral, there is a progressive spiritual movement.[29]

In contrast, the Hindu cycle can never become a spiral, for time is beginningless and thought itself is beginningless: There is not a notion of progress. For Eliade, "The conception of the four *yugas* in fact contributes a new element: the explanation (and hence the justification) of historical catastrophes, and of the progressive decadence of humanity, biologically, sociologically, ethically, and spiritually."[30]

Eliade even sees the basic theory as "invigorating and consoling for man under the terror of history."[31] For now, humans have the information that they are to suffer in this epoch and they must either resign themselves or take the opportunity to enter the spiritual path and escape through *sadhana* (struggle to achieve liberation).

However, liberation can also be, as with Smith, economic. For example, while most Indian thinkers argue that India is currently in the midst of the darkest *kali* period, Buddha Prakash takes a more technocratic view.[32] He argues that after the era of sleep of British imperialism (*kali*), India awakened (*dvapara*) and moved through nationalism (*treta*) to high-tech industrialism (*krta*). The golden age is thus not a spiritual era but the coming post–industrial society.

For Sarkar, the fourfold pattern from gold to iron and back is useful in providing inspiration to change social conditions, but they should not be seen as actual historical eras. As a macrohistorian, Sarkar uses the Hindu model of history as a point of departure and then attaches a new range of meanings to it, some additive and some organic. For Sarkar, time is used in different ways. There is the cosmic cycle at one level, the generation, degeneration, and regeneration of time; and at another level, there is the individual escape from time and entrance into no time or infinite time. Finally, there is social time (his spiral), where the time of exploitation can be reduced through social transformation, thus, in the long run, allowing for the increased possibility of individual escape from time. By bringing in historical structure—his theory of epistemic/*varna* stages—he transforms traditional Indian time and rescues it from its fatalism.

Besides Indians, ancient Greeks also used this fourfold division. For example, Ovid had his four ages. "In the beginning was the Golden Age when men of their own accord, without threat of punishment, without laws, maintained good faith and did what was right. . . . The people of the world, untroubled by fears, enjoyed a leisurely and peaceful existence, and had no use for soldiers."[33] From the golden age came the age of silver. In each subsequent age, struggle increases, resources decrease, and moral virtues decrease. In the final iron age, "the land, which had previously been common to all, like the sunlight and the breezes, was now divided up far and wide by boundaries. . . . All manner of crime broke out; modesty, truth and loyalty fled. Treachery and trickery took their place, deceit and violence and criminal greed."[34] The comparisons to the present serve as further proof for millennialists that we are at the end of a major era in history and about to begin a new era.

Marx also saw the division of property as central to the decline in civilization and, as with Ovid, his cycle concludes with a return to a golden age when all property is shared. For Marx, it is individual humans, albeit the select vanguard as a class and not any particular redeemer, who will return us to the golden age. While the classical Hindu and Ovid's four ages are useful comparative distinctions, they do not comprise a social theory. We are not told why time degenerates. The causes and mechanisms are left vague. Nonetheless, this fourfold model of degeneration keeps returning in the works of other macrohistorians. From Sorokin, we can see how the spirit descends from the mountaintop of ideational to the plateau of integral to the valley of sensate. Foucault would categorize these ages as increases in difference (from high level of conformity and homogeneity), and thus not necessarily as a decline. For Ssu-Ma Ch'ien, however, social decline is evidenced by disagreement among schools of thought and of a lack of harmonious and conceptual unity in explanations of philosophy.

As this illustrates, there are many types of time. There is the million-year time of the cosmos, which is useful for spiritual theory but not for social macrohistory. There is individual timelessness or spiritual time, useful for mental peace but not for social development. There is also the classic degeneration of time model from heaven to hell, from the golden to the iron. There is the Chinese model, wherein time is correlated with the stars with thus has no beginning and no end. There is Occidental time, which traditionally started with the birth or some other event related to the life of the Prophet. It now relates to the birth of the nation-state. There is also archeological time, used by Eisler, which is midway between astronomical time (billions of years) and social time (the last few thousand).

In contrast to the linear model and the four-stages model, which implicitly use the metaphor of the seasons, there is the biological and sexual model. The rise and fall of nations, dynasties, and families can be related to the rise and fall of the phallus. The phallic movement is dramatic and has a clear beginning and a clear end. Men, it can be argued (using the linear model), prefer the first part of the cycle, imagining a utopia where the phallus never declines. The historical empirical data suggests, however, that endless rise does not occur.

In contrast, and not as obvious to men (and those involved in statecraft and historiography), the female experience is wavelike, with multiple motions. Time slows and expands. Instead of a rise and fall model, what emerges is an expansion and contraction model. Galtung, for instance, uses the expansion and contraction metaphor to describe Western cosmology. He also suggests that there might be a relationship between different cosmologies (for example, as Christian cosmology declines, Islamic cosmology might expand).

Expansion and contraction also reminds us that there are benefits in each phase of the cycle. In the contraction, for example, the poor do not suffer as proportionally as the rich who have less speculative wealth available (although certainly the wealthy attempt to squeeze the middle class and the poor as much as possible, especially the poor in the periphery). The expansion and contraction metaphor is also used by Kondratieff and Wallerstein, but for them key variables in the model are prices and the flow of goods, not individuals or social organisms.

Biological time can also be used to understand the future. Ibn Khaldun uses the idea of generational time, of unity and creativity declining over four generations.

The central metaphor used by all cyclical theorists is the lifecycle. Spengler, in particular, uses this perspective, arguing that each individual culture has a unique personality with various distinguishing characteristics. But the cycle has a downward spiral. First, there is the stage of culture. This stage eventually degenerates into mass civilization, wherein the force of the money spirit leads to imperialism and the eventual death of the culture. For Toynbee, civilizations have particular cycles they must go through. Some elites respond to challenges through their creative faculties and others do not meet these challenges. The former expand mentally while the latter intellectually decline. Civilizations that meet challenges expand in size and wealth. Those that do not meet internal or external challenges slowly decline (unless there is rejuvenation from within, as Ibn Khaldun argues).

Within the unit of episteme there can be different types of time. The modern episteme, for example, is particularly strong on quantitative, scientific, and linear time, but weak on mythological, spiritual, and seasonal time. For Sarkar, each *varna* has a different sense of time: the warrior more mythological and the intellectual more philosophical, for example. Sorokin's stages also exhibit different models of time. The ideational era, for example, is strong on transcendental time while the sensate is strong on quantitative time.

The best or most complete macrohistory must be able to negotiate the many types of time: seasonal, rise and fall, dramatic, mythological, expansion and contraction, cosmic, linear, and social-cyclical, as well as the intervention of the timeless in the world of time. These must be associated with notions of social structure and individual and transcendental agency. In what ways is time personal, in what ways do macrostructures give us time, and how does the role of the transcendental reshape time? The ancient cycle alone leads to fatalism (unless redefined, as by Prakash), and the linear pattern alone leads to imperialism, wherein particular collectivities can be placed along the ladder of economic success. Transcendental time alone leads to a focus on the cosmos and neglect of economic progress and social development. For empowering macrohistory, all three are needed. But few manage to include all these characteristics; rather, macrohistorians privilege certain types of time and avoid or marginalize others. Developing a theory of history that coherently integrates these many types of time is not an easy task.

## 3.7 THE ROLE OF THE VANGUARD

A complete theory of macrohistory also requires the links through which the pattern of history can be transformed. There are three levels to this. The first is the transformation which ends one cycle or stage and begins the next one, such as the end of one dynasty and the beginning of a new one. The second is when the macrohistorian develops a theory of history but posits an exit from history in which a vanguard plays the central role of leading history into a future out of its past and present limitations. The epistemological problem of finding exits from one's theory of history is the third dimension, which was touched on earlier: the classic question of the relationship between episteme and theory building. We will examine the first two in the section, focusing on the second. The third dimension will be developed in the next section.

For Ibn Khaldun, once a dynasty is in its final phases governors from one of the provinces or a rebel from the periphery attempts to gain royal authority and political power. This new leader will succeed if the group from which he emerges has a high degree of unity. *Asabiya* is developed through kinship, religion, and struggle against the desert environment and other tribes. When successful, a new leadership cycle is born.

For Ssu-Ma Ch'ien, the cycle begins with the next sage-king, the learned man attuned to the tao. Writing much later in the modern period, Chang Hsüeh-Ch'eng argues that the sage-king restores the link between government and learning. The officials follow the tao and are wise. Government should be run by the wise, not the rich or the powerful. This is similar to Sarkar's *Vipran* system, but ethical guidelines and social structure are more important in the Chinese system than a complex theory of the transcendental and the structure of hierarchy that has access to it, as with the Indian system.

For Khaldun and Ssu-Ma Ch'ien, there is no way to construct an eternal dynasty (unlike Western thought, where the goal is to stay on top forever through nation, evolution, or God). For Khaldun, the polity declines as luxury and sedentary life increases. The ties that bind leaders and followers decline. Religion, as in the case of Islam, may increase these ties and stall the decline, but the cycle of the rise and fall of dynasties and civilizations cannot be escaped. This is the same for Ssu-Ma Ch'ien. The universe exhibits a waxing and waning: a yin and yang. While balance is desirable, an eternal peace is impossible, as the history of empires, sages, and tyrants suggests. For Vico, it was only a Christian spirituality that could lead humans out of the Age of Barbarism. The truly religious could lead humanity to the next level of knowledge.

For Toynbee, as well, a creative minority responds to an external or internal challenge and rises in power, but eventually its creativity is lost and it becomes merely a dominant majority. Toynbee's question is if the nemesis of failing creativity can be averted. For Toynbee, through spiritual rebirth civilizations can move from strength to strength without resting on their oars. It is the spiritual dimension that can solve the problems of the future and lead humanity onward.

For Sarkar, the spiritual dimension is best represented by *sadvipras*. They are leaders who have characteristics of each era (the characteristics of worker, warrior, intellectual, and entrepreneur), whose actions are selfless and moral, who understand the patterns of history and a sense of the possible futures ahead, and are committed to spiritual realization. Leadership must then have several dimensions to transform the cycle of history into a spiral, but becoming a *sadvipra* is an arduous task full of personal sacrifice and social struggle.

Marxists have learned this in their failure to develop nonexploitive forms of leadership. For Marx, the link to the contradictions of the present and the unitary state of the future could be realized through the proletariat. They would smash the edifices of capitalism and bring on the next and final stage of human civilization. Through the theory of Marxism, the structure of the party, and the struggle of organizing workers and consciousness, the vanguard would emerge to lead the world onward. They would bring about the new man and the new day.

For Gramsci, developing on Marxism, it is the organic intellectuals who would counter the capitalist project and bring on the new era. According to interpreter Carl Boggs, "The more 'advanced intellectuals' would presumably take on a large number of indispensable ideological-cultural projects: subverting the illusions of conventional ideologies, introducing and disseminating critical view of social reality, presenting an alternative vision of the future."[35]

Contrast this with Hegel's view of leadership. World historical leaders (such as Alexander or Napoleon) would continue the onward march of the spirit in state after state. But while they believed they were acting for themselves, for Hegel it was the cunning of Reason, the larger motivation, that transformed history. For Hegel, there is no need to exit history, rather the present in the body of the Prussian State was humanity's finest development. From Prussia, Hegel postulated that the spirit would move to America next, although, if one follows his logic, the final freedom should be in a world state since it is only at the global level that the contradictions between the individual and society can be resolved. But living in the context of the nation-state, the idea of a world state was not easily available to Hegel.

In addition, this contradiction can be expected, for in linear theories there is no functional need of a special vanguard—in need of theoretical and social creation—that must be created to aid in the escape of the cycle; rather, there is merely a need for a push into the next stage, whether through the freeing of productive sources, the expansion of power through world leaders, or the refinement of science and positive philosophy, as in the case of Comte. For Spencer, this push in evolution comes not from value-oriented intellectuals but from corporations. Successful businessmen are the chosen agents that will lead society to a new evolutionary stage and to a world without government.

For Khaldun, Ssu-Ma Ch'ien, and Toynbee, leadership brings on the next stage in history; for Marx, Sarkar, and Eisler, properly developed leadership can transform history and create a new future; for Hegel, world historical leaders continue the onward progressive march of history; but for Pareto and Mosca, leadership is not the way out of history; rather, history itself is the circulation of leadership. The best polity has a high circulation of elites so that excellence can flower. Excellence, then, is based on merit, not moral or spiritual qualities. Pareto does not have a concept of leadership to bring on a permanent stage of equilibrium. He argued against the effort (the communist experiment in particular), claiming that all polities are elite and history is the graveyard of aristocracies.

Sorokin takes an alternative strategy in his discussion on the ways to elude history. He does not call for a new type of leadership, rather he tells us the type of leadership we might most likely see in particular mentalities (ecclesiastical authorities during Ideational eras, for example). As we might expect given the generality of Sorokin's theory, there is no vanguard that will bring on the new era. The future comes about because of the principle of limits, not because of the actions of any particular individual.

For Eisler and Boulding, what is needed is not great leaders but nongovernmental organizations (the peace, ecology, spiritual, and women's social movements) working together to slowly transform gender relations, the military–industrial complex, and social injustice so as to create a global civil culture.

For Eisler, as well as Sarkar, Marx, and Gramsci, the links between leadership and structure are critical. Those who explicitly desire a new civilization find ways to create leadership that can break the cycle or transform the cycle or any other patterns of history. Others show how even when leaders create the future they are bounded by the structures of history, the rise and fall of virtue, *dharma, asabiya* or the pendulum swings of materialism and idealism. Leadership and the exit of history is the least developed dimension of macrohistory. Since macrohistory privileges structure we should not be surprised at the underdevelopment.

## 3.8 EXITS FROM THE THEORY OF HISTORY

Beyond exits to the stages of history, there are exits to the theories of macrohistory. This includes questions of whether the macrohistorian or believers of a particular macrohistory can see other views of history; whether there is only one true macrohistory and macrohistorian; or whether there are a plurality of truths. While we touched on this issue earlier, through the argument that all macrohistory is totalizing and that macrohistory removes agency, using the works of Ashis Nandy we will continue this discussion by focusing on leadership and the vision of the future within macrohistories.

Ashis Nandy, among others, explores grand theory in the context of utopian thought, especially linear theories of development, liberal or socialist. For Nandy, a realized utopia, a realized vision of the ideal society, can be another source of terror, since "rarely have utopians and visionaries built escape clauses into their charters for the future. One can enter their utopias; one cannot emigrate from them."[36] His question is this: Can we construct a set of criteria to assess the utopias of others without violently imposing our own utopian tendencies? Generally, while no "utopia can give a guarantee against its misuse by over-zealous ideologues, utopias can build conceptual components which sanctify self-doubts, openness and dissent."[37] A theory must be more of a vision than a finished blueprint. There need to be spaces left for interpretation, dialog, and dissent, thus creating the necessary conditions for epistemological and ontological pluralism.

Utopias must be open to dialog between other utopias, but this is unlikely, as most attempts at utopian thinking make knowledge claims in which those outside the grand theory cannot understand themselves because they exist in prehistory. For example, monotheists claim not only to understand their world better, but they claim also to understand the world of the paganists more fully. Science exalts itself to the objective and reduces magic to the irrational and marginal. This, as we might expect, is the sort of knowledge imperialism that so easily develops from a linear theory of progress. It is only recent efforts within the sociology and politics of knowledge discourse that have attempted to place both accounts of the real within historical practice; each knowledge system finds its meaning in the particular era of the time.

Even if, as Nandy writes, "Yesterday's dissent is often today's establishment and, unless resisted, becomes tomorrow's terror," and the past is a consensual fable, "waiting to be interpreted and reinterpreted as an alternative in the future," theorists still develop grand visions of history and the future based on natural laws that are space/time and observer invariant.[38] Without a utopian knowledge claim, their theories would not be able to mobilize activism; their efforts would be merely intellectual discourse. As discussed earlier, ideologies and movements are significant because of their grandness. Without their unproblematic representations of the real, of the natural, and of the belief that their movements are guided by destiny, they would not be able to sustain the "myth" needed for individual and social transformation. Thus the paradox; to change history, texts must stand outside of history. Unfortunately, it is this very placement that can cause misuse and often terror.

Nandy's way out of this problem is similar to Voegelin's—the evocation of the eternal cycle. As written in the *Mahabharata*, "Alas, having defeated the enemy, we have ourselves been defeated. . . . The . . . defeated have become victorious. . . . Misery appears like prosperity, and prosperity looks like misery. Thus our victory is twined into defeat."[39] Identification with human suffering (and the view that all utopias will cause it) is one step out of totalizing discourse. Indeed, the beginning and end of macrohistory has to be about human suffering and its alleviation.

Our own perspective is that while empirical truth claims are useful, as they aid the move from theory to data and back (between the vision and the reality), the comparative is even more useful, as it places the real in the context of other similar efforts and allows an interdiscursive civilizational dialog. With a comparative framework and layered framework (as Spengler tries to develop, as opposed to Spencer's unified theory of reality), exits to a particular theory of history are implicit and critique is implicit.

A third approach and perhaps most useful is the view that sees theory as an asset; macrohistorical works can be seen as projects that develop new meaning systems outside of their tradition, yet inclusive of their cultural history. Ultimately, the asset that historians like Vico, Marx, Eisler, "Gaia," Teilhard de Chardin, and Steiner are manufacturing is a new language, a new interpretation of the real, and an ensuing new politics, economics, and culture: a new discourse. It is in this context that we choose to read macrohistory and macrohistorians. Exits from theory become new points of beginning and new frames of analysis, thus allowing one to move out of linear theories (even though they are gradual and have no exit), cyclical theories (where the exit is based on the tragedy of history, or the repeatability of our mistakes), and transcendental theories (where the exit is individual not social). What is needed are multiple entrances and multiple exits to macrohistory.

## 3.9 MACROHISTORY AND THE FUTURE

The future can certainly be an exit for macrohistory. The vanguard attempts to create a new future by breaking out of the confines of history. But we need not focus only on the vanguard to understand the diverse understandings of the future embedded in theories of macrohistory. We can also ask what role their theories have in terms of better future possibilities. To do this, we first need to develop a theory of understanding the future.

We can develop three frames in which to contextualize the future: the predictive, the interpretive, and the critical.[40] In predictive types of futures studies, the goal is to make true predictions—ones that match the empirical world. Language is transparent and does not constitute the real. It merely describes the real in a neutral manner. The cultural perspective takes a diverse view of the future, searching for commonalities in the midst of differences and looking at the way different cultures construct the future. The goal is not prediction but insight and revelation. The third approach examines not the problems of the empirical nor the view of culture, but asks how meanings are constituted in different statements of the future. What is the epistemological price of the future: Who gains from a particular image? Who loses? In short, it is the politics of temporality.

In the section that follows, our goal is merely to use our legion of grand thinkers to point us in the appropriate future direction. Using these thinkers, we can ask what the "world" might look like in the future. We can also use their unique cultural perspective to recover futures and visions that have been hidden by the present dominant view of the future, and we can use their work as an interpretive asset to shed light on the present and possible futures. To do this, we take selected macrohistorians and summarize the key variables they use to explain social change and forecast the future. We will attempt to recontextualize their thought in light of the categories of the modern world (nation-state system, world capitalist system, structures of core and periphery, information and technological revolutions).

This task can initially be divided into linear and cyclical categories. From Ibn Khaldun we can use three ideas: *asabiya*, the rise and fall of dynasties, and the theory of four generations. Our questions then become as follows: Who are the new Bedouins? Which collectivities are building unity and are ready to sacrifice the present for the future? Which ones have struggled a great deal and still retain the warrior spirit? How long will they stay in power? One answer is that the new Bedouins are Japan and the tigers. The Confucian culture provides the unity and hierarchical structure, and defeat in war provides the struggle. But moving away from nation-state analysis, it is social movements that could be the new leaders: environmental movements, women's movements, and various spiritual movements. Their unity may develop from struggle against the status quo.

From Sorokin, we can use the principle of limits and the pendulum theory of history. What is the next stage in human history? Have we reached the limits of sensate civilization? If we have, what are the outlines of the emerging ideational or mixed-idealistic civilization? Sorokin also gives us a pattern for the future from which we can understand the formation of the next integrative phase. He places this pattern not at the level of the supersystem (sensate, idealist/integrative, and ideational) but at the level of civilization.

Since Western civilization so strongly corresponds with sensate civilization (i.e., since the West has assumed the form of the universal system), Sorokin speaks directly to the future of the West. The pattern he gives is crises, catharsis, charisma, and resurrection. At present, the West stands in the middle of sensate civilization, awaiting the final two stages of charisma and resurrection. The West awaits new leadership that can inspire and lead it to a rebirth in spirit and society, mind and body, individual and collective. But eventually, since each stage is temporary, the next stage (ideational) will emerge from the integrated stage and the pendulum will continue. But can these categories themselves be transcended? Given the empirical evidence of history and the structure of the real, for Sorokin the answer would be in the negative, at least at the level of the social system. Individually, one might adopt a view of the real that is neither ideational, integrated, or sensate, but nihilistic. This latter view, however, does not lead to a social system.

Sarkar is particularly rich as a predictive and interpretive theory of the future. We have his theory of social cycle, his theory of civilization, and his vision of the future. Appropriate questions to begin an analysis include the following: Which *varna* will lead next? Which stage are we in now? Will the cycle move forward or will there be a reversal? Which civilizations or ideology will continue and which will collapse or cause oppression? Certainly, from the Sarkarian view, the communist (*ksattriyan*) nations are now moving into their *vipran* era. Will this era be dominated by the church or the university, and how long will it be before these new intellectuals become technocrats for the capitalist era to emerge? For the nations or groups presently in the capitalist cycle, where will the new workers' evolution or revolution come from? And what of the centralization of power that ensues? What will a *Ksattriyan* United States look like? Batra reminds us that, historically, it is these *ksattriyan* eras that are often seen as the golden ages, as they provide security and welfare for citizens and expand wealth. *Ksattriyan* nations also expand physically. Will space be the final frontier?

We can also use Sarkar's theory of civilizations and movements to gauge their possible success. Do these new movements—feminist, ecological, ethnic, regional, and consumer—have the necessary characteristics to create a new system? Do they have an authoritative text, a leadership, and a theory of political economy, spiritual practices, fraternal universal outlook, and being and consciousness? Are there any ideologies that fulfill this criteria for success? Answering these questions would aid in understanding the long-term future of the new movements.

From Toynbee, we can ask which civilizations can meet the numerous technological and ecological survival challenges facing humanity. Which civilizations will find their development arrested as they are unable to deal with the coming challenges? Will there be a spiritual rebirth that revitalizes the present? Is a Universal State next? Or is the next stage a Universal Church? Who and where are the upcoming creative minority? Will Western civilization survive, or will it go the way of historical declines? If there is a spiritual rebirth, who will lead it and how will it come about?

Braudel, Kondratieff, and other world system theorists offer a theory of economic cycles and war. Are we ready to enter a new expansion or a contraction? If a contraction, should we anticipate a global depression? Is war the most likely future, since there is no longer a dominant hegemony? What will be the form of the new expansion and where will it be located? For Kondratieff and other long-wave theorists, it is these questions of power and control that derive from the economic and must be asked.

From Ssu-Ma Ch'ien, the economic is not an important variable; rather, questions of leadership and the balance of nature are. For example, who will be the sage leader that will return the tao and restore balance in China–West relations? In Russia, is Yeltsin the new sage-king that ends the tyrannical dynasty or merely a short-term revival in the longer-term degeneration? Who is the sage-leader (king) that will provide the similar restructuring for North–South relations? Which nations have moved away from virtue and are now ruled by tyrants? Is the world system moving according to tao or are there other forces at work? Can government and learning be restored so that there is social balance? How can unity among schools of thought, in the nation and in the family, become the dominant trend? As important, how can we reorder our understanding of history and the future so as to more accurately reflect the lessons of virtue and morality?

From Spengler, the critical variable or tool for understanding the future is the life cycle of culture. Following Spengler, we would attempt to locate cultures in the pattern of the life cycle. We would ask which cultures are in the final days and which cultures are renewing themselves through interaction with other cultures. We could also ask which cultures are rising and which new cultures are emerging. For example, is Islamic culture in its final stages because of the new religiosity, or is it still expanding because of emergence of the money spirit? Indeed, world fundamentalism could be seen from a Spenglarian view as the last breath of dying cultures. Given that great souls create new cultures, we can survey the world landscape and speculate which thinkers, activists, or leaders might potentially create a new culture.

For Vico, the next stage in history can be delayed or even eliminated. The final stage of barbarism can be avoided by a warrior king, a mythic hero. There are also breakouts or disjunctions in these stages. As with other macrohistorians, we should not attempt to develop empirical indicators for each era—stages of gods, heros, men, and barbarism—rather, the effort is insight and interpretation. But we can ask what stage we might be in: Are we in the age of barbarians now? Is there a spiritual (Christian) revitalization that can move us out of the cycle? Is the age of the gods next?

To Pareto and Mosca, the theory of elites is paramount. What will be the level of elite circulation in the future? Will it be rapid or fixed? Representations of democracy and widespread participation notwithstanding, who are the real functioning elites? Who will the future elites be? Is elite rule the only possible governance design? Also of importance is Pareto's different types of elites: the innovators and consolidators. With respect to Mosca, we can ask whether we are moving from a society of the wealthy to a society of warriors.

From Comte, we can ask if we have reached the end of the Positive stage. Or, since only a few nations have completely entered the Positive stage, is there still a long wait until the rest of the world joins in and become developed? Does the collapse of communism and decline of Islam (in political power if not in mass numbers) signify the continued movement of positivism? Indeed, the present can be construed as a validation of Comte and Smith, among others. Liberalism has become the dominant ideology; the scientific worldview remains the official global ideology.

From Hegel, we search for the location of the *Geist*. Which society has solved basic historical contradictions? We can argue that the Geist has shifted from the United States to Japan, as perhaps the Japanese conquered the contradictions of individual and family in the form of their state. Who will the new world historical leaders be? And, if we follow Hegel's conclusions, should we not see the ultimate resolution of the *Geist* in the form of a world state, either through the victory of one state or through some type of consolidation? In the Hegelian view, the variables that we should focus on are the dialectics of the spirit, the power of the state, and rare world leaders.

From Marx (with renewal from Wallerstein), we can ask if the end of communism has mainly furthered commodification of the world (the proletarization of Eastern Europe). Will the dramatic and total success of capitalism and its eventual transformation lead to socialism? Are we closer to global socialism than ever before? Will the new electronic and genetic technologies change social relations, or will they merely further commodify workers?

From Adam Smith, it is not only the future of the market as a hegemonic metaphor and a site of economic exchange that we should look for, but Smith's other key category as well: that of love for the other and love for self as the causal mechanisms of social change. Will the future see a society that combines love or self-love, or will this combination fail to emerge and lead to civilizational decline?

Spencer's theory and his biological metaphor predicts a world government which would function as the brain of civilization. This world government would also end the rebarbarization of civilization (world wars). Spencer also predicts a new societal stage, neither barbarous, militant, nor industrial.

For Eisler, the relevant questions relate to gender. What might the partnership society look like? What are its contours and contradictions? How will it come about? What are the supporting trends? What of the contradictory trends, which show increased androgyny throughout the planet? Will the partnership society then revert to cyclical or pendulum social formations or will it continue unabated through the future?

Polak focuses specifically on the image of the future. Those collectivities with no vision of the future decline; those with a positive image of the future—transcendental and immanent—advance. Humanity, especially now, needs a positive image of the future to create a new tomorrow.

For Boulding, given the power of human agency, the future cannot be forecasted. The image of the future cannot be predicted. As with cultural historian William Irwin Thompson, the image emerges organically at an unconscious mythological level. Mythology cannot be categorized nor rationally created; it is constantly changing, always more than what we can know. But although the future cannot be predicted, we can assert that history follows a rise and fall related to the image of the future.

We can also ask why some societies develop compelling images of the future and others do not. Answering this question would lead to a more complete theory of history. Like Eisler, Boulding's view of the future leads her to develop political strategies in which associations attempt to imagine and commit to their preferred future. A central part of this imagination is faith in the realization of the preferred future. To develop this faith—a concrete belief in a future possibility—Boulding advocates developing future histories in which individuals, after imagining their vision, develop strategies for how this vision can come to be. From these timelines, hope that tomorrow can be changed is gained. Agency thus overcomes structure.

Sarkar advocates global *samaj* (society, people) movements that challenge nationalism, capitalism, and the dogma of traditional religions. Locally and globally active, these movements, Sarkar believes, will transform the inequities of the current world capitalist system. Coupled with spiritual leadership, Sarkar is hopeful that a new phase in human history can begin.

These macrohistorians aid in transforming the discourse away from the litany of minor trends and events to a macro level of stages and grand causes. While their stages do not provide concrete data for policy making, they provide an alternative way of thinking about the future. The stages also give the study of the future an anchor, a structure from which debate or dialog becomes possible. Otherwise, thinking about the future remains idiosyncratic and overly values based.

## 3.10 VIEWS ON HISTORIOGRAPHY

As important as macrohistorians' thinking on the future are their views on historiography. Vico attempted to create an alternative science of humans, since the natural sciences deal with the passive environment while humans actively make history. Hegel sought to explain history, "to depict the passion of mankind, the genius, the active powers that play their part on the great stage."[41]

Sarkar aims to write a history that does not privilege one class. For Sarkar, history should not be a history of kings and queens or intellectuals; rather, history should show how individuals braved physical, social, and spiritual challenges and how humanity excelled in the face of collective agony. History should provide lessons and inspiration.

Ssu-Ma Ch'ien believed that good history should make sense of otherwise meaningless events and trends. The historian must develop a script of history so as to elucidate the lessons of virtue.

Marx sought to develop a history that clearly showed what makes humans different: how through production they differentiate themselves from each other. What is important is labor and its division.

Galtung uses the metaphors of street level and sky level to grapple with the problem of levels of history. As with Spengler, it is not that one is false and the other true (the usual distinction), but rather that one is deep and the other shallow. They complement each other. Spengler and Toynbee attempted to give us a sense of this deeper history, to search for a more comprehensive unit of analysis and pattern. Khaldun wrote that most people merely come to the Earth to live their lives and quietly die. Historians have merely recorded the dates of their deaths; they have not searched for the more general patterns that give meaning to life and death. Nor do most historians take the next level of analysis that Foucault does, searching for the boundaries of culture, history, and the knowledge that gives us these particular boundaries. For Foucault, it is the way power is dispersed in systems of thought and in social arrangements that constitutes good historiography.

While Foucault privileges epistemology, most macrohistorians, even as they develop alternative ways of knowing, make specific ontological claims as to the truth of history itself. Classical thinkers believe human history cannot be divorced from deeper universal structures. Given this isomorphism, what emerges is a science of society. But this science does not necessarily have to be an empirical science. It can be a science that has different pillars; for example, it could be a science of interpretation (Vico), of intuition (Sarkar), of historical materialism (Marx), of supersensitivity (Steiner), or of nature and the tao (Ssu-Ma Ch'ien).

For Sorokin, the key in writing history is finding the appropriate unit of analysis and the appropriate form of science. Most historians choose a unit of analysis that has no logical or meaningful relationship. Most writers use units that have no causal relationship or are related because of some external factor. But once the true unity—logically, causally, and meaningfully related—is discovered, a more fruitful history can be written.

For us, what is essential is that history in itself should, like the future, be pluralized and placed in a nexus of self-interpretation. A science of society (with stages of history and causes of change) is important in that there is closure at the level of the social. At the same time, there is a need to have escapes so that change is possible, if not the likelihood of ever new stages, social creations, macroforces, internal and external explanatory variables, and theories of leadership. Macrohistory should not close the debate of science, interpretation, temporality, power, and spatiality; rather, it should make it increasingly diverse. To be transformative in creating alternative politics and alternatives futures, macrohistory must make necessary and important links with the present and the future.

## CONCLUSION

Are there any final conclusions that we can draw? First, one central variable is creativity. This is counterposed to imitation. Creativity leads to expansion, growth, more wealth, more power, or inner development. Creativity comes from challenge and is gained through experience. External factors such as resources, geography, and invasions are important to macrohistorians, but they are not central.

Second, the double dialectic is central. William Irwin Thompson, in his review of macrohistory, says it like this: "The model of four seems to be a persistent one; it recalls the rule of four in the Indian caste system, Plato, Vico, Blake, Marx, Yeats, Jung and McLuhan. So many people look out at reality and come up with a four-part structure that one cannot help but think that it expresses the nature of reality and/or the Kantian apriori pure categories of understanding. But whether the structure exists in reality or is simply a project of the categories of the human mind is, of course, the traditionally unanswerable question of science."[42]

Sorokin has his three stages, but there is a fourth stage, a kind of chaotic stage where reality is not fixed at any particular point. This is Sarkar's *Shudra* era, Galtung's notion of plastic time, or Foucault's postmodern world. Steiner argues that we need a balanced society with three autonomous spheres: the economic, the cultural, and the political. All these three interact with the fourth, the environment. In any case, the notion of stages is critical. History must be placed into categories which, while simplifying the real, at the same time give us more information about a particular age than a mere summation of the particular events of the time.

These stages also directly relate to various metaphysical causes or positions (contradictions or dilemmas): mind/body, good/evil, internal/external, expansion/contraction, accumulation/distribution, absolute/relative, and theory/data, to mention a few. These stages relate empirically to the great events of history. The great religions and their institutions must be explained. The grand empires and their fall must be explained. The contradiction between city and pasture too must be explained; between the civilized and the barbaric, the courageous and the weak, and the unified and fragmented.

For Khaldun, it was clear that the urban world brought about the end of *asabiya*. Indeed, this concept is central for Spengler's theory of history. Urbanization led to the decline of culture and to mass civilization for Spengler. For others, such as Durkheim and Smith, it was the urban world that brought about progress; reduced disease led to economic growth and rationalized the irrationality of pagan religions. The city aided in the development of democratic society and helped move away from traditional society.

As mentioned earlier, there must be ways to link the stages. How does each one emerge? The pattern most often used is the dialectic. Each stage emerges naturally out of the previous because of the internal contradictions in the previous stage. Sorokin has his limits, Marx and Hegel their dialectics, Ssu-Ma Ch'ien has his yin and yang.

Thus, we have creativity, four stages, the dialectic, and basic dilemmas. When macrohistory has a new society which is to be created—that is, a utopia—then we have the vanguard. These are always the minority, as Pareto and Mosca have pointed out. They have special access to the real, whether because of transcendental reasons, reasons of struggle, or because the system in itself creates their possibility.

The pattern most used to describe these stages is none other than the life cycle, although others are used (e.g., the river). In general, it is the birth and death of the individual and the natural world (changing seasons) that is accessible to us through the gaze. For some, there is a golden time to return to. For others, borrowing from Darwin, the past should be forgotten, it was a time of barbarism. History is evolutionary, with teleology existing not in God but in the interaction of humans and nature. History is progressive with increasing levels of complexity and differentiation. Macrohistorians thus have an initial stage from which history begins, often an age of chaos or confusion or barbarism. For some, this age is repeated, serving as a bifurcation point for a new future; for others, this initial prehistorical period is forgotten in humanity's evolutionary march onward.

Finally, each macrohistorian speaks from a view outside of history. While leading to a certain arrogance, this also gives the theory a certain legitimacy. History is spoken of in dramatic terms, as art, as poetry, indeed, as prophecy; otherwise it would be a mere academic treatise that reflects upon history but does not recreate it. Macrohistory is intended to recreate history.

But the skeptical critic is also necessary. Jose Ortega y Gasset questions the civilizational biases of macrohistory. Ashis Nandy asks if there are escapeways from the particular theory. Once one enters a particular utopia, whether linear, cyclical, or transcendental, is there a way out? Or is the theory constructed so airtight that no ways out are possible? Is the system so comprehensive that only acceptance or rejection is possible? Is the framework of analysis too narrow and exclusive, and biased toward one gender, civilization, metaphor, or structure?

For us, these theories need not be rejected or accepted in total; rather, they can be used as interpretive assets to rethink the past, present, and future and to recreate the past, present, and future. Our own preference is for an empowering macrohistory that has linear, cyclical, and transcendental dimensions; that is inclusive of agency, structure, and superagency; and that uses multiple metaphors of time and space.

## NOTES

1. Michel Foucault, *The Archaeology of Knowledge and the Discourse of Language*, trans. A. M. Sheridan Smith (New York: Pantheon, 1972), 4.
2. See John Barrow, "Platonic Relationships in the Universe," *New Scientist*, 20 April 1991, 40–43.
3. Attila Faj, "Vico's Basic Law of History in Finnegans Wake," in *Vico and Joyce*, ed. Donald Phillip Verene (New York: State University of New York Press, 1987), 22–23.
4. See Karl Popper, *The Poverty of Historicism* (New York: Basic Books, 1957).
5. See Anthony Giddens, *Central Problems in Social Theory* (Berkeley and Los Angeles: University of California Press, 1979).
6. Fernand Braudel in Peter Burke, *Sociology and History* (London: George Allen and Unwin, 1980), 94.
7. Richard Ashley, "Living on Borderlines," in *International/Intertextual Relations*, ed. Michael Shapiro and James Der Derian (Lexington, Mass.: Lexington Books, 1989), 261.
8. Auguste Comte, *The Positive Philosophy*, trans. Harriet Martineau (London: Trubner, 1875), 132.
9. Oswald Spengler, *The Decline of the West*, trans. Charles Atkinson (New York: Alfred A. Knopf, 1962), 3.
10. Herbert Spencer, *First Principles* (1862; reprint, Osnabruck: Otto Zeller, 1966), 432.

11. Karl Marx, *Karl Marx: The Essential Writings*, ed. Frederic Bender (New York: Harper and Row, 1972), 164.
12. Immanuel Wallerstein, preface to *Revolution in the Third World*, by G. Challiand (New York: Viking Press, 1977).
13. Erwin Laszlo, "Footnotes to a History of the Future," *Futures* 20 (1988): 479–493.
14. See Richard Gauthier, "The Greenhouse Effect, Ice Ages and Evolution," *New Renaissance* 1, 3 (Summer 1990): 19–21.
15. See Rupert Sheldrake, *A New Science of Life: The Hypothesis of Formative Causation* (Los Angeles: Jeremy P. Tarcher, 1981).
16. Amitai Etzioni and Eva Etzioni-Halevy, eds., *Social Change* (New York: Basic Books, 1973), 4.
17. Ibid., 5.
18. See Stephan McNight, ed., *Eric Voegelin's Search for Order in History* (Baton Rouge: Louisiana State University Press, 1978).
19. Eric Voegelin, *The New Science of Politics* (Chicago: University of Chicago Press, 1987), 166.
20. Fred Polak, *The Image of the Future*, trans. Elise Boulding (San Francisco: Jossey-Bass, 1973), 2.
21. Elise Boulding, "Futuristics and the Imaging Capacity of the West," in *Human Futuristics*, ed. Magoroh Maruyama and James Dator (Honolulu: University of Hawaii, 1971), 31.
22. Pitirim Sorokin, *Social and Cultural Dynamics* (Boston: Porter and Sargent, 1970), 10–11.
23. Gaetano Mosca, *The Ruling Class*, trans. Hannah Kahn, intro. Arthur Livingston (New York: McGraw-Hill, 1939), 59.
24. Burton Watson, *Ssu-Ma Ch'ien: Grand Historian of China* (New York: Columbia University Press, 1958), 4–5.
25. Ibid.
26. Mircea Eliade, *The Myth of the Eternal Return* (Princeton, N.J.: Princeton University Press, 1971), 114–115.
27. Ibid.
28. Romila Thapar, "Society and Historical Consciousness: The Ithasa–Purana Tradition," in *Situating Indian History*, ed. Bhattacharya Sabyasachi and Romila Thapar (New Delhi: Oxford University Press, 1986), 376.
29. Ibid.
30. Eliade, *Myth of Eternal Return*, 118.
31. Ibid.
32. Buddha Prakash, "The Hindu Philosophy of Thought," *Journal of the History of Ideas* 16, 4 (1958).
33. Ovid, *Metamorphoses*, trans. Mary. M. Innes (Middlesex, England: Penguin, 1955), 31.
34. Ibid.
35. Carl Boggs, *The Two Revolutions: Antonio Gramsci and the Dilemmas of Western Marxism* (Boston: South End Press, 1984), 222–223.
36. Ashis Nandy, *Traditions, Tyranny, and Utopias* (New Delhi: Oxford University Press, 1987), 2.

37. Ibid., 7.
38. Ibid., 13, 19.
39. Ibid., 20.
40. See Sohail Inayatullah, "Deconstructing and Reconstructing the Future," *Futures* 22, 2 (1990).
41. George Wilhelm Friedrich Hegel, *Philosophy of History*, trans. J. Sibree (London: George Bell and Sons, 1888), 87.
42. William Irwin Thompson, *At the Edge of History* (New York: Harper and Row, 1971), 78.

Chapter *4*

# *Macrohistorians Combined: Toward Eclecticism*

*Johan Galtung*

## 4.1 TWENTY MACROHISTORIANS, TWENTY *FORCES MOTRICES*

These are people who have shaped our entire way of conceiving of ourselves. They have mapped us on trajectories with the most intriguing curve shapes, even if the linear and the cyclical tend to dominate. Giants as they are, there is always the temptation to yield to any one of them, like people in the Occident (and not only there) have done to Smith and to Marx. There is the temptation to adopt the biblical approach and see their main work as the *Book*, even *the* book; the trajectory looks self-evident, in need of no further axiological, axiomatic, or empirical validation. It also looks self-fulfilling; if sufficiently many believe in it, it will be so. Moreover, it looks self-rewarding; for ourselves, or at least for the initiated.

This is not the approach that will be taken here. To the contrary, all these macrohistories will be seen as inspiring and important except when or if people really start believing in them in the triple sense mentioned. From that point on they become dangerous, as seen by the tendency for liberalism and socialism to become the self-appointed "end of history," *secundum non datur* (there is no second opportunity). To see much is not to have seen it all. Even the highest mountain offers a limited view of the earth; the earth itself is limited; and many people enjoy views only in one direction. Greatness can be shared, as there is much room at the top of Mt. Olympus.

One way of opening for a polytheist as opposed to a monotheist approach to this pantheon of social philosophers would be to play them out, two and two, not against each other but with each other. They generally do not refer to each other, and not only for reasons of distance in space and/or time. So we do not know how they would have behaved in dialogues with each other; nor is that so important, since they probably would mainly have given voice to their own inner thoughts and inner dialogues.

What we can do here starts with a very simple question: How can the key theme of macrohistorian X be combined with the key theme of macrohistorian Y? That theories are different does not imply that they are incompatible or even irreconcilable; among other reasons, because they may refer to different phenomena or different aspects of the same phenomenon. Moreover, they are not necessarily theories, in the strict sense of a body of thought that in principle can be invalidated by one single disconfirmation of one single hypothesis correctly derived from the theory. Rather, they are perspectives, in the more generous sense of announcing that, when studying social history, here is the unit of special concern and here are the variables to watch, and, in general, the unit will move through time in the way suggested by the macrohistorian.

For this purpose let us focus on ten of the macrohistorians, simplifying their *forces motrices* to a naked skeleton of thought. To begin with, we have selected five cyclical (Khaldun, Spengler, Sorokin, Toynbee, and Sarkar) and five linear (Smith, Comte, Spencer, Marx, and Weber). Two are non-West: Khaldun and Sarkar. The rest are Westerners, but, three of them being predominantly cyclical, there is at least some variation.

Here is the list of key themes to be paired with each other:

Khaldun (*Kh*) rise and fall of *asabiya* (unity); dynastic successions
Spengler (*Sg*) culture versus civilization; cultural life cycles
Sorokin (*So*) principle of limits; epistemic–cultural cycles
Toynbee (*To*) challenge/response; civilizational cycles
Sarkar (*Sa*) epistemic–social *varna* (collective way of knowing) cycles
Smith (*Sm*) self-interest/moral sentiments; division of labor
Comte (*Co*) positive knowledge; epistemic stages
Spencer (*Sc*) evolutionary differentiation; socioeconomic stages
Marx (*Ma*) means and modes dialectics; socioeconomic stages
Weber (*We*) cultural primacy; rise of rationality/bureaucracy

These will not necessarily be presented in this order, as there is an important cyclical–linear dialectic we would like to elucidate. For each author, a two-letter acronym has been given to enable us to refer to the *force motrice* as the Kh factor, and so on. With ten authors we have, in principle, forty-five pairs to explore, above all for possible synergies (had we taken all 20, there would have been 190). Actually, as will be seen, there are even more possibilities, as each pair can be read both ways:

How could Khaldun enrich Smith and how could Smith enrich Khaldun (the systematically minded might even add, how could Khaldun enrich Khaldun; for example, by having minicycles inside the stages he is elaborating)? There are ninety jobs to do, maybe one hundred. Of course, we will not attempt that, nor pay equal attention to each pair. The reader is invited to fill in the gaps, and we hope that this exercise in dialogues that never took place will prove sufficiently appetizing.

## 4.2 TEN MACROHISTORIANS: AN EXPLORATION OF SYNERGIES

First on the list historically is Ibn Khaldun, which begs the question: How could the nine macrohistorians following Khaldun add something that might fill in gaps in the thinking of the great Tunisian statesman and philosopher? How could we today combine the insights of two or more, not only one at the time?

Starting with Smith, the individual enters. Smith has an element of *asabiya* in the moral sentiments that balance self-interest as the driving force in a society characterized by division of labor (or differentiation, in general, as Spencer would have said), with everybody able to find a niche. Khaldun could have admitted this factor of individual hard work, as opposed to the example set by some prince. But he would have added his doubts as to whether the moral sentiments would survive that much self-interest. But if Smith had picked up this point from Khaldun, his theory would have been cyclical. And Smith would not have been Smith.

Comte introduces an epistemological perspective: positivism in the sense of basing science on the empirically existing and in applying this to society, paving the way for modern sociology. Comte might have said that Khaldun had positive knowledge, but in a theological/metaphysical era. Had the era been positivist, the attitude to his knowledge would also have been different, to the point of "doing something about it." Khaldun states a social law but not such conditions for its validity as the epistemological climate. What would have happened to Khaldun's societies if they had read the *Muqaddimah* as more than a wise man's musings?

Spencer would probably have advised a higher level of differentiation as a way out of the weakening *asabiya* problem. He might have argued that there can be ups and downs everywhere, like disease in some parts of the body. But the higher the differentiation, the more likely that some parts are healthy even if others are not. Khaldun could have answered that he is not talking about parts of the social body (or any other body), but of stages in its life cycle. All parts eventually grow old; maybe not at the same time, but the general principle applies to them all.

Marx could have admonished Khaldun to pay more attention to the specificity of the socioeconomic formations involved. The Bedouins coming in from the outside may have exhibited a tribal, essentially primitive communism with a high level of communal sharing; the city they cracked open may have been feudal with a highly unequal property distribution. Such exploitative societies may have been weakened by their own exploitation, collapsing even at a soft push from a far less sophisticated and numerically inferior outside force. However, getting into the shoes of the system they conquer, they will be marked by the same acute inner contradictions and that, rather than the general formula of decreasing *asabiya*, is what ultimately brings it down. Marx might have added that the new power holders should be the internal, exploited victims of the old system, as carriers of the next historical stage, not outsiders who fall into the trap of imitating the present. History is brought forward through inner dialectics, not through any outer conflict; through birth, not onslaught. But at that point Khaldun would have disagreed. His empirical observation of the human condition was the renewal from the outside and that the renewal has a short half-life.

Weber would emphasize culture. He might have asked for the specifics of the cultures of the Eastern Mediterranean area at Khaldun's time. No Protestantism, no capitalism; no capitalism, no growth. With no growth, decline and fall may look more normal, or at least less abnormal. Given that, what happens happens.

So much for the five linear theories. How about the four other cyclical macrohistorians? With their inclusion, immediately the compatibility level increases. Linear macrohistorians, working on physical time, would offer alternative recipes to get out of the decline and fall so eloquently promised by Khaldun; cyclical macrohistorians, working on biological time, would offer additional reasons why some decline is unavoidable; not how it can be foreseen and forestalled.

Spengler would point to the degeneration of culture into mass civilization, maybe precisely in a city-based culture. Sorokin would see decline as inevitable if the barbarians are materially motivated; in any case, each social formation has its limitations. Toynbee would point not to the lack of objective challenge but to the lack of subjective perceived challenge, the inability to read the famous handwriting on the wall and to respond creatively to it. Sarkar would simply say that a *varna* has run its course, the time is here for another *varna*. Khaldun would have no problem with his four cyclical *confrères*, seeing them as enriching his theory by pointing out more aspects of the mechanisms leading downward.

But let us now turn the tables around and ask what the others could have learned from Khaldun, like we did for Smith. In short, curing the linearists of some of their wildest fantasies about progress and *endzustand* (end of history), and giving the cyclicists another mechanism to consider, conjointly with their own favorite factors.

More particularly, from Khaldun (and from many others for that matter), Comte could have picked up the simple idea of linkage between his epistemological stages and socioeconomic stages. He might have almost been forced to consider making his theory cyclical, depending on external social circumstances. Thus, could it be that people start collecting data and become empirical, "positivist," simply because they are trying to prove some points about their own lack of power and privilege? Could it be that empiricism is the voice of the dispossessed believing in material change of some kind, and the theological–metaphysical molds the voice of those who either do not believe in material cures for spiritual problems or do not want any change finding this world, their world, essentially acceptable or even very just?

In the same vein, both Spencer and Weber might feel challenged to consider the limits to differentiation. Weber actually does, pointing out that one part of a highly differentiated society may put the other in the famous "iron cage." But Khaldun might go deeper. He could have argued that differentiation is also degeneration, that sophistication brings in its wake a yearning for simplicity, whether referred to with Durkheim's dysphemism "mechanical solidarity" or Tönnies's euphemism *Gemeinschaft* (community).

But how about Marx, with a linear theory superimposed on a number of successive social cycles except one: communist society. He has something very important to learn from Khaldun that might have saved people in the twentieth century from enormous suffering. However correctly society has been organized according to theory, with the basic contradiction between means and modes of production engineered away through collectivization, there may still be elites on top of the most perfect system, resting on their laurels. In the beginning they can kill the barbarians (read, the dissidents) knocking on the gates, or expel them to remote corners of the realm. But in the longer run the protest may reach stormlike proportions until the hurricane cleans up the whole place.

Khaldun might have added that this would not only have applied to the highly imperfect Soviet Union but even more so to a more perfect Soviet Union giving people no hopes or illusions that with deficits removed the system could nevertheless work. No system is immune from social attrition when *asabiya* weakens. Khaldun is remarkable also in being a pure sociologist: The explanatory factor is neither cultural nor economic, but the sum total of individual psychology at the social level.

The four other cyclicists definitely have something to learn from Khaldun because they are as one-sidedly cultural as three of the linearists, Smith, Spencer, and Marx, are economic. Spengler could have used Khaldun for rich images of the transition from culture to civilization and back again. The Bedouins have their culture intact, but then it degenerates. New supplies are needed.

For Sorokin, Khaldun could offer a major theoretical input, even if it may be rejected for the reason argued by Marx. Sorokin presupposes an enormous quantum jump of a sociocultural formation, from the gutters of the super-sensate to the celestial spheres of the super-ideational (whereupon it starts running downhill again). Where does the energy for that jump come from? How can a system undergo a transition of that magnitude, especially when it is utterly exhausted by its own acts of self-destruction? Khaldun could say, through outside supply of energy, with barbarians of any kind knocking down the gates. In the fatigued Western societies today, filled with self-doubt behind all the braggery and *braggadocio*, there are many candidates as there are many repressed, exploited, or at least marginalized categories: women, children, retired people, non-Whites, the working class, the non-believers, or other countries. Of these seven possibilities, women appear to be announcing themselves today as possible renewers of society, especially if they set their goals higher than parity with men inside the present formation. The younger generation is, of course, the institutionalized renewal; the problem is that they may be too young to be pregnant with a well worked-out blueprint (and the retired too tired). The working class may be said to have been tried in this troubled century and found wanting, possibly for lack of alternatives except becoming middle class and bourgeois, which leaves the society where it was, only more so. Some hopes, in the United States more than in racist Europe, focus on non-Whites from East Asia as a source of spiritual and cultural renewal (although any thought of "new blood" would in itself have racist overtones).

The problem with that entire approach, Sorokin might respond, lies in the crucial distinction between inner and outer dialectic. The quantum jump from sensate to ideational comes about through intense disgust with the sensate mode, and that disgust has to be converted into a yearning for the celestial alternative. The jump has to be in the society and by the society, and preferably in the person and by the person who was once in that gutter. That Paul gets disgusted with a materialistic Saul is obvious; what makes the Damascus story interesting is that Paul equals Saul; two souls inhabiting the same body. Paul comes from the inside, not the outside.

In the outer dialectic, there is also a change in society, possibly also in the persons; but the changes are of the society, not by the society or by some outside forces. An array of sources or forces of renewal have been mentioned; each one carrying a potential, with some reservations for the younger generation and the working class. They may be forces, but not for renewal. A regular invasion by other countries could have been included, but in that case there is no element of inner dialectic.

But what if the outsiders enter legally or illegally, invited or not, and stay sufficiently long to become insiders, yet not so long as to represent no challenge? This can only happen if they have firm imprints on their minds, strong alternative cultures that can be used to replenish and refresh Western/European culture in a deeply multicultural world. With that formula, frequently found in the United States, Khaldun's and

Sorokin's positions become compatible, even if Khaldunian renewal comes more quickly than that of Sorokin.

How could Toynbee's and Sarkar's theories be enriched with the Kh factor? The answer is relatively clear. Toynbee needs a theory for why the ability to respond adequately, meaning creatively, to challenge should decline; Sarkar needs a theory of how the power position of a given *varna* declines. This is exactly what Khaldun offers, since his theory does not presuppose any particular cultural or economic structure, only that, over time, contentment sets in. People at the top become too much victims of their own worldly success to sense the suffering around them and to respond creatively before it is too late.

Toynbee and Sarkar might also object less than Sorokin to an outer dialectic of change or renewal through conquest, including through colonization. Even Marx was inclined to view colonization of the archaic non-West by the more advanced capitalist West positively, as a way of bringing them (Mexico by the Americans, Algeria by the French, India by the British) into history. The colonial countries probably still have to learn how grateful they should be to Marx for offering such justifications. Let us then try the same exercise for the second-in-line historically: Adam Smith, searching for synergies. Smith was, like Khaldun, an empiricist, reporting what he saw and interpreting. He saw an agenda for humanity, or at least for the British: increasing the division of labor, and with that, increasing wealth. He did not really see any strong limits to that process, only weaker limits that could be overcome. How could we enrich this simplistic image?

The cyclicists will always be there with their ready-made promises, not of doom and gloom (that is only another linear theory with negative *endzustand*, not progressive but regressive), but of decline and much of it before it gets better. Marx and Sarkar will promise class revolts, Marx within a broad linear scheme where no stage is repeated, while for Sarkar the revolutions will come and go and true progress is ultimately spiritual. Spengler, Sorokin, and Toynbee will promise decline if the cultural capital is not constantly renewed or at least replenished. Clearly, Smith did not pay sufficient attention to such factors, all of them accompanying in various ways the tremendous economic growth that has taken place since the days of Smith and to a large extent because of his thinking, due to *Smithism* ("capitalism" is a much too narrow term for his broad theories).

Khaldun, Marx, Sarkar, Spengler, Sorokin, and Toynbee all were right. Whole countries have gone down as victims of capitalist success; there certainly have been working class revolts; the West is declining at least relatively speaking; there has been a tremendous increase in individualist materialism (or materialist individualism), often called a culture of consumption or mass culture; and there are clear signs (eco-catastrophes, alienation and modernization diseases, increasing gaps between rich and poor within and between countries, increases in warfare) that the elites, the political classes or castes, have not been able to come up with sufficiently creative answers within their own civilizations, or from elsewhere for that matter. And this seems to hold for all types of political elites—cultural, military, and economic—to bring us into Sarkar's very fruitful *problématique*.

But at the same time, and that is the interesting point, Smith was also right: A tremendous and astounding accumulation of wealth has occurred through the division of labor. The six clear critics just mentioned can certainly be seen as standard-bearers of different but complementary types of opposition to the world dominant system, but the system persists. It must possess some primordial strength beyond the obvious to provide well for the strong people on top of the strong countries on top of the world pyramid of power and privilege. If total truth belonged to anyone of the cyclicists, the societies generated along the lines of Smithism would have disappeared long time ago. Could an explanation be found in the theories of the other linearists?

Comte brings in positivism, which is more than empiricism. There is an implicit doctrine, not only that what is is possible (otherwise it would not have been), but that it continues once the conditions for its existence, generally held to be understandable, are understood. Mainstream economics picks up the Smithian promise and adds to the faith the Comtean positivism as one more promise.

Spencer reinforces that faith even further, coining the term "social Darwinism" and thereby making the dominant economic system look natural, a continuation of the evolutionary chart for life with other means, through ever more differentiation, including the total autonomy of the economy from the polity in the sense of the state. His reasoning, based on biological metaphors and the distinction between the central and the autonomous nervous systems, is not used heuristically but as apodictic truth that is in no need of confirmation.

Weber reinforces Smith further, pronouncing the cultural background for capitalism just right; in fact, implicitly promising that there will never be any serious competitors since they do not have that background. He also delivers a concept of rationality compatible with self-interest maximization, and sees bureaucracy as providing means, not ends; in other words, as servants for capital and civil society. This is at the risk of the iron cage, though.

The general image is clear. The linearists reinforce each other, lining up together; the cyclicists go up and down together; and the two camps are each other's most fervent critics. Behind the ideological debate in the West between well publicized linear positions like Smithism and Marxism lurks a deeper debate between linear and cyclical worldviews. Since the premises of the debate are unclear, the debate itself runs in circles.

And if the premises are made clear, the debate will also run around in circles because the question of which is the correct view, linear or cyclical, cannot be answered within Western logic. The West simply *is* linear.

This leads us straight to the question of what the critics can learn from Smith. The answer is this: Keep going; invest, not rest, giving capitalism eternal life (Co) and making the social body ever young (Sp, We). More money means more problems solved. Expand all the time (Kh); welfare state for the working class (Ma); keep the masses at bay (Sa); at the very least do not decline militarily (Sg); make materialism entertaining, *panem* and *circenses* (bread and circuses) (So); and create a class of idea makers for the elites (To). All of this is done today. It costs, but the wealthy can afford it.

We now make a jump in the chronology, not according the same attention to all the luminaries. The time has come to pose the same questions to Karl Marx. What could he have learned from the others, and what could he have taught them; leaving aside the obvious comment that these people neither learn nor teach in the usual sense. The points about Khaldun and Smith are easily repeated. How is *asabiya* possible at all across class borders with flagrant inequalities due to massive exploitation? For Smith, there is a surprise: History is not smooth and linear (today we might have said exponential). There are ruptures and changes of the course. There are ups and downs.

Marx could have said much the same to Spencer and Weber, both of them so weak on the vertical dimension of the social order, the classes, and so strong on the horizontal dimension, the institutions. Again, this is a good example of how macrohistorians often do not exclude each other but complement each other simply because they are addressing different problems. They are incomplete rather than wrong, which again has something to do with the entire human condition: so complex that there is more than enough for all to reflect on, and also much too much for any totalitarian claim.

More interesting is the relation to the cyclicists, perhaps indicative that Marx, being both but with an overriding linearity, is also very much in the cyclical school. He addresses some of the same problems of rise, decline, and fall, and is more interesting as a cyclical critic of one of the six stages, capitalism, than for his whole *Stufengang* (stairway or stepwise progression) theory of linear history.

Spengler's primacy of culture would have been unacceptable to Marx the materialist, although there is also a strong streak of idealism in a philosopher who puts so much emphasis on the creation of means of production as a basic component in his *force motrice*. But Marx might have seen both Spengler's civilization in the sense of mass culture, and Toynbee's universal church, as some kind of all-encompassing effort to coopt everybody within reach, across all class borders; as opium for the people. Marx's truth does not exclude Spengler's and Toynbee's.

But much more can be said about the relation between Marx and Toynbee. If Toynbee needs a major challenge for his elites to remain creative, then Marx certainly offers him a recipe. But Marx himself then underestimates by far the To factor: The elites learn from the challenge, sometimes responding really creatively, a good example being the social democrat compromise and the welfare state. Thus, it is not strange that members of Marxist parties all over the world saw the social democrats as their major enemies, since they stood in the way of the prediction coming true. The elites let the working class in after adequate filtering, as represented by the labor movements, the same way they are now trying to let nature in as represented by ecological movements, or at least by ecologists (and indigenous people by anthropologists). The elites are strengthened, not only in the eyes of weary electorates, but more important in their own eyes, growing by taking on and handling challenges and feeling they can handle anything. Sooner or later they fall, but maybe later rather than sooner. That distinction matters, particularly to those who live today.

Marx with Sarkar is also an interesting combination to explore. Sarkar is broader than Marx, building his theory on a *vidya/avidya* dialectic that operates at the physical and idea level as well as acknowledging the role of the spiritual in human evolution. But at the same time there is the clear class aspect, only Sarkar operates more symmetrically, with three upper classes employing cultural, military, and economic power, where Marx brings all these power dimensions together in one unified upper class with primacy of the economy. Maybe Marx could have profited from that insight, seeing the three types of power as representing separate class dimensions inside a social formation, exploiting people in three different ways, as slaves, serfs, and workers (or as citizens in a Marxist state, we might add). There is no need to accept Sarkar's time-ordering military–cultural–economic people power, and then military again. Marx might have put economic exploitation in the center as the major articulation; either preceded by cultural legitimation and then protected by the military in the end, or vice versa, launched by military conquest and then vainly legitimated culturally in the end. Or both. Or any other of the six possible orders. All shed some light on the intricacies of class within, and imperialism between, societies.

In the same vein, Sarkar might perhaps have picked up from Marx at least the possibility of asymmetric thinking, exploring the consequences of seeing one of the three forms of power as more basic than the other. With his spiritual inclination, it would probably have been cultural power, setting the framework and the discourse for a spiritual dialectic and possible leadership, which his solution to the cycle, the *sadvipra* or spiritually oriented intellectual, transforms into a progressive spiral.

Let us conclude by using Pitirim Sorokin as a way of reflecting on the others and as a way of reflecting the others. His principle of limits is a stroke of genius that can be used as a metatheory on top of all others, regardless of what kind of *endzustand* the linearists envisage, or what kind of explanation the nonlinearists envisage for their lack of *endzustand*.

What Sorokin says is similar to Sarkar's theory. A simple version runs as follows. Human beings are potentially so rich and complex, with so many drives, needs, desires, and faculties, that it is impossible for any social order (being precisely that—an order) to provide space, let alone satisfaction, for them all. Moreover, what is provided for and what is not will probably easily submit to classification and hence to divisive ideologies, like needs of the body versus needs of the mind, the economy versus the military, and the like.

So Sorokin could have told Khaldun that in the process of entering the city, the new group gives up their freedom, their desert life. They change as they lose the unity they gained through struggle. And once the decay sets in, there is no way back; over time, the new generations forget their past desert life. He could have told Smith that people will sooner or later tire of producing and consuming things; your view is too materialistic. He could have told Comte that there are limits to empirical truth; people will want other truths (theological, metaphysical). He could have told Spencer that people want a sense of wholeness, not only of ever more differentiated parts. He could have told Marx what he told Smith, and he could have told Weber the same as he told Comte: There are limits to rationality. There cannot be any *Endzustand*.

This is no news to his cyclical colleagues. So what does he tell them? Essentially, that they are focusing on only one aspect of ever-changing reality: Khaldun too one-sidedly on solidarity; Spengler and Toynbee too one-sidedly on culture; and Sarkar too one-sidedly on psychological adequacy. Where the others focus on one bundle of factors in the human condition, Sorokin tries to focus on the totality, hence his very "thick" holistic description of the ideational versus sensate antinomy. He brings in cohesiveness, material as well as nonmaterial aspects of sociocultural life, and the depth of human satisfaction. Sorokin might say that these are the major dimensions, but no social order can realize all points on those dimensions simultaneously (the principle of limits applied to social orders), and no author can accommodate all possible dimensions, not even Sorokin (the principle of limits applied to authors). Hence, social orders fail. And authors fail.

Can this principle be applied to Sorokin himself? Sorokin against Sorokin? Of course it can, using simple taoist logic. The principle of limits applied to itself should sensitize us to the possibility that there might, somewhere out there, be that social order that nevertheless is satisfactory: the right culture (Sg), elites (To), balance (Sa), empirical (Co), differentiated (Sc), beyond material problems (Ma), and rational (We)—paradise, utopia, and pluralism, whether achieved by increasing satisfaction or decreasing needs. Sorokin may actually have chosen the cyclical approach prematurely and too one-sidedly, not contemplating the possibility of a humankind at rest. That opens for *le grand débat*, pursued in Section 4.4.

## 4.3 THE OTHER TEN MACROHISTORIANS

What kind of qualitatively new insights can the other ten macrohistorians bring to bear on the kind of issues that have been raised? Ssu-Ma Ch'ien has a point of departure for his cyclical thinking even broader than Sorokin's: the yin–yang contradiction itself, in its most universal form. He applies it in a way which may sound reductionist: history as an endless succession of good and evil kings; sage-kings and tyrants. But king means reign, and that is a very holistic variable. Many people probably have this in mind when they think of history: good years and bad years. In that sense, Ssu-Ma Ch'ien is the primordial macrohistorian. The others in the cyclical school are all variations on that theme, spelling out the yin and the yang, the good and the bad, in various ways.

Augustine gives the Occidental/Manichean version of the same, contrasting sin with Jesus and bringing in the Christian idea of individual choice and hence of individual responsibility. In doing so, he individualizes history. Clearly, sinful choices may be made under good reigns, and Jesus may be chosen during the bad ones. In Augustine, the micro level of the individual is on par with, if not above, the macro level of concern for almost all the others.

Vico is concerned with the disintegration of Christianity much the same way as Khaldun's basic concern is the decline of Islam. The stages run downward, from the age of Gods via the Heroes and Man to the Barbarians and then a Sorokin-type quantum jump upward again. But the same problem remains: Where does the energy for rejuvenation come from?

Pareto may be said to combine the individualism of Augustine with the collectivism, or perhaps sociologism, of almost all the others by focusing on the elites. Toynbee may be said to have done the same, an inclination that comes easily to a professional historian of his generation. But Pareto's solution is different: Do not even try to bet on the same elites responding creatively to new challenges; they will not. Rather, the elites have to circulate in such a way that new elites can accommodate new challenges. And by "new," he means considerably more than the newness provided by democratic elections in Western countries, rotating members of the political classes within the partocracy. Pareto is thus more like Sarkar.

Hegel differs from all the others in being the only one to bring in the world system; talking not about the society or the state, but about all states. There is a clear theory of progress, a linear evolution of states ending with one on top (the Prussian State, playing a role in Hegelian political thought very similar to the role the United States plays in American political thought). There are *Herr* and *Knecht*, top-dog and underdog. But Hegel did not see that they could be related through an invisible system of transfer of wealth from *Knecht* to *Herr*: exploitation. That major insight is found in Marx. And the same applies, of course, to the relation between states in the world system; a relation explored by Lenin but not by anyone on our list of macrohistorians. Hegel produces a ranking of states without exploring the relation between them; in other words, an ideal ideological discourse for the post–socialist world.

Gramsci combines a basically Marxist–Leninist understanding of the world with culture and intellectuals (provided they are "organic") as the carriers of a new social formation. The struggle for cultural hegemony, hence, becomes as important as, or a substitute for, the struggle for control over the means of production. The media and the publishing houses become the battlefields for the conquest of the future, not only the factories. What this means in concrete terms is that Gramsci differs from Marx in placing one of the elites, the holders of cultural power, in the vanguard position rather than the "people" in the sense of the proletariat. But he also differs from the pure culturalists like Comte and Spengler, and perhaps Toynbee, in seeing the mechanism in concrete social terms, as a struggle for hegemony among people and groups of people.

Steiner, like Marx, is cyclical with an overriding linearity and combines a high number of the metaphors and archetypes of the others, being a live bridge between Orient (particularly India) and Occident. Most interesting in this context is his division of society into three parts—spiritual-cultural, legal–political, and economic—and his basic thesis: Each part should be autonomous, and be based on freedom, equality, and brotherhood, respectively. In doing so, he in a sense solves Sarkar's problem, giving each of the three power groups its own sphere with no overriding power system where they are vying with each other for ultimate power. Whether they can really be autonomous yet sufficiently symbiotic is not obvious; none of them can do without the other two.

Teilhard de Chardin is the supreme linearist with the most final *Endzustand* among the twenty; Omega, the end point of evolution, somewhat similar to that other great Christian, Augustine, and reminiscent of the Hindu– Buddhist concept of *moksa–nirvana* (unspeakable bliss and love, the final liberation). Teleology like that does not easily blend with the diachronic social science theories most of the others engage in. But Teilhard had another kind of problem: how to reconcile his scientific ego believing in evolution and his religious Jesuit ego believing in Christ. The answer is Christ as Omega. But on the way there are antievolutionary dangers: egoistic individuation instead of personalization and socialization and a depersonalized human mass subordinated to some totalitarian social arrangement. Here he touches the ground of the others.

Comte bids farewell to theology and metaphysics; Smith and Spencer promise some kind of individuation through an ever more differentiated division of labor but do not guarantee personalization and sociation; Marx and Sarkar promise conflict and struggle rather than love and harmony, although they both have their Omega points; Weber rattles with the iron cage of totalitarianism; and Khaldun, Spengler, Sorokin, and Toynbee see the whole enterprise on its way down, as antievolution, rather than on its way up, as evolution. Teilhard must have shared these pessimisms, otherwise he would not have written so much on antievolution. His was a more holistic perspective, with Omega and Christ as goals and evolution as the way. The other macrohistorians at most serve as his assistants, spelling out some of the humps on this rather grandiose road.

Eisler (following the seminal work of Elise Boulding) adds a perspective missing completely in all the others with no exception: one half of humanity—women. This is a telling indictment of the rest, who very willingly talk about humanity and then of man, meaning the male gender or humanity in general, making no differentiation. For Eisler, the contrast is not between a patriarchy (suppressing so much of the life-sustaining capacity of human beings and not only the women) and matriarchy, but between patriarchy and a gylanic world of partnership where humanity can express itself fully as enlightened peaceful humans. All cyclical macrohistorians could make use of this insight in their search for the hidden energizer providing energy for quantum jumps upward, and all linear theorists should reconsider their *endzustand* from the angle of women. For these are all macrohistories produced by men, and to a major extent for men.

We conclude with the Gaia hypothesis, belonging to no author in particular since personification and deification of the earth and the universe must be about as old as humankind itself. There are both cyclical elements in Gaian macrohistory and linear elements, the big question being whether the latter is inclined up or down. In the latter case, the subject matter of all theories, including Steiner and de Chardin, will be extinguished; a catastrophe for all macrohistorians. However, we can have good theories of both dinosaurs and Aztec society without having either of them around, so maybe there is still some hope. Who will hold these theories is another matter. Maybe some being more evolved than us, viewing us like we tend to view dinosaurs and Aztecs: from above.

## 4.4 *LE GRAND DÈBAT*: THE LINEAR VERSUS THE CYCLICAL SCHOOLS

The first general conclusion is clear: These macro theories and perspectives are complementary, not contradictory. Theories $T_1$ and $T_2$ contradict each other *strictu sensu* when we can derive proposition $P_1$ from one and its negation, $-P_1$ from the other. If somebody had said, "More division of labor, less creation of wealth," this would have contradicted Smith; if somebody had said, "Each generation within a dynasty remains automatically equally creative," Khaldun would have been shrieking from the deeper recesses of history. But no one in this exclusive company has come up with such stupidities.

What about Smith and Marx; is that not a clear case of contradiction? In the sense of social conflict yes, and not only the conflict Smith predicted between competing enterprises, nor the one Marx predicted between antagonistic classes, but between Smith adherents and Marx adherents, whatever either camp means by that. But this does not mean that the theories are contradictory. As mentioned, Smith and Marx look at different aspects of the socioeconomic formation that fascinated them: early industrial capitalism. Smith had a good horizontal look, Marx looks at it vertically. Two noncontradictory truths emerge. Why do so many conclude that different means contradictory? Do they conclude the same looking at crystals from different angles? Or is it rather that there is no concept of any totality too complex even for giants to fathom?

Consequently, let us be grateful for this rich set of superb theoreticians in our tool chest, and rather focus on how to synergistically use several of them, not only one at a time. However, then comes the second general conclusion: The linear and the cyclical theories and perspectives do, indeed, differ. They are contradictory *strictu sensu* because a linear trajectory either descends or ascends, whereas a cyclical trajectory has to ascend and descend to be recognized as cyclical. In addition, the worldviews of the carriers of linear and cyclical views are so different that they simply pick up different aspects of that infinitely complex reality human beings inhabit. That they complement each other in the sense that the linearists have ideas about how to postpone any downswing and the cyclicists have ideas about how to deny the linearists their *endzustand* is obvious.

But behind that there is something more subtle than the contrast between *khronos* (the passage of time, the inexorability of time) and *kairos* (the right time); between physical and biological time. There is a whole cosmology lurking underneath: the Occidental view of life as preparation for an *endzustand* here or there, progress or regress; and the Oriental view of being given a second chance, a third, and a fourth. In the long run, Orientals may agree, there is an exit from the cycles, from the *samsara* (endless cycle of cause and event), as nirvana; but in the much longer run. And the Occidentals might also agree that there may be ups and downs in paradise, perhaps even in hell, and perhaps even tend toward the Viking view of transitions between hell and heaven or even via more earthly forms of existence—eternal life versus transmigration and rebirth; Christianity/Islam versus Hinduism/Buddhism.

That debate is eternal. There is no *experimentum crucis* (decisive experience) that can help us decide. So let us keep the debate, and keep it *grand*. There are good arguments on both sides, and we can grow with the arguments. It is a good contradiction to keep unresolved.

## 4.5 MACROHISTORIANS LEARNING FROM EACH OTHER: A SUMMARY

*Khaldun could teach*
Spengler why the transition comes about
Sorokin the source of energy for the quantum jump upward
Toynbee why elites often are unable to respond creatively
Sarkar why a *varna* starts declining
Smith why accumulation of wealth cannot go on forever
Comte how epistemic stages reflect interests of social carriers
Spencer that the whole body, being organic, dies in the end
Marx that any stage will ultimately wear out, including the communist stage
Weber that people may yearn for simplicity, and there are limits to differentiation

*Khaldun could learn from*
Spengler that culture tends to be replaced by mass civilization
Sorokin that urbanization is too materialist
Toynbee that there is a limit to how much elites can handle
Sarkar that any *varna* runs its course
Smith to cultivate the individual entrepreneur and accumulate
Comte to find empirical laws and act accordingly to forestall
Spencer to make society more differentiated
Marx that real change is only possible through an internal dialectic
Weber to change to a growth-oriented culture

*Sorokin could teach*
Spengler that human life is not only culture/ideational
Toynbee that human life is not only culture/ideational
Sarkar that the human mind is too complex for spiritual adequacy
Smith that human life is not only economic/materialist
Comte that people want more than only empirical truths
Spencer that people want not only parts but also wholeness
Marx that human life is not only economic/materialist
Weber that human life is not only rational/scientific

*Sorokin could learn from*
Spengler to protect the culture from becoming a civilization

Toynbee that renewal of the creative energies of the elites
Sarkar to find an equilibrium between the *varnas*
Smith to make materialism more challenging (and entertaining)
Comte to be always aware of the facts and change accordingly
Spencer to make society more differentiated, more pluralist
Marx to solve the problems of material production, then spiritual
Weber to be more rational; do not just let things happen

*Smith could teach*
Spengler that if you decline, at least keep the military
Toynbee to pay idea makers to rescue the elites
Sarkar to pay off the discontented
Comte that accumulation is the condition for facts to endure
Spencer that social differentiation knows no limits
Marx to transform workers into entrepreneurs
Weber to continue expanding; repression comes with economic decline

*Smith could learn from*
Spengler that the West is in for a decline for noneconomic reasons
Toynbee that the system produces more crises than elites can handle
Sarkar that there will be revolts along the three power dimensions
Comte to learn from the facts and there will be no problems
Spencer that survival of the fittest is the law of natural life
Marx that the proletariat will revolt; there will be severe ruptures
Weber that the culture has to be right; the Protestant ethic

*Marx could teach*
Spengler that the dominant culture is the culture of the dominant class
Toynbee that the capitalist system will produce overabundant challenges
Sarkar that economic power relations steer cultural and military power
Comte that epistemology depends on whether you want change
Spencer that the hands and feet may revolt against the brains
Weber that rationality is not abstract but tied to class position

*Marx could learn from*
Spengler that culture serves as cement for society
Toynbee that the church serves as cement for society
Sarkar that cultural and military power are as important as economic power
Comte to learn from the facts and there will be no problems
Spencer to make society more differentiated
Weber to be more rational; do not just let things happen

# Chapter 5

# *Social Macrohistory as Metaphor for Personal Microhistory*

*Johan Galtung*

### 5.1 BIOGRAPHY AS MICROHISTORY: HUMAN LIFE-CYCLE PHASES

History is the story of how "things human" hang together through time diachronically, and, more particularly, how they change. The individual is the most micro, even indivisible, human thing there is, so evidently the story of the individual through time, with particular emphasis on change, is microhistory. Of course, like for all other good efforts to write history, there will be a context. The individual will be seen partly as self-driven, and partly as driven by inner and outer "forces" impinging on him or her. The context will be in terms of nature, or, more particularly, the life cycle of the human body, including how it is affected by outside nature. Then there is structure, particularly the microstructure of G. H. Mead's "significant others," but also the macrostructure of local, domestic, and global society. Finally there is culture, the values, norms, and rules; both the microculture of the immediate age, gender, race, class, and ethnic surroundings, and the macroculture or civilization in which the individual is embedded, with an inner core of "deep culture" or "cosmology."[1]

Some kind of core personality, somewhat similar to the cosmology of a civilization, takes shape fairly early in life. The personality generates fairly uniform responses to similar situations, reducing the complexity of decision making in everyday life. In some personality disorders, the response is the same, regardless of stimulus. But the mature human individual has the capacity to reflect on and, to some extent, modify, the personality, thereby correcting such (and other) pathologies.

The core may survive inner and outer changes intact, but may also undergo changes that are usually so discontinuous that they can be referred to as (personal) transformations. These transformations may or may not be related to the more obvious changes of the human body from conception, foetus and birth, infancy, childhood and adolescence, maturity, old age, and death. Whether the personality also has an independent existence as a "soul" prior to conception and after death is probably the hottest disputed item on the human agenda. There is also the opposite view, that the personality emerges after and not at birth and may dwindle down to very little or nothing before and not at death (hence the expression "vegetable," and comparisons with early infancy).

All this gives rise to a number of theories of phases in human life; here limited to a discussion of the birth to death interval. The first is a very simple division of human life into four stages which are useful in discussing contemporary issues, but have broader implications.[2]

### Life Phases I:
### Childhood–Education–Work–Retirement (CEWR)

An individual in modern society is surrounded by the inner structure of the family and the outer structure of society at large. There is an exchange going on with input and output. Modern society allocates about five years to childhood, with input mainly from the family and little output. Then there are up to twenty years of education, with input from society and little output; followed by about forty years of work, with output to family and/or society (the individual is paying back); and maybe fifteen years on top of that in retirement, with little input and even less output.

Evidently, the CEWR stages primarily relate the individual to society. Childhood is preparation for schooling, which may be a more appropriate term than "education." And schooling, in turn, is preparation for work: learning time and space, when to be where, discipline, orderly behavior, competition, and some teamwork. None of this is preparation for retirement, which is socioeconomic death if not yet death in the family (the microstructure similar or identical to where the individual came from, and to which he or she retires). Retirement is essentially preparation for biological death. Only norms of sacredness of life saves the individual from being put to biological death. There are some signs today that these norms are weakened, yielding more and more to euthanasia as assisted suicide or genuine suicide.

### Life Phases II: *Dharma–Artha–Kama–Moksha* (DAKM)

Let us now contrast the standard Western life cycle with what could be called the standard Hindu life cycle or scheme of life. Again, there is an input–output relation to society defining the phases; they are not generated out of inner human concerns only. The building blocks for the phases are four Hindu modes of behavior. In the *dharma* (duty, righteousness) mode the focus is on values, norms, and rules; on doing one's duty, to put it that way. In the *artha* mode the focus is on money, property, and what is needed for sustenance. In the *kama* mode the focus is on worldly pleasures and enjoyments (sexual passion being well described in the famous *Kama Sutra*). In the *moksha* mode the focus is on self-realization and god-realization.

In these four phases, of approximately equal duration, there is a shift of emphasis, roughly speaking, from *dharma* via *artha* and *kama* to *moksha*. The four phases in the life cycle are as follows:

1. *Brahmacharyashrama*, the first quarter of life for education and character-building ("student")
2. *Arthastshrama*, for material enjoyment and material progress with due regard to righteousness ("family")
3. *Vanaprashtashrama*, for disinterested service of humanity and cultural growth ("social service")
4. *Sanyastashrama*, for reaching the peak of inwardliness and godwardliness in this world ("enlightenment"). This stage is eternal, continuing after the death of the body.

Thus, the Hindu wants to see the death of death itself before the death of the physical body actually occurs. As it is put in the *Upanishads*, "Lead me from appearance to Reality, from darkness to Light, and from death to Immortality."

Schematically the life phases would look like this:[3]

|  | *dharma* | *artha* | *kama* | *moksha* |
|---|---|---|---|---|
| *brahmacharyashrama* | maximum | nil | minimum | implicit |
| *arthastashrama* | uncompromising | maximum | maximum | implicit |
| *vanaprasthashrama* | predominant | nil | minimum | implicit |
| *sanyastashrama* | minimum | nil | minimum | maximum |

As life unfolds, *moksha*—liberation as a mode—is itself liberated. In the first phase the focus is on *dharma* alone, in the second the individual is fully launched in this world, in the third the focus is on service in this world, and in the final phase on self-realization. *Moksha* is implicit all the time.

CEWR and DAKM both have four stages and there is an obvious similarity in first things first: learning correct behavior and how to make a living. But from that point on Hindu life seems superior to Western life. There is room for enjoyment, and on top of that a fourth stage of wisdom and liberation, transcending in this physical life the limitations of the body. This gains in perspective when we remember that each phase is supposed to last one-quarter of a life—say, twenty years, or forty years for the first two phases—as opposed to C + E + W = sixty-five years. This leaves half of the Hindu life cycle for pleasure and self-realization, as opposed to less than one-quarter of the Western cycle. Of course, it is unfair to compare a secular Western life scheme and a nonsecular Hindu life scheme. Western retirement may also stand for pleasure and wisdom, but it is less than one-fifth of the life span. And the Hindu cycle ends on a participatory note, whereas the Western life cycle ends in a void, very different from the Western "idea of progress." The microhistory is neither cyclical nor linear. It just ends.

### Life Phases III: The Ten Greek Phases

Following Bernard Lievegoed let us now look at another way of dividing the individual life cycle, keeping in mind the need not to be limited to contemporary and/or Western views.[4] The Greek phases are seven years each; in other words, a quite realistic life expectancy of seventy years. More interesting is the description of the phases: fantasy life, self-presentation, puberty and adolescence, exploring the life basis, reinforcement and verification of the life basis, second puberty with possible reorientation, the manic–depressive period (at the 42 to 49 years interval), images of one's own decline and fall, reconsideration, and a second youth and possible new climax.

The basic difference from the others is the camel shape (two humps), as opposed to the dromedary-shaped image of the life cycle found in CEWR and the ever-progressing life image found in the Hindu model. If the Greeks had had a shorter life expectancy, more like thirty-five years, then there would have been no time for two humps. But Greeks at the top of society lived longer and were introspective; they had time enough to accommodate two life cycles in their composite cycle. Life is more than biological flow. The human psyche enters, possibly interacting with outer circumstances and bringing out contradictions showing up as (midlife) crisis, and then there is a second puberty in this life.

### Life Phases IV: Rudolf Steiner's Ten Phases

Rudolf Steiner's ten phases of seven years each are based on complex interactions between biological, psychological, and spiritual factors.[5] The first three are for the development of the body, the next three for the development of the mind, the next three for the development of the spirit, and then comes a tenth phase of consolidation. But life does not end at seventy: At this point, the person has achieved personhood and can give back the fruits of his life. In this, we sense the influence of Hindu thought on Steiner; a man bridging the Occident–Orient divide.

There is much wisdom in these phase models. In Freudian terms, they all try to accommodate the Superego from family and society, the Id of the body, and the Ego of mind and spirit, seeing them both as autonomous and as malleable, interacting with each other in conflict and cooperation. One of them may yield to the other, and ultimately the body yields, first socially and then biologically.

One crucial point from CEWR can now be formulated. The phases are socially defined as interaction patterns of Self with family and society. But why should the phases be taken in that order? Why should there be any order at all? Why not start with a year or two of childhood, then straight into work as human beings used to do, then some years of education, then maybe some retirement when it can still be fully enjoyed? Sabbaticals could be available to all, not only to high-status persons. Thus, cyclicity can be built into the CEWR system by seeing C, E, W, and R as different ways of relating to self and others. By shortening the phases, great varieties of lifestyles can be constructed, reproducing the other life phase models above. Why does the West not do that, except for strong and possibly marginal individuals? Because Western time is linear.

The objection would be that *nirvana* endows Hindu and Buddhist microhistory with an *Endzustand* (end of history). But the time perspective is staggering, like the Occidental figure "at the end of time." The Hindu model sees each life as preparation for the next and for *nirvana*, with any number of cycles before one gets a "pass." In the Occident, with only one physical life to prepare for eternity, linear lifestyles must prevail. Time is cyclical in the Orient, and mixed and linear in the Occident.

## 5.2 MACROHISTORY AS SOCIOGRAPHY: SOCIAL LIFE-CYCLE PHASES

Societies also exhibit birth and death, the latter sometimes with a whimper, sometimes with a bang. Their "biography" is here referred to as "sociography." A division into phases is one of the major intellectual tools of the macrohistorians, but it is not indispensable. There can also be models with no discontinuities—only growth, for instance—or business cycles—only *khronos*, no *kairos*. But the idea of social life cycles with recognizable and generalizable phases between coming into being and going out of being is found all over in human thought.

There can be little doubt that macrohistorians have gotten some of their inspiration from biological time, projecting human cycles on social cycles, with birth, adolescence, maturity, old age, and death. The human mind works to a large extent by imputing isomorphisms—using something as a model, or at least a metaphor, for something else—and the closest point of departure for model building would be oneself. There is also physical time, annual cycles, seasons, day, and night, not to mention sexual time, with its rise and fall (male) and expansion and contraction (female).[6]

Time does not come to macrohistorians like a tabula rasa, but has been prepared for them by the civilization in which they live. Nature prepares all humans everywhere for some cyclical time perspectives, as has been argued. Bodies come, bodies go; new bodies created out of the old appear. In the Orient this is reinforced by Hindu and Buddhist images of transmigration and rebirth: spirits come, spirits go; new spirits are created out of the old.[7] As a consequence, life cycles do not end with death.

Not so in the Occident, and particularly not in the dominant Occidental religion—Christianity. There is no return of the spirit. Migration to paradise or inferno is one-way. Even in the short run, after human life, there is either heaven and progress or hell and regress; up or down. There may be cyclical aspects of life before that, but the total time *Gestalt* is not only linear, with up or down varieties, but comes equipped with final states; *Endzustand* with no more transformation. Biography has an end; so does a sociography inheriting this scheme. There is an end to history.

We would expect secularization to work for even more linearity, simply because afterlife with *Endzustand* has to be mirrored on earth. As a matter of fact, all the linear macrohistorians may be seen as products of the Enlightenment, which brought in its wake an explosion of linear thought. The logical sequel to eternal and perfect afterlife was the same on earth.

What remains when Occidental linear thought comes down on earth is, of course, the distinction between eternal optimists and apocalyptic pessimists, between perfect heaven and perfect hell on earth. Both Smith and Marx are good examples of the former; for the latter, late twentieth-century ecologically inspired gloom and doom thinking might serve as an example. Fertile minds will profitably cross the biography–sociography border.

## 5.3 MICROHISTORY AND MACROHISTORY AS EACH OTHER'S METAPHOR

Let us now do something similar to the analysis in Chapter 4, and ask how the macrohistorians can enrich human life-cycle theory and practice. Are there some ways of using human life-cycle theories to enrich macrohistory? In what follows, we first focus on Khaldun, Spengler, Sorokin, Toynbee, and Sarkar from the cyclical camp, and then on Smith, Comte, Spencer, Marx, and Weber from the mainly linear camp. The question to be addressed is what we can learn about human biography translating the core of the theories and the mechanisms of change from the social to the individual, focusing on the human core, the personality. More particularly, could there be some hidden message of a more normative character, not only about how humans live their lives and run through phases concurrently and/or serially, but also how they should or might do so?

The cyclical thinkers combine threat and promise: There is a buildup to climax and then decline, even fall, but up it comes again. Like transmigration and rebirth, there is a second chance or a third, with the promise of an exit from *samsara* (endless cycle of action and reaction, cause and effect) when the job has been completed and maturity has been achieved.

From a biographical point of view, no conversion of the Occidental person to Oriental philosophy is necessary. The perspective can also be built into biography, as mentioned in Section 5.1, where it was referred to as a camel-shaped life cycle. More fanciful animals could also be imagined. The Greeks saw this as normal, but standard Western life-cycle theory (so far) does not.

But the insight becomes more commanding if we understand the mechanisms behind cycles of rise, decline, and fall. Khaldun's answer is to take new energy and people from the outside. The new cycle starts with the Bedouins knocking on the gates, even knocking them down; and the new rule flourishes until people deplete the economic and cultural capital and degeneration sets in.

What does this remind us of? A marriage that has gone stale, irreversibly past its climax, and then a "fresh" spouse knocking down the defenses already weakened by the degeneration, infusing new energy through new love and love rekindled? Or the old spouse, renewing himself or herself? A brutal metaphor to some, but full of promise to others. What Khaldun teaches us is that some *asabiya* renewal is indispensable to stave off decline and fall.

Just as societies may conform to Khaldun's cycles within different chronological time spans because some change quickly and some slowly, so may human beings. The metabolism is different; there may be accelerated as well as retarded history at work. The metaphor does not unambiguously point to *eros* and *sexus* as the renewers. The other who knocks at the door could be new children or new friends. The basic truth of the metaphor lies in the notion of decline, fall, and waiting for or inviting the renewal, even if painful, from the outside, (exogenously).

A new *Leitmotif*, a new sociocultural mentality, is another source of renewal, picked up by both Spengler and Sorokin. To them, the cycles start at a very high pitch. Sorokin stresses the ideational, the other worldly side of the human personality, building society around that theme. The principle of limits then enters the picture: A society playing on too narrow a band of the total human spectrum will be punished. The repressed and neglected spectral lines and bands will revolt and fight their way through, like weeds through asphalt. The sensate or this worldly aspects of human beings will make themselves seen, heard, and felt. For a short period, an idealistic compromise or combination, an *eclecticum*, may be found, but the general thrust is toward a more sensate existence. And from there the decline leads to Spengler's civilization, and Sorokin's chaos which ends in the gutter of material totalitarianism; his version of decline and fall. The principle of limits applies again: Like a Phoenix, society rises from the sensate ashes, or Spengler's new cycle starts. This can be illustrated of one famous biography: Saul on the way to Damascus, becoming Paul by being disgusted with himself, and being helped by God. But Sorokin does not presuppose any God. Humanity has sufficient endogenous strength to bring about that qualitative jump upward, although he never really discusses where that energy comes from. Individual conversion is Sorokin's metaphor for fundamental social renewal, based on disgust, endogenously perceived and endogenously brought about. So his contribution to lifestyle theory might run something like this: Build your life around a *Leitmotif*, a basic theme; start high up, but do not expect one theme to last your entire life span. Be prepared to change your theme by inner force, not waiting for the other to stave off the depravity of uncontrolled sensualism.

Toynbee's answer to the same problem—how to be born again—differs from both Khaldun's and Sorokin's: His focus is on the challenge and response and the creative minority-imitative majority. There is decline and fall, but that is not the end. There will always be new challenges, and the possibility of new groups responding to them creatively. Like Sorokin, he sees the response as coming from the inside, endogenously, not from outsiders from heaven or from hell, changing the order: Pull yourself together and respond to the challenge. This reminds us of the person who may be aging but is always looking out for new challenges to respond to; in short, the innovator. The mentality has vitality as long as the responses are still creative. In principle, the individual can continue evolving until death claims the body.

But where is Toynbee's imitative majority? Toynbee has a social context for the creative minority; how about the human context for the creative individual? The answer is simple: Creativity in one field may have a spillover to other parts of the personality imitating that creative core. The economic entrepreneur may also become creative in the art of living, possibly by dabbling in the arts, engaging in sports, doing some research, or the other way around. There is a carryover effect.

Sarkar adds another touch to the same theme, in a sense combining the ideas of his three cyclical colleagues. His cycles are also based on the principle of limits, not so much to the cultural mentalities as to occupational structures. The archetype is the military–priest/scholar–merchant–people cycle, with the military providing law and order but so culturally inept that the priest/scholars take over. After they have wrecked the economy, the merchants take over, but they exploit the people so mercilessly that the people take over. At that point, the military are reinstated in power, bringing about law and order.

What can we learn from this at the level of individual biography? Maybe that our specialized occupation structures, built according to the one person–one job principle, will never satisfy a person whose potential richness in terms of talent waiting to flourish transcends what an occupational structure can satisfy. Unless, that is, there is either a change of occupation or the person holds more than one. Nowadays, both patterns seem to be increasingly frequent, and life-cycle theory informs us when to expect the change: at the mid-life crisis, from the late forties to the early fifties.

Sarkar's answer can be practiced without limiting the choice to Sarkar's occupations from the classical Hindu *varna* system, and particularly not in Sarkar's sequential order. But there is a more general lesson to be drawn. Some jobs are more brainy, others more brawny. Some are high and some are low in society. Combine these two dichotomies and Sarkar's system is, to some extent, reproduced. Maybe the message is this: Do not scorn the low, nor fail to aim for the high; use both your body and your mind in your life. As a result, your inner self and outer society will be deeply rewarded; your life will be rich indeed and you will have much to give. To every such inclination there is *kairos*, the right time; order them into your *khronos*, the physical passage of time, and develop a sense of when the limit has been reached and the time for a change has come. But there is no transformation before its time has come, otherwise the change is only a restless back and forth with no organic rhythm of *kairos* in *khronos*. In doing so, you exit from *samsara* by becoming its master.[8]

Thus interpreted, the four cyclical macrohistorians give us ample insight into how we could live our lives with multiple peaks, knowing that this also means multiple troughs: Let new or renewed persons into your life; renew yourself by converting to new *Leitmotifs*; pick up challenges, respond, and never give up; and change occupations, not only once but several times. A rich life menu indeed, probably lived by some of the macrohistorians themselves. Most of them also lived in social niches where this was possible, reminiscent of Marx's famous hunting in the morning, then shepherd and fisherman, and finally social critic at night. This is maybe also a reason why they thought rich thoughts, living in both worlds, macro and micro.

Let us then proceed to the linear macrohistorians. Their message sounds less interesting. There is progress and regress, usually Adam Smith–type progress. Christianity, after all, focuses more on how to end in heaven than in hell. The final state, although in this world, is remote; somewhere and when, like "communist society." That state, then, becomes the goal, the teleological purpose of the whole analysis. And that is where a certain reductionism sets in; seeing society as striving through history to achieve that goal like a person striving to achieve salvation. In the long run, Oriental thought also has this idea, but much has to happen before that.

To Comte, the road to maturity goes through three stages: a theological stage, with belief in the transcendental; a metaphysical stage, with belief in ideas as reality; and, finally, the positive stage, with belief in positively existing observed phenomena. To Comte, the third stage is simply the final stage, with a positive science of society, sociology, providing answers to questions of harmony, conflict resolution, peace, and the like.

How would this message translate into human biography? No doubt there are individuals who have gone through these stages, and in that order in their life; maybe even as a revolt against theological indoctrination, with idealism as an interlude. But just as many or more might have done the opposite, entering the theological stage when they feel closer to having their souls released from their bodies. Maybe Comte's message could be made less linear, focusing on the three modes of coming to grips with reality. But then it is no longer Comte, and merely a typology.

Comte knows which stage is the highest. But how about the other four possible sequences, using Comte's three stages as answers to the basic and universal questions of "Who am I," "Where am I," and "Where am I headed?" Translated from sociography to biography, it looks like Comte puts the human being in some kind of straitjacket or iron cage: This is where you are supposed to end up as a positivist. Comte's reaction to the theology and the metaphysics of his day is understandable. But his stages taken as human prescription would lead us straight to Sorokin's dilemma: Once you have entered materialism, shedding all other worldly and idealist beliefs, where do you end? Where do your values, norms, and rules come from?

To such questions, Spencer does not provide much of an answer either. History is one-way evolution, and evolution is differentiation with increasing autonomy between parts. There is the right, even duty, of the strong to prevail over the weak in the struggle for Spencer's "survival of the fittest." Spencer uses the ontobiological distinction between ectoderm and endoderm, with the mesoderm located in-between, and makes it normative for society: If the brain (corresponding to the state) cannot control the intestines (corresponding to industry), then the state should not control industry (the intestines should be governed by the autonomous, not by the central nervous system).

Spencer became, and still is, one of the high priests of liberal society in that particular sense, providing biological premises for Adam Smith's laissez-faire conclusions one century earlier. But what is there to learn from this at the personal, but not necessarily biological level? Differentiation can be interpreted as ever higher discrimination—in emotions, cognitions, and volitions—with a capacity to respond with finer tuning to ever finer nuances in perceptions. This might tally well with many notions of maturity, and is observed empirically by comparing the newborn with the highly seasoned individual. But the cyclically oriented would immediately temper that insight with the observation that there can be limits to refinement, and that the refined can also produce a longing for the crude and the undifferentiated in a never-ending dialectic. If there are limits to everything, then they apply also to *le cru* and *le cuit* (the raw and the cooked), or to any pure yin or pure yang, as the daoist would insist.

There is also Spencer's penchant for autonomy and his general effort to prove his own ideological convictions as expressing the "natural order." But ecosystems seem to be at their most mature or resilient when the parts are not only diverse (which could be taken to mean differentiated), but are also symbiotically related; in other words, far from autonomous. To use Spencer's illustration, what is called for would be state and industry cooperating rather than being mutually independent of each other. That, in turn, would actually call for a negotiation economy harmonizing private and public, capital and state, and market and plan at high levels (Japan) or medium levels (social democracy), rather than separation.

This type of imagery may also produce more interesting insights at the personal level. Cognitions, emotions, and volitions separated from each other in splendid, autonomous isolation do not convey an image of maturity. Moreover, this is Spencer's final stage, not an early or intermediate one. The society is not supposed to move from there, as any move from a state of perfection would be irrational. Translated into a biography, Spencer's message suffers from exactly the same basic shortcoming. The final state of affairs is too static.

Does Marx fare much better?[9] He is more subtle, and the answer depends on how we choose to interpret him. Let us try to express quintessential Marx as follows: There is one basic endogenous contradiction located in the very core of society, between means of production (above all technology) and modes of production (above all ownership patterns). More particularly, whereas the mode has a tendency to remain fixed for long periods of time, the means are continuously changing with innovations, sometimes in jumps, sometimes slowly, and sometimes continuously. If something is constant and something else is changing, then sooner or later there will be a rupture. The mode will have to yield, simply because counterproductive social patterns stand in the way of what has become technically feasible. Thus it is and thus it will always be, for any society at any time, at any point along the primitive communism–slavery–serfdom–capitalism–socialism–communism trajectory, until, in the end, the drama is over and the fit has been obtained in communist society. The technology is given free reins to satisfy ever higher human needs; from *Notwendigkeit* to *Freiheit*, necessity to freedom.

What could this mean when translated into a biography? The notion of contradiction between the constant and the changing, and the constant ultimately undergoing rupture like a branch overloaded with snow, makes sense also at the individual level, like anywhere else. But Marx's techno-economic interpretation makes no particular sense, and the contradiction-free person, like contradiction-free society, sounds like a dead person deprived of the dynamism of life; a zombie without personality. The end of history, to individual and society, may turn out to be the beginning of death, even with a bang rather than a whimper.

Weber introduces a surprising element in this linear approach to macrohistory: regress instead of progress.[10] There is emphasis both on Comte's rationality and on Spencer's differentiation. They meet in bureaucracy. But bureaucracy can become counterproductive, too powerful and overpowering, and an iron cage for the rest of society.

This also makes good sense at the personal level. If a person steers personal development in the direction of the supremacy of the cognitive over the emotive and the volitional modes, foreseeing all possible situations and developing rules for all of them, thereby ruling out in advance all surprises, chances are that the person will either be as surprise-free as the system he or she designed to foresee and counter surprises (meaning unable to undergo any transcending change or even learn from anything new), or undergo basic rupture the moment this inflexible system is exposed to an overload of surprises. In other words, this is a person with the iron cage inside the head rather than the head inside the cage. It makes a difference: In the latter case, the head knows what is going on; in the former, the ability to understand what happens may already have been lost somewhere in that inner cage (the United States versus the Soviet Union).

How does one exit from Weber's cage? Can we retreat from communist society? "Yes," Eastern Europe said in the fall of 1989. Can we de-differentiate and make the parts less autonomous? Can we become metaphysical and theological again? Yes, but the problem with the linear theorists is that their paradigm prevents them from seeing or even exploring how. Essentially, all linear theories are cage theories, with no built-in escapes or exits.

The preliminary conclusion must be that the human individual has more to learn from cyclical than linear macrohistory. But linear theories are not completely ruled out. In Comte, there is also a theory of cognitive development of the individual, worthy of taking seriously as an hypothesis, that is reminiscent of Jean Piaget. Spencer opens for a theory of refinement, reminiscent of Norbert Elias. Marx has a general theory of rupture and transformation. And Weber issues a general warning, including against himself.

Modern Occidental, secular, socially, and individually linear thinking comes out very barren indeed. Human life heads for retirement along a simple rectilinear curve, with nothing beyond. Social life proceeds toward a final state of affairs doomed to induce yawns of boredom once it is realized. Given such secular micro and macro futures, people of course turn to religion, to dream again the dream of an afterlife. Cyclical sociographies produce histories with no final chapters. And cyclical lifestyles would produce much more interesting biographies without that brief or long interval between retirement and obituary.

What could macrohistorians pick up from microhistorians? Even though individuals are many and societies are few, there should be much to learn. But we are comparing theories, or rather paradigms, and it is less obvious which discipline has attracted the more gifted thinkers. Moreover, as has been lamented many times, biology imposes something finite on biography, bracketed between birth and death. Society is more like God, transcending the life span of individuals, comprising any number of us, and providing an abode for all who belong, in time and in space. It is like God (possibly an even more attractive subject of study); moreover, in Hindu terms society is a Creator, a Protector, and a Destroyer.

This points to the standard Hindu scheme of life as the most interesting microhistory from the point of view of macrohistory, including those Western schemes that have some similarities: the Greeks and Rudolf Steiner. In all of them we detect resistance against yielding to biology by modeling the spiritual cycle on the physiological with maturation, senescence, and death. They all pack much more complexity into this one life by placing the spirit and wisdom in command. In relation to the individual search for wisdom they probably, in the back of their minds and sometimes on the tip of the tongues, thought of wisdom (in a broad sense) as something not only to be carried by the individual into the individual afterlife, but to be shared with others, thereby enriching the collective Being, the society that transcends individuals. In doing so, they highlight a problem overlooked by macrohistorians: How should society be in order to sustain not only life, but also the afterlife, here, there, or both? We shall return to this in Chapter 6.

## 5.4 ON THE LIMITS TO ISOMORPHISM

The purpose of this analysis is to bring two fields, obviously related, closer to each other; letting them play with each other so to speak, shedding light on each other, and then letting that light be reflected, refracted, and diffracted. It is like comparing theories of peace and theories of health: The are similar, and yet dissimilar. This corresponds to that and that to this, yet never completely; only up to a certain point, but they are sufficiently similar for any insight relatively well rooted in one field to become a fruitful hypothesis when translated into the other. To say "you cannot prove anything about one from the other" is as obviously true as "any insight in one field is automatically valid in the other" is obviously false.

Microhistory and macrohistory have, in common, the effort to make visible or transparent both the structure of some basic processes and the process that some core structures undergo, such as personalities for individuals and cosmologies for civilizations. The biographical phases and processes of Section 5.1 and the sociographical phases and processes of Section 5.3 can all be seen as archetypes, even as metaphors. The intellectual danger is less located in jumping too quickly to conclusions across the micro–macro divide than in elevating any one of these powerful archetypes to the position of Arch-archetype, the only one. Marxists did that, and it became their undoing. Why did they do that? Probably because they were influenced by other archetypes in the Occident, such as religions with monopoly on truth and monotheism with only one God and, just as important, only one prophet—mono-prophetism.[11] Marxism met the bill.

Better, then, to enter any concrete historical process with a toolchest richly stuffed with many such archetypes, using them also across the divide; seeing Sarkar in the individual and Steiner in the society.[12] A rich toolchest should be carried by all, but generously; not complaining if all tools do not fit all problems. Hammers are as bad for sewing as needles for hammering. To complain that Comte does not fit human biography, or Steiner human sociography, may be mistakes of the same order.

And yet we have a right to ask for a Swiss army (or non-army) knife, the multi-tool that fits all problems. Moreover, if a theory developed for biography or sociography makes no sense when reasonably translated into the other field, this could be an indicator that it is simply a bad theory. Take Comte again as an example: He hardly makes any sense as biography, neither empirically nor normatively. But if society consists (also) of individuals, how can he make sense socially? Should there not be some common logic to organic, live, even human systems, at least at the general level of these theories?

Conversely, take Steiner and his three phases, first focusing on the body, then on the mind, and then on the spirit. Are we to understand that a society should first focus on basic material needs, then move on to basic nonmaterial needs, and finally develop an ability to reflect on it all? Why this order? Why not the other way round? Or, still better, why not do all of this concurrently rather than serially, as indicated at the end of Section 5.1? Why should we assume more separation of these processes than the absolute minimum necessary, given the limited capabilities of the newborn or our images of them as limited?

However that may be, let us end on a very constructive note. The toolchest of archetypes referred to can be expanded; new tools can enter and less desirable old tools can be discarded. Each one makes us see and do something obscured by other tools. Each one enables the biographer or sociographer to ask this question: Could this factor have been operating? If the answer is no, then comes the counterfactual question, always fruitful in historical research. What if it has been operating? Should it?

The objects of the analysis, the individual and the society of individuals, themselves historical subjects, may ask exactly the same questions, perhaps focusing on the normative more than the empirical and building a future in addition to understanding the past. In so doing, they would be better served by multiple than by single tools. Imagine that the Marxists in the ex-Soviet Union had been willing to learn more from the other macrohistorians, including Adam Smith, and imagine that the Smithians in the United States (and in Russia today) had been more open to others, including Karl Marx. Then they might not have been so overtaken by another country—Japan—which is much higher in eclectic ability, capable of operating both plan and market, and more, simultaneously.

The moral is to pick tools carefully and to beware of the shiny and the modish. This applies to the subjects as well as to the students who turn the subjects into objects of study, and most particularly to the relation between them when the subject becomes introspective, retrospective, and prospective.[13]

## NOTES

1. Johan Galtung, *Peace by Peaceful Means*, part 4 (London: Sage, 1996), particularly Chapter 4, 2.

2. See Johan Galtung, "Structural Pluralism," in *Challenges from the Future: Proceedings of International Futures Research Conferences*, ed. Japan Society for Futurology (Tokyo: Kodansha, 1970); and Johan Cullberg, *Kris och utveckling: en psykoanalytisk och sosialpsykiatrisk studie* (Crisis and development: A psychoanalytic and social psychiatric study) (Stockholm: Naturoch Kultur, 1976).

3. I am indebted to Professor J. A. Yajnik, Director of the University School of Psychology, Education, and Philosophy of Gujarat University, Ahmedabad, for his observations.

4. Bernard Lievegoed, *De Levensloep van de mens* (The life cycle of human beings), 15th ed. (Rotterdam: Lemniscaat, 1988).

5. Rudolf Steiner, *Grundlinien einer Erkenntnistheorie der Goetheschen Weltanschauung* (Basic aspects of the epistemology of Goethe's worldview) (Stuttgart: Verl Freies Geistesleben, 1961).

6. I am indebted to Sohail Inayatullah for this notion.

7. For one presentation, see Johan Galtung, *Buddhism: A Quest for Unity and Peace* (Colombo, Sri Lanka: Sarvodaya Vishva Lekha, 1993).

8. As an example, I offer a private story. Once, probably in some early "midlife crisis" at the end of my thirties, I had a very concrete vision at an *hacienda* at the pampas in Argentina. Cattle which were about to be butchered were driven by the *gauchos* between two fences that come closer and closer—a Y-shaped arrangement—with less and less latitude for the cattle. At the end was an axe. A small cow managed to jump the fence. At that time, I saw my own life narrowing in options and I exited.

9. Like the others, Marx was also fascinated with the idea of *Naturgesetzlichkeit*—how society evolves according to "scientific" laws. The events in Europe during 1989 might have made Marx contemplate cyclical theories and voluntarism more.

10. See Max Weber, "Zur Lage der bürgerlichen Demokratie in Russland" (The state of bourgois democracy in Russia), *Archiv* 22 (1905–1906), quoted in Gunther Roth and Wolfgang Schluchter, *Max Weber's Vision of History, Ethics and Methods* (Berkeley and Los Angeles: University of California Press, 1979), 201.

11. See Johan Galtung, "Theory Formation in Social Research: A Plea for Pluralism," in *Comparative Methodology: Theory and Practice in International Social Research*, ed. Else Öyen (London: Sage, 1990).

12. There are others, like Charlotte Bühler, *The Course of Human Life: A Study of Goals in the Human Psychology* (New York: Springer, 1968); Romano Guardini, *The World and the Person* (Wuerzburg: Werkbund-Verl, 1939); Martha Moers, *Die Entwicklungsphasen des menschlichen Lebens* (Development stages in the human life cycle) (Ratingen: Henn, 1953). Also interesting is an article by Johan Jensen, "Ritualer, Födselsdagsforelesning" (Rituals: An anniversary lecture) (Arhus: NYT fra Center for Kulturforskning, 1989), following the tradition of Arnold van Gennep, *Les rites de passage* (Transition rituals), trans. Monka Vizedom and Gabrielle Cafee, intro. Solon Kimball (London: Routledge and Kegan Paul, 1972); and Victor Turner, *Drama, Fields and Metaphors: Symbolic Action in Human Society* (Ithaca, N.Y.: Cornell University Press, 1974). Jensen focuses more on the transitions between the phases; the border territory, the liminality. In the CEWR system, these are birth, school entry, final exams, retirement, and death; in Japan, entrance exams substitute for final exams; in more traditional societies (closer to reproduction), puberty and marriage would play similar roles. Birthdays make a person accountable, to self and others, particularly publicly celebrated birthdays (in the West, fifty, sixty, seventy, and then every fifth year; in Japan, sixty, seventy-seven, and eighty-eight).

13. For a superb general exploration along the lines of this chapter, see Christie W. Kiefer, *The Mantle of Maturity* (Albany: State University of New York Press, 1988).

# Chapter 6

# *Social Macrohistory as Metaphor for World Macrohistory*

*Johan Galtung*

### 6.1 TWENTY MACROHISTORIANS LOOK AT THE WORLD

Can social macrohistorians make us see world society differently? This is the guiding question for this concluding chapter. The answer is yes, but not all of them. For example, Ssu-Ma Ch'ien's theory is, to a considerable extent, a theory of rulers and dynasties, and the world does not have a ruler (yet). Both Augustine and Aquinas operate within a Christian logic, and the world as a whole is not Christian and will probably never be. Khaldun is also problematic, as he believes in change from the outside and there is no outside (yet). The perennial reference to an invasion of Martians as unifying, transcending East–West conflict and the like, testifies to the significance of this factor, although it should be noticed that Khaldun focuses on renewal through takeover, not just a unifying external threat. The Tunisian upper-class diplomat seems to have been less afraid of Bedouins than the U.S. public was of Martians in the Orson Welles broadcast, or as Ronald Reagan diplomacy in one of the last United States–Soviet dialogues. However, we certainly cannot count on them to energize the Khaldun cycle. Some of the same applies to Vico. It is hard to believe in gods or heroes on top of the world system, since our leaders look and act highly human. The Vico cycle looks heavily curtailed, between chaos and humans and back again.

But after this negative opening, many of the other macrohistorians are very relevant. They shed considerable light on the condition of the world system, doing so often in unexpected ways, as one might expect from great thinkers.

Smith, Comte, and Spencer belong together, as they all focus on economic growth—stick to the facts, unsentimentally, and ever-increasing differentiation, they argue. If anything is the salient, dominant feature of the world system today, transcending all kinds of orders, this is it. We live in their capitalist–positivist–evolutionist world. Their words came true. This does not necessarily mean that they were the greatest of the great, but they certainly formulated theories compatible with dominant Western cosmology, presumably the cosmology of the dominant class, meaning the dominant class of the dominant countries at the time.[1] If this is what they predicted would happen, they were good guessers. But as we know, they did not only predict. Like most macrohistorians, they were also great moralists, and prescribed at the same time.

That is where the doubts emerge and multiply. Up come five, perhaps even more, preeminent macrohistorians with their counterarguments formulated as theories: Marx, Weber, Spengler, Sorokin, and Gramsci. They point to the blatant exploitation in the wake of unabated growth-positivism–division of labor trends. For Marx, it is class struggle. Mao Zedong brings in the landless masses of the world, switching the attention from cities to villages, possibly a little too easily since the former are now more than 50 percent of the world population. But Mao's former friend, Lin Biao, had an important world system formulation: The class struggle, according to him, was in terms of the "world village" against the "world city," the latter being located predominantly in the world Northwest—the Smith–Comte–Spencer world. Concretely, this means world terrorism against counterterrorism, with state torture as one important form of the latter.

But Marx also had a world system formulation: "Proletarians all over the world, unite!" They did not, partly because the capitalists were strong, and through their secret services killed off much of the opposition; but also, while Marx's analysis pointed to their common class interests, he forgot the importance of gender and generation, race and nation, and distance.[2] Women have common interests, so does the younger generation, and so do people of the same race. Finally, people of the same nation have a cultural coherence missing among "proletarians all over the world." This is the reason why so many contemporary "liberation fronts" are "FNL" (*Front National de Liberation*).

In short, the Marxist formulation, while brilliant in its brevity, misses quite a few points. "Underdogs of the same type around the world, unite!" makes some sense, though. And this is what is happening in the world system today: feminist and women's movements, youth revolts, and nationalism (purely racial solidarity being less prominent so far). But it is not proletarians all over the world; and if proletarians, then it is less transnational, isolated, and limited to their own gender, generation, and nation. Often, they have had to fight proletarians from oppressive nations, like Vietnamese peasants fighting French workers.

In a certain sense, Gramsci has more insight to offer in today's world. His implicit critique of Marx is more over methods than over goals. To him, class struggle is more in terms of intellectuals conquering the cultural infrastructure (media, publishing houses, etc.) than workers conquering factories. In today's world, with global networks defining what is and what should be, this *primauté de la culture* (primacy of culture) makes very good sense.[3]

Weber's iron cage at the world level translates into a stifling world bureaucracy, which is not what the United Nations is today. The United Nations can be accused of inefficiency, but (maybe precisely for that reason) not of being humanity's iron cage. The point is Weber's premonition that this would happen, and there is no reason why world society should be exempt from such social regularities.

For Spengler, like for Gramsci, the discourse is cultural. There are creative elites and there is mass culture and even "civilization," for Spengler a very derogatory word. With the mass media, and above all the most widely dispersed mass culture, particularly among the young American culture, the conditions for a Spengler problematic are already there. The problem is, as with Vico, the truncated cycle: not the whole cycle, but rather some oscillation between lower rungs of culture and civilization, perhaps because an incoherent world has to rally around least common denominators. The United States, itself a multicultural and not always cohesive society, produces exactly that. The top creative elite demands a setting more cohesive and coherent than the world offers today. But tomorrow, that might change.

Then comes Sorokin, with all his thunder. Like the others, he also has four phases: ideational, idealistic, sensate, and chaos. The diagnosis would probably be that the world as a whole is culturally somewhere between the last two. In that case, where is the energy for the quantum jump upward to the higher level of human existence? Where is the motivation? The answer is probably precisely where the West does not want and cannot see an answer: among the "fundamentalists," the true believers, in their religion.

The Toynbee factor is one of the most relevant of them all: the challenge, and then the creative responses, from a creative minority followed by a mimetic majority. There is sufficient challenge in the world, much of it arising from the quadruple patterns of exploitation (use beyond the capacity to reproduce): exploitation of nature, of Toynbee's inner proletariat (the working classes), of Toynbee's outer proletariat (the Third World), and, last but not least, exploitation of Self in the "rat race," showing up in psychosomatic modernization diseases.[4] There are many creative people ready to take up the challenge. The problem is, however, as Toynbee states clearly (like all good macrohistorians he not only unravels patterns and cycles but also tells us where it may go wrong): the universal state and the universal church. If the world becomes a society with one overarching ruling minority, the question is to what extent its creativity can be maintained.

As Pareto points out, the elites will circulate, possibly oscillating between democratic and authoritarian, like Ssu-Ma Ch'ien postulated. The Pareto factor will hardly disappear on the way to a world state. But the problem from Toynbee's point of view would be routinization and the universal state–universal church syndrome, now truly universal, going stale and nonresponsive, mimetic only of the past. This may happen at any level of social organization; if at the world level, then so much worse, with no alternatives to learn from and be challenged by. In this lies a warning against ever bigger units. As Toynbee shows, it may go wrong and does in the end. The bigger, more cohesive, and more coherent the system, the more people will suffer.

Sarkar, as usual, provides insights, also in the context of a world society, that may not have been originally in his thoughts. His psychosocial occupational cycles—*varna*—combined with his inner and outer dialectics, contain a message for world society. His military–intellectuals–business–workers (and military again, because people produce chaos, most feared by the other three) cycle rings true. During the Cold War, the world was dominated by the military and their (defense) intellectuals, and now we are in a phase dominated by merchants and their (economist) intellectuals. According to Sarkar, a major people's revolution may come from people who would have been sacrificed to the gods of nuclear weapons had the Cold War turned hot and are now sacrificed to the gods of economic growth.

But this is more than a change of occupations, there is an underlying epistemic dialectic. The four *varnas*, the occupations mentioned, are both negative and positive; *vidya/avidya* in Sarkar's language, inner-directed and outer-directed. There is personal and social agony. The exit—the linear side of Sarkar, so to speak—is not the rule of the brahmins, as that is only one more form of one-sidedness, but to develop in each person the entire gamut of entrepreneur, intellectual, service, and protection to others, or at least in a creative spiritual minority. We sense both the Hindu life cycle and Marx's utopia in this vision. There is also a major challenge to intellectuals, but maybe most of them are no longer intellectuals but intelligentsia in the service of the military and corporate elites. In that case, not much creativity is to be expected from them. However, they certainly could integrate activities from other *varnas* and remain autonomous within the totality, not servants to one or the other.

What about Hegel, Steiner, and Teilhard de Chardin? The primacy of the spirit is basic to all of them. Hegel's predilection for the Prussian

State as the place where the *Weltgeist* finds a more permanent abode is disturbing, to say the least. But his metaphor contains a deep message, exactly because he was thinking in terms of the world system in which the world spirit traces its trajectory.

Today, we sense how the world spirit, or whatever we might call it, may be moving from Occident to Orient, bestowing the gift of initiative and creativity on new peoples and places. But the question is whether this is a zero-sum game as the metaphor suggests, the *Weltgeist* moving not only to, but also away from, leaving the vacated place impoverished. Hegel is monocentric, as expected, but at least has the center moving—a key message in the contemporary world. The implications for the location of the United Nations are obvious: Move along with the world spirit.[5]

The spiritual careers of humankind, as seen by Steiner and Teilhard de Chardin, transcend distinctions between micro (the individual), local, macro, and mega social formations, and for that reason may be less interesting here. But feminist macrohistorians, like Eisler (and Boulding), may be the most interesting of them all. They point to a basic source of renewal right here, available any time patriarchy steps down, collapses of its own weight, or is torn down: the women of the world, not as matriarchy but in partnership. It is concrete, endogenous to the world and any part of it, overlooked by Marx, and even more revolutionary. Moreover, it is happening right now, possibly with the United States as the epicenter of the feminist movement. The movement is a world system transnational movement, a true aspect of world society.

What will the movement bring in its wake? Of course, it is too early to say. But Mother Gaia will probably be treated better, meaning a deeper, more harmonious relation between her needs and basic human needs. Women, being much less violent physically than men, will probably also bring with them more peace. In addition, women, being more basic needs and care oriented and less given to intellectual abstractions than men, will probably also bring with them a more real development, meaningful for the human beings worst hit by the present patterns of development.

Of course, we find the relevance of the macrohistorians for world society to be uneven. Other commentators might lift into high relevance Augustine and Aquinas, or Steiner and Teilhard de Chardin. The biases of the present author were perhaps more suited to the others. However, the relevance, though sometimes negative, is amazing:

*Khaldun* We have no outside-the-world challenge to renew us

*Vico* We cannot rely on the gods and the heroes to bail us out

*Smith, Comte, Spencer* The world is not made for linear processes

*Marx* Solutions to exploitation not only from the exploited

*Gramsci* Conquering the positions of high cultural command

*Weber* Beware of the iron cage of a stifling world bureaucracy

*Spengler* Rise of the East may follow the fall of the West
*Sorokin* A spiritual renewal is needed from the materialist gutter
*Toynbee* Beware of the universal state and universal church
*Sarkar* Reduce division of labor, integrate, develop spiritual culture
*Eisler* Gender partnership (and Boulding with her underside of history)
*Gaia* A deeper contact, symbiosis, harmony

These are simplifications of complex thinkers, but they can produce a wealth of ideas.

## 6.2 JOSE ORTEGA Y GASSET AS ANTI-MACROHISTORIAN

To bring in a fresh perspective, let us now reflect on a macrohistorian who has not been discussed so far, since he is more of an anti-macrohistorian. For Jose Ortega y Gasset (1883–1955) the basic metaphor is the river of history, into which each individual has to plunge for the river to be adequately understood. The river is formed by the succession of generations (fifteen years), the group of people who share a certain historic experience. But within that river, in Ortega's imagery, there is another metaphor operating: a pendulum swinging, for instance, from masculine to feminine, or from *kitra* periods of recreation to *kali* periods of degeneration.[6] Generations follow each other like the swinging of the pendulum.[7] The task of discovering the great historical rhythms Ortega refers to as "meta-history."

One problem is whether these periods can be evaluated. Are there "good" and "bad" ones, "superior" and "inferior" ones? The temptation to rank them is very strong and later periods are often considered better than earlier periods. Ortega rejects it all, since methodologically "the assessment of different cultures, their ranking on a scale of status, assumes the previous understanding of all of them," an impossible task.[8]

What Ortega found in 1924 still holds: Our idea of the world is limited by our knowledge, our history, and our geography; our assumptions remain so obviously hidden from us, yet we continue to build grand schemes. One of the criticisms of many macrohistorians is precisely that they do not cover the whole world. A very interesting case is Greek culture, whose African roots have been systematically denied, not because of any empirical evidence, but because of the ethnocentric prejudice of the researchers.[9]

Ortega raises the same question about Toynbee, arguing that of Toynbee's thirty-four civilizations, at least twenty-five are of the white race. That this is not noticed is quite remarkable. Furthermore, Ortega does not accept the terms "transition" and "decadence," frequent among macrohistorians, as pertinent:

Transition is everything in history to such a degree that history can be defined as the science of transition. Decadence is a partial diagnosis, when it is not an insult dedicated to an Age.... There is no doubt that at certain stages Man has lived with the awareness that he was between a great past already in ruins and a great future.... The historian should take this into consideration because this idea, although it may be a mistaken one, (and sometimes has been), belongs to the reality which he is going to write up as history. He should, then, take it into consideration, but he should not take it as the title or definition of a historic period.[10]

At any rate, all macrohistorians fail to locate the possible role of knowing that the process is as they themselves describe it. Ortega believes that the ultimate reality cannot be reduced to an idea or a theory, but that ultimate reality consists of countless personal lives. The historic flow is not the result of successive generations which gradually disappear. The historic flow is those generations. History is not something to be known about. History is to be lived in. At heart, Ortega is not a macrohistorian, even though we can learn a great deal about macrohistory from Ortega.

## 6.3 SOME IMPLICATIONS FOR THE FUTURE

Macrohistorians have insights, but they are in no way infallible guides; certainly not singly, but not combined either. Eventually, we are to live in the future—only then will we know, and our knowledge will then be recast by the next generation and probably be discarded. Not only the future is unknowable in the sense of irresistible, unshakeable, and final truth. Also the present. Even the past.

Ortega's points are important. There is a strong Western (and male) bias, not in our sample of macrohistorians but in the whole macrohistory enterprise (although we have tried to correct for this). There is much moralism in the way "bad" and "good" stages are evaluated; this goes for the cyclical as well as for the linear schools. But above all, we need to ask what the basis is for the idea that humans always want to create and then protect. Maybe they want equally much to destroy, and, like Hindu gods dividing the three tasks of creator, protector, and destroyer between the three gods (Brahma, Vishnu, and Shiva), divide the tasks among generations, making it look like cyclical history. Certainly, this is a theme we find among all members of the cyclical school.

Does this make Ortega a macrohistorian or an anti-macrohistorian, like politics and antipolitics in Eastern Europe at the end of the Cold War? Maybe both at the same time. If no macrohistory is absolute truth, nor is any anti-macrohistory. His view is one, like Foucault and other post–modernists who discount grand narratives, to be added to the others. The Western bias remains important and the Western mind enjoys architectonics, whether in space and time or in the tradition of *grande théorie* for anything (for instance, peace, development, and the future).

In spite of Ortega and others who argue against a grand theory of macrohistory, it is hard to believe that insights cannot be used, but in plural and with caution. We simply want the world to survive, to reproduce itself, to be sustainable, and to have a future, to put it in the simplest possible terms. Peace and development are contained within this formulation. The opposite of reproducibility is exploitation, by definition, use beyond reproducibility. But then nature starts wilting and cracks; people starve, suffer, and die at the margin of societies; and countries dissolve and engage in internal and external wars under burdens of debts and traumas. The center of the whole enterprise also suffers. There is peacelessness and maldevelopment all over.[11]

Would not "proceed with caution" be one simple rule? Do not exploit? And maybe a certain conservatism. Of course, we shall strive to get out of all the gutters the macrohistorians have described and analyzed for us, all the troughs on their explicit or implicit curves. But a striking point is the inability to recognize the "good" stages when they are there, and then try to conserve them. Is this, as Ortega intimates, because we are also destroyers at heart—"Man . . . the barbarian destroy[ing] wherever he goes: he is the great manufacturer of ruins"[12]—and that defining and identifying "good" and "bad" and "decadent" is impossible anyhow? Or could more insights have been helpful?

One key is, of course, the yin–yang nature of things; good for some, bad for others, good in this way, bad in that. And yet there is something absolute about trying to remove unnecessary suffering (negative peace), to enhance well-being (positive peace and development) and to make peace and development sustainable. More than the positive advice from macrohistorians, their warnings of what can go wrong should be taken seriously.

## NOTES

1. See Johan Galtung, Claus Otto Scharmer, and Katrin Kaufer, "Mainstream Economics and Occidental Cosmology," chap. 2.6 in *Economics in Another Key* (London: Polity Press, forthcoming).

2. For one estimate of CIA activities, see the report on the organization of former CIA agents, ARDIS (Association for Responsible Dissent), in *The Guardian Weekly*, 30 December 1987: "At least six million people have died as a consequence of U.S. covert operations since World War II." See John Stockwell, *The Praetorian Guard: The U.S. Role in the New World Order* (Boston, Mass.: South End Press, 1991), and *In Search of Enemies* (New York: Norton, 1978). Also see, on the world wide web, http://www.magnet.ch/serendipity/cia/stock1/html and, for a list of death squads supported by the CIA (as compiled from newspapers around the world [*Washington Post*, etc.), see http://www.chemengr.ucsb.edu/~chaubal/issues/ciabase.txt.

3. The right understood this a long time ago, partly inspired by Gramsci. For consequences in terms of media images of the world, with particular refer-

ence to peace, war, development, and the environment, see Johan Galtung and Richard Vincent, *Global Glasnost* (Cresskill, N.J.: Hampton Press, 1992).

4. Cardiovascular diseases, malignant tumors, and mental disorders all have stress components in their etiologies.

5. Hence, one suggestion would be to put the U.N. headquarters in East Asia; for instance, in Hong Kong or Okinawa.

6. Jose Ortega y Gasset, "La Espana Invertebrada" (Spain without a backbone), in *Obras completas* (Collected works), 5th ed., vol. 3 (Madrid: Revista de Occidente, 1965), 97–99.

7. "Each generation represents a certain vital height," and there are "cumulative periods" and "eliminatory and polemic periods," according to the type of dominant generation. Ibid., 148–149.

8. Ibid., 312

9. See Martin Bernal, *The Fabrication of Ancient Greece 1785–1985*, vol. 1 of *Black Athena: The Afroasiatic Roots of Classical Civilization* (London: Free Association Books, 1987).

10. Ortega, "Historia de la filosofia de Emile Brehier" (History of the philosophy of Emile Brehier), in *Obras Completas*, vol. 6, 378.

11. These useful terms were coined by the late Bengali, Professor Surendra Dasgupta.

12. Ortega, "Un diccionario enciclopedico abbreviado" (An abbreviated encyclopedia), in *Obras Completas*, vol. 3, 59, 107.

*Appendix A*

# Chart of the Twenty Macrohistorians

| Author | Shape | Key | Unit or Stages |
|---|---|---|---|
| Ssu-Ma Ch'ien | Cycle | Yin–Yang of virtue | Dynasty–sage king–tyrant–sage king |
| Augustine | Linear | Good/Evil | Individual–Creation–Christ–Judgment |
| Khaldun | Cyclical | *Asabiya* | Dynasty: decline over four generations |
| Vico | Cycle/River | Soft laws: *Corsi / Recorsi* | Ages: gods, heroes, man, barbarians |
| Smith | Linear | Self-love/Love for other | Economic stages: hunter, pasturage, agrarian, commerce |
| Hegel | Linear | States/World leaders | Geist in nations |
| Comte | Linear | Positive knowledge | Theological, metaphysical, positive |
| Marx | Linear/Spiral | Tech/economic dialectics | Historical economic stages |
| Spencer | Linear | Evolutionary differentiation | Primitive to modern |
| Pareto | Oscillation | Circulation of elites | Innovate/Consolidate |
| Weber | Linear | Cultural primacy | Rationalization towards the iron cage |
| Steiner | Linear | Individual and cosmic evolution | Planetary stages: Universe, Man, and Nature |
| Spengler | Life cycle | Maturation and decline of cultures | Cultures: decline from culture to civilization |
| Teilhard | Evolution | Linear | Individuals: pull of God towards Omega |
| Sorokin | Pendulum | Principle of limits | Supersystems: sensate, idealistic, ideational |
| Toynbee | Rise and Fall | Challenge and response | Civilizational cycles |
| Gramsci | Linear/Spiral | Cultural forces/hegemony | Intellectuals create new society |
| Sarkar | Cycle/Spiral | *Vidya/Avidya* dialectics | *Varna:* Social Cycle |
| Eisler | Multilinear | Gender | Partnership, Dominator, Partnership |
| Gaia | Equilibrium/Cycle | Planetary evolution | Geophysiology/Cosmic |

# Appendix B

# Pictorial Representations of the Twenty Theories

*Daniela Rocco Minerbi*

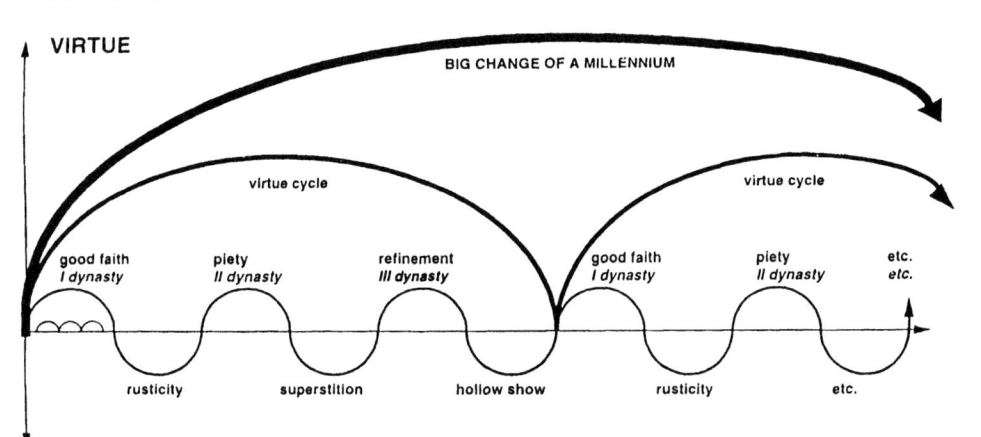

**Figure B.1**
**Ssu-Ma Ch'ien**

VIRTUE

BIG CHANGE OF A MILLENNIUM

virtue cycle          virtue cycle

good faith    piety         refinement    good faith    piety       etc.
I dynasty     II dynasty    III dynasty   I dynasty     II dynasty  etc.

rusticity     superstition  hollow show   rusticity     etc.

DECLINE

⌒ = 30 YEARS, SMALL CHANGE, duration of a ruler's reign

⌐ = 100 YEARS, MEDIUM CHANGE, duration of a dynasty and of the virtue characterizing it

⌐ = 300 YEARS, GREAT CHANGE, full historical cycle, cycle of a virtue

⌐ = 1000 YEARS, "Three big changes equal to one millennia *[sic]* "

**Figure B.2**
**Augustine**

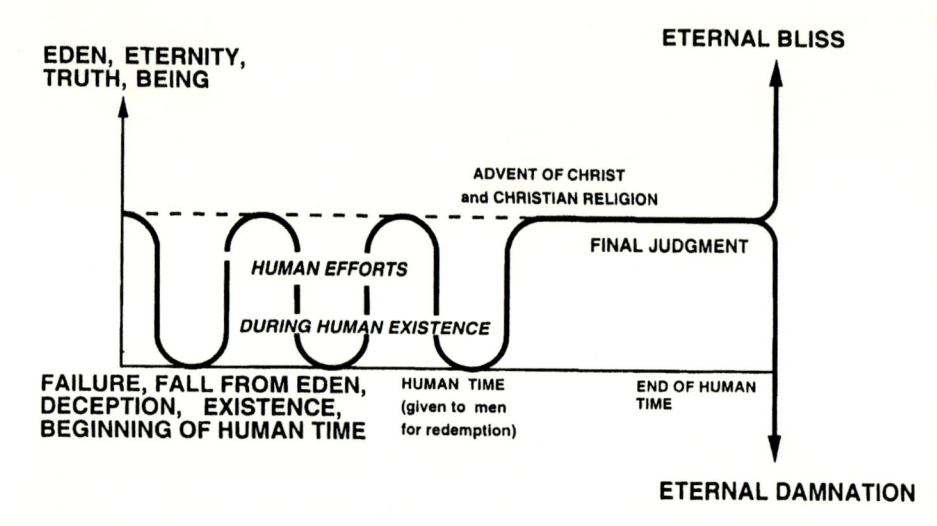

EDEN, ETERNITY,
TRUTH, BEING

ETERNAL BLISS

ADVENT OF CHRIST
and CHRISTIAN RELIGION

FINAL JUDGMENT

*HUMAN EFFORTS*
*DURING HUMAN EXISTENCE*

FAILURE, FALL FROM EDEN, DECEPTION, EXISTENCE, BEGINNING OF HUMAN TIME

HUMAN TIME
(given to men for redemption)

END OF HUMAN TIME

ETERNAL DAMNATION

**Figure B.3**
**Khaldun**

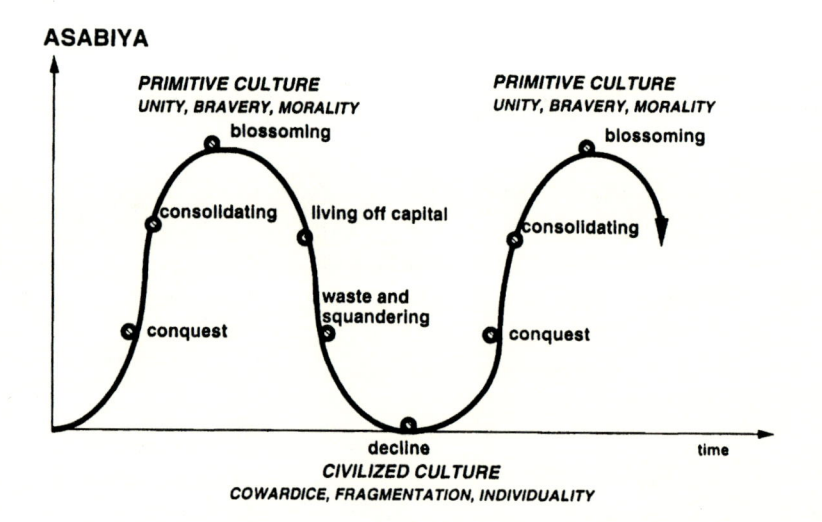

ASABIYA

PRIMITIVE CULTURE
UNITY, BRAVERY, MORALITY
blossoming

consolidating     living off capital

conquest          waste and squandering

PRIMITIVE CULTURE
UNITY, BRAVERY, MORALITY
blossoming

consolidating

conquest

decline
CIVILIZED CULTURE
COWARDICE, FRAGMENTATION, INDIVIDUALITY

time

**Figure B.4**
Vico

REASON AND WISDOM
KNOWLEDGE OF TRUTH
DEVELOPMENT OF HUMAN MIND

ADAM'S FALL

**RECOURSE**
II AGE OF MEN
(contemporary time of Vico, age of new sciences)

**COURSE**
AGE OF MEN
(reason, making of law)

II AGE OF HEROES
(feudalism)

AGE OF HEROES
(fantastic knowledge, lasted 200 years)

AGE OF GODS
(creativity, lasted 900 years for the Greeks and Latins)

II AGE OF GODS
(age of Christianity in Euope)

time

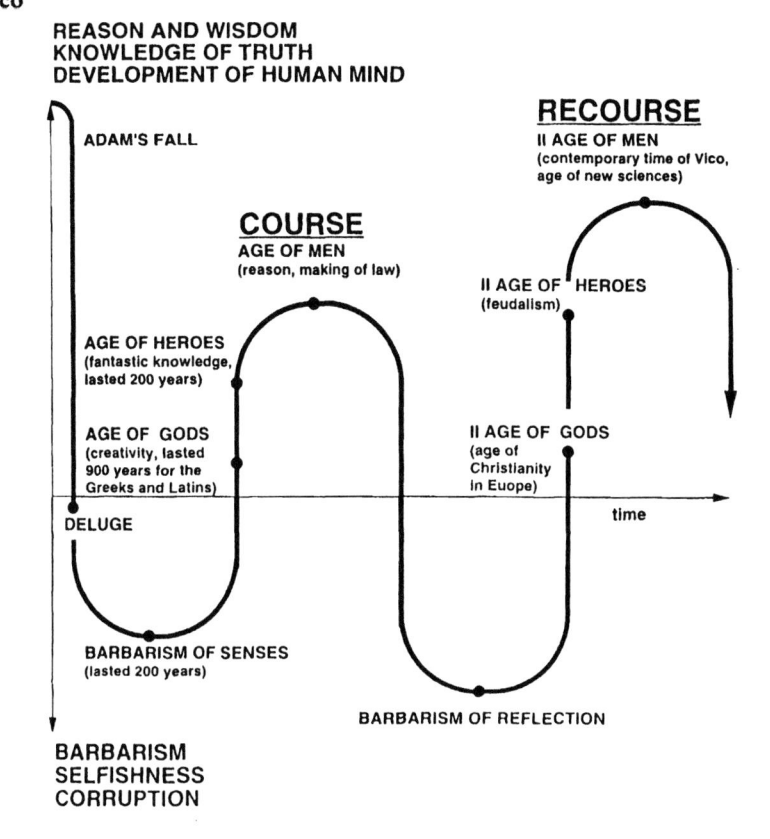

DELUGE

BARBARISM OF SENSES
(lasted 200 years)

BARBARISM OF REFLECTION

BARBARISM
SELFISHNESS
CORRUPTION

**Figure B.5**
Smith

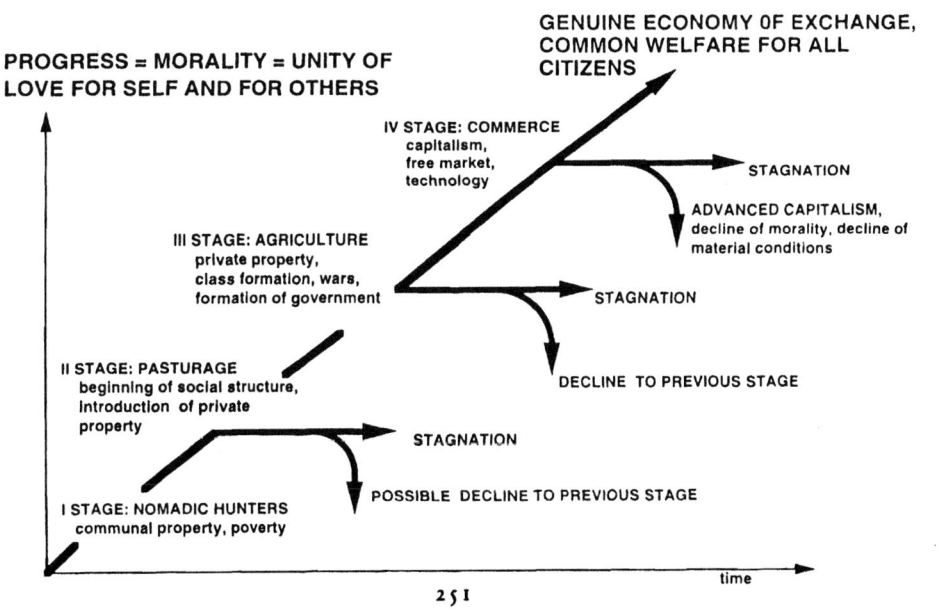

PROGRESS = MORALITY = UNITY OF
LOVE FOR SELF AND FOR OTHERS

GENUINE ECONOMY OF EXCHANGE,
COMMON WELFARE FOR ALL
CITIZENS

IV STAGE: COMMERCE
capitalism,
free market,
technology

STAGNATION

ADVANCED CAPITALISM,
decline of morality, decline of
material conditions

III STAGE: AGRICULTURE
private property,
class formation, wars,
formation of government

STAGNATION

II STAGE: PASTURAGE
beginning of social structure,
introduction of private
property

DECLINE TO PREVIOUS STAGE

STAGNATION

I STAGE: NOMADIC HUNTERS
communal property, poverty

POSSIBLE DECLINE TO PREVIOUS STAGE

time

**Figure B.6
Hegel**

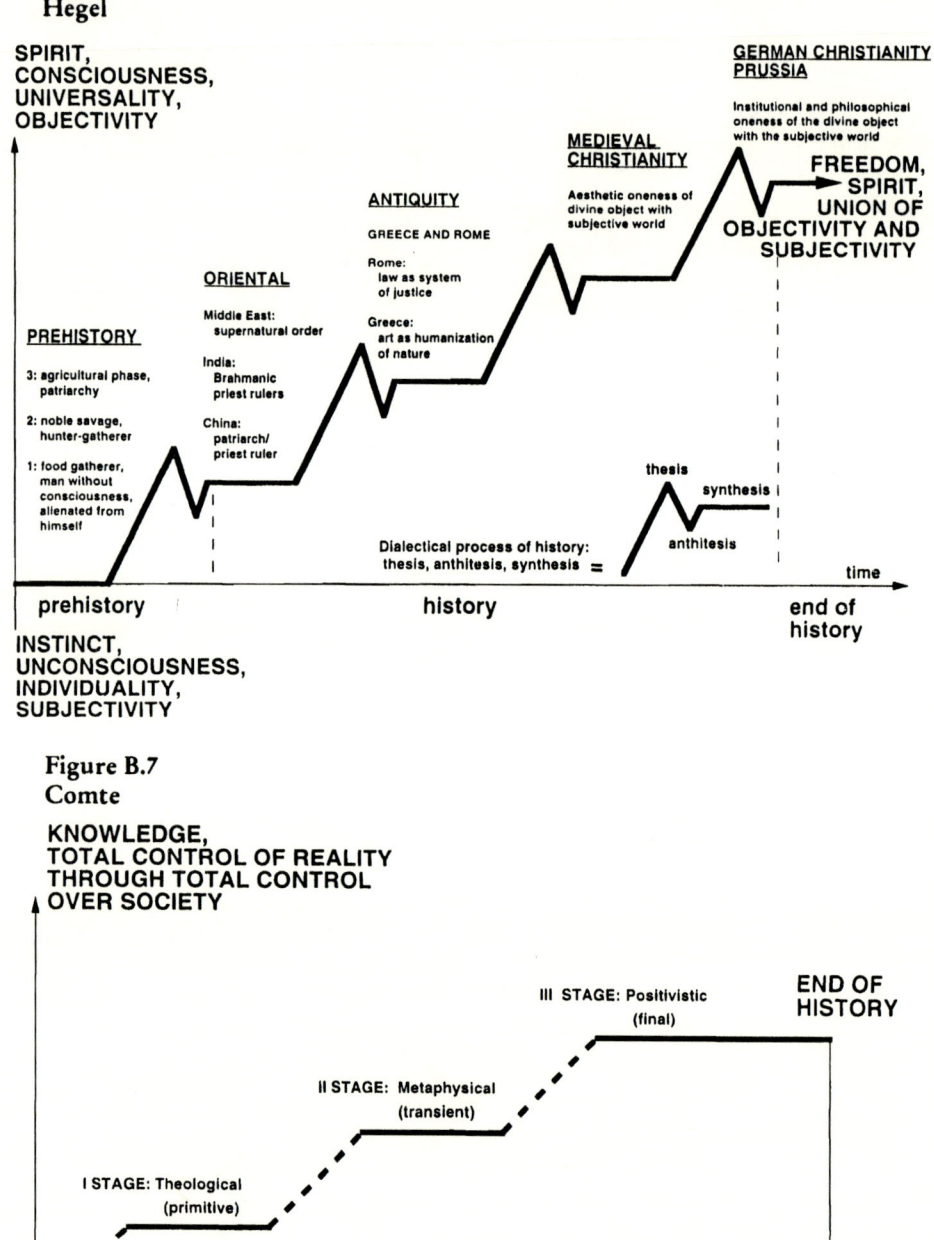

SPIRIT,
CONSCIOUSNESS,
UNIVERSALITY,
OBJECTIVITY

GERMAN CHRISTIANITY
PRUSSIA
Institutional and philosophical oneness of the divine object with the subjective world

MEDIEVAL CHRISTIANITY
Aesthetic oneness of divine object with subjective world

FREEDOM,
SPIRIT,
UNION OF OBJECTIVITY AND SUBJECTIVITY

ANTIQUITY
GREECE AND ROME
Rome: law as system of justice
Greece: art as humanization of nature

ORIENTAL
Middle East: supernatural order
India: Brahmanic priest rulers
China: patriarch/priest ruler

PREHISTORY
3: agricultural phase, patriarchy
2: noble savage, hunter-gatherer
1: food gatherer, man without consciousness, alienated from himself

Dialectical process of history:
thesis, anthitesis, synthesis =

thesis
synthesis
anthitesis

time

prehistory | history | end of history

INSTINCT,
UNCONSCIOUSNESS,
INDIVIDUALITY,
SUBJECTIVITY

**Figure B.7
Comte**

KNOWLEDGE,
TOTAL CONTROL OF REALITY
THROUGH TOTAL CONTROL
OVER SOCIETY

III STAGE: Positivistic (final)

END OF HISTORY

II STAGE: Metaphysical (transient)

I STAGE: Theological (primitive)

until A.D. 1300 | 1300 -1800 | 1800

time

UNKNOWABLE,
MYSTERY,
INTELLECTUAL DISORDER

**Figure B.8**
**Marx**

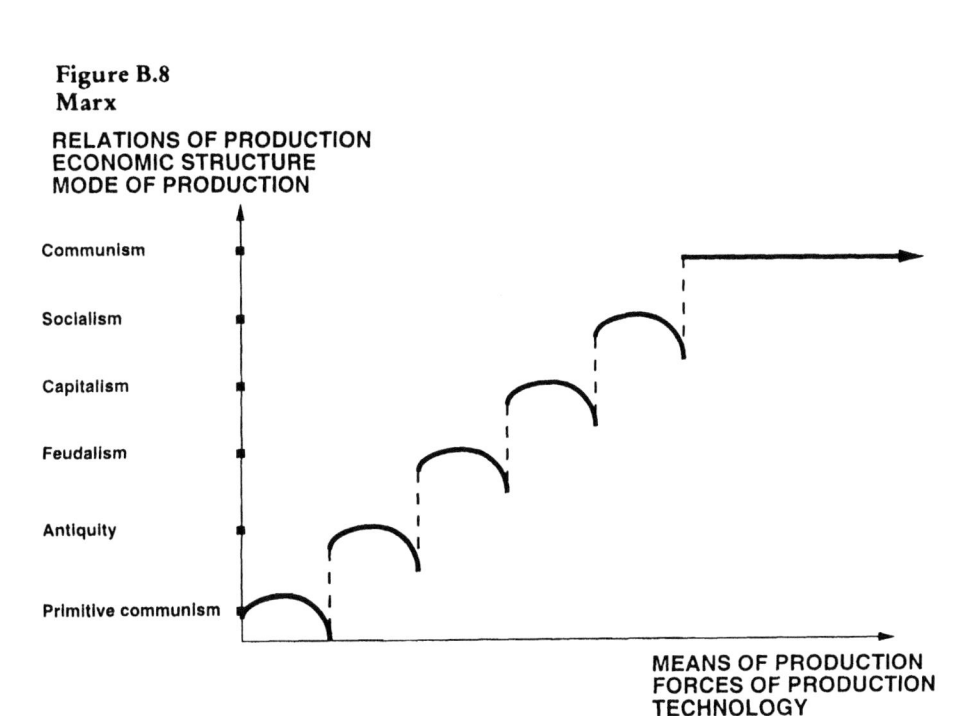

RELATIONS OF PRODUCTION
ECONOMIC STRUCTURE
MODE OF PRODUCTION

- Communism
- Socialism
- Capitalism
- Feudalism
- Antiquity
- Primitive communism

MEANS OF PRODUCTION
FORCES OF PRODUCTION
TECHNOLOGY

**Figure B.9**
**Spencer**

GREATEST DIFFERENTIATION
LEADING TO GREATEST SOCIAL INTEGRATION

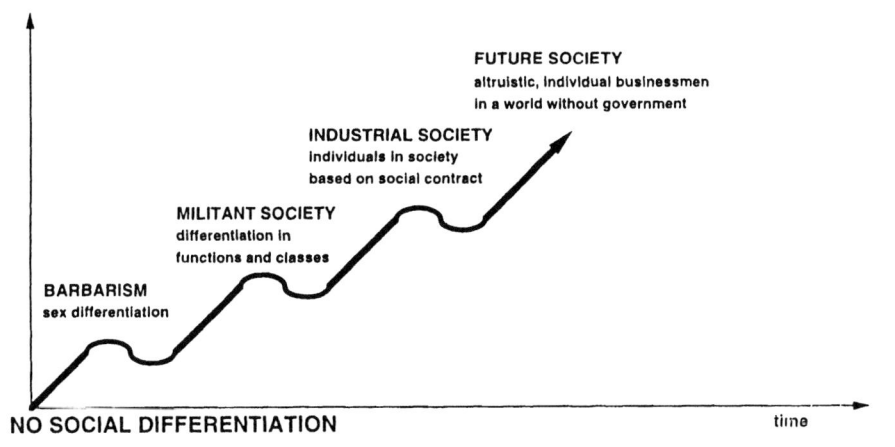

FUTURE SOCIETY
altruistic, individual businessmen
in a world without government

INDUSTRIAL SOCIETY
individuals in society
based on social contract

MILITANT SOCIETY
differentiation in
functions and classes

BARBARISM
sex differentiation

NO SOCIAL DIFFERENTIATION

time

**Figure B.10
Pareto**

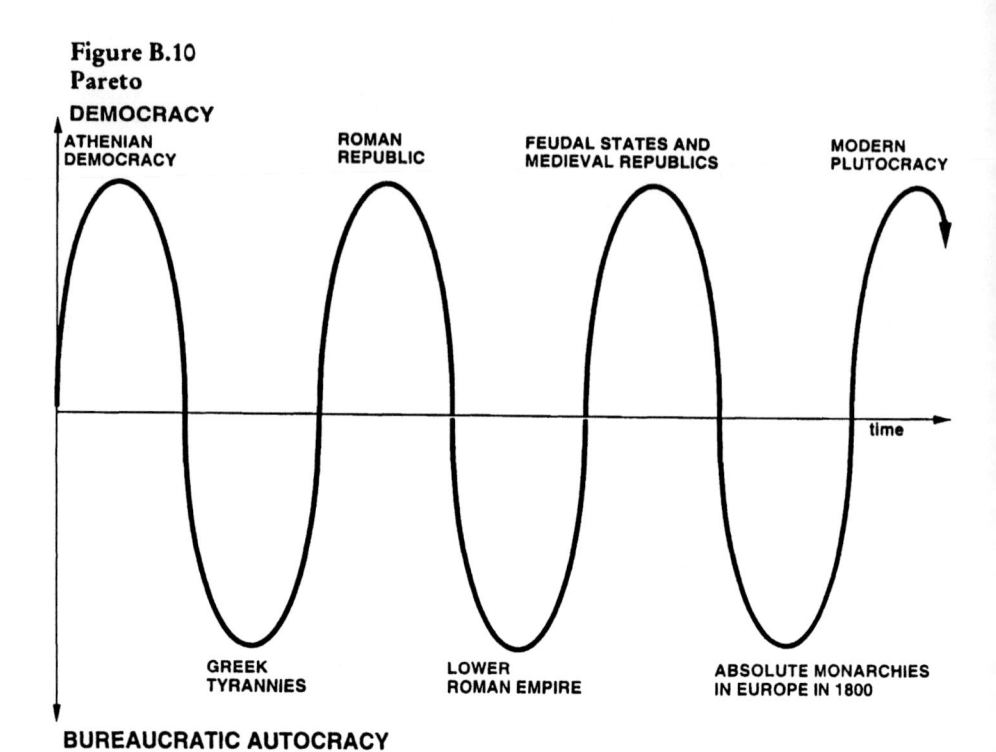

DEMOCRACY

ATHENIAN DEMOCRACY — ROMAN REPUBLIC — FEUDAL STATES AND MEDIEVAL REPUBLICS — MODERN PLUTOCRACY

time

GREEK TYRANNIES — LOWER ROMAN EMPIRE — ABSOLUTE MONARCHIES IN EUROPE IN 1800

**BUREAUCRATIC AUTOCRACY**

**Figure B.11
Weber**

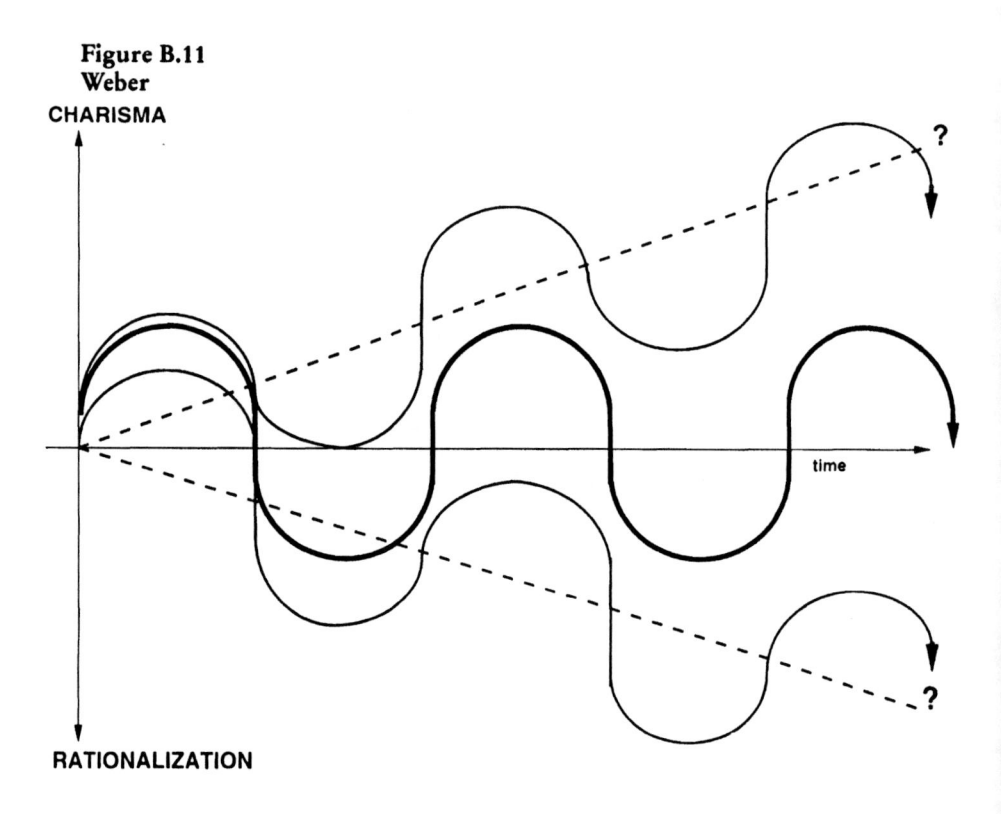

CHARISMA

?

time

?

**RATIONALIZATION**

**Figure B.12**
Steiner

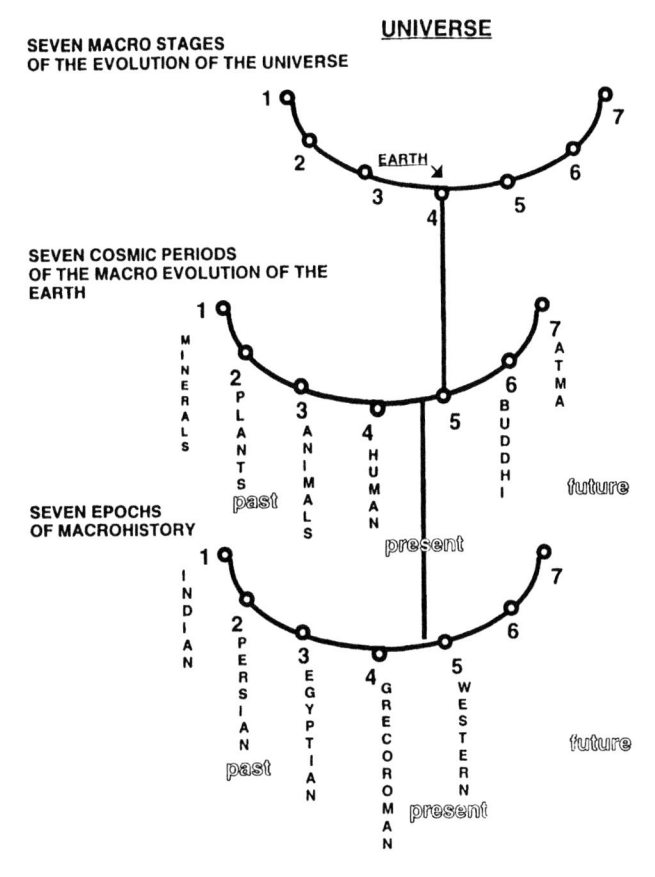

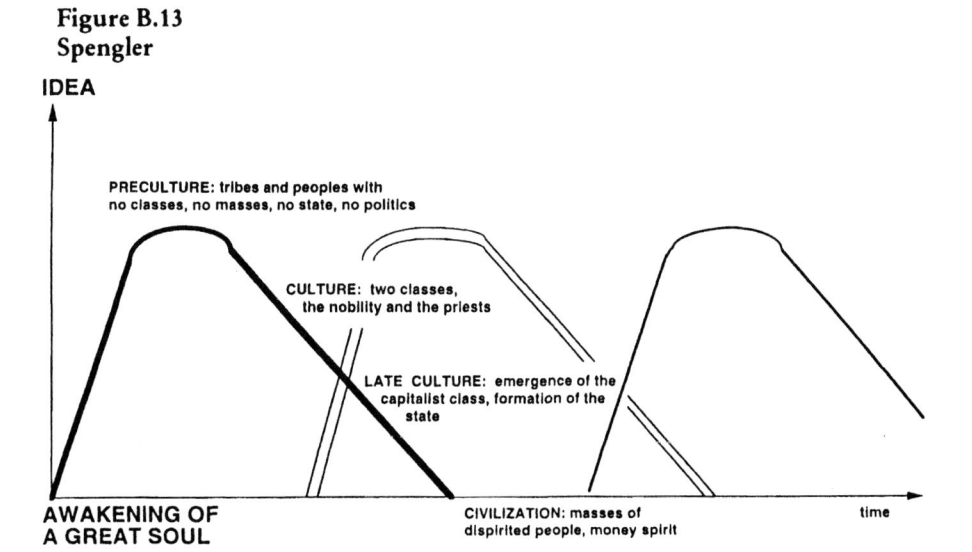

**SEVEN MACRO STAGES OF THE EVOLUTION OF THE UNIVERSE**

UNIVERSE

1, 2, 3, 4 (EARTH), 5, 6, 7

**SEVEN COSMIC PERIODS OF THE MACRO EVOLUTION OF THE EARTH**

1 MINERALS, 2 PLANTS, 3 ANIMALS, 4 HUMAN, 5, 6 BUDDHI, 7 ATMA

past — present — future

**SEVEN EPOCHS OF MACROHISTORY**

1 INDIAN, 2 PERSIAN, 3 EGYPTIAN, 4 GRECOROMAN, 5 WESTERN, 6, 7

past — present — future

**Figure B.13**
Spengler

IDEA

PRECULTURE: tribes and peoples with no classes, no masses, no state, no politics

CULTURE: two classes, the nobility and the priests

LATE CULTURE: emergence of the capitalist class, formation of the state

AWAKENING OF A GREAT SOUL

CIVILIZATION: masses of dispirited people, money spirit

time

**Figure B.14**
**Teilhard**

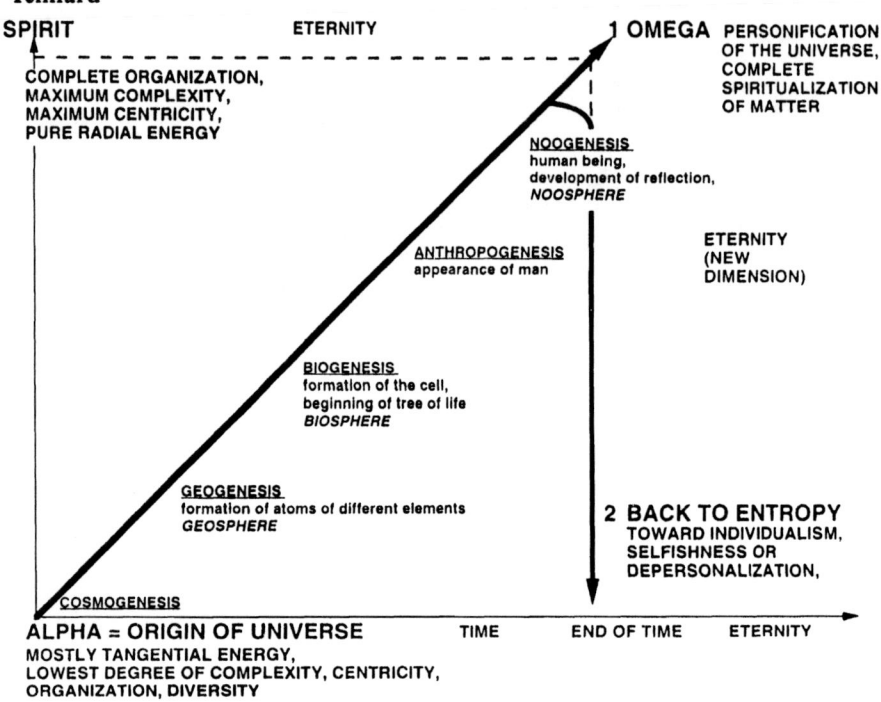

**SPIRIT** — ETERNITY — **1 OMEGA** PERSONIFICATION OF THE UNIVERSE, COMPLETE SPIRITUALIZATION OF MATTER

COMPLETE ORGANIZATION, MAXIMUM COMPLEXITY, MAXIMUM CENTRICITY, PURE RADIAL ENERGY

**NOOGENESIS** human being, development of reflection, **NOOSPHERE**

ETERNITY (NEW DIMENSION)

**ANTHROPOGENESIS** appearance of man

**BIOGENESIS** formation of the cell, beginning of tree of life **BIOSPHERE**

**GEOGENESIS** formation of atoms of different elements **GEOSPHERE**

**2 BACK TO ENTROPY** TOWARD INDIVIDUALISM, SELFISHNESS OR DEPERSONALIZATION,

**COSMOGENESIS**

**ALPHA = ORIGIN OF UNIVERSE**     TIME     END OF TIME     ETERNITY
MOSTLY TANGENTIAL ENERGY, LOWEST DEGREE OF COMPLEXITY, CENTRICITY, ORGANIZATION, DIVERSITY

**Figure B.15**
**Sorokin**

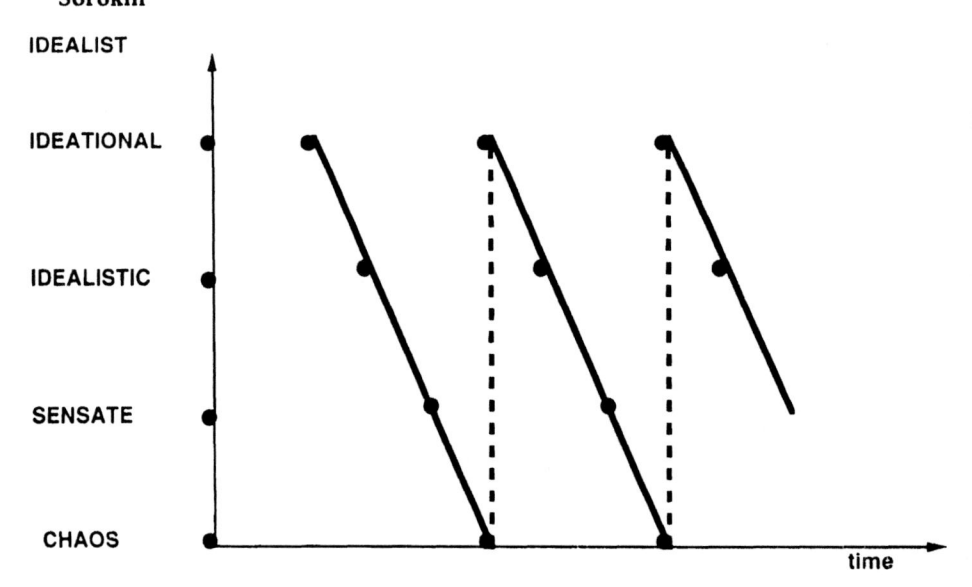

IDEALIST

IDEATIONAL

IDEALISTIC

SENSATE

CHAOS

time

**Figure B.16**
**Toynbee**

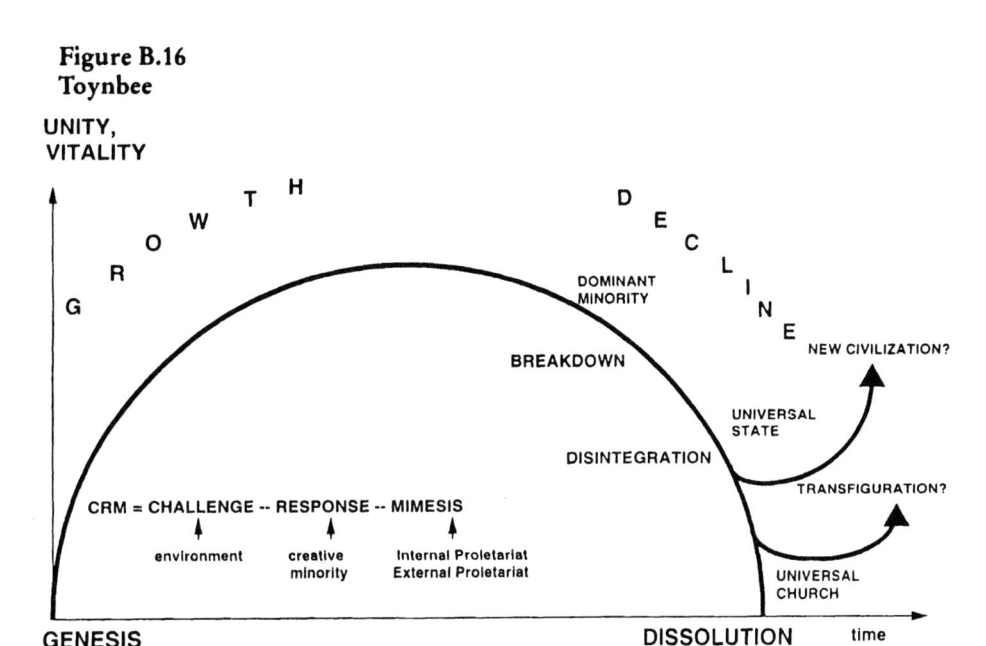

UNITY, VITALITY

GROWTH  DECLINE

DOMINANT MINORITY

BREAKDOWN

UNIVERSAL STATE → NEW CIVILIZATION?

DISINTEGRATION

CRM = CHALLENGE -- RESPONSE -- MIMESIS
- environment
- creative minority
- Internal Proletariat / External Proletariat

TRANSFIGURATION?

UNIVERSAL CHURCH

GENESIS — DISSOLUTION — time

**Figure B.17**
**Gramsci**

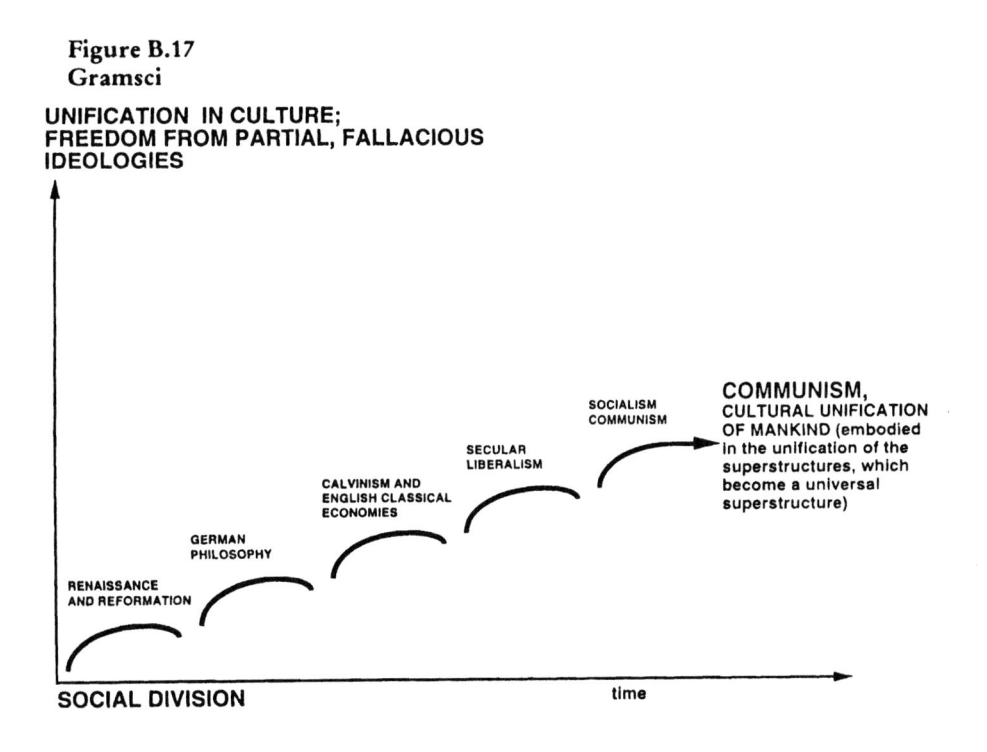

UNIFICATION IN CULTURE; FREEDOM FROM PARTIAL, FALLACIOUS IDEOLOGIES

- RENAISSANCE AND REFORMATION
- GERMAN PHILOSOPHY
- CALVINISM AND ENGLISH CLASSICAL ECONOMIES
- SECULAR LIBERALISM
- SOCIALISM COMMUNISM
- **COMMUNISM,** CULTURAL UNIFICATION OF MANKIND (embodied in the unification of the superstructures, which become a universal superstructure)

SOCIAL DIVISION — time

**Figure B.18**
**Sarkar**

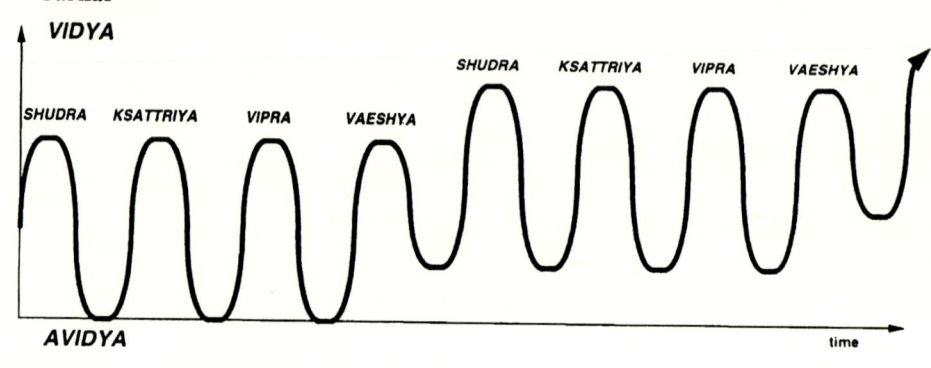

*VIDYA*

SHUDRA — KSATTRIYA — VIPRA — VAESHYA — SHUDRA — KSATTRIYA — VIPRA — VAESHYA

*AVIDYA*                                                                 time

**WARRIOR**
**KSATTRIYA**
Struggles and dominates environment

**WORKER**
**SHUDRA**
Dominated by environment

**INTELLECTUAL**
**VIPRA**
Struggles and dominates ideas

**CAPITALIST**
**VAESHYA**
Struggles with and dominates environment and ideas

**Figure B.19**
**Eisler**

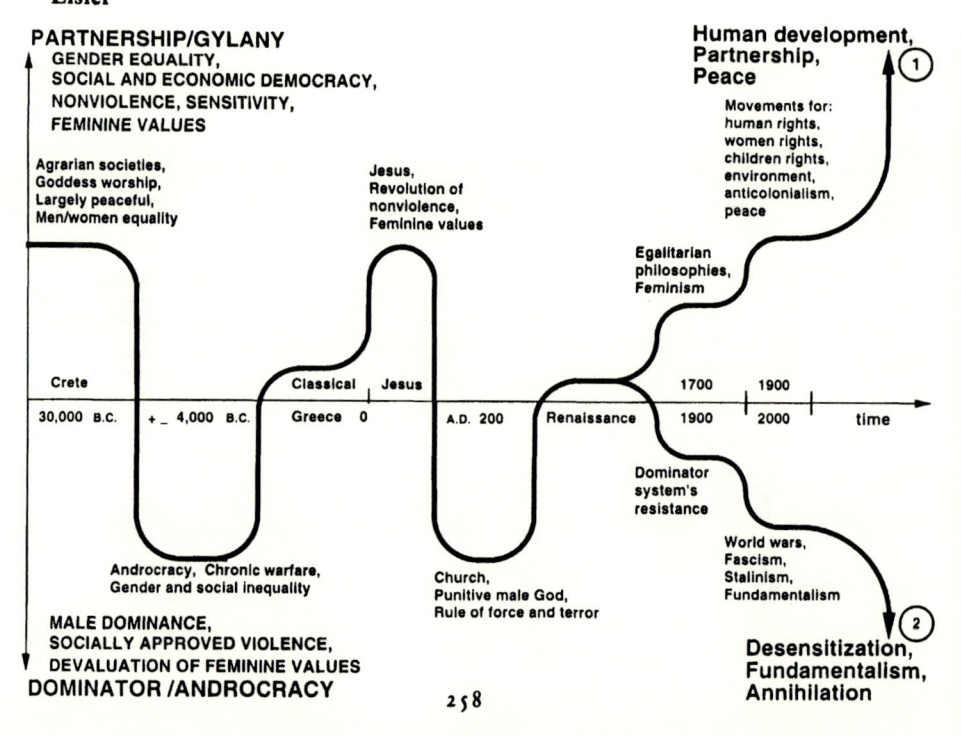

**PARTNERSHIP/GYLANY**
GENDER EQUALITY,
SOCIAL AND ECONOMIC DEMOCRACY,
NONVIOLENCE, SENSITIVITY,
FEMININE VALUES

Human development,
Partnership,
Peace
①

Agrarian societies,
Goddess worship,
Largely peaceful,
Men/women equality

Jesus,
Revolution of
nonviolence,
Feminine values

Movements for:
human rights,
women rights,
children rights,
environment,
anticolonialism,
peace

Egalitarian
philosophies,
Feminism

Crete        Classical  Jesus                    1700    1900
30,000 B.C.  +_ 4,000 B.C.  Greece  0  A.D. 200  Renaissance  1900  2000  time

Dominator
system's
resistance

Androcracy, Chronic warfare,
Gender and social inequality

Church,
Punitive male God,
Rule of force and terror

World wars,
Fascism,
Stalinism,
Fundamentalism

**MALE DOMINANCE,**
**SOCIALLY APPROVED VIOLENCE,**
**DEVALUATION OF FEMININE VALUES**
**DOMINATOR /ANDROCRACY**

②
**Desensitization,**
**Fundamentalism,**
**Annihilation**

**Figure B.20**
**Gaia**

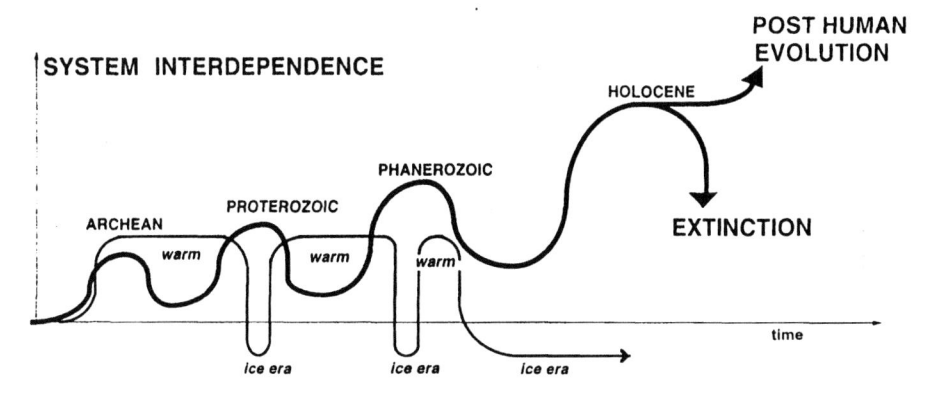

# Selected Bibliography

Adams, Henry. *The Life and Writings of Giambattista Vico*. London: George Allen and Unwin, Ltd., 1935.
Albini Grimaldi, Alfonsina. *The Universal Humanity of Giambattista Vico*. New York: S. F. Vanni, 1958.
Allaby, Michael. *A Guide to Gaia: A Survey of the New Science of Our Living Earth*. New York: E. P. Dutton, 1989.
Amin, Samir. *Eurocentrism*. London: Zed, 1989.
Antonio, Robert, and Robert Glassman, eds. *A Weber–Marx Dialogue*. Lawrence: University of Kansas Press, 1985.
Ashley, Richard. "Living on Borderlines." In *International/Intertextual Relations*, edited by Michael Shapiro and James Der Derian. Lexington, Mass.: Lexington Books, 1989.
Augustine, *Basic Writings of Saint Augustine*. Vols. 1–2. Edited by Whitney Oates. New York: Random House, 1948.
Baltazar, Eulalio. *Teilhard and the Supernatural*. Baltimore: Helicon Press, 1966.
Barrow, John. "Platonic Relationships in the Universe." *New Scientist*, 20 April 1991.
Batra, Ravi. *The Downfall of Capitalism and Communism*. 2nd ed. Dallas: Venus Books, 1990.
Batra, Ravi. *Muslim Civilization and the Crisis in Iran*. Dallas: Venus Books, 1980.
Becker, Kurt E. *Anthroposophie—Revolution von Innen, Leitlinien im Denken Rudolf Steiner's* (Anthroposophie—Revolution from within, guidelines in thinking of Rudolf Steiner's thinking). Frankfurt: Verlag Freies Geistesleben, 1988.

Bernal, Martin. *Black Athena: The Afroasiatic Roots of Classical Civilization*. London: Free Association Books, 1987.
Berry, Thomas. *The Historical Theory of Giambattista Vico*. Washington, D.C.: Catholic University of America Press, 1949.
Bocock, Robert. *Hegemony*. London: Tavistock Publications, 1986.
Boggs, Carl. *The Two Revolutions: Antonio Gramsci and the Dilemmas of Western Marxism*. Boston: South End Press, 1984.
Borkenau, Franz. *Pareto*. New York: John Wiley and Sons, 1936.
Boulding, Elise. *Building a Global Civic Culture: Education for an Interdependent World*. Syracuse: Syracuse University Press, 1990.
Boulding, Elise. "Futuristics and the Imaging Capacity of the West." In *Human Futuristics*, edited by Magoroh Maruyama and James Dator. Honolulu: University of Hawaii Press, 1971.
Boulding, Elise. *The Underside of History: A View of Women through Time*. 2nd ed. Newbury Park, Calif.: Sage, 1992.
Braudel, Fernand. *Civilization and Capitalism*. Vols. 1–3. New York: Harper and Row, 1981–1984.
Braudel, Fernand. *The Mediterranean and the Mediterranean World in the Age of Philip II*. New York: Harper and Row, 1972.
Bridenthal, Renate, and Claudia Koonz, eds. *Becoming Visible: Women in European History*. Boston: Houghton Mifflin, 1977.
Brown, Irene. "Ibn Khaldun and African Reintegration." Paper presented at the 1971 Universities Social Sciences Council Conference, Makerere, December 1971.
Bucolo, Placido, ed. *The Other Pareto*. New York: St. Martin's Press, 1980.
Burke, Peter. *Sociology and History*. London: George Allen and Unwin, 1980.
Burke, Peter, ed. *The New Cambridge Modern History, Companion Volume*. Cambridge: Cambridge University Press, 1979.
Butler, Clark. *G. W. F. Hegel*. Boston: Twayne, 1977.
Caird, Edward. *Hegel*. Edinburgh and London: William Blackwood and Sons, 1883.
Campbell, Joseph. *The Hero with a Thousand Faces*. Princeton, N.J.: Princeton University Press, 1968.
Campbell, Joseph. *The Masks of God*. Vol. 4. New York: Penguin, 1968.
Caponigri, Robert. *Time and Idea: The Theory of History in Giambattista Vico*. London: University of Notre Dame Press, 1968.
Caute, David, ed. *Essential Writings of Karl Marx*. New York: Collier Books, 1967.
Clark, M. T., ed. *An Aquinas Reader*. New York: Fordham University Press, 1995.
Cohen, G. A. *Karl Marx's Theory of History: A Defence*. Oxford: Clarendon, 1979.
Collingwood, R. G. *The Idea of History*. Oxford: Oxford University Press, 1946.
Comte, Auguste. *The Positive Philosophy*. Translated by Harriet Martineau. London: Trubner, 1875.
Coser, Lewis. *Master of Sociological Thought*. New York: Harcourt Brace Jovanovich, 1971.
Croce, Benedetto. *The Philosophy of Giambattista Vico*. New York: Russell and Russell, 1964.
Debary, Wm. Theodore. *Sources of Chinese Tradition*. New York: Columbia University Press, 1960.
Ederhard, Wolfram. *A History of China*. Berkeley and Los Angeles: University of California Press, 1969.

Eisler, Riane. *The Chalice and the Blade: Our History, Our Future*. San Francisco: Harper and Row, 1987.
Eisler, Riane. *Sacred Pleasure: Sex, Myth, and the Politics of the Body*. San Francisco: HarperSanFrancisco, 1995.
Eliade, Mircea. *The Myth of the Eternal Return*. Princeton, N.J.: Princeton University Press, 1971.
Elias, Norbert. *The Civilizing Process: The Development of Manners*. Translated by Edmund Jephcott. Oxford: Basil Blackwell, 1994.
Etzioni, Amitai, and Eva Etzioni-Halevy, eds. *Social Change*. New York: Basic Books, 1973.
Fabel, Arthur. *Cosmic Genesis*. Teilhard Studies, No. 5. Chambersburg: Anima Books, 1981.
Faghirzadeh, Saleh. *Sociology of Sociology: In Search of Ibn Khaldun's Sociology*. Tehran: Soroush Press, 1982.
Fairbank, John K. *Chinese Thought and Institutions*. Chicago: University of Chicago Press, 1957.
Faj, Attila. "Vico's Basic Law of History in Finnegans Wake." In *Vico and Joyce*, edited by Donald Phillip Verene. New York: State University of New York Press, 1987.
Farina, Giulio. *Vilfredo Pareto Compedium of General Sociology*. Minneapolis: University of Minnesota Press, 1980.
Finer, S. E. *Vilfredo Pareto: Sociological Writing*. New York: Frederick A. Praeger, 1966.
Foucault, Michel. *The Archaeology of Knowledge and the Discourse of Language*. Translated by A. M. Sheridan Smith. New York: Pantheon, 1972.
Foucault, Michel. *The Order of Things*. New York: Vintage Books, 1973.
Frank, Andre Gunder, and Barry K. Gills, eds. *The World System: Five Hundred Years or Five Thousand*. London: Routledge, 1993.
Galtung, Johan. "Cultural Violence." *Journal of Peace Research* 27 (1990): 291–305.
Galtung, Johan. *Essays in Peace Research*. Vols. 1–6. Copenhagen: Ejlers, 1975–1988.
Galtung, Johan. *Members of Two Worlds: A Development Study of Three Villages in Western Sicily*. Oslo: Universitetsforlaget, 1971.
Galtung, Johan. *Methodology and Development*. Copenhagen: Ejlers, 1988.
Gardner, Patrick, ed. *Theories of History*. Glencoe, Ill.: The Free Press, 1959.
Giddens, Anthony. *Central Problems in Social Theory*. Berkeley and Los Angeles: University of California Press, 1979.
Gillespie, Michael. *Hegel, Heidegger and the Ground of History*. Chicago: University of Chicago Press, 1984.
Gilligan, Carol. *In a Different Voice*. Cambridge: Harvard University Press, 1982.
Gimbutas, Marija. *The Goddesses and Gods of Old Europe*. Berkeley and Los Angeles: University of California Press, 1982.
Goodman, Lenn. "Ibn Khaldun and Thucydides." *Journal of American Oriental Society* 92 (1972): 250–270.
Gramsci, Antonio. *The Modern Prince and Other Writings*. Translated by Louis Marks. New York: International Publishers, 1957.
Gray, Donald. *The One and the Many*. New York: Herder and Herder, 1969.
Hegel, George Wilhelm Friedrich. *Lectures on the Philosophy of World History*. Translated by J. Sibree. London: George Bell and Sons, 1888.
Hegel, George Wilhelm Friedrich. *Phenomenology of Spirit*. Translated by A. V. Miller. Oxford: Clarendon Press, 1977.

Hegel, George Wilhelm Friedrich. *Philosophy of History*. Translated by J. Sibree. London: George Bell and Sons, 1888.
Heidegger, Martin. *Hegel's Concept of Experience*. New York: Harper and Row, 1970.
Hofstadter, Richard. *Social Darwinism in American Thought*. New York: Brazilla, 1959.
Hucker, Charles O. *China's Imperial Past*. Stanford: Stanford University Press, 1975.
Inayatullah, Sohail. "Sarkar's Spiritual-Dialectics: An Unconventional View of the Future." *Futures* 20 (1988): 54–65.
Inayatullah, Sohail. *Situating Sarkar*. Singapore: Ananda Marga, 1997.
Inayatullah, Sohail. "Understanding Prabhat Rainjan Sarkar." Ph.D., Department of Political Science, University of Hawaii, 1990.
Inayatullah, Sohail, and Jennifer Fitzgerald, eds. *Transcending Boundaries: Prabhat Rainjan Sarkar's Theories of Individual and Social Transformation*. Singapore: Ananda Marga, 1997.
James, E. O. *The Cult of the Mother Goddess*. London: Thames and Hudson, 1959.
Joseph, Lawrence E. *Gaia: The Growth of an Idea*. New York: St. Martin's Press, 1990.
Kaufmann, Walter. *Hegel: Reinterpretation, Texts, and Commentary*. New York: Doubleday, 1965.
Khaldun, Ibn. *The Muqaddimah*. Translated by Franz Rosenthal, edited by N. J. Dawood. Princeton, N.J.: Princeton University Press, 1967.
King, Thomas, and James Salmon, eds. *Teilhard and the Unity of Knowledge*. New York: Paulist Press, 1983.
Koestler, Arthur. *The Yogi and the Commissar*. New York: Macmillan, 1946.
Laszlo, Ervin. "Footnotes to a History of the Future." *Futures* 20 (1988): 479–492.
Laszlo, Ervin, Ignazio Masulli, Robert Artigiani, and Vilmos Csanyi, eds. *The Evolution of Cognitive Maps: New Paradigms for the 21st Century*. New York: Gordon and Breach, 1993.
Lovelock, James. *The Ages of Gaia: A Biography of Our Living Planet*. New York: W. W. Norton, 1988.
Lovelock, James. *Gaia: A New Look at Life on Earth*. Oxford: Oxford University Press, 1979.
Macfie, A. L. *The Individual in Society: Papers on Adam Smith*. London: George Allen and Unwin, 1967.
Mahdi, Muhsin. *Ibn Khaldun's Philosophy of History*. London: George Allen and Unwin, 1957.
Manicas, Peter. *A History and Philosophy of the Social Sciences*. New York: Basil Blackwell, 1987.
Manson, Richard. *The Theory of Knowledge in Giambattista Vico*. Hamden, Conn.: Archon Books, 1969.
Marx, Karl. *A Contribution to the Critique of Political Economy*. Translated by S. W. Ryazanskaya, edited by Maurice Dobb. New York: International Publishers, 1970.
Marx, Karl. *Karl Marx: The Essential Writings*. Edited by Frederick Bender. New York: Harper and Row, 1972.
Marx, Karl, and Frederick Engels. *Manifesto of the Communist Party*. Beijing: Foreign Language Press, 1975.
McKinney, Ronald H. "The Origins of Modern Dialectics." *Journal of the History of Ideas* 44 (1983): 179–190.
McNight, Stephan, ed. *Eric Voegelin's Search for Order in History*. Baton Rouge: Louisiana State University Press, 1978.

Min, Jiayin, ed. *The Chalice and the Blade in Chinese History: Gender Relations and Social Models.* Beijing: China Social Sciences Publishing House, 1995.
Mosca, Gaetano. *The Ruling Class.* Translated by Hannah Kahn, with an introduction by Arthur Livingston. New York: McGraw-Hill, 1939.
Murti, K. Satchidananda, ed. *Readings in Indian History, Philosophy and Politics.* Delhi: Motilal Banarsidass, 1974.
Nandy, Ashis. *Traditions, Tyranny, and Utopias.* New Delhi: Oxford University Press, 1987.
Nivision, David. *The Life and Thought of Chang Hsüeh-Ch'eng.* Stanford: Standford University Press, 1966.
O'Donnell, J. J. *Augustine.* Boston: Twayne, 1985.
Ortega y Gasset, Jose. *Obras Completas.* 5th ed. Vols. 1–9. Madrid: Revista de Occidente, 1965.
Ovid. *Metamorphoses.* Translated by Mary M. Innes. Middlesex, England: Penguin, 1955.
Pareto, Vilfredo. *Manual of Political Economy.* New York: A. M. Kelley, 1971.
Pareto, Vilfredo. *The Mind and Society: Trattato di Sociologia Generale.* Vols. 1–4. New York: Harcourt, Brace and Company, Inc., 1935.
Pareto, Vilfredo. *The Rise and Fall of the Elites.* With an introduction by Hans Zetterburg. Totowa, N.J.: Bedminister Press, 1968.
Polak, Fred. *The Image of the Future.* Translated by Elise Boulding. San Francisco: Jossey-Bass, 1973.
Pompa, Leon. *Vico: A Study of the New Science.* New York: Cambridge University Press, 1975.
Popper, Karl. *The Poverty of Historicism.* New York: Basic Books, 1957.
Prakash, .uddha. "The Hindu Philosophy of History." *Journal of the History of Ideas* 16 (1958): 494–505.
Sabyasachi, Bhattacharya, and Romila Thapar, eds. *Situating Indian History.* Delhi: Oxford University Press, 1986.
Sarkar, Prabhat Rainjan. *The Human Society.* Rev. ed., pt. 2. Calcutta: Ananda Marga, 1984.
Sarkar, Prabhat Rainjan. *The Liberation of Intellect—Neo-Humanism.* Calcutta: Ananda Marga, 1982.
Sarkar, Prabhat Rainjan. *PROUT in a Nutshell.* Vols. 1–25. Calcutta: Ananda Marga, 1988.
Sarkar, Prabhat Rainjan. *Proutist Economics: Discourses on Economic Liberation.* Calcutta: Ananda Marga, 1992.
Scheirer, Sheila Marie. *The World View of Pierre Teilhard de Chardin.* Ann Arbor, Mich.: University Microfilms International, 1980.
Sheldrake, Rupert. *A New Science of Life: The Hypothesis of Formative Causation.* Los Angeles: Jeremy P. Tarcher, 1981.
Smith, Adam. *The Theory of Moral Sentiments.* Edited by D. D. Raphael and A. L. Macfie. Oxford: Clarendon Press, 1976.
Smith, Adam. *The Wealth of Nations.* Edited by Andrew Skinner. 1776. Reprint, Middlesex, England: Penguin Books, 1986.
Sorokin, Pitirim. *Social and Cultural Dynamics.* Boston: Porter and Sargent, 1970.
Sorokin, Pitirim. *Social Philosophies of an Age of Crisis.* Boston: Beacon Press, 1951.
Sorokin, Pitirim. *Sociological Theories of Today.* New York: Harper and Row, 1966.
Spencer, Herbert. *First Principles.* 1862. Reprint, Osnabruck: Otto Zeller, 1966.
Spencer, Herbert. *Social Statics.* 1850. Reprint, New York: Appleton, 1897.

Spencer, Herbert. *Structure, Function and Evolution*. London: Michael Joseph, 1971.
Spengler, Oswald. *The Decline of the West*. Translated by Charles Atkinson. New York: Alfred A. Knopf, 1962.
Spengler, Oswald. *Today and Destiny*. With an introduction by Edwin Franden Dakin. New York: Alfred A. Knopf, 1940.
Steiner, Rudolf. *Die Geheimwissenschaft im Umriß* (An overview of Geheimwissenschaft). Dornach: Rudolf Steiner Verlag, 1962.
Steiner, Rudolf. *The Philosophy of Spiritual Activity and Truth and Knowledge*. Translated by Rita Stebbing, edited by Paul Allen. New York: Rudolf Steiner, 1963.
Teilhard de Chardin, Pierre. *Activation of Energy*. London: Collins, 1970.
Teilhard de Chardin, Pierre. *The Future of Man*. New York: Harper and Row, 1964.
Teilhard de Chardin, Pierre. *The Heart of the Matter*. New York: Harcourt Brace Jovanovich, 1976.
Teilhard de Chardin, Pierre. *Human Energy*. New York: Harcourt Brace Jovanovich, 1969.
Teilhard de Chardin, Pierre. *On Love and Happiness*. San Francisco: Harper and Row, 1984.
Teilhard de Chardin, Pierre. *The Phenomenon of Man*. New York: Harper and Row, 1961.
Teilhard de Chardin, Pierre. *Science and Christ*. New York: Harper and Row, 1965.
Teilhard de Chardin, Pierre. *Toward the Future*. New York: Harcourt Brace Jovanovich, 1975.
Teilhard de Chardin, Pierre. *The Vision of the Past*. New York: Harper and Row, 1966.
Thapar, Romila. *A History of India*. Baltimore: Penguin Books, 1966.
Thompson, William Irwin. *At the Edge of History*. New York: Harper and Row, 1971.
Thompson, William Irwin, ed. *Gaia: A Way of Knowing*. Great Barrington, Mass.: Lindisfarne Press, 1980.
Toynbee, Arnold. "After the Age of Influence." *Observer*, 14 April 1974.
Toynbee, Arnold. *A Study of History*. 1st ed. Published in 12 vols. 1934–1961. Oxford: Oxford University Press, 1934.
Toynbee, Arnold. *A Study of History*. Illustrated. Oxford: Oxford University Press, 1971.
Varma, Vishwanath Prasad. *Studies in Hindu Political Thought and its Metaphysical Foundations*. Delhi: Motilal Bararsidass, 1974.
Vico, Giambattista. *The Autobiography of Giambattista Vico*. Ithaca, N.Y.: Cornell University Press, 1944.
Vico, Giambattista. *On the Study Methods of Our Time*. Indianapolis: Bobbs-Merrill, 1965.
Vico, Giovanni Battista. *The New Science of Giambattista Vico*. Translated by Thomas Goddard Bergin and Max Harold Fisch. 3rd ed. Ithaca, N.Y.: Cornell University Press, 1968.
Voegelin, Eric. *The New Science of Politics*. Chicago: University of Chicago Press, 1987.
Walsh, W. H. *Philosophy of History*. New York: Harper and Row, 1958.
Watson, Burton. *Ssu-Ma Ch'ien: Grand Historian of China*. New York: Columbia University Press, 1958.
Wiltshire, David. *The Social and Political Thought of Herbert Spencer*. Oxford: Oxford University Press, 1978.
Worsley, P. *Marx and Marxism*. London: Havistock, 1982.

# Index

*Ananda Marga*, 132. See also Prabhat Rainjan Sarkar
Androcracy, 142–144. See also Riane Eisler
Anti-macrohistory: Aristotelian, 166–167; critical theory, 169–70, Ortega, 200, 242–243
Aquinas, Thomas, 18, 21, 23–24, 106
Asabiya: and bedouins, 27; and class, 206, 211; defined, 28; desert conditions, 30; kinship, 28; in marriage, 227; religion, 28. See also Ibn Khaldun
Ashley, Richard, 169
Augustine, 8, 18–24, 167, 215; biography, 19–20; God, 22–24; theory of knowledge, 20–21; theory of macrohistory, 21–23
Aurobindo, Sri, 138

Barrow, John, 166
Batra, Ravi 193
Biao, Lin, 238
Biography, 221–225. See also Microhistory

Boulding, Elise, 9n.12, 159, 165, 178–179, 196, 241
Braudel, Fernand, 168–169, 194
Brian Question, 119–120n.6
Buddhist epistemolgy, 179
Buddhist time, 183–184

Camus, Albert, 52
Capitalism, 45, 170, 196, 209, 211, 238
Causes and mechanisms in macrohistory, 166–172. See also Macrohistory
Chang Hsüeh, Ch'eng, 11
Chaos theory, 141
Chinese time, 182, 185
Christ, 22, 108, 110, 215, 216
Christianity, 20–21, 23, 26, 144, 147, 163, 165, 178, 195, 215, 229
*City of God*, 20. See also Augustine
Civil society, 131
Communist Party, 17, 63
Communist society, 207, 229
Computer, personal, 64–65
Comte, Auguste, 54–61, 163, 169, 229–230; biography, 54–56; cerebral hygiene, 56; and Clotilde de Vaux, 55;

Comte, Auguste (*continued*)
compared to Hegel, 60; critique, 58–59; European history, 58; law of the hierarchy of sciences, 57–58; law of the three stages, 56–57; and Caroline Massin, 55; universal law of nature, 57–58
Confucianism, 13–14, 16, 192
*Contribution to the Critique of Political Economy, A*, 67. *See also* Karl Marx
Copernican view of history, 100
*Cours de Philosophie Positive*, 55. *See also* Auguste Comte
Culture, primacy of, 211, 239
Cyclical theories of macrohistory, 15–16, 22, 25, 27, 31, 38, 46, 81, 136, 156, 168, 172–175, 239, 243. *See also* Shape of macrohistory

Daisyworld model, 154
Darwin, Charles, 106, 165, 199, 210
Decline of civilization: critique of, 243; Khaldun, 28–31, 187; Spengler, 102–103, 194; Sorokin, 116–117; Ssu-Ma Ch'ien, 187–188; Toynbee 122, 126; Vico, 37; Weber, 86–87
*Decline of the West, The*, 169. *See also* Oswald Spengler
Descartes, 21
Diachronic, 1–3, 5, 159
Dialectical theories of macrohistory, 168. *See also* Shape of macrohistory
Dialectics, 129–130, 133, 139, 198–199, 208
Dilthey, William, 1
Doom and gloom, 6
Durkheim, Emile, 199, 207

Eisler, Riane, 141–150, 165, 173, 196, 216, 241; cultural transformation theory, 141; dominator model, 142–143, partnership model, 143–144, 193, 241; technological phase changes and cultural shifts, 144–149
Eliade, Mircea, 137, 183
Elias, Norbert, 232
Elites and decline, 29. *See also* Ibn Khaldun; Vilfredo Pareto

*Endzustand*, 65, 88, 206, 209, 213, 215–217, 225–226
Episteme and context in macrohistory, 163–166. *See also* Macrohistory
Epistemological exclusivity, 170
Epistemological skepticism, 171, 200. *See also* Anti-macrohistory
Equilibrium theories of macrohistory, 168. *See also* Macrohistory
*Erklären*, 1
Evil, 15, 110–111, 168, 199
Evolution, 56, 68, 70–72, 73–75, 93–96, 106–107, 109–111, 136, 199. *See also* Auguste Comte; Herbert Spencer; Rudolph Steiner; Pierre Teilhard de Chardin

Faj, Attila, 166
Feminist movement, 66, 192–193, 241
*Forces motrices*, 64, 88, 203–204, 211
Foucault, Michel, 164, 167, 175, 185, 197–198, 243
Future, and macrohistory, 192–197. *See also* Macrohistory
Futures studies, 192, 196, 198

Gaia, 151–158, 169–170, 241; exogenous and endogenous, 156; futures, 157; as hypothesis, 152, 158; macrohistory and geophysiology, 15; regulatory processes, 153–154; as synthesis of linear, cyclical, and spiral patterns, 155. *See also* James Lovelock
*Gaia: A New Look at Life on Earth*, 154. *See also* James Lovelock
Gandhi, Mahatama, 97;
*Geist*, 170, 195. *See also* George Wilhelm Friedrich Hegel; *Weltgeist*
Giambutas, Marija, 144, 146
Gibbon, Edward, 174
Giddens, Anthony, 167
Gilligan, Carol, 9n.12
Golden age, 15, 163, 184, 193, 199
Golding, William, 158
Gramsci, Antonio, 128–132, 188, 215; biography, 128; compared to Marx, 128–129; dialectics, 129, hegemony, 131

Grand theory, 139, 169–171, 243
*Gylany*, 143, 150n.5. *See also* Riane Eisler

Habermas, Jürgen, 89
Hegel, George Wilhelm Friedrich: 47–54, 163, 165, 188–189, 195; biography, 47–48, dialectical resolution, 50–52, 163; future, 51; spirit, 50, 52 (*See also Weltgeist*); stages of history, 50–52; theory of knowledge, 48–50
Historiography, 130, 163, 197–200

Ideographic, 1–4, 8–9n.5
Indian episteme, 179. *See also* Prabhat Rainjan Sarkar
Indian time, 182–184
International Monetary Fund, 148
Islamic time, 182

Jain epistemology, 179

Kant, Immanuel, 163
Khaldun, Ibn, 25–32, 162, 205–209, 213, 217–218; biography, 25–26; comparisons with other macrohistorians, 31; elites and decline, 29; endogenous versus exogenous, 31; generational time, 30–31; God and history, 25; and microhistory, 227; primitive-civilization cycle, 27–28; rise and fall of *asabiya*, 28–30; royal authority, 28. *See also Asabiya*
Koestler, Arthur, 115, 119n.5

Laszlo, Erwin, 172–173
Laws: of history, 3, 70, 121, 134; of imitation, 124; of nature, 57, 64; of progress, 59; universal, 6, 57–58, 63, 70, 162–166
Leadership: in Comte, 60; creative minority, 122, 188, 194; degenerative monarch, 15; organic intellectuals, 188, 215; in Pareto, 195; royal authority, 28; sage-king, 15, 18, 171, 187, 194; *sadvipra*, 134–135, 140, 188, 212; savior, 122; in Spencer, 73; *Taraka Brahma*, 137; warrior king, 194; world historical leaders, 188

*Leitmotif*, 227–229
Life cycle: Greek, 224; Hindu, 222–223; human phases, 221–225; Steiner, 224–225; Western 222, 225
Linear theories of macrohistory, 6, 22, 56–57, 59, 75, 97, 155, 168, 172–175. *See also* Shape of macrohistory
Linear versus cyclical theories of macrohistory, 174, 216–218. *See also* Shape of macrohistory
Lovelock, James, 151–154, 157–158. *See also* Gaia

Macrohistorians: age, 7; blindspots, 5; gender, 4, 7, 9n.12; guide to social space-time, 4; implications for the future, 243–244; learning from each other, 218–219; Occident/Orient, 7; synergies between, 205–216; views on the future, 191–197; views on historiography, 197–198
Macrohistory: and anti-macrohistory, 166–167, 169–170, 242–243; causes and mechanisms, 166–172; cyclical theories of, 168; defining factors, 159–162; diachronic, 1, 3–5, 159; dialectical theories of, 168; episteme and context, 162–166; equilibrium theories of, 168; exits from, 190–191; and the future, 191–197; male bias, 7, 243; metaphors of time, 182–187; metaphysical choices and the role of the transcendent, 176–179, 186; and nation-building, 6; nomethetic, 1, 3, 5–6, 159; Platonic approach, 35, 166–167; role of the vanguard, 187–190; stages and patterns, 172–175; transcendental theories, 168, 191; unit of analysis, 179–182; Western bias, 243; women, 7, 243. *See also* Metaphors; Shape of macrohistory
*Mahabharata*, 191
Manicheism, 19
Mao Zedong, 17, 65–66, 238
Marx, Karl, 40, 61–68, 163, 165, 167, 195, 219, 238, 241; biography, 61; critique, 64–65; and Hegel, 67n.5; and micro-history, 229–231; and Sarkar, 63

Marxism: gender relations, 66; reasons for decline; revival, 67
Materialistic conception of history, 41, 128
Matriarchy, 143, 241
Mead, G. H., 221
Metaphors, 4, 160, 199; circulatory system, 154; *kitra* to *kali*, 242; lifecycle, 99, 186; masculine to feminine, 242; mirror, 14; oceans of eternity 22, 242; pendulum, 242; Phoenix, 117; rise and fall, 14, 139; river 8, 22; seasons, 100; sexual, 225; Sisyphus, 117; society as living body, 70; waves 139
Microhistory: 221–236; Buddhist, 225; Comte, 229–230; cyclical theory, 232; Hindu, 225; Khaldun, 227; linear theory, 232; and macrohistory, 226–233; Marx, 229, 231; Occident, 225; Sarkar, 228–229; Sorokin, 227–228; Spencer, 230; Toynbee, 228
Model of four, 184, 198–199, 239
*Modern Prince, The*, 129. See also Antonio Gramsci
Mosca, Gaetona, 11, 159, 175, 180–181
*Muqaddimah, The*, 26, 205. See also Ibn Khaldun

Nandy, Ashis, 190–191, 200
Nehru, Jawaharlal, 139
Nomethetic, 1, 3–5, 159
Non-Western cosmologies, 59

Occident/Orient, 7, 224, 229, 241
Ortega y Gassett, Jose, 169, 200, 242–244
Ovid, 184–185

Pareto, Vilfredo, 76–84, 175, 181, 214; biography 76–77; circulation of elites, 80–82; concept of history, 77–81; debt to Lamarck and Spencer, 83; fluctuation between democracy and autocracy, 82
Parsons, Talcott, 119
Patriarchy, 142, 216, 241

Paul, 208
Peace, positive and negative, 241, 244
*Phenomenology of Spirit*, 48. See also George Wilhelm Friedrich Hegel
Plato, 24
Platonic philosophy, 35
Polak, Fred, 159, 178–179, 196
Popper, Karl, 166–167
Prakash, Buddha, 138, 184, 186
Progress, 6, 44, 66, 70, 232. See also Adam Smith; Auguste Comte; Herbert Spencer
PROUT (Progressive Utilization Theory), 132–134. See also Prabhat Rainjan Sarkar
Ptolemaic system of history, 100

*Rta*, 171

*Sadvipra*, 134–135, 140, 188, 212. See also Sarkar, Prabhat Rainjan
Saint-Simon, Claude Henry, 55
*Samsara*, 217, 228
Sarkar, Prabhat Rainjan, 132–140, 163–165, 181, 184, 196, 210; biography, 132–133; dialectics, 233, 139; Indian episteme; 136; larger civilizational project, 133–134; and microhistory, 228–229; neohumanism, 133; *sadvipra*, 134–135, 188, 212; theory of history, 134–136; *varna*, 134–135, 180, 186, 193, 206, 209, 229; *vidya and avidya*, 18, 133, 168, 212; view of the future, 193
*Satya*, 171
Schelling, Friedrich, 47–48, 106
Science, different pillars, 197–198
Science of history: as contradiction, 99; as myth, 170
Science of society, 166
*Scienza Nouva*, 36. See also Giambattista Vico
*Scienza Nouva Seconda*, 36. See also Giambattista Vico
Shape of macrohistory, 160; cyclical, 15–16, 22, 24, 25, 27, 31, 38, 46, 81–83, 103–104; 122, 136, 156, 168, 172–175,

## Index

Shape of macrohistory (*continued*) 239, 243; dialectical, 50–52, 62–63, 67, 86; linear, 6, 22, 56–57, 59, 60, 70–73, 75, 97, 111–112, 155, 168, 172–175; linear versus cyclical, 174, 216–218; multilinear, 141; pendulum, 115–116, 193; rupture, 67, 211; spiral, 135; synthesis, 155

Sheldrake, Rupert, 174

*Shi Ji*, 12–13, 15. See also Ssu-Ma Ch'ien

Si-Ma Tan, 12, 13

Smith, Adam, 40–46, 174, 195–196, 205, 211, 219; biography, 40–41; decline of the age of commerce, 45–46; feudalism, 43; induction in Smith's thought, 45–46; morality and the love of the other, 43–44; stage theory, 41–43

*Social and Cultural Dynamics*, 113. See also Pitirim Sorokin

Social movements, 66, 192–193, 196, 238, 240–241

Sociology, 18, 58, 74, 162; as the ultimate science, 55, 57

Sorokin, Pitirim, 113–120, 166, 180, 189, 218–219; biography, 113; cultural mentalities, 113–114; historical dynamics, 116; and Marx, 119; and microhistory, 227–228; Orient, 118; sensate gutter, 117; view of the future, 193; world macrohistory, 118–119

Spencer, Herbert, 68–76, 165–166, 169, 196, 238; biography, 68–69, comparisons with other macrohistorians, 74–75; evolution, general laws of, 69; future stages, 73; and microhistory, 230–231; survival of the fittest, 68, 71, 165, 230; ultimate cause, 70

Spengler, Oswald, 98–104, 169, 194; biography, 98–99; comparison with Hegel, 101; comparison with Khaldun, Sarkar, and Sorokin, 103–104; culture and the great soul, 101; future, 102; lifecycle of cultures 100–102; money spirit and the decline of

Spengler, Oswald (*continued*) culture, 102; stages of history, 102–103; types of history, 99–100; understanding versus explanation, 100

Ssu-Ma Ch'ien, 12–18, 102, 162, 168, 181, 184, 194, 197; biography, 12–13; comparisons with Confucian, Taoist, and Yin-Yang schools of thought, 13–14; Confucian episteme, 14–15; philosophical background, 13–14; sage-king, 15, 18, 171, 187, 194; theory of history, 15–16

Stages and patterns in macrohistory, 172–175. See also Macrohistory

Steiner, Rudolf, 90–97, 215; Anthroposophy, 92–93; biography, 90–93; compared to Marx, 96; future stages, 94; historic method, 97; phases of microhistory, 224–225; planetary stages, 95–96; reincarnation and karma, 95; spiritual hierarchy, 96; stages of macroevolution, 93–94

*Study of History, A*, 120. See also Arnold Toynbee

*Stufengang*, 211

Subaltern, 139

Synergies between macrohistorians, 205–216. See also Macrohistory

*Synthetic Philosophy*, 69. See also Herbert Spencer

*Systeme de Politique Positive*, 56. See also Auguste Comte

Tamerlane, 26
Tantra, 18, 168
Tao, 101, 163, 165, 170, 176, 182, 198
*Tao Te Ching*, 144
Taoist schools of thought, 13
Teilhard de Chardin, Pierre, 81, 105–113, 167, 172, 174, 215; biography, 105; end of time, 112; evil, 110; evolution, 106–107, 109–110, 112; Omega point, 106–107, 110–112, 215; rejection of scholasticism of Thomas Aquinas, 106; suffering and evolution, 111; theory of knowledge, 105–107

*Theory of Moral Sentiments*, 40–41, 43, 45. *See also* Adam Smith
Thompson, William Irwin, 196, 198
Time, 138; Buddhist, 183–184; Chinese, 182; diachronic 1–3, 5, 159; generational, 186; Indian, 183; Islamic, 182; kairos, 217, 225, 229; khronos, 217, 225, 229; plastic, 198; sexual, 185–186, 225; syncronic, 1–3, types of, 138
Tönnies, Ferdinand, 207
Toynbee, Arnold: 120–127, 242–243; biography 120; challenge–reponse–mimesis, 122; compared with other macrohistorians, 123–124; creative minority, 122–123, 125–126; critique, 124–125, critique by Sorokin, 121; and macrohistory 121–123; and microhistory, 228; universal church, 122, 126
Transcendental, role of in macrohistory, 176–179, 186
Transcendental theories of macrohistory, 168, 191. *See also* Macrohistory

*Übermensch*, 64
Underdogs, 238. *See also* social movements
Urbanization and decline, 103, 199. *See also* Ibn Khaldun; Oswald Spengler
Utopian thinking, 191

Vanguard, role of the, 187–190. *See also* Leadership
Varna, 134–135, 180, 186, 193, 206, 209, 229. *See also* Prabhat Rainjan Sarkar
*Vedas*, 176, 182
*Verstehen*, 1

Vico, Giambattista, 32–39, 194–195, 214; ages of history, 36–38, 164; biography, 33; concept of history, 33–34; course and recourse, 38–39, 164, 166; *famuli*, 35–37; history and true knowledge, 35; mythology and fables, 35; providence in history, 38–39; theory of knowledge, 34–35
*Vidya and avidya*, 18 133, 168, 212
Voegelin, Eric, 11, 159, 177–178, 191

Waldorf school movement, 92, 97
Wallerstein, Immanuel, 2–3, 170, 186, 195
Watson, Burton, 15
*Wealth of Nations, The*, 40–43, 45–46. *See also* Adam Smith
Weber, Max, 84–90, 174, 232; biography, 84–85; compared with Marx and Nietzsche, 86–86; critique of, 89; linear versus cyclical, 87–88; rationalization and charisma, 87
*Weltgeist*, 60, 64, 165, 170, 193, 195, 241. *See also* Geist; George Wilhelm Friedrich Hegel
Western history, comparison to Chinese and Indian, 101, 163
Western model, compared to Indian, 133
Windelband, Wilhelm, 1
Women's history, 165
World Bank, 148
World history, 2, 237–242
World village versus world city, 238

Yeltsin, Boris, 194
Yin–yang: as metaphor, 16, 18; nature of things, 244; schools of thought, 13–14
*Yogi and the Commisar, The*, 15, 119n.5. *See also* Arthur Koestler

# About the Editors and Contributors

JOHAN GALTUNG is the author of seventy-one books and hundreds of articles on topics such as peace studies, alternative development, social science methods, and civilizational studies. Most recent books include *Human Rights in Another Key* and *Peace by Peaceful Means*. He is Professor of Peace Studies at the University of Hawaii, Universitet i Tromsö, and Universität Witten/Herdecke, F-01210 Versonnex (ain), France. In addition to his many professorships, Galtung has worked extensively for the United Nations family of organizations. He is the founder of the International Peace Research Organization and *Journal of Peace Research*. Galtung is recipient of numerous honorary doctoral degrees, the Right Livelihood Award, the Norweigian Humanist Prize, and the Alo'ha International Award.

SOHAIL INAYATULLAH is senior research fellow at The Communication Centre, Queensland University of Technology, GPO Box 2434, Brisbane, Qld 4001, Australia. He is the author of numerous books and over 150 articles, book chapters, and magazine pieces. In addition to two books exploring the works of Prabhat Rainjan Sarkar, *Situating Sarkar* and *Transcending Boundaries* (edited with Jennifer Fitzgerald), Inayatullah has recently finished *Islam, Science, Postmodernism and the Future*. In preparation is *Theorizing Futures*. He is on the editorial board of the journals *Futures, Journal of Futures Studies*, and *Periodica Islamica*, associate editor of the European alternative quarterly, *New Renaissance*, and senior writer for the newsmagazine, *Global Times*. Inayatullah is a fellow and executive council member of the World Futures Studies Federation.

**DANIEL J. CAMPBELL** is a former Ph.D. philosophy student, now at 2204 Madeira Drive NE, Albuquerque, NM 87110.

**RIANE EISLER** is the author of numerous books, including *The Chalice and the Blade* and, most recently, *Sacred Pleasure*. She is director of the Centre for Partnership Studies, 25700 Shafter Way, Carmel, CA 93923.

**MARSHA HANSEN** is an A.b.D. in Sociology and currently works for the San Diego Unified School District. She has a Masters in Human Relations from Pacific Lutheran University. 860 Hazy Glen Court, Cula Vista, CA 91910.

**CHRISTOPHER B. JONES** is Assistant Professor of Political Science at Eastern Oregon State University, 1410 L Avenue, School of Arts and Sciences, Eastern Oregon State College, La Grande, OR 97850-2707.

**DANIELA ROCCO MINERBI** is an architect, a concert pianist, and a writer—a true renaissance woman. 2444 Hihiwai St. #2005, Honolulu, HI 96826.

**CLAUS OTTO SCHARMER** is a lecturer at the Center for Organizational Learning, Massachusetts Institute of Technology, E60-301 Sloan School of Management, 30 Memorial Drive, Cambridge, MA 02142.

**BRIAN SHETLER** is a private attorney living at 1544 Johnson Ave, Sartoga, CA 95070.

**CHANG XIE** is Director of the Brooklyn Branch of the Chinese–American Planning Council. He has a Masters in Education from the University of Hawaii. Brooklyn Branch, Chinese–American Planning Council, Sunset Park Office, 6022 7th Avenue, 2nd Floor, Brooklyn, NY 11220.